ECOFEMINISM
and the
SACRED

Edited by
Carol J. Adams

CONTINUUM · NEW YORK

1999

The Continuum Publishing Company
370 Lexington Avenue, New York, NY 10017

Printed in the United States of America

Library of Congress Cataloging-in-Publication Data

Ecofeminism and the sacred / edited by Carol J. Adams
   p.   cm.
   Includes bibliographical references
   ISBN 0-8264-0586-X; 0-8264-0667-X (pbk.)
   1. Ecofeminism—Religious aspects.   I. Adams, Carol J.
HQ1233.E25   1992
305.42—dc20   92-36883
                                                         CIP

Portions of Sallie McFague's "An Earthly Theological Agenda" appeared in *The Christian
Century,* January 2–9, 1991 © 1991 Christian Century Foundation, reprinted with permission
of the foundation. Other portions appeared as an article in *Spirit and Nature: Why the
Environment is a Religious Issue,* ed. Stephen C. Rockefeller and John Elder, © 1992 Beacon
Press, and are reprinted with the permission of the publisher.

Jane Caputi's "Nuclear Power and the Sacred: Or, Why a Beautiful Woman is Like a
Nuclear Power Plant," is based on an article that appeared originally in *Women's Studies
International Forum,* vol. 14, no. 5 © 1991 Pergamon Press, and is reprinted with permission
of the *Forum.*

Ellen Cronan Rose's "The Good Mother: From Gaia to Gilead," first appeared in *Frontiers:
A Journal of Women Studies,* vol. 12, no. 1, and is reprinted with permission of *Frontiers.*

Excerpts from Charlene Spretnak's *States of Grace: The Recovery of Meaning in the Postmodern Age* © 1991, HarperCollins Publishers, are reprinted with the permission of the
publisher.

Judith Plaskow's "Feminist Judaism and Repair of the World" is excerpted and adapted
from *Standing Again at Sinai* © 1990, HarperCollins Publishers, and is reprinted with the
permission of the publisher.

"Carol J. Adams," "Ecofeminisn and the Sacred,"
 reproduced with permission from, "Bloomsbury Publishing Group."

CMID#159695.

 Printed on
Recycled Paper

In Memory of
PETRA KELLY

1947-1992

"We must make it clear
that we will not
just go away. . . ."

[Earth] is perceived, ironically, as other, alien, evil, and threatening by those who are finding they cannot draw a healthful breath without its cooperation. While the Earth is poisoned, everything it supports is poisoned. While the Earth is enslaved, none of us is free.

Our thoughts must be on how to restore to the Earth its dignity as a living being; how to stop raping and plundering it as a matter of course. We must begin to develop the consciousness that everything has equal rights because existence itself is equal. In other words, we are all here: trees, people, snakes, alike. We must realize that even tiny insects in the South American jungle know how to make plastic, for instance; they have simply chosen not to cover the Earth with it.

Beyond feeding and clothing and sheltering ourselves, even abundantly, we should be allowed to destroy only what we ourselves can re-create. We cannot re-create this world. We cannot re-create "wilderness." We cannot even, truly, re-create ourselves. Only our behavior can we re-create, or create anew.

—excerpts from Alice Walker's
"Everything Is a Human Being"
in *Living by the Word: Selected Writings, 1973-1987*

We women want to call attention to the fact that environmental issues also have to do with human solidarity and with the distribution of wealth and equity. . . . A social order created by a culture lacking fundamental values of human solidarity gives rise to the conditions that perpetuate poverty. Both poverty and environmental deterioration are products of the same world view of how human beings should cohabit the earth. Nothing short of a transformation of our culture is needed.

—Margarita Arias, the first woman candidate
for President of Costa Rica,
keynote speaker at the 1991 Women's World Congress
for a Healthy Planet

Contents

Acknowledgments

In 1972, Francoise d'Eaubonne set up "Ecologie-Féminisme," arguing that "the destruction of the planet is due to the profit motive inherent in male power." D'Eaubonne's book *Le féminisme ou la mort [Feminism or Death]* introduced the term *ecofeminism* [*eco-féminisme*] two years later upon publication in France. She envisioned a planet that was "green again for all" and in which human beings were treated as people first, and not marked as male or female. Only women, she argued, could bring about such an ecological revolution.

I vividly remember learning about d'Eaubonne's ideas in the fall of 1974. I was taking Mary Daly's Feminist Ethics class at Boston College as a second-year divinity-school student. Mary translated parts of *Le féminisme ou la mort* and interpreted d'Eaubonne's insights.

The field of ecofeminism has grown immensely since the early 1970s. As a feminist divinity school student during that time, I was exposed to many of the early texts as they appeared, most notably the writings of Mary Daly and Rosemary Radford Ruether. When my own book, *The Sexual Politics of Meat: A Feminist-Vegetarian Critical Theory,* appeared in 1990, it too joined the ranks of ecofeminist texts. In many ways it fulfilled the insights that occurred as I took Mary Daly's class, as it first began as a paper for her. I am thankful for her prescience about ecofeminism and her early support.

Curiously, though, while I agreed with many ecofeminist analyses, I did not feel completely comfortable with the idea that feminism needed to be modified by the term *eco.* After being graduated from divinity school, I worked against racism and sexual and domestic violence with grass-roots, community action groups in upstate New York. Ecofeminism did not seem to speak to this work. Ecofeminist philosopher Karen J. Warren's writings changed my mind. Her 1987 and 1990 articles in *Environmental Ethics* offered an interpretative analysis of the logic of domination that illuminated the scope of ecofeminism's critique. She has contributed immensely to shaping my understanding of ecofeminism and my own writings on the subject.

Rosemary Radford Ruether's analysis of the relationship between structures of social domination and the domination of nature confirmed for me that *"eco"* was an appropriate modifier for *feminism.* I have appreciated her support of my work, as well.

The editing of this anthology has been an experience of grace and revelation: I thank Jay McDaniel for suggesting that I edit a volume on this subject, and for his constancy along the way; Tom Regan, supportive friend, for introducing us; Dieter Hessel for a prophetic word at an appropriate moment; Mary Hunt for her "fierce tenderness"; and the staff at Crossroad and Continuum for their embrace of this project. The contributors have been a joy to work with: responsive and thoughtful, conscientious in meeting deadlines, and thorough in their responses to my suggestions. They have deepened my admiration for the work and vision of ecofeminism. I thank them for joining in this venture.

My support group of friends who have helped me sort out ideas about ecofeminism and the sacred has been immeasurably helpful, especially Mary E. Hunt, Marjorie Procter-Smith, and Nancy Tuana. Charlene Spretnak, Jay McDaniel, and Bill Eakin suggested names for contributors; I appreciate their assistance. I gratefully acknowledge others who were helpful as I considered the shape of this anthology: Chellis Glendinning, Joanna Macy, Josephine Donovan, and Marti Kheel. Thanks to Alicia Gray for transcribing the Avery-Hunt conversation quickly, Elizabeth Archer for proofreading, and Gene Mason for guiding me through computer glitches. Rebecca Johnson, Catherine Keller, Stephanie Kaza, Sallie McFague, Cathleen McGuire, Rosemary Ruether, Carol Lee Sanchez, Charlene Spretnak, Nancy Tuana, Karen Warren, Bill Eakin, and Jay McDaniel offered helpful comments on different parts of the anthology.

Anthologies can disrupt one's life, and this one was, at times, no exception. My partners in shaping a sustainable life-style, Bruce, Douglas, and Benjamin Buchanan, were flexible and accepting of such disruptions. Bruce has helped to create the space and time for me to engage in this project, and I am thankful for this support, as I know the demands it has placed on him. Douglas has revealed the challenges of working out these ideas as a seven-year-old, and confirms for me that including children in the issue of environmental ethics from an early age is an essential part of transforming the world.

Finally, I wish to acknowledge you, the reader. By being concerned about the environment, and by recognizing the importance of an ecofeminist analysis, you assist in bringing a book such as this into being. I hope that you will help it bear fruit.

ECOFEMINISM
and the
SACRED

Introduction

CAROL J. ADAMS

For many years now, women around the world have worked to transform a social order that sanctions human oppression and environmental abuse. We see the interrelationship of social domination and the domination of the rest of nature, such as deforestation that displaces indigenous peoples; hazardous waste sites located near poor and Black neighborhoods; industrialized factory farms that eliminate the small family farmer; and international policies of free trade that hurt poor people and the earth. Women are the major caretakers of victims of pollution, and along with the poor they are the primary victims of industrial pollution. The overwhelming majority of the millions of people denied the basic rights of clean air, water, food, shelter, health, and well-being are women. Aimed at both preventing and solving environmental problems, our responses have included designing solar cookers and greenhouses, transforming farming methods that damaged the environment, challenging loggers, analyzing economic policies that fail to measure environmental protection (or housework) as "productive," holding vigils outside of slaughterhouses, investigating chemical dumping, protesting war and the military-industrial complex.

The term *ecofeminism* defines these global activisms and analyses.

Ecofeminisms might be more accurate in conveying the diversity of these responses to environmental exploitation.

Ecofeminism identifies the twin dominations of women and the rest of nature. To the issues of sexism, racism, classism, and heterosexism that concern feminists, ecofeminists add naturism—the oppression of the rest of nature. Ecofeminism argues that the connections between the oppression of women and the rest of nature must be recognized to understand adequately both oppressions.

Some of the earliest feminist theologies in this wave of feminism examined attitudes toward the rest of nature, and some of the earliest ecofeminist texts critiqued religion.[1] They demonstrated how metaphors of patriarchy simultaneously feminize nature and naturalize women. When patriarchal spirituality associates women, body, and nature, and then emphasizes transcending the body and transcending the rest of nature, it makes oppression sacred. Thus,

1

since the publication in the 1970s of Rosemary Radford Ruether's *New Woman/New Earth* and Elizabeth Dodson Gray's *Green Paradise Lost*, analysis of theological constructs that contribute to women's and the rest of nature's oppression has been a vital part of ecofeminist writings.

In describing ecofeminism's focus, Karen J. Warren has identified a "logic of domination," according to which, "superiority justifies subordination":

> Ecofeminists insist that the sort of logic of domination used to justify the domination of humans by gender, racial, or ethnic, or class status is also used to justify the domination of nature. Because eliminating a logic of domination is part of a feminist critique — whether a critique of patriarchy, white supremacist culture, or imperialism — ecofeminists insist that *naturism* is properly viewed as an integral part of any feminist solidarity movement to end sexist oppression and the logic of domination which conceptually grounds it. (Warren 1990, 132)

This logic of domination is often expressed in dualisms.

Dualisms reduce diversity to two categories: A or Not A. They convey the impression that everything can then be appropriately categorized: *either* it is A *or* Not A. These dualisms represent dichotomy rather than continuity, enacting exclusion rather than inclusion. Ecofeminists analyze many restrictive dualisms that uphold a logic of domination: independence/interdependence; heaven/earth; male/female; culture/nature; mind/body; white/"non-white"; humans/animals; humans/nature.

Ecofeminism has traced the dualisms that characterize Eurocentric patriarchal culture to (1) classical thought and Jewish and Christian religious traditions (see the work of Ruether and Gray), (2) the modern European mechanistic science and Enlightenment philosophy emphasizing autonomy and objective knowing (see the work of Merchant and Easlea), or (3) the desacralization of the Earth in favor of a sky-god (Spretnak, Starhawk).

False dualisms result in several patriarchal theological tenets: transcendence and domination of the natural world, fear of the body, projection of evil upon women, world-destroying spiritual views. Moreover, the second part of the dualism is not only subordinate but *in service* to the first. Women serve men; nature serves culture; animals serve humans; people of color serve white people. Ecofeminists seek a transformed consciousness that eliminates the dualisms that undergird dominance. We note, for instance, that the same dominant mind-set that separates humans from the rest of nature divides politics from spirituality, as though humans are not a part of nature and politics is not integrally related to spirituality. The matter/spirit, politics/spirituality dualisms are a product of Western theology and philosophy. The voices of women of color and women from other philosophical traditions offer alternative metaphysical viewpoints in which the matter/spirit dualism evaporates.

Because of the ecofeminist analysis that attributes the degradation of nature to the dominant Euro-American worldview, indigenous and nontechnological cultures have been sources for the creation of syncretistic ecofeminist spiritualities. Many ecofeminists look to earth-based spiritualities as alternatives to dominant theologies. *How* to incorporate diverse cultural and religious traditions within ecofeminism is an important ethical/political question to raise about these syncretistic efforts. The more diverse the sources for envisioning ecofeminist spiritualities, the more opportunities exist for either succumbing to racism or exposing racism in this syncretism.

What Eurocentric outsiders identify as the "spiritual" dimensions of a culture may actually be a thoroughly eviscerated spirituality that a dualistic worldview cannot even perceive. And regrettably, some aspects of Euro-American ecofeminism have "borrowed" from these cultures those parts that resonate with a noninstrumental view of nonhuman nature and have depoliticized the context for these views. In many instances, cultures that are struggling for physical survival against genocide are romanticized, their spirituality misappropriated and misunderstood. When Euro-American ecofeminists elevate some of the spiritual aspects of these cultures above those political struggles, they perpetuate dualisms while ignoring the fact that it is dominant cultures that have necessitated such struggles for survival in the first place.

Ecofeminists who have addressed the issue of white racism respond to the charge of cultural insensitivity by pointing to the witchhunts in which a prepatriarchal spirituality met the same fate as many Native cultures. They argue that gynocentric spiritualities (such as Goddess worship and the practice of Wicca) share an earth-based focus and basic metaphysical assumptions with Native spirituality (see Todd). As the pre-Columbian world in which indigenous cultures flourished was under siege from European colonialism, the European world itself was participating in an attack on women and their earth-based healing and nature-based spirituality through the witchcraft "craze." Because of this connection between the destruction of indigenous cultures and the persecution of women healers as witches they argue that it is logical for ecofeminism to turn to both sources for spiritual guidance. However, "that shared historical oppression does not excuse white women from working on their own racist behavior" (Ecofeminist Visions Emerging 1992).

Ecofeminist theories resist dividing a culture into separate enclaves—separating politics from spirituality, human from the rest of nature—and name such divisions patriarchal dualisms. Ecofeminist spiritualities must challenge any syncretism that disregards the political dimensions of a culture. In fact, ecofeminists around the world are analyzing the interrelated aspects of social domination and domination of nature. We are deeply engaged with political and economic struggles, as well as with the challenge to articulate ecofeminist theory. This is why ecofeminism has been called the third wave of feminism. Ecofeminism may have grown out of earlier feminist theory, but it revises this theory by its position that an environmental perspective is necessary for feminism. In demonstrating how a patriarchal culture "naturalizes" the domination of nature, of women, and of different races, this third wave of feminism can play "an important role in connecting feminist with other social movements" (Plumwood 1992, 13).

Ecofeminism does not presuppose or posit a unitary voice of women. Its theory making and activism is global in perspective and authorship. We are not talking about a unity with other women that would erase differences among us, especially those of race and class (Lugones 1987). We are talking about solidarity. Ecofeminism's engagement with the world involves recognizing the maldistribution of wealth and power and its relationship to the abuse of nature. As Sheila Collins pointed out in 1974, "racism, sexism, class exploitation, and ecological destruction are four interlocking pillars upon which the structure of patriarchy rests" (Collins 1974, 161). The notion of interdependent communities leads to acknowledging the unequal power that currently separates communities.

As women protest, analyze, reform, and envision, there has been no one perspective on the place of spirituality in ecofeminism. Some ecofeminists act from specific religious traditions; others have seen themselves as rebelling against these traditions. For some, the spiritual aspect of ecofeminism is integrally a part of their ecofeminism. For others, spirituality is thought to derail the ecofeminist engagement with the social conditions and political decisions that tolerate environmental exploitation, encourage unbridled consumerism, and fail to rein in military spending.

The discussions and debates that revolve around the issue of spirituality and the sacred manifest ecofeminism's diversity. Women act environmentally as Buddhists, Hindus, Jews, Christians, post-Christians, and from within specific Tribal traditions. In answer to those who depict ecofeminist spirituality as escapist, we see our environmental actions as deeply related to our idea of the sacred. This anthology demonstrates how environmental exploitation, unbridled consumerism, military spending, apocalypse, exploitation of animals, pollution of the Ganges, and other environmental issues are precisely the concerns of ecofeminist spiritualities.

This book is the first anthology devoted entirely to the issue of ecofeminism and spirituality. Its main precept parallels an ecological insight: diversity amidst relationship. It does not presuppose or posit a unitary voice of women, but enacts a complex interweaving of race, class, and national boundaries. The authors represented here share certain commonalities: We are all women concerned about environmental issues, and we are all actively involved with improving women's status in a world that still holds us as second-class citizens. Furthermore, we recognize that social domination enables environmental abuse. We reject an either-or approach; we do not believe that we must decide between working to help human beings or working to stop environmental abuses, between politics and spirituality, between humans and the rest of nature. We recognize that addressing issues related to the sacred furthers ecofeminist goals. We do not dematerialize the sacred or despiritualize matter. The idea of diversity amidst relationship does not erase differences among us; nor does it deny our commonalities.

Just as there are many ecofeminisms, there are wide varieties of ecofeminist spiritualities.

This anthology communicates the diversity of ecofeminism in several ways. It is unique in going beyond critiques of Judaism and Christianity. Writers from different religious traditions engage their heritage and assess whether it contributes to or challenges environmental exploitation. Some write from a post-Christian perspective. Just as we speak from various religious perspectives, so we speak in different voices. One article is co-authored; another is an edited transcript of a conversation; a third interweaves poetry and reflection on social and environmental oppressions; yet another is a philosophical assessment of ecofeminist spiritualities as empowering responses to sexist oppression and environmental destruction. The contributors consider the role of metaphor and symbols, ritual and myth, engaging theological questions of creation and eschatology, transcendence and immanence, salvation and repentance, purity and pollution. Some appraise specific manifestations of alienation from women and the rest of nature, such as nuclear metaphors, the language of Christian communion, the antiabortion movement. The transformations envisioned by the authors are inextricably both political and spiritual. They emphasize mutuality and a noninstrumental view of both "nature" and marginalized people at many levels.

The theme of relationships and mutuality reappear in many of the articles. Ecofeminism stresses relationship, not solely because it has been women's domain, but because it is a more viable ethical framework than autonomy for transforming structures that are environmentally destructive.

While this volume offers an extensive representation of issues associated with ecofeminism and spirituality, it cannot be exhaustive. Nor need it be. It joins its voice with many valuable works that are now available or are in press. I see this volume as a conversation representing a particular historical point in what is an ongoing process.

Some of the writers in this anthology speak from within a specific religious framework such as Buddhism, Hinduism, Judaism, Christianity, Native American Tribal cultures, post-Christian, or Goddess Spirituality.[2] They evaluate these frameworks as to whether they impede or foster ecojustice or environmental compassion that is sensitive to race, class, and sex. Part 1, Revisioning Religion, groups together articles whose general themes involve the assessment of various religious traditions from a feminist or womanist politics and theology. These authors consider whether and how these traditions are detrimental or beneficial to eliminating environmental exploitation. Revisioning means looking again, "in order to correct or improve." This is an important aspect of ecofeminism.

In her article for this volume, Rosemary Ruether traces the historic development of a process that has made oppression sacred by separating matter from mind, nature from culture, women's labor from men's. She also introduces us to central ecofeminist tenets. Next, Delores Williams extends Ruether's examination by exploring the connection between the United States' exploitation of the natural environment with its historic abuse and exploitation of enslaved African-American women's bodies. Further, Williams explains why Black women's defilement has been invisible to mainstream America. Catherine Keller addresses the question of whether the Christian notion of eschatology has made us sanguine about the environmental apocalypse that looms so threateningly near: How do we respond to an apocalypse now colored green, to a loss of innocent weather talk?

Stephanie Kaza examines the intersection of Buddhist and feminist emphases on interrelationship as a foundation for environmental ethics and believes that "embodied knowing of *any* person is a direct link to experience of relationship with the earth." Her examples of wide-ranging Buddhist environmental work by feminists demonstrates her claim that those trained in the self-discipline, analysis, and reflective processes of Buddhism and feminism have a powerful contribution to make in addressing the enormous challenges of environmental degradation. From the position of feminist Judaism, Judith Plaskow develops a sophisticated argument for the connection between faith, politics, and feminism, into which she then sets the issues of environmental exploitation. For instance, Plaskow examines the proposal to turn Tu Bishvat, a minor Jewish holiday marking the new year of trees, into a major environmental holy day.

Theology is an "earthly" affair, according to Sallie McFague, and she shows precisely how to articulate this earthly engagement: Theology needs to see human beings as earthlings, God as immanently present, and redemption as including all dimensions of creation. Lina Gupta uses the pollution of the Ganges to assess Hindu notions of purity and pollution and their relationship to concepts of nature and the feminine.

Part 2, Envisioning Ecofeminism, offers descriptive interpretations and sympathetic critiques of ecofeminist spiritualities. Karen J. Warren argues that, properly understood, ecofeminist spiritualities do or could play an important role in advancing the ecofeminist project of exposing and replacing harmful interconnected practices toward women and nonhuman nature. Succeeding essays in Part 2 examine specific aspects of ecofeminist spirituality, to determine whether they advance or impede the ecofeminist project. Teal Willoughby analyzes ecofeminist rituals that treat nature instrumentally, when, for instance, water is symbolized as a source of purity that can accept human beings' pollution. She recommends developing rituals that are based on mutuality with nature rather than use of nature.

Ellen Cronan Rose reflects on what she calls reproductive anxieties and raises concerns about gendered representations of nature, such as "mother earth" and the Gaia hypothesis (the notion that the whole earth is a living creature). She argues that such concepts may be hazardous for women, encouraging the view of our procreative capacities as "reproductive environments" that can be expropriated. She urges instead finding nonanthropomorphic, gender-free ways of representing nature.

Whether Euro-Americans can meaningfully encounter Tribal spiritualities is emphatically questioned by Andy Smith. She argues that approaching Indians and their traditions solely for their spirituality trivializes the oppression of Indian women, diverts Indian women from organizing within their own communities, makes Indian spirituality a consumable item separable from communities, and results in white women acting in racist ways toward individual Indians and their communities.

Gloria Orenstein extends Smith's insights to the growing interest in Shamanism. Because Shamans appear to provide answers about how to live in balance on the earth, ecofeminists may be drawn to Shamanism. Yet, this interest has also resulted in a trivializing and misunderstanding of Shamanism; Orenstein seeks to correct this by setting out some ethical considerations and ways of approaching Shamanism in a holistic, respectful, nonracist manner.

Shamara Shantu Riley explores how the emergent environmental activisms by Black women in both the United States and Africa are linked to social justice issues. She draws upon West African spiritual principles to lay the groundwork for seeking human interdependence with the rest of nature, juxtaposing them with the logic of domination that attaches determinative importance to the variables of race, class, gender and species.

In Part 3, Embodying Ecofeminist Spiritualities, Carol Lee Sanchez takes up the issue of how cross-cultural sharing can occur and offers some guidance on the issue. While underscoring that she is not suggesting stealing Native American spiritual practice or dances or songs, she proposes what she calls a "living philosophy" from people who have lived on the North American land base for thousands of years.

Just how one might make technology sacred is pursued by Jane Caputi, as she considers how nuclear technology and patriarchal views of the sacred are interrelated, so that nuclear apocalypse is associated with male orgasm and religious ecstasy. Caputi contends that we should neither worship nor demonize technology, drawing upon the writings of Native American women to understand atomic power through sacred gynocentric metaphors.

Rebecca Johnson, using the full moon as an organizational tool, maintains that the city is where fundamental change can and must take place to save the land. Urban dwellers must recall the "fundamental orientation" of Black people toward land as a resource to be protected and conserved, in opposition to the life-style of dominance and destruction which arises out of the history of European imperialism.

Patriarchal spirituality emphasizes transcending the body and transcending nature. Charlene Spretnak proposes a path that goes into nature and the body. She sees patriarchy as a reactive cultural response to the elemental power of the female body and believes that any cultural or religious orientation that demonizes or denies the elemental power of the female serves patriarchy. She explores specifically "Gaian spirituality" as the path into nature and "Grace embodied" as the path into the body.

The Mary Hunt and Byllye Avery dialogue is a pioneering effort, placing abortion rights within an ecofeminist spiritual viewpoint. Avery speaks as an African American health activist, Hunt as a white Catholic theologian. They see their position as resonating with respect for life, including all the life that already exists on the planet. To convey that the position of abortion rights is the position that respects life, they develop the metaphor of recycling experience. Through this metaphor they are able to explore the way women integrate the experience of abortion into their lives and their community.

In my paper with Marjorie Procter-Smith, we build on previous ecofeminist writings and environmental theologies that situate animals as a part of environmental concerns. We explain the absence of animals from feminist, womanist, mujerista, and other liberation theologies, and propose that animals should be seen as new theological subjects. We explicitly locate the essay within an analysis of the interlocking oppression of marginalized people and the animals we consume.

Zoe Weil applies what she sees as an ecofeminist pedagogy to her efforts to educate adolescents about the issues of the exploitation of animals and nonhuman nature. This pedagogy is suffused with implications for spirituality, due to the many "ways of knowing" she pursues with her students. Weil describes how a "Council of All Beings" enables linking spiritual experiences with purposeful action and responsibility.

The reader may encounter a note of urgency in the pages that follow. This urgency represents an ecofeminist response to traditional theory, which we see as having been cut off from feeling. There are some things that we are learning about that it would be wrong not to be upset about. Moreover, this volume may make some of us uncomfortable. After all, it speaks to the fortunate about their practices of consumption and environmental abuse. Industrialized Northern countries have unjustly exploited both human and natural resources of poor Southern nations. Stopping such exploitation is not an armchair phenomenon. A simple formula for environmental change is "Anything the absence of which would cause daily discomfort probably represents something that is environmentally exploitative."

The transformations envisioned in these pages represent spiritual practices that are practical and environmental practices that are spiritual. Solidarity is one aspect of this spiritual practice. Solidarity does not require complete understanding of those who are victimized by social domination; it entails respect and a willingness to assess one's own role in perpetuating domination and, upon discovering what that role is, changing it. Social domination is a palpable phenomenon, and it requires a sense of compassionate solidarity with its victims.

Solidarity enacts an ecofeminist recognition: Our embodiment takes place somewhere. We are situated here and now; we cannot abstract this embodiment and the consequences of what we do as embodied persons. Acknowledging our embodiment directs us to our interdependent relationship with the human and the nonhuman world and the uses we make of other people and the rest of nature.

Interrelationship, solidarity, transformation, embodiment: These are a few of the themes that recur in the following pages. The diversity of ecofeminist spiritualities that you will find here does not mean a dilution of or instability of ecofeminism. Instead they manifest the global phenomenon of ecofeminism. As with the ecological insight of relationship in the midst of diversity, in reading the following pages, honor the diversity, embody the interrelationships.

NOTES

1. I note Salleh's concern that English-speaking ecofeminists have tended to get their views broadcast first, and thus their statements came to be canonized

as the "classic" ones, i.e., Ruether, Gray, and Merchant (Salleh 1991, 206). Notwithstanding this process of canonization, that these writers focus attention on the Euro-American culture—which is widely held to be the source of the philosophical and religious legitimations of environmental destruction—means that their critiques maintain their value wherever these Euro-American values prevail.

2. I use the term *religious* loosely, since some of these traditions do not adhere to or aspire to be seen as adhering to the prevailing notions of religion.

PART 1

REVISIONING RELIGION

1

Ecofeminism

Symbolic and Social Connections of the Oppression of Women and the Domination of Nature

ROSEMARY RADFORD RUETHER

What is ecofeminism? Ecofeminism represents the union of the radical ecology movement, or what has been called "deep ecology," and feminism. The word "ecology" emerges from the biological science of natural environmental systems. It examines how these natural communities function to sustain a healthy web of life and how they become disrupted, causing death to the plant and animal life. Human intervention is obviously one of the main causes of such disruption. Thus ecology emerged as a combined socioeconomic and biological study in the late sixties to examine how human use of nature is causing pollution of soil, air, and water, and destruction of the natural systems of plants and animals, threatening the base of life on which the human community itself depends (Ehrlich et al. 1973).

Deep ecology takes this study of social ecology another step. It examines the symbolic, psychological, and ethical patterns of destructive relations of humans with nature and how to replace this with a life-affirming culture (Devall and Sessions 1985).

Rosemary Radford Ruether is Georgia Harkness Professor of Applied Theology at the Garrett-Evangelical Theological Seminary in Evanston, Illinois, and a faculty member in the joint doctoral program with Northwestern University. A contributing editor to *Christianity and Crisis* magazine, she is also the author of *Gaia and God: An Eco-feminist Theology of Earth Healing* (forthcoming), *Sexism and God-Talk: Toward a Feminist Theology, New Women/New Earth*, and several other books and numerous articles.

Feminism also is a complex movement with many layers. It can be defined as only a movement within the liberal democratic societies for the full inclusion of women in political rights and economic access to employment. It can be defined more radically in a socialist and liberation tradition as a transformation of the patriarchal socioeconomic system, in which male domination of women is the foundation of all socioeconomic hierarchies (Eisenstein 1979). Feminism can be also studied in terms of culture and consciousness, charting the symbolic, psychological, and ethical connections of domination of women and male monopolization of resources and controlling power. This third level of feminist analysis connects closely with deep ecology. Some would say that feminism is the primary expression of deep ecology (see Doubiago 1989, 40–44).

Yet, although many feminists may make a verbal connection between domination of women and domination of nature, the development of this connection in a broad historical, social, economic, and cultural analysis is only just beginning. Most studies of ecofeminism, such as the essays in *Healing the Wounds: The Promise of Ecofeminism*, are brief and evocative, rather than comprehensive (Plant 1989).

Fuller exploration of ecofeminism probably goes beyond the expertise of one person. It needs a cooperation of a team that brings together historians of culture, natural scientists, and social economists who would all share a concern for the interconnection of domination of women and exploitation of nature. It needs visionaries to imagine how to construct a new socioeconomic system and a new cultural consciousness that would support relations of mutuality, rather than competitive power. For this, one needs poets, artists, and liturgists, as well as revolutionary organizers, to incarnate more life-giving relationships in our cultural consciousness and social system.

Such a range of expertise certainly goes beyond my own competence. Although I am interested in continuing to gain working acquaintance with the natural and social sciences, my primary work lies in the area of history of culture. What I plan to do in this essay is to trace some symbolic connections of domination of women and domination of nature in Mediterranean and Western European culture. I will then explore briefly the alternative ethic and culture that might be envisioned, if we are to overcome these patterns of domination and destructive violence to women and to the natural world.

PRE-HEBRAIC ROOTS

Anthropological studies have suggested that the identification of women with nature and males with culture is both ancient and widespread (Ortner 1974, 67–88). This cultural pattern itself expresses a monopolizing of the definition of culture by males. The very word "nature" in this formula is part of the problem, because it defines nature as a reality below and separated from "man," rather than one nexus in which humanity itself is inseparably embedded. It is, in fact, human beings who cannot live apart from the rest of nature as our life-sustaining context, while the community of plants and animals both can and, for billions of years, did exist without humans. The concept of humans outside of nature is a cultural reversal of natural reality.

How did this reversal take place in our cultural consciousness? One key element of this identification of women with nonhuman nature lies in the early human social patterns in which women's reproductive role as childbearer was tied to making women the primary productive and maintenance workers. Women did most of the work associated with child care, food production and preparation, production of clothing, baskets, and other artifacts of daily life, cleanup, and waste-disposal (French 1985, 25–64).

Although there is considerable variation of these patterns cross-culturally, generally males situated themselves in work that was both more prestigious and more occasional, demanding bursts of energy, such as hunting larger animals, war, and clearing fields, but allowing them more space for leisure. This is the primary social base for the male monopolization of culture, by which men reinforced their privileges of leisure, the superior prestige of their activities, and the inferiority of the activities associated with women.

Perhaps for much of human history, women ignored or discounted these male claims to superiority, being entirely too busy with the tasks of daily life and expressing among themselves their assumptions about the obvious importance of their own work as the primary producers and reproducers (Murphy and Murphy 1974, 111–41). But, by stages, this female consciousness and culture was sunk underneath the growing male power to define the culture for the whole society, socializing both males and females into this male-defined point of view.

It is from the perspective of this male monopoly of culture that the work of women in maintaining the material basis of daily life is defined as an inferior realm. The material world itself is then seen as something separated from males and symbolically linked with women. The earth, as the place from which plant and animal life arises, became linked with the bodies of women, from which babies emerge.

The development of plow agriculture and human slavery very likely took this connection of woman and nature another step. Both are seen as a realm, not on which men depend, but which men dominate and rule over with coercive power. Wild animals which are hunted retain their autonomy and freedom. Domesticated animals become an extension of the human family. But animals yoked and put to the plow, driven under the whip, are now in the new relation to humans. They are enslaved and coerced for their labor.

Plow agriculture generally involves a gender shift in agricultural production. While women monopolized food gathering and gardening, men monopolize food production done with plow animals. With this shift to men as agriculturalists comes a new sense of land as owned by the male family head, passed down through a male line of descent, rather than communal landholding and matrilineal descent that is often found in hunting-gathering and gardening societies (Martin and Voorhies 1975, 276–332).

The conquest and enslavement of other tribal groups created another category of humans, beneath the familiar community, owned by it, whose labor is coerced. Enslavement of other people through military conquest typically took the form of killing the men and enslaving the women and their children for labor and sexual service. Women's work becomes identified with slave work (Lerner 1986, ch. 4). The women of the family are defined as a higher type of slave over a lower category of slaves drawn from conquered people. In patriarchal law, possession of women, slaves, animals, and land all are symbolically and socially linked together. All are species of property and instruments of labor, owned and controlled by male heads of family as a ruling class (see Herlihy 1988, 1–28).

As we look at the mythologies of the Ancient Near Eastern, Hebrew, Greek, and early Christian cultures, one can see a shifting symbolization of women and nature as spheres to be conquered, ruled over, and finally, repudiated altogether.

In the Babylonian Creation story, which goes back to the third millennium B.C.E., Marduk, the warrior champion of the gods of the city states, is seen as creating the cosmos by conquering the Mother Goddess Tiamat, pictured as a monstrous female animal. Marduk kills her, treads her body underfoot, and then splits it in half, using one half to fashion the starry firmament of the skies, and the other half the earth below (Mendelsohn 1955, 17–46). The elemental mother is literally turned into the matter out of which the cosmos is fashioned (not accidentally, the words *mother* and *matter* have the same etymological root). She can be used as matter only by being killed; that is, by destroying her as "wild," autonomous life, making her life-giving body into "stuff" possessed and controlled by the architect of a male-defined cosmos.

THE HEBRAIC WORLD

The view of nature found in Hebrew Scripture has several cultural layers. But the overall tendency is to see the natural world, together with human society, as something created, shaped, and controlled by God, a God imaged after the patriarchal ruling class. The patriarchal male is entrusted with being the steward and caretaker of nature, but under God, who remains its ultimate creator and Lord. This also means that nature remains partly an uncontrollable realm that can confront human society in destructive droughts and storms. These experiences of nature that transcend human control, bringing destruction to human work, are seen as divine judgment against human sin and unfaithfulness to God (see Isaiah 24).

God acts in the droughts and the storms to bring human work to naught, to punish humans for sin, but also to call humans (that is, Israel) back to faithfulness to God. When Israel learns obedience to God, nature in turn will become benign and fruitful, a source of reliable blessings, rather than unreliable destruction. Nature remains ultimately in God's hands, and only secondarily, and through becoming servants of God, in male hands. Yet the symbolization of God as a patriarchal male and Israel as wife, son, and servant of God, creates a basic analogy of woman and nature. God is the ultimate patriarchal Lord, under whom the human patriarchal lord rules over women, children, slaves, and land.

The image of God as single, male, and transcendent, prior to nature, also shifts the symbolic relation of male consciousness to material life. Marduk was a young male god who was produced out of a process of theogony and cosmogony. He conquers and shapes the cosmos out of the body of an older Goddess that existed prior to himself, within which he himself stands. The Hebrew God exists above and prior to the cosmos, shaping it out of a chaos that is under his control. Genesis 2 gives us a parallel view of the male, not as the child of woman, but as the source of woman. She arises out of him, with the help of the male God, and is handed over to him as her Master.[1]

THE GREEK WORLD

When we turn to Greek philosophical myth, the link between mother and matter is made explicit. Plato, in his creation myth, the *Timaeus*, speaks of primal, unformed matter as the receptacle and "nurse" (Plato, 29). He imagines a disembodied male mind as divine architect, or Demiurgos, shaping this matter into the cosmos by fashioning it after the intellectual blueprint of the Eternal Ideas. These Eternal Ideas exist in an immaterial, transcendent world of Mind, separate from and above the material stuff that he is fashioning into the visible cosmos.

The World Soul is also created by the Demiurgos, by mixing together dynamics of antithetical relations (the Same and the Other). This world soul is infused into the body of the cosmos in order to make it move in harmonic motion. The remnants of this world soul are divided into bits, to create the souls of humans. These souls are first placed in the stars, so that human souls will gain knowledge of the Eternal Ideas. Then the souls are sown in the bodies of humans on earth. The task of the soul is to govern the unruly passions that arise from the body.

If the soul succeeds in this task, it will return at death to its native star and there live a life of leisured contemplation. If not, the soul will be reincarnated into the body of a woman or an animal. It will then have to work its way back into the form of an (elite) male and finally escape from bodily reincarnation altogether, to return to its original disincarnate form in the starry realm above (Plato, 23). Plato takes for granted an ontological hierarchy of being, the immaterial intellectual world over material cosmos, and, within this ontological hierarchy, the descending hierarchy of male, female, and animal.

In the Greco-Roman era, a sense of pessimism about the possibility of blessing and well-being within the bodily, historical world deepened in Eastern Mediterranean culture, expressing itself in apocalypticism and gnosticism. In apocalypticism, God is seen as intervening in history to destroy the present sinful and finite world of human society and nature and to create a new heaven and earth freed from both sin and death.[2] In gnosticism, mystical philosophies chart the path to salvation by way of withdrawal of the soul from the body and its passions and its return to an immaterial realm outside of and above the visible cosmos.[3]

CHRISTIANITY

Early Christianity was shaped by both the Hebraic and Greek traditions, including their alienated forms in apocalypticism and gnosticism. Second-century Christianity struggled against gnosticism, reaffirming the Hebraic view of nature and body as God's good creation. The second-century Christian theologian Irenaeus sought to combat gnostic anticosmism and to synthesize apocalypticism and Hebraic creationalism. He imaged the whole cosmos as a bodying forth of the Word and Spirit of God, as the sacramental embodiment of the invisible God.

Sin arises through a human denial of this relation to God. But salvific grace, dispensed progressively through the Hebrew and Christian revelations, allows humanity to heal its relation to God. The cosmos, in turn, grows into being a blessed and immortalized manifestation of the divine Word and Spirit, which is its ground of being (Richardson 1953, 1:387–98).

However, Greek and Latin Christianity, increasingly influenced by Neoplatonism, found this materialism distasteful. They deeply imbibed the platonic eschatology of the escape of the soul from the body and its return to a transcendent world outside the earth. The earth and the body must be left behind in order to ascend to another, heavenly world of disembodied life. Even though the Hebrew idea of resurrection of the body was retained, increasingly this notion was envisioned as a vehicle of immortal light for the soul, not the material body, in all its distasteful physical processes, which they saw as the very essence of sin as mortal corruptibility.[4]

The view of women in this ascetic Christian system was profoundly ambivalent. A part of ascetic Christianity imagined women becoming freed from subordination, freed both for equality in salvation and to act as agents of Christian preaching and teaching. But this freedom was based on woman rejecting her sexuality and reproductive role and becoming symbolically male. The classic Christian "good news" to woman as equal to man in Christ was rooted in a misogynist view of female sexuality and reproduction as the essence of the sinful, mortal, corruptible life (see Vogt, 1990).

For most male ascetic Christians, even ascetic woman, who had rejected her sexuality and reproductive role, was too dangerously sexual. Ascetic women were increasingly deprived of their minor roles in public ministry, such as deaconess, and locked away in convents, where obedience to God was to be expressed in total obedience to male ecclesiastical authority. Sexual woman, drawing male seminal power into herself, her womb swelling with new life, became the very essence of sin, corruptibility, and death, from which the male ascetic fled. Eternal life was disembodied male soul, freed from all material underpinnings in the mortal bodily life, represented by woman and nature.

Medieval Latin Christianity. was also deeply ambivalent about its view of nature. One side of medieval thought retained something of Irenaeus's sacramental cosmos, which becomes the icon of God through feeding on the redemptive power of Christ in the sacraments of bread and wine. The redeemed cosmos as resurrected body, united with God, is possible only by freeing the body of its sexuality and mortality. Mary, the virgin Mother of Christ, assumed into heaven to reign by the side of her son, was the representative of this redeemed body of the cosmos, the resurrected body of the Church (Semmelroth 1963, 166–68).

But the dark side of Medieval thought saw nature as possessed by demonic powers that draw us down to sin and death through sexual temptation. Women, particularly old crones with sagging breasts and bellies, still perversely retaining their sexual appetites, are the vehicles of the demonic power of nature. They are the witches who sell their souls to the Devil in a satanic parody of the Christian sacraments (Summers 1928).

THE REFORMATION AND THE SCIENTIFIC REVOLUTION

The Calvinist Reformation and the Scientific Revolution in England in the late sixteenth and seventeenth centuries represent key turning points in the Western concept of nature. In these two movements, the Medieval struggle between the sacramental and the demonic views of nature was recast. Calvinism dismembered the Medieval sacramental sense of nature. For Calvinism, nature was totally depraved. There was no residue of divine presence in it that could sustain a natural knowledge or relation to God. Saving knowledge of God descends from on high, beyond nature, in the revealed Word available only in Scripture, as preached by the Reformers.

The Calvinist reformers were notable in their iconoclastic hostility toward visual art. Stained glass, statues, and carvings were smashed, and the churches stripped of all visible imagery. Only the disembodied Word, descending from the preacher to the ear of the listener, together with music, could be bearers of divine presence. Nothing one could see, touch, taste, or smell was trustworthy as bearer of the divine. Even the bread and wine were no longer the physical embodiment of Christ, but intellectual reminders of the message about Christ's salvific act enacted in the past.

Calvinism dismantled the sacramental world of Medieval Christianity, but it maintained and reinforced its demonic universe. The fallen world, especially physical nature and other human groups outside of the control of the Calvinist church, lay in the grip of the Devil. All who were labeled pagan, whether Catholics or Indians and Africans, were the playground of demonic powers. But, even within the Calvinist church, women were the gateway of the Devil. If women were completely obedient to their fathers, husbands, ministers, and magistrates, they might be redeemed as goodwives. But in any independence of women lurked heresy and witchcraft. Among Protestants, Calvinists were the primary witch-hunters (Perkins 1590, 1596; see also Carlsen 1980).

The Scientific Revolution at first moved in a different direction, exorcizing the demonic powers from nature in order to reclaim it as an icon of divine reason manifest in natural law (Easlea 1980). But, in the seventeenth and eighteenth centuries, the more animist natural science, which unified material and spiritual, lost out to a strict dualism of transcendent intellect and dead matter.

Nature was secularized. It was no longer the scene of a struggle between Christ and the Devil. Both divine and demonic spirits were driven out of it. In Cartesian dualism and Newtonian physics, it becomes matter in motion, dead stuff moving obediently, according to mathematical laws knowable to a new male elite of scientists. With no life or soul of its own, nature could be safely expropriated by this male elite and infinitely reconstructed to augment its wealth and power.

In Western society, the application of science to technological control over nature marched side by side with colonialism. From the sixteenth to the twentieth centuries, Western Europeans would appropriate the lands of the Americas, Asia, and Africa, and reduce their human populations to servitude. The wealth accrued by this vast expropriation of land and labor would fuel new levels of technological revolution, transforming material resources into new forms of energy and mechanical work, control of disease, increasing speed of communication and travel. Western elites grew increasingly optimistic, imagining that this technological way of life would gradually conquer all problems of material scarcity and even push back the limits of human mortality. The Christian dream of immortal blessedness, freed from finite limits, was translated into scientific technological terms (Condorcet 1794).

ECOLOGICAL CRISIS

In a short three-quarters of a century, this dream of infinite progress has been turned into a nightmare. The medical conquest of disease, lessening infant mortality and doubling the life span of the affluent, insufficiently matched by birth limitation, especially among the poor, has created a population explosion that is rapidly outrunning the food supply. Every year 10 million children die of malnutrition.[5] The gap between rich and poor, between the wealthy elites of the industrialized sector and the impoverished masses, especially in the colonized continents of Latin America, Asia, and Africa, grows ever wider (Wilson and Ramphele 1989).

This Western scientific Industrial Revolution has been built on injustice. It has been based on the takeover of the land, its agricultural, metallic, and mineral wealth appropriated through the exploitation of the labor of the indigenous people. This wealth has flowed back to enrich the West, with some for local elites, while the laboring people of these lands grew poorer. This system of global affluence, based on exploitation of the land and labor of the many for the benefit of the few, with its high consumption of energy and waste, cannot be expanded to include the poor without destroying the basis of life of the planet itself. We are literally destroying the air, water, and soil upon which human and planetary life depend.

In order to preserve the unjust monopoly on material resources from the growing protests of the poor, the world became more and more militarized. Most nations have been using the lion's share of their state budgets for weapons, both to guard against one another and to control their own poor. Weapons also become one of the major exports of wealthy nations to poor nations. Poor nations grow increasingly indebted to wealthy nations while buying weapons to repress their own impoverished masses. Population explosion, exhaustion of natural resources, pollution, and state violence are the four horsemen of the new global apocalypse.

The critical question of both justice and survival is how to pull back from this disastrous course and remake our relations with one another and with the earth.

TOWARD AN ECOFEMINIST ETHIC AND CULTURE

There are many elements that need to go into an ecofeminist ethic and culture for a just and sustainable planet. One element is to reshape our dualistic concept of reality as split between soulless matter and transcendent male consciousness. We need to discover our actual reality as latecomers to the planet. The world of nature, plants, and animals existed billions of years before we came on the scene. Nature does not need us to rule over it, but runs itself very well, even better, without humans. We are the parasites on the food chain of life, consuming more and more, and putting too little back to restore and maintain the life system that supports us.

We need to recognize our utter dependence on the great life-producing matrix of the planet in order to learn to reintegrate our human systems of production, consumption, and waste into the ecological patterns by which nature sustains life. This might begin by revisualizing the relation of mind, or human intelligence, to nature. Mind or consciousness is not something that originates in some transcendent world outside of nature, but is the place where nature itself becomes conscious. We need to think of human consciousness not as separating us as a higher species from the rest of nature, but rather as a gift to enable us to learn how to harmonize our needs with the natural system around us, of which we are a dependent part.

Such a reintegration of human consciousness and nature must reshape the concept of God, instead of modeling God after alienated male consciousness, outside of and ruling over nature. God, in ecofeminist spirituality, is the immanent source of life that sustains the whole planetary community. God is neither male nor anthropomorphic. God is the font from which the variety of plants and animals well up in each new generation, the matrix that sustains their life-giving interdependency with one another (McFague 1987, 69–77).

In ecofeminist culture and ethic, mutual interdependency replaces the hierarchies of domination as the model of relationship between men and women, between human groups, and between humans and other beings. All racist, sexist, classist, cultural, and anthropocentric assumptions of the superiority of whites over blacks, males over females, managers over workers, humans over animals and plants, must be discarded. In a real sense, the so-called superior pole in each relation is actually the more dependent side of the relationship.

But it is not enough simply to humbly acknowledge dependency. The pattern of male-female, racial, and class interdependency itself has to be reconstructed socially, creating more equitable sharing in the work and the fruits of work, rather than making one side of the relation the subjugated and impoverished base for the power and wealth of the other.

In terms of male-female relations, this means not simply allowing women more access to public culture, but converting males to an equal share in the tasks of child nurture and household maintenance. A revolution in female roles into the male work world, without a corresponding revolution in male roles, leaves the basic pattern of patriarchal exploitation of women untouched. Women are simply overworked in a new way, expected to do both a male workday, at low pay, and also the unpaid work of women that sustains family life.

There must be a conversion of men to the work of women, along with the conversion of male consciousness to the earth. Such conversions will reshape the symbolic vision of salvation. Instead of salvation sought either in the disembodied soul or the immortalized body, in a flight to heaven or to the end of history, salvation should be seen as continual conversion to the center, to the concrete basis by which we sustain our relation to nature and to one another. In every day and every new generation, we need to remake our relation with one another, finding anew the true nexus of relationality that sustains, rather than exploits and destroys, life (Ruether 1984, 325–35).

Finally, ecofeminist culture must reshape our basic sense of self in relation to the life cycle. The sustaining of an organic community of plant and animal life is a continual cycle of growth and disintegration. The western flight from mortality is a flight from the disintegration side of the life cycle, from accepting ourselves as part of that process. By pretending that we can immortalize ourselves, souls and bodies, we are immortalizing our garbage and polluting the earth. In order to learn to recycle our garbage as fertilizer for new life, as matter for new artifacts, we need to accept our selfhood as participating in the same process. Humans also are finite organisms, centers of experience in a life cycle that must disintegrate back into the nexus of life and arise again in new forms.

These conversions, from alienated, hierarchical dualism to life-sustaining mutuality, will radically change the patterns of patriarchal culture. Basic concepts, such as God, soul-body, and salvation will be reconceived in ways that may bring us much closer to the ethical values of love, justice, and care for the earth. These values have been proclaimed by patriarchal religion, yet contradicted by patriarchal symbolic and social patterns of relationship.

These tentative explorations of symbolic changes must be matched by a new social practice that can incarnate these conversions in new social and technological ways of organizing human life in relation to one another and to nature. This will require a new sense of urgency about the untenability of present patterns of life and compassionate solidarity with those who are its victims.

NOTES

1. Phyllis Trible (1973) views the story of Eve's creation from Adam as essentially egalitarian. For an alternative view from the Jewish tradition, see Reik 1960.

2. For the major writings of inter-testamental apocalyptic, see Charles 1913.

3. For the major gnostic literature, see Robinson 1977.

4. Origen (1966, Bk. 2, ch. 3, 83-94). Also Nyssa, 464-65.

5. Cited in a talk in London, May 29, 1989, by Dr. Nafis Sadik, head of the United Nations Fund for Population Activities. See Broder, 1989.

2

Sin, Nature, and Black Women's Bodies

DELORES S. WILLIAMS

As early as the 1960s, people in the Western world were beginning to realize that technology was developing to the point of dismembering the natural environment, of rendering the planet uninhabitable. Many Americans were beginning to realize that the preservation of what was known as "The American Way of Life" (i.e., luxury and comfort, compared to poverty in the two-thirds world) was rapidly depleting the world's natural resources. Some scholars even contended that Christianity's encouragement of technological invention was, in part, responsible for the environmental crisis (White 1967, 1205).

However, very few people made the connection between America's contribution to the abuse and exploitation of the natural environment today with the dominating culture's historic abuse and exploitation of African-American women's bodies in the nineteenth century. Just as technology's rapid and often unchecked contribution to the destruction of nature is rationalized on the basis of technology providing greater profits, comfort, and leisure for more Americans, the exploitation of the black woman's body was rationalized to the advantage of white slave owners. Female slaves were beaten, overworked, and made to experience excessive childbearing in order to provide income, comfort, and leisure for slave-owning families. Because, in the nineteenth century, slave owner consciousness imaged black people as belonging to a lower order of nature than white people, black people were to be controlled and tamed like the rest of the natural environment. Black women (and black men) were

Delores Williams is Associate Professor of Theology and Culture at Union Theological Seminary in New York City. She is the author of the forthcoming book *Daughters of Hagar: The Challenge of Womanist God-Talk* (Orbis Books). Her articles have appeared in the *Journal of Feminist Studies in Religion, The Journal of Religious Thought, Christianity and Crisis, Christian Century,* and in several books.

"viewed as beasts, as cattle, as 'articles' for sale" (Nichols 1963, 12). The taming of these "lower orders of nature" would assure the well-being of both master and slave—so slave owner consciousness imagined. Put simply, the assault upon the natural environment today is but an extension of the assault upon black women's bodies in the nineteenth century.

Within the last ten years, African-American women have begun developing Womanist Theology and have labeled this assault upon the environment and upon black women's bodies as sin. In some womanist theological quarters, this sin has been named "defilement."[1] Different from the traditional theological understanding of sin as alienation or estrangement from God and humanity,[2] the sin of defilement manifests itself in human attacks upon creation so as to ravish, violate, and destroy creation: to exploit and control the production and reproduction capacities of nature, to destroy the unity in nature's placements, to obliterate the spirit of the created.[3]

Assuming a relation between the defilement of earth's body and the defilement of black women's bodies, this article will attempt one task. That is to show the correlations between the defilement of aspects of the natural environment today and the defilement of black women's bodies in the nineteenth century. Finally I suggest how American national consciousness has been shaped so that Christians do not readily see the manifestations of the sin of defilement in relation to black women's experience and to nature.

STRIP-MINING AND BREEDER WOMEN

As the environmental crisis became more obvious, strip-mining was recognized as a problem, as an assault upon the earth. Richard Cartwright Austin describes strip-mining as "Modern technology in the form of giant shovels, bulldozers, and other ... equipment ... at war with the earth to extract coal. The people who lived among these once-beautiful hills [of West Virginia] often became casualties along with the landscape" (Austin 1988, 3). Because of the use of explosives and heavy machinery, strip-mining on top of the earth's surface "helped" the mine owners realize faster and larger profits than could be realized with men furnishing the energy for releasing the coal from beneath the earth's surface. Austin testifies that "those with capital were dismembering the hills, using dynamite and bulldozers to harvest coal cheaply" (Ibid., 4). Strip-mining ultimately exhausts the earth's capacity to produce coal. The bottom line here is regular and consistent defilement and abuse of the earth's body (the land) for the sake of economic profit—destroying the earth's production capacities for the benefit of a few people with money.

Just as strip-mining exhausts the earth's body, so did the practice of breeding female slaves exhaust black women's bodies. One slave woman tells of her aunt, who was a breeder woman during slavery and "brought in chillum ev'y twelve mont's jes lak a cow bringing in a calf" (Lerner 1973, 48). This practice was continued until many of the breeder women were no longer able to have children. Breeding women with men one already owned was a much cheaper way of obtaining more slaves than buying them on the slave market. The violation of the land's production capacities in strip-mining is no more severe than the violation of black women's bodies and reproduction capacities during slavery. Frances Kemble, a British actress who married a Georgia planation owner, had this to say about her interview with slave women:

> [One woman has a particularly dismal story to tell.] She has had sixteen children, fourteen of whom were dead; she had had four miscarriages: one had been caused with falling down with a very heavy burden on her head, and one from having her arms strained up to be lashed ... She said their hands were first tied together ... and they were then drawn up to a tree or post ... and then their clothes rolled around their waist, and a man with a cowhide stands and strips them. ... She did not speak of this as anything strange, unusual ... and when I said: "Did they do that to you when you were with child?" she simply replied: "Yes, missis." (Lerner 1973, 49-50)

Just as the land is vulnerable to all kind of uses by those who own the means of production in our society, the nineteenth-century slave woman's body was equally as vulnerable. "Black women ... were sexually available to any white man who cared to use them. ... The sexual exploitation of black women by white men was so widespread as to be general" (Ibid., 45-46).

DESTROYING THE UNITY IN NATURE'S PLACEMENTS

Violation and exploitation of the land and of women's bodies is, in part, caused by widespread human disrespect for the unity of nature's placements. This disrespect has led to the destruction of natural processes in nature. In 1973, Alan Hayward cited instances of the destruction of this unity by humans. He said:

> We cut down trees and plant crops on hillsides where nature intended that only trees should grow. But our crops cannot hold the soil together as nature's trees did. Muddy torrents cascade down the slopes until nothing but bare rock remains.
> Or we plough up the great prairies, where the soil and climate are suited for growing grass. Short-sighted methods of husbandry soon exhaust the soil, until the hot winds of summer are able to blow it away. The great dust bowls of the U.S.A. and Kazakhstan in the U.S.S.R. were created within living memory in this way. (Hayward 1973, 16)

This disrespect and destruction of nature's placements with regard to the land and its vegetation has a parallel in the disrespect seventeenth-, eighteenth- and nineteenth-century Western white men had for the natural location of the earth's peoples. Snatching African bodies, female and male, from their homeland in order to enslave them and make a profit, Western white males depleted the African continent's human resources that had been fundamental for institutional life in many African villages. These "body snatchers" not only captured ordinary Africans for slavery, they also snatched rulers, kings, and queens. In the middle passage, as these captured Africans were sailing to America, the black women's bodies, regardless of their former social status, were raped by crewmen. Thus many African women arrived on American shores pregnant.

ATTACK UPON NATURE'S SPIRIT AND THE HUMAN SPIRIT

There can be little doubt that this Western disrespect for the unity of nature's placements, for nature's own cycles of production and reproduction, has emerged with the growth and development of biblical monotheism. Lynn White, Jr., was correct when he said that the spread of this monotheism stamped out the animism present in the popular religious consciousness. Austin, reporting White's ideas, says common people believed "that spirits inhabited trees, springs, hills and other features of the landscape . . . [therefore] common people had traditionally empathized with their environment and had sought to placate it while they used it" (Austin 1988, 2). White says that "By destroying paganism, Christianity made it possible to exploit nature in a mood of indifference to the feelings of natural objects" (Ibid.). The present environmental crisis, perceived in the context of animistic faith, has resulted from Western assault upon the spirits of nature. (It is not uncharacteristic of some of African-American and African-Christian faith to believe that the spirit of God created nature and prevails in it. Therefore, the assault upon nature is an attack upon both the creation and the divine spirit.)

Many African-American slave narratives mention the work of men called "Negro breakers" or "Spirit breakers," who were hired by slave owners "to break" the spirit of slaves on the plantation who seemed to have too much self-esteem, too much sense of independence, who seemed to be "uppity." Often the slave master, himself, broke the spirit of such slave women by constantly raping them. Ex-slave Solomon Northup told the story of the slave woman Patsey, who was "slim and straight. . . . There was an air of loftiness in her movement, that neither labor, nor weariness, nor punishment could destroy." Northup says Patsey was "naturally . . . a joyous creature, a laughing, light-hearted girl, rejoicing in the mere sense of existence." But Patsey suffered more than any of the other slave women, because "it had fallen her lot to be the slave of a licentious master and a jealous mistress. Finally, for a trifling offense, Patsey was given a savage whipping, while her mistress and the master's children watched with obvious satisfaction. She almost died." Northup says "From that time forward she was not what she had been . . . the bounding vigor, the sprightly . . . spirit . . . was gone."[4] In his narrative, the ex-slave Frederick Douglass told of the "Negro Breakers" whom slave owners hired to break the spirit of "uppity" slaves.

Breaking the spirit of nature today through rape and violence done to the earth, and breaking the spirit of nineteenth-century slave women through rape and violence, constitute crimes against nature and against the human spirit.

Inasmuch as some Christianity has historically advocated that God gave man [sic] dominion over nature to use to his own advantage, it has not been difficult to create rationales to support this rape and violence. Christian slaveholders, believing they had ownership over the lower orders of nature (i.e., lower than themselves, who were the "highest" order of nature), assigned black men and women to the order of subhuman, on par with the lower animals. Thus these black people needed to be controlled.

INVISIBILIZING THE DEFILEMENT OF BLACK WOMEN

American national consciousness has been structured so that the defilement of black women is invisible due to the kind of associations made with the color of their black skin. In North America, popular culture, religion, science, and politics have worked together to assign permanent negative value to the color black. This has led to the formation of a national consciousness that considers black frightening, dangerous, repulsive, and a prime candidate for destruction. In this kind of consciousness, nothing black can be violated, because illegality and disaster are associated with blackness. For instance, blackmail and the black market are illegal. When the stock market fell in 1987, the day was referred to, in the media and elsewhere, as Black Monday. When the movie Ghost showed in American movie houses recently, whiteness was associated with heaven, while blackness was associated with hell. The hero in the movie died and ultimately walked into a bright, white light apparently leading to heaven. When the villains in the movie died, jet-black figures escorted them, apparently into hell.

Not only today, but also in earlier times, negative associations were made with the color black. The American economic crash of 1873 was referred to as Black September. In the early days of the Industrial Revolution in America, when the factory system was emerging, management circulated blacklists. On these lists were the names of workers whom management designated as troublemakers or undesirable for one reason or another. Antipathy toward blackness was expressed as early as the first century, in an early Christian document titled The Epistle of Barnabas. This document provided the following "portrait" of the devil:

> The way of the Black One [i.e., the devil] is crooked and full of cursing, for it is the way of death eternal with punishment, and in it are the things that destroy their soul: idolatry, forwardness, arrogance of power, hypocrisy, double-heartedness, adultery, murder, robbery, pride, transgression, fraud, malice, self-sufficiency, enchantments, magic, covetousness. (Lake 1919, 1:407)

In the nineteenth century, the newly developing science called physical anthropology went to great lengths to "prove" the intellectual and moral inferiority of black people, including black women (Stanton 1960). Put all this structuring of the national consciousness about blackness with the structuring of the national consciousness to devalue black womanhood,[5] and it is not difficult to understand why black women's defilement is invisible to mainstream America. Then put all of this together with the practice of controlling and using nature, which many Christians have believed to be their God-given right, and it is not difficult to understand why Westerners did not recognize in the early stages of technological development the defilement of nature that could and surely would occur.

This defilement of nature's body and of black women's bodies is sin, since its occurrence denies that black women and nature are made in the image of God. Its occurrence is an assault upon the spirit of creation in women and nature. Whereas theologians such as Paul Tillich spoke of sin as man's [sic] estrangement from God and from other humans, womanist theologians can claim that humanity in the Western world has fallen to deeper states of degradation and depravity. Western Christians, some of whom are the manipulators of technology and concepts of development, no longer have to struggle only with the despair of being alienated from God (or the ground of being). They must now struggle with the attack Western man has waged against creation itself. They must struggle against the sin of defilement (evidenced today in nature and in the history of black women)—the sin that now threatens to destroy all life on the planet.

NOTES

1. See Williams 1991.

2. Paul Tillich identified sin as estrangement from God and humanity in his *Systematic Theology*. See Saiving 1992, 25-42. Saiving provides new understanding of the human situation that challenges the relevance of traditional notions of sin for women's experience.

3. In Western culture, even the ancients believed that their gods considered defilement a serious act for which one received severe punishment. In Homer's *Iliad*, the gods become angry with Achilles not because he killed his opponent, Hector, but because he defiled Hector's body after he killed him. To defile a person after death deserved the punishment of being cut off from eternal life—which, of course, was the punishment Achilles received. He lost his invulnerability, and his heel became his vulnerable spot which, if properly wounded, could lead to his death.

4. Northup 1853, 188-90, 198, 156-59. Northup's story was quoted in Lerner 1973.

5. See bell hooks's (1981) description of the devaluation of black womanhood.

3

Talk about the Weather

The Greening of Eschatology

CATHERINE KELLER

You know how to interpret the appearance of earth and sky; but why do you not know how to interpret the present time?

Luke 12:56

What do you think of when you hear the phrase, "the end of the world?" A premillennialist horror fantasy of final tribulation, complete with planes crashing as born again pilots join the rapture of the true Christians? The final heat death of the universe? The smoke and fire of nuclear war, and endless winter afterwards?

Let me guess that as the nineties count down to the millennium, the rhetoric of "the end of the world" stimulates for most white middle-class North Americans, male or female, anxious ecological associations. Apocalypse is getting colored green. "Increasingly, apocalyptic fears about widespread droughts and melting ice-caps have displaced the nuclear threat as the dominant feared meteorological disaster," notes Andrew Ross in his aptly titled *Strange Weather* (1991). Consider what it means that—among the religious and the irreligious alike—phrases like "the destruction of the earth" or "save the planet" have within a few years become commonplace. But if apocalypticisms have become casual, so has the casual become apocalyptic. You exchange pleasantries with

Catherine Keller, author of *From a Broken Web: Separation, Sexism, and the Self,* teaches feminist theory and constructive theology in the Graduate and Theological Schools of Drew University. She is completing work on *Apocalypse Now and Then: A Feminist Approach to the End of the World.*

a stranger and find a casual allusion to the weather—for instance when it is unseasonably warm, or cold, or when the weather weirdly bounces—rudely insinuating the end of the world. The foreboding feeling of irretrievable and unforeseeable damage reverberates in the brief silences, as we nod and shake our heads, break eye contact, change the topic.

Talk about weather has lost its innocence. Such a loss poses a social crisis for human discourse. How but through the weather do we move beyond the formalities? What other topic everywhere and always connects us, whoever we are, whether we are strangers thrown together for a few moments or partners rising from the same bed? The great inclusive "it" of "it's looking like rain," "it's gorgeous," has always bound us, with accompanying sighs, groans, and grimaces. It embeds our relations to each other in nature—that materiality which is shared, no matter what, across every arbitrary human division. In the commonplace medium of the weather we encounter the ever mobile face of the creation here and now. This encounter, and the eschatological threat to human meaning posed by its material devastation, places the present theological enquiry within the realm of daily experience.

What weather talk means differs quite precisely according to our cultural as well as geographic location. Thus elite Western cultures tend to scorn weather-talk as banal. This superiority to small talk about the weather symptomatizes a kind of relationship to the planetary condition. Thus it is important to ask who benefits from a relationship of distance from the rest of creation. Who profits from the so-called transcendence of nature? However piously couched in the language of higher, eternal and invisible preoccupations, such transcendence correlates nicely with western technological practices. Freedom from nature implies, for instance, freedom from the vicissitudes of weather. It therefore facilitates practices of control of the environment and the exploitation of the earth's energies to sustain artificial environments with homogenized, central-ized, steady, comfortable weather. Who can better afford to experience "nature" as banal, exterior, outside of immediate importance than those urban elites who seem to have severed the immediate bonds of dependency upon weather conditions? But have they not therefore also forfeited the subtle shift-ing consciousness of our connections to all the earth creatures who share the dependency? This means most of us in the Northern Hemisphere. Nonetheless, even in the banality of our clipped connections, we talk about the weather. We are somehow still at home together in it.

The weather is at once a metaphor for the ecological crisis in which the planet finds itself, and its most inescapable symptom. The weather, like "nature," has readily been woman-identified—alternately enchanting and frightening, nurturing and withholding, rhythmic and capricious, moody and unstable, subject to the modern and "manly" sciences of meteorology, climate control, and other modes of social management. Talk about the weather there-fore becomes ecofeminist discourse. Theologically, because it is about the end of the world as we know it, it falls under the heading of eschatology—talk about end things. More precisely, I am situating it within the theological topic of "apocalyptic eschatology." It revolves around "apocalypse" meaning disclosure or revelation; around "eschatology" meaning discourse about the ultimate or the end; and around "end" coming from the Greek *eschatos* for a temporal or spatial end, edge or horizon. This essay considers the link between ecology and eschatology. Apocalypse is a type of eschatology. The ecological trauma apocalyptically encoded in the weather may clue us into our eschatological missions, as theological practitioner—our missions not to a life after life but to life itself. Eschatology is discourse about the collective encounter at the edge of space and time, where and when the life of the creation has its chance at renewal.

It was the change in weather patterns that inspired Bill McKibben to title his work on the ecological crisis *The End of Nature*. The book displayed on its black cover an image of the earth ringed by a fiery haze—as though the planet is on fire. The publisher chose to inflame the ecologically endearing photo of our common home with apocalypse. Though the biblical "apocalypse" does not (contrary to popular usage) necessarily imply the "end of the world," any imagery of "the end of . . ." certainly taps the fantasy of apocalypse. It is not necessary to suggest some sort of absolute annihilation of all planetary life in order to imagine the destruction of *this* world, this fragile, resilient interplay of human culture and the rest of creation. Apocalypse, the edgiest of eschatologies, always reveals the threat to a *particular* world.

In what sense does McKibben's text develop an apocalyptic discourse? Referring to what scientists call the "large-scale geophysical experiment" entailed by the accumulation of carbon dioxide in the atmosphere, he makes his interpretive move, saying, "While there are other parts to this story—the depletion of the ozone, acid rain, genetic engineering—the story of the end of nature really begins with that greenhouse experiment, with what will happen to the weather" (McKibben, 10). Why? Mainly because the changing of the atmosphere and the subsequent warming, changes everything. These changes will be on an unprecedented scale. The chain reactions of heat, drought, rising ocean levels, catastrophic storm systems, mass species extinctions remain in a certain sense incalculable. Yet the signs of the time are already manifest. Jesus had seemed to scold his questioners for reading weather indicators but not the signs of the time—of the end of the age. The current configuration seems to require both readings at once—the signs of the times are written in the sky. Moreover, Jesus, in classic eschatological form, also grasped at women's experience to find hope amidst the prospect of greater doom, likening tribulations to a woman's travail: "all this is but the beginning of the birth-pangs" (Mt. 24:8). McKibben inadvertently draws upon the same metaphor. "To declare, as some editorialists have done, that the warming has not yet appeared and therefore the theory is wrong is like arguing that a woman hasn't yet given birth and therefore isn't pregnant" (McKibben, 29).

While certainly not intending to design an eschatology, McKibben uses his apocalyptic language with precision. For him, "the end of nature" does not mean "the end of the world"—for there will still be rain and snow, summer and winter, if not the "same" rain and snow, summer and winter. He means the end of that to which the *idea* of nature refers. He understands that idea as "our sense of nature as eternal and separate," in some fundamental way independent of our influence, autonomous and powerfully over and against us. McKibben's definition of nature is not without serious problems for the present argument, as we shall see. But it has disclosive power. Once the atmosphere is changed, nothing is "untouched." (Loss of innocence indeed!) For instance, "summer is going extinct, replaced by something else that will be called 'summer.' This new summer will retain some of its relative characteristics—it will be hotter than the rest of the year, for instance, and the time of year when crops grow—but it will not be summer, just as even the best prosthesis is not a leg." In other words, human culture now determines—haphazardly, recklessly, but effectively—the course of everything "natural." There is no mountain peak where the wind blows or a stream flows uninfluenced by human input. "By changing the weather, we make every spot on earth man-made [sic] and artificial. We have deprived nature of its independence, and that is fatal to its meaning."

In other words the problem of ecological destruction is not just a global rat's nest of gruesome facts. It is at the same time a problem of meaning. Christian theology trucks in nothing if not meaning questions. McKibben's view of nature has tremendous implications for any theological attention to the future of creation, that is, to eschatology (See Moltmann 1979). The end of nature's analysis stands as a prophetic, properly apocalyptic text, representative of an entire genre of ecological discourses. Like the Book of Revelation, it involves a certain determinism. Sin, corruption, and exploitation have wreaked irreversible evil, and human effort cannot return the earth to any pristine Edenic conditions; yet they also sound the conditional doom which calls, rather dubiously, for conversion. Its hope of course is not for a miraculous new heaven and earth, but for change—enough, and soon enough—that the changes of sky and earth already in process can be minimized and their effects handled with maximum decency (which would be something of a miracle anyway). The best to be hoped for is a kind of well managed planetary park. In this sense the vision resonates sadly to the artificiality of the vision of John of Patmos rather more than to the eschatological hope of the classical prophets, who did not quite envision universal doom as the precondition of renewal. The New Jerusalem of the Apocalypse has no sea, no natural sun, and little geography beyond a lush architectural miracle through which supernatural rivers lined by unnaturally fecund trees offer nourishment to all. John of Patmos of course does not, like McKibben, lament the prospective loss of "nature" but rather celebrates the artifice of God.

Back to the weather. Theologically it is crucial to distinguish between man-made (yes, sic) and God-made conditions. Nature itself consists of spontaneous vitalities which cannot—according to orthodoxy, as well as to process theology—be read as simple mirrors of divine will. But nature at the end of the twentieth century, as McKibben has so cogently argued, can only be understood as a product of human agency. Thus its destructiveness cannot be understood as judgment but rather as that for which we will be judged. But the punishment seems to be—with a terrifying indifference to individual human agents—already contained in the sin. As I first considered these connections, Bangladesh was suffering the hideous aftermath of a calamitous storm. The poverty which causes the population to mount uncontrollably and to crowd the coastal areas worked in tandem with apparently "natural" disaster in this case. The 1990 State of the World foresaw just such a disastrous storm surge, not as natural at all, but as an effect of the rising planetary heat, which is so ominously accompanied by rising oceans. The higher the sea level, the more catastrophic the storms. Recalling the worst storm of the century, which hit Bangladesh in 1970, the author wrote that "as the region's population mounts, so does the potential for another disaster" (Brown 1990).

Human injustice here shows a cosmic face set especially toward poorer southern nations which are most vulnerable to rising sea levels caused by the industrial north's greenhouse gases—and least able to do anything to stop it. Some islands will simply disappear by the turn of the next century at present rates. Low-lying coastal ecological systems, of which Bangladesh tops the list as an example, will suffer ever more apocalyptic weather.

The very notion of a "natural disaster," like what the insurance companies designate "act of God," may soon sound like nostalgia for a lost universe, where innocent humans heroically stood their ground against cosmic caprice, finding solace in some sense of a divine controlling providence behind the assaults of wild weather or wild beasts. Ecological analysis displays a morass of "man-made" factors vastly exacerbating any so-called "acts of God." Indeed it reveals—*apokalypsis*—the interstructured density of oppressions for which North American political theology at the end of the millennium senses its accountability. The intertangling strands of the so-called "issues" begin to stretch out into their own eschatological horizon. The mix of obstacles to the goal which the World Council of Churches has dubbed "justice, peace, and the integrity of creation" creates a formidable threat of doom. But at the same time the growing consciousness of the deadly mixture of economics, race, gender, nationality and religion creates a true *apokalypsis,* or revelation. It discloses the just demand for a radically inclusive horizon of practice.

This revelatory moment renders the best contemporary prophecy horizonal—attentive to the perspective within which we live and relate to the rest of creation. It also draws it horizontal—the divine is encountered in our relations to each other and the other creatures upon the earth rather than in sheerly vertical moments of transcendence. Nowhere is the density of the tangle more clearly manifest than in the planetary ecological crisis. After all, ecology is the discipline of interrelatedness par excellence, and in its increasing exchange with the varieties of social analysis, begins to contribute to a richly textured social ecology. Thus at the same time that the crisis of nonhuman communities requires prophetic human attention, the human communities traditionally understood in terms of oppression can no longer abstract their historical issues from the bioregions in which they seek to survive. But also our own human relations of domination or of solidarity gain illumination from the ecological model. From the perspective of an earth-bound eschatology, there may be no more disclosive field right now than that generated by the intersections of the "issues."

Sexism is just one such vantage point for observing the ecological intersections of both modes of oppression and modes of solidarity. It remains the privileged issue for ecofeminism, that is, its entry point into analysis of the multiple oppressions. The "man" of the "man-made apocalypse" does not implicate all males of our species any more than it exonerates all women. However, it does allow us to discern that gender imbalance may lie at the heart of the ecological imbalance. Take, for instance, the rising global population rate, a catastrophic trend variously underplayed both by right wing anti-abortionists and feminists combating the misogyny implied by monofocal emphasis on population (often encouraging female infanticide and forced sterilization). It brings the gender dimension of ecological crisis into focus. For poverty and population growth are positively correlated with each other and inversely proportional to women's status. The way to an enlightened population policy is clear:

> [S]tudies on every continent show that as female literacy rates rise so do income levels, nutrition levels, and child survival rates; at the same time, population growth slows, as women gain the self-confidence to assert control over their bodies. (Brown 149)

The bodily self-confidence of women flows directly and eschatologically against the currents of the artificial apocalypse.

The "end of nature," which poses threats to all bodies—but to some much sooner and more than others—seems to be the product of the same worldview which has subordinated all women to men and most men to a few pale and privileged ones. So environmental racism and the police state policies here and abroad which enforce it enter the picture as well.[1] Like a shadow-side of our unacknowledged web of connections, the tangle of "isms" underlying the ecological crisis twists endlessly round the planet. It stirs up strange weather. My point is not to enumerate them here but to point to the horizon of assumptions by which they enclose our vision—and open it up radically when exposed.

Apocalypse means literally "to unveil." In exposing and disclosing, it leaves no hiding place. The text in Revelation 6:12ff, mocks the very effort to hide, when, at the opening of the sixth seal, "the kings of the earth and the great men and the generals and the rich . . ." call to the mountains, "Fall on us and hide us . . ." That seems to be our situation, when even weather patterns threaten the future life of human civilization. In North America, we normally think of cozily hiding in our houses from bad weather. But the ecological vision reveals, in a less mythological sense than apocalypse, that there is no home to hide from the weather in. The home of the human species is the planet. The ravaged air and water and earth are the elements in which we move and live and have our being. We can't keep the weather out. There is no "out."

Ecology—etymologically it means "talk about home"—has become talk about the planetary home of homes, the ultimate "habitat for humanity." It has developed as a discourse only because there is no longer any notion of home, like weather, which can be taken for granted. The weather itself poses the need to talk about the rapid deterioration of the home-spaces, deterioration to the point that without radical and rapid renovation, our terrestrial habitat will soon be uninhabitable to most of us except the rich, the armed, and the insect. Talk about home merges with talk about the end of the world—the ultimate case of homelessness.

Apocalyptic eschatology, which entertains the vision of the imminent collapse of the world (the sum of nature and civilization), appears at moments irresistible. This is both mythically appropriate and historically dangerous. And precisely therefore must those who practice spiritualities of justice within Christian contexts consider the theological force field of the weather and other ecological traumas. This means doing our apocalyptic "home-work."

But, after all, what about eschatology? Can Christian talk about ultimacy help to inspire the needed clean-up? Or do eschatological beliefs about our ultimate home only mess things up worse on earth? Eschatology, I have suggested, is the doctrinal lens through which Christian culture, consciously or not, imagines any "end of the world." Yet since *eschaton* does not simply refer to a final, temporal end, but alludes at the same time to the spatial image of an end, an edge, so the moving, and therefore endless, spatial horizon of the earth presents itself both as metaphor and as content of any adequate eschatology. The edge of life takes on the charge of an ultimate encounter, a kind of discourse that takes place and takes time at the edge of wherever we as a people are. Because the very notion of the end of the world has been distorted by the modern capacity to bring that end about—that is, to effect a man-made apocalypse—the meaning of eschatology must also be fundamentally renegotiated. Unless it can meaningfully and effectively address the green apocalypse, Christian theology becomes a trivial pursuit at the end of the second millennium.

Let me then suggest the following criterion: *a responsible Christian eschatology would be an ecologically sound eschatology, one that motivates work to save our planet.* It quite simply must be good for the earth, and must inspire and challenge the caretaking, biblically referred to as stewardship, to which we, the human component of creation, are called. For we find ourselves at the edge of history, where history threatens to consume nature and therefore itself. We can entertain the prospective of a retrospective judgment upon human stewardship by extrapolating statistical trends as well as by mythologizing final judgement. Responsible theology recycles its own resources. Therefore, rather than seeking to junk the doctrine, a sound theology requires an earth-bound eschatology.

But is this reconstruction of eschatology possible? Or is it another case of liberal Christian wishful thinking? Does not Christian eschatology gather under its wings precisely that array of doctrinal symbolics which have drawn interest *away from* the earth, from natural conditions, from finitude and flesh? Has Christian reflection on the ultimate destiny of redeemed humanity sucked the best of life toward a heaven which only deathless and fleshless souls are fit to inhabit? Sometimes eschatology has retained the biblical imagery of the resurrected body as the inhabitant of the new creation, attempting to emphasize that wholeness becomes incarnate. Early theologians such as Tertullian argued hard on behalf of the goodness of the material creation against the flesh-despising "heretics," in order to affirm the bodiliness of the resurrection not just of Jesus but of all humans. Yet this spiritual body has been conceived as free of natural limits and geographical ecologies, hence perhaps again—tragically—feeding the Christian tendency to substitute supernature for nature.

One can argue that this addiction to the unnatural is unbiblical, that Hebrew scripture and much early Christian thought is far earthier than its Hellenized later theologies. But are not the biblical roots of Western civilization themselves ecologically ambiguous, casting stewardship in terms of dominion? Lynn White's classic essay, less dismissive of Christianity than the defenses from Christian apologists would suggest, first got this case a wide hearing (White 1967). He claims that the environmental crisis has roots in Judeo-Christian attitudes toward nature as placed under human dominion.

Dominion means in its original context, quite precisely, domination and subjugation. Human subjugation of the other creatures thus mirrors the creator's controlling power over creation. Will such a doctrine of creation inevitably justify human irresponsibility precisely in the name of responsibility, as it does now in the hands of anti-environmentalist lobbyists? If so, then it always finally necessitates a "new creation" by the same omnipotent Creator. Is the biblical understanding of history as moving toward the "new thing" which God will do already problematic? Does it indirectly teach us to undervalue the present tense of the earth and its cycles of renewal—never forgetting their pagan associations? Does it thus prepare the way for the throw-away culture in which we live from one "new thing" to the next? With the apocalyptic emphasis upon the new heaven and earth, this new creation comes about by the supernatural intervention of the omnipotent God. Is not the new earth, with its new Jerusalem, so incomparably more perfect than the first creation as to make this one out to be a crummy little earth ball? In other words, when Christian hope basks in such resplendent supernatural futures, why would it worry much about mere nature? Indeed, serious concern with the natural world, like too much occupation with one's own bodily processes, indicates within this framework a lack of faith.

There are many varieties of what we may call the unearthly eschatology. At their best they sin by omission—by draining energy away from our earth-home, living life in orientation toward a many-mansioned heavenly home. But at a certain point, the indifference toward nature implied in traditional eschatology becomes lethal. That is, its distraction from the earth complies with the destruction of the earth. This need not be so bald as Reagan's infamous appointment to the Environmental Protection Agency of James Watts, a Mormon who used dominion language couched within the premillennialist apocalypse of the imminent end of the world to justify the rapid exploitation of all planetary resources. It also plays itself out in continual casual references to right to use, now called "wise use," (that is, to "use up" the rest of the creation, because of "mankind's" privilege at the apex of the created universe. The strange failure to develop practices of sustainable use within a culture in which Christian eschatology has shaped our view of the future is, accordingly, not so strange. For there is no need for endlessly renewable resources if the earth is not an endless proposition. The end is in sight. Sooner or later, but within the foreseeable future, God will create a new heaven and earth. Thus it so happens that the neo-fundamentalist fantasy of the rapture out of this world, just as the going gets bad, followed by a supernatural new creation, claimed such public power in the eighties. This was precisely the time of the most profligate development of the throw-away consumer culture.

Has a set of apocalyptic codes—more subliminal than intentional—embedded itself deep in the subtext of western culture? If so, is it altogether surprising that the doomsday text of apocalyptic mythology can function as self-fulfilling prophecy, realizing itself with all the techno-power of late modern literalism? The disregard of the creation seems to be endemic to the culture which has called itself Christian. In other words, the assumption of the imminent end of the world, however indefinitely deferred, may be the ultimate self-fulfilling prophecy.

But why this temptation to flee the earth, whether in a rapture that awaits the supernatural new creation, or in an afterlife expectancy which always for orthodoxy suggests the final resurrection of the dead at the end of history? Why has faith for most Christians through most of our history come down simply to hope for an *after*-life, not for life? How did Christian fantasy get addicted to visions of heaven and hell, sucking the meaning out of our lives as earthlings? How did popular religion come to mean so little more than this—be good enough in your private life so that you can get your personal reward at the end of your life? How did eschatology come to function as the great magnet of future reward, sucking all embodied life toward a fantasmagoric future, making the earth and all its delicate, voluptuous, daunting, dynamic ecologies into nothing but material means to immortal ends?

The Marxist answer, that religion has provided the opiate for the people, now appears as quaint as the Soviet army belt buckles and other Second World memorabilia on sale at tourist shops throughout Europe. Materialism, even the apocalyptic-prophetic materialism of the socialist vision, has overreacted against otherworldliness and thus done violence at once to spirit and to the nuances of its *matter*. It has totalized the worst anthropocentrism and technological utopianism of modernity. Yet it does address the power of an addictive vision to distract from the real needs of human bodies and spirits. It bears witness to the suffering which religion has tried, however pathologically, to address.

To decry this flight from the earth as western, indeed, as patriarchal dualism (which includes the Marxist vision), may come close to the truth but remains too foggy. The habit of transcendence upwards, boredom and alienation in relation to nature seems to be a symptom of systemic suffering, of fissures within the self and its community, from which selves can find no earthly relief. But viewed from the vantage point of late North American modernity, we cannot but be suspicious that the construction of salvation as supernatural has helped to cause the very destruction of nature from which the earth now needs saving. When salvation means removal from the earth to a heavenly home, then our *oikos* is abandoned to the assaults of those whose ultimate concern is neither heaven nor the earth, but the power and wealth of their particular households. These households, however, drain heaven and earth of what used to be called their "glory" and that of their creator—their energy, their beauty, their disclosiveness. This makes for lousy weather.

Before we can decide to what extent Christian eschatology may share in the culpability for the present eco-apocalypse, and to what extent it may redemptively address the crisis, we need to understand better the crisis itself. What kind of late modern secularized "eschatologies" are at work in the structures which facilitate eco-apocalypse? What sense of home?

A recent cover of *Life* magazine (May 1992) featured in bold display type "OUR NEXT HOME." Beneath it floated in cosmic black the photograph of a planet which at first glance could be the earth. But the caption read "MARS: Bringing a dead world to life." NASA's "young Turks" are pushing a project called "the terraformation of Mars," the greening of the red planet. "It's ridiculous to go all the way to Mars just to plant the flag, grab a few rocks and come home," biophysicist Robert Haynes is quoted as saying. "Humanity needs a new vision, a new challenge, not a cosmic park. Mars could provide that challenge." Rather than construing problems like the present perils to our own planet to be worthy challenges, the argument cuts in the opposite direction: precisely in the light of ecological and nuclear threat, the chief of research for NASA's life sciences branch opines that "it is foolish to put all our eggs in one basket. It would be wise to look for a place other than Earth where this species could make a home. It would be wise to learn how to terraform Mars."

This flagrantly secular vision of the new—"*man-made*"—creation, the "new heaven and earth" has metastasized as the new earth in the heavens. Earth, no longer worthy of the manly imagination, is disdained as a mere "basket" in which we may or may not invest all of "our eggs" (truly far from Jesus' mother hen apocalypse of Matthew 23: 37ff., which does not boldly stride towards new worlds but rather laments the self-destructiveness of this one). Why clean up our home when we can make a new one? Here we have an ultra-modernist technological utopianism at work, willing to accept apocalyptic consequences for the earth while transferring traditional American optimism about progress into the heavens. It carries early modern colonialist millennialism of the new world literally beyond all horizons. Indeed it frees itself from limits precisely by its exultant idolatry—an idolatry which proclaims the next giant step for mankind. Life's writer blandly notes, with no criticism intended, that the new challenge is "to re-create Creation—to play God."

This utopianism exemplifies what we may call the eschatology of progress, an apocalypse without judgment, an apocalypse, therefore, that blithely furthers the green apocalypse. Even without Martian visions, various modes of this irresponsible futurism thrive in the technocratic hopes of an ever unrepentant modernism. But the fantasy of the terraformation of Mars offers itself as a metaphor and a caricature of the colonizing optimism of modernity. The degree to which the modern technological utopianism has begun to give up on the earth itself. Indeed it suggests the desperate level of failure and of denial encoded in this eschatology.

More common among the range of modernist eschatologies is the well-organized and well-funded "wise use" movement, the free enterprise attack on environmentalism. Again the terms are unavoidably theological. But here they are pointedly *anti*-utopian, as the following article from *Forbes* demonstrates (Nelson 1990). This is because the right wing now identifies various progressive movements (not technologism) as the utopians to contend with. Nelson is appalled at such environmentalist rhetoric as the notion that "humanity is the destroyer of the earth." He lambastes one such ecologist as follows: "[he] doesn't want to settle for cleaner air; he wants to *roll back man's conquest of nature*" (my emphasis). Indeed! *Forbes* goes on to identify "eco theology" with the "quasi-religious fervor" of the "new gospel of ecology," analyzing both Judeo-Christian and pantheist modes of environmental religion as irrational fanaticisms, which he sees as heretical divergences from the interests of late capitalism. His coup de grace comes in his revelation that dialectical materialists in search of a new cause are joining the ecological crusade:

> Environmental theology, like Marxist theology, teaches that human greed and exploitation have infected the world with sin, yielding a condition of human alienation. Both are fundamentally utopian expressions of the desire for heaven on earth.

Indeed the argument seems well prepared to characterize any prophetic analysis of structural sin as Marxist and utopian.

The capitalist alternative, interestingly, gets justified in Christian terms—the starkly anti-apocalyptic eschatology of Aquinas "and other medieval scholastics" is vaguely alluded to as the basis for the market theory. The Forbes article goes on to say that

> As against this fanatical religiosity, there fortunately exists in Western theology a pragmatic tradition that regards the pursuit of self-interest, the maintenance of property rights, the desire for the good life and the institutions of the marketplace as the best available accommodation to the facts of human nature. Heaven will not be realized on earth for at least some time to come. . . .

Indeed the Angelic Doctor did stand with orthodoxy against the radical apocalyptic movements of his day, like the radical Franciscans. These groups, inspired by a new wave of apocalyptic new age prophecy, rejected private property as sub-Christian. But this pro-capitalist Aquinas is about as historically accurate as portrayals of Jesus in a business suit.

So we have here examined two varieties of secular eschatology, the first utopian-apocalyptic in its willingness to give up on the earth and expect a new one; the second realist-triumphalist in its business as usual attitude and its vested interest in the endless "delay of the *parousia*." The first sees a need to "boost morale" in North America—in the light of the apocalyptic levels of destruction, no doubt—by proposing a highly unrealistic and heavenly vision of hope. The latter, which represents more or less the status quo of economic thinking in North America, construes not the destruction of the ecology but those who warn of its destruction as the problem. The apocalypse it opposes is not that of the NASA scientists—this project, if it stimulated the GNP, might well appeal. Rather, it pits itself against the sort of secular apocalypticism which stems from the Hebrew prophetic tradition of the denunciation of sinful exploitation. To this it juxtaposes its free market "realism", which accommodates "the facts of human nature," by which are meant no doubt precisely the self-interest the prophets have traditionally felt themselves called to denounce. Indeed this free market triumphalism pronounces its own pragmatism environmentally more sound, because the environmentalist visionaries will "one day create a backlash."

Note that each of these bastardized eschatologies relies on the imagery of " 'man's' conquest of nature," either in the colonization of Mars or the Earth, to stimulate the proper attitude. The first gleams with its visionary futurism, the second holds doggedly to the status quo, but both aggressively ignore the real apocalypse, the one pointed to by McKibben's burning earth. Each of them acquiesces in the present levels of terrestrial deterioration as inevitable byproduct of "progress." Indeed, it is progress defined as the unimpeded, indeed accelerating, "conquest" of terrestrial and extraterrestrial nature that must yield the solutions to present problems. That, at any rate, is the basis of the modernist faith in technology, growth and the market.[2]

There are, as we shall see in the concluding section, premodern, theistic antecedents for the eschatologies of utopia and of the status quo. But a peculiar "thrust" toward independence from the materialized "Nature" (helped by the male God) and then from God himself (revolt of the sons from the Father) characterizes the process of secularization by which modernity shapes its futures. Despite some begrudging steps toward ecological globalism, the project of Western modernity still thrives on dominance of and independence from the physical world, then, rather than creative cooperation among its interdependent members.

Let us then agree: *the cause of the ecological crisis is precisely " 'man's' conquest of nature."* All that is not of the God-identified pale male ruling class gets situated in "nature," or as "more natural." Such more natural beings—women, darker persons, and animals—are, naturally, suited to perform the alienated physical labor by which raw "nature" is cooked, both by production and reproduction, into "culture."

Feminist commentators have not missed the implications of " 'man's' conquest of nature." Ecofeminisms takes their rise from our analysis of the parallelism of the subjugation of women and nature. Whether the feminist strategy is to celebrate or to dispute women's so-called closeness to nature, any feminism will acknowledge that the fates of women and of nature have lain on the same side of the cultural dualism which pits an alienated mind against its own matter. Analysis of this dualism provides a key to the interstructured oppressions constituting the momentum of the man-made apocalypse. Gender dualism rehearses at the most intimate level of relation to one's own body and relation to the closest other body a foundational practice of disconnection. " 'Man's' conquest of nature" begins at home. The *oikos* of intimate violence seems to provide an inner landscape of apocalypse. Private and yet becoming, in its revelation, startlingly public, the ecology of abuse discloses the lie by which the illusion of separateness is maintained. Within the matrix of interdependent life, abuse seems to control the flesh and the spirit of that upon which the controller is unconsciously dependent. The outer landscape of an abused planet discloses the cosmic results. An attitude of disconnection of the subject from an object allows the subject to *subject* the object, that is, to make it into a mere means for the subject's end. Subjection of nature and nature-identified beings to " 'man's' ends" drives the mainstream eschatology of Western civilization.

The sorry paradox revealing itself to us at the end of our millennium is this — to make nature a means to anthropo/androcentric ends is to realize "the end of nature." The end of nature as an idea, the end of "nature" defined as something separate and independent of us? No. Here McKibben's diagnosis becomes itself symptomatic of the problem. The conceptualization of nature as independent of us humans is the flip side of our quest for independence from nature—an independence pursued with the aggression of the preoedipal son seeking his freedom from mom. To construe our right relation to nature as one of transcendence is to reconvene the project of modernity. Nostalgia for nature's independence from us is the mirror reversal of the scientific project of independence from nature—both reflect the same presupposition. The presupposition of ontological independence, far from guaranteeing respect for radical difference, carries with it the dualist substructure of all modernism. It suggests first of all that nature is something that we are not. The difference of the human as subject from nature as object is protected, indeed barricaded, by an ontology of separation. In the modern dualist sensibility which seems to begin philosophically with Descartes one senses the character of a male defense against threat, indeed fear of a feminized nature, of chaos, of finitude and uncertainty. Susan Bordo has called this Cartesian anxiety a "postparturition crisis." It sets in as the more organic medieval (indeed, Thomist) relation to nature fades.

One may argue that all ideology of separation and independence is maintained as a defense against difference and violently simplifies the character of freedom in relation—and that such ideology orders the thought-patterns of patriarchy. (I argued this in my book *From a Broken Web*.) McKibben's focus on wilderness and mountain peaks rings at moments precariously masculinist, suggesting the sportsman's conquest of the peaks, the elite adventurer's escape upwards from mundane, homebound, traditionally feminine, concerns. We are again in the grips of a late modern apocalypticism—his end of nature is the end of the modern view of nature.

A self-healing respect for nonhuman nature will not be to return to a view of its separateness. That is what allowed us to wreck its weather in the first place. Rather it means allowing all kinds of earthlings— winged, horned, creepy and crawly, two-legged and four-legged, dark and light, female and male—the space and time they require to be who they are. But human earthlings will not grant such permission without restoration of ourselves—ourselves in the light of our interdependence with all the creatures who together with us *are* "the creation."

Such reconstruction is not a matter of nostalgia for the way the weather used to be, for seasonal rhythms and climatological stabilities which may be changing now forever. Not that grief for the lost innocence of weather might not offer an apt starting place. But—finally and first of all—the human sense of what satisfies, the human sense of ultimacy, requires what Rosemary Ruether called "the conversion to the earth" (See Ruether, 1983; and Ruether in Thistlethwaite, 1990, 111-24). That is, the metanoia will only be large enough to make a difference if it redeems our sense of shared human purpose and future: our *eschaton*. It will only be powerful enough to save the time and space in which that future can unfold if our work on collective structures taps the energy at once of judgment and of hope. So eschatology itself needs reconstructing, if it is not to sabotage its own work.

What would such a reconstruction of eschatology be like? Earlier we wondered if any such redemption of eschatology is worth the effort. Is eschatology itself hopelessly addicted to the end of nature? Can there be a greening of Christian theology? If so, a new kind of theological self-understanding, one with a method expressive of its content, must develop. We need a theological practice of recycling. It will issue from a kind of ecology of discourse. Discerning the toxins at work in Christianity and its cultures allows us, or rather requires us, to break down the elements of the Christian hope, to cleanse them where possible of their own patriarchal poisons and late modern capitalist deteriorations. An ecology of discourse requires the recycling of the elements of what we are—as persons grown in a culture replete with Christian influences, however disconnected these influences may be from their healthier contexts and communities of origin. Those of us somehow called or situated to recycle the Christian theological heritage must understand this work and have it understood as a needful and radical contribution to our relevant subcultures, not as some Sunday School nostalgia.

The biblical array of *eschata* present a complex picture incapable of homogenization (despite the attempts of modern fundamentalists designing those complex charts of the seven dispensations of creation to reconcile the different biblical accounts). But one thing is clear: there is no biblical reference to "the end of the world." Rather, one reads of anticipating a day of judgment and of a subsequent renewal of the entire creation. That is, the prophetic tradition focuses the uniquely biblical passion for the "new," the future. Its futurity feeds upon that rage at systemic injustice and hope for a repentance of the people that will allow the restoration of wholeness. This wholeness does not look supernatural. Rather it expresses *shalom* in intensely natural and historical terms. Hope in the Hebrew scriptures is not for life without death but for a long, full life, lived under the shade of one's own vine and in the fullness of a community healed of the alienation of nature and culture (the lion and the lamb cohabiting, the little child leading . . .). In a way not unlike that of Native Americans today, the prophetic vision harkened back to a tribal sense of "the land," imagined as new Israel, new heaven and earth, new Jerusalem. In their incipience, this imagery has little unearthly about it (and hence it was often deemed too materialistic by later, especially 19th century, Christian interpreters, who preferred eschatologies of the next world.) Yet the Hebrew images of home, dreamed in exile, became frantic when the homecoming itself disappoints. Then it is that apocalyptic eschatology begins to emerge, bringing with it a desperate, totalizing hope, a new sort of hope, for a once-for-all supernatural action of punishment and restitution (See Hanson 1975). But still the call for the conversion of the people resounds, and still the hope does not leave the earth except to find the agent powerful enough to create the desired new heaven and earth. It is still a hope for the radical reformation of life on earth, a hope for a home that can be lovingly and equitably cohabited by all creatures.

What about the eschatology of Jesus? Surely the *basileia tou theou* provides fresh imagery for the already ancient expectation of the new Jerusalem. His reliance on the form of the parable—replete with ecological imagery of seeds and growth—provokes a process that is neither merely individual nor merely political, neither merely realized nor merely futurist, a process of mutual engagement quietly unfurling to include all time and space in its celebration. The Pauline notion of the new creation transfers this tension into a christocentric messianism of which of course Jesus himself was incapable. In both Jesus and Paul there is an occasional recourse to the apocalyptic anticipation of utter annihilation, which in Jesus means the prediction of the destruction of Jerusalem Temple (the center of the Jewish world) and in Paul even extends to include the cosmos.

Only in the Book of Revelation do we find a full-blown New Testament apocalyptic narrative. Here there linger few traces of the subtlety and gradualism of the parables of the divine commonwealth, nor of the traditional prophetic trust in the power of repentance to turn around impending destruction. Now fear rather than love seems to motivate fidelity, and justice is depicted not by a radically disarmed power from below, but by a cosmically armed overpower.

And what of nature in the Book of Revelation? Here we have the ultimate case of bad weather. It is seen in hideous tribulations that result in the death of one third of the life of the seas, the fresh waters, the arable fields, the trees.[3] Yet the element of divine judgment intends "the destruction of the destroyers of the earth," not the earth itself. There is intuition here into the profound interlinkage of the economic and political injustice of Rome/Babylon and the devastation of nature. After the cosmic violence of the final solution, the New Jerusalem appears, now dressed up as "bride of the lamb." She "comes down from heaven" as an architecture of wish-fulfillment, a place of "no more tears," where food and drink are free, and where there is "no more ocean" (the salt water of tears and oceans both evoke maternal chaos and threat). Beauty manifests itself in supernal jewels rather than a regenerated ecology. Nonetheless, the imagery remains so mythic and the structure so non-linear as to leave this extremist eschatology open to endless reclamations—those of liberationists as well as reactionaries, of those whose faith works for "justice, peace and the integrity of creation" as well as for those whose faith awaits Armageddon with the assurance of those for whom nature and its history have become expendable, soon to be replaced. But however desperate, dualistic, determinist and far-fetched the hope of John's Apocalypse appears, it does not in itself require an otherworldly or unearthly reading. Its New Jerusalem can be placed in the context of prophetic hope for a radical renewal of this creation.

After the biblical period, especially after the conversion of Constantine in the fourth century, Christian history would never settle the tension between an explosive apocalyptic utopianism, which carried within itself the prophetic social critique, and a conservative ecclesial triumphalism. Augustine split the eschatological hope for a new age of justice and cosmic harmony within history into the "city of God" transcending nature and history and the "city of Man" within them and ending soon. Christianity as the religion of the Empire could too readily acquiesce in this static dualism, which undermines any motivation to struggle with the institutional causes of suffering. The eschatological triumphalism of orthodoxy emerges on this basis. The city of God could not be better realized on earth than it already is in the church; true fulfillment is only attainable individual by individual in heaven. Almost a thousand years later, a new rash of apocalyptic movements, inspired by Joachim's prophecy of a "third status," an age of the free spirit about to break in, reopened history. Yet these insurrectionist movements and their anti-Augustinian view of history were by the time of Münzer definitively relegated to the far margins of history.

These currents provide theistic antecedents for the self-interested modernist distortions discussed above. Belief in technological progress for the creation of heaven of earth—and failing that, earth *in* heaven—uses the old energy of apocalyptic hope for the qualitative leaps of real-world change. Yet it skips the step of judgment against the status quo, which, after all, it seeks merely to reinforce. Capitalist triumphalism, on the other hand, rests easily on the long Constantinian tradition of conservative realism that pits itself against any call for radical transformation of the social order. Both, precisely in their aggressively secular colonialist modalities, move to the conquest of the universe freed from the inhibitions of theistic doctrines of creation and new creation. They exploit the danger already inherent in biblical texts—the patriarchal recourse to moral dualism, to control from above, to coercive power, and to hopes for a future dissociated from present processes. Though in their secular forms they are supremely "worldly"—committed to economic self-interest and its symbiosis with political and technological prowess—they heighten the Christian tendency to take the earth for granted, indeed to disdain the claims of its multiple creatures.

Let me suggest, as a speculative hypothesis, that the ever hovering Christian (if minimally biblical) expectation that history will end soon has shaped the horizons of modernity in peculiar ways. Late modern capitalism tortures time into something endless and undifferentiated like a line. Yet its actual praxis uses the creation as means to its own ends and brings about the very future-lessness it denies. Its currently climaxing passion for short term gain seems subliminally to presuppose the imminent end of the world. And through the "conquest of nature" involved in the endless stress of development and exploitation, it is bringing that end about.

Christianity cannot be held unilaterally accountable.for the modern distortions of its messages. Yet it is surely not accidentally the culture whose holy book happens to culminate in a vision of the imminent devastation of the earth, the culture that has developed the technologies and politics capable of Armageddon—nuclear or greenhouse. To the extent that the expectation for the cataclysmic end, the redemption through cosmic violence, did indeed inspire apocalyptic hope, to that extent the task of theologians at the end of the millennium is to take responsibility for defusing the self-fulfilling prophecy of worldly doom. Thus the recycling of eschatology becomes precisely a means of the metanoia of theology itself—returning to the earth. It is not that there can be no responsible sense of life after life and of spirit-existence; after all, most of the indigenous traditions we praise for the intimacy with their own ecological realities also entertain complex connections to ancestral and other denizens of the spirit-world. A gaiocentric eschatology need not bang the spoons of reductionism. Eschatology has been about life after death, and may find new earth-embracing ways of affirming the sustaining and renewing powers of the Spirit and the spirits of life. Still—reconstructing the Western relationship to the earth must mean nothing less than understanding the earth as our ultimate home— a major come-down to all conservative and most liberal theology.

Home however does not mean "end"—indeed home allows the rootedness by which we grow through endings and beginnings. Home takes on the edginess of eschatology only when it is itself threatened. Jürgen Moltmann has argued that Christian eschatology is not a matter of *end* but of *hope* (see Moltmann, 1976).[4] We are therefore in the position of hoping against hope—against the false hopes of modernity which are destroying the nature out of which future lives. Christian attention to the promised future, the future of universal fulfillment, shalom, resurrection—certainly can and does serve, by default or direction, the ends of the " 'man'-made" apocalypse. The question is whether Christian hope can also energize work on our home or not. The ultimacy, the *eschaton,* of eschatology designates the radically inclusive spatio-temporal edge of our existence and therefore the shared future of our earth-creaturely existence.

All creatures—the all upon whom falls the rain and shines the sun, the all who share the weather: the endless species, threatened with premature endings, who together constitute both the habitats and the inhabitants of the creation. Indeed there is no creature who is not also home to many other creatures. Inhabitant is also habitat. Being at home means home. "The human is less a being on the earth or in the universe than a dimension of the earth and indeed of the universe itself" (Berry 1988, 195).

The Greek word *oikumene* from which "ecology," "economy," and "ecumenism" stem, makes *oikos,* home, into "the inhabited earth." This is the earth not as a geological formation but as that portion of the creation for which we have a steward's accountability, precisely not as passing outsiders but as paramount insiders. The Greek word *oikonomos* means "house steward." The old term "ecumenacy" added the theological dimension. The *Oxford English Dictionary* defines it, oddly, as "the ecclesiastical primacy or supremacy of the world." (One would expect rather "the universal primacy or supremacy of the church.") This trope invites us to understand ultimacy in terms of the primacy of the inhabited earth. Here pulses the central insight for a recycled eschatology—an *eco-eschatology* that will not content itself with interfaith, interreligious or multicultural exchange, but will call forth a *green ecumenacy,* the earthly ecclesia of all creatures.

Eschatology, as a doctrine, cannot be conceived apart from the doctrine of creation. By the same token, the doctrine of creation appears as irresponsible apart from eschatology, that is, the new creation. Yet this responsibility, because it roots eschatology in the ongoing, albeit so far hideously neglected and thwarted, call of stewardship for the ecumenacy, is a matter of *response* to the groaning of the creation. This particular dimension of an eschatological ethic is clear. It is revealed to us, in fact, in a way that it could not have been during the biblical periods, when nature still laid claim to a certain ferocious inexhaustibility. Yet biblical authors display occasionally passionate sensitivity to the effects of systemic greed upon their fragile and desertifying ecology: "Woe to those who join house to house, who add field to field, until there is no more room . . ." (Is. 5:8). Hence the eschatological imperative of the jubilee year's sabbath rest of the land, correlated with the liberation of the oppressed and the interruption of the economic system.

We ourselves are also in the consciousness of a prophetic minority. We are called to the work of the new creation, the renewal of creation. But this work only breeds futility if not done in and with the Spirit—which refracts in a multitude of spirits—of the creation.

We cannot create or recreate this life. Our responsibility for the new creation is not to terraform planets and otherwise play God. It is to participate in our finite, interconnected creatureliness with metanoic consciousness—that is, facing up to the " 'man'-made" apocalypse, resisting the North American array of post-utopian cynicisms, pessimistic determinisms, reactionary Christian messianisms, and business-as-usual realisms. All together these spell out the omega points of culpable doom. As earth-bound Christians, we may indeed embrace a utopian realism, bound to the rhythms of earth and its indelible history, but nonetheless still "bound for the promised land"—a promising place and time which is the possible healing of this one.

The realistic hope for ecology today lies not in miraculous interventions, supernatural or techno-capitalist. It lies in the still-greening mass consciousness that the apocalypse is unacceptable, that its causes are analyzable, and that we the people can make a difference. Who the "people" is makes a difference as well. Perhaps the most moving case studies in eco-hope come from the far and southern reaches of the planetary ecumenacy. For instance, the grass roots Chipko movement in India, the tree-hugging women who are using Gandhian techniques to save trees from the bulldozers of development and therefore have been renewing the face of the earth by reversing erosion and desertification, for the sake of creating a sustainable village economy (Weber 1988). Similarly, an even more pointedly woman-centered movement, that led by Wangaari Mathai in Kenya, has planted millions of trees, created jobs, accessible fuel and renewable agriculture, leading the way toward the desirable future in spite of persecution.

For North Americans, especially white urban ones, the prospect of sacrifices in lifestyle required to redress the injustices to the other peoples and nonhuman species — indeed just to save ourselves — increasingly brings on numbness. Such eco-numbness, akin to the "psychic numbing" of nuclearism (Lifton 1979), spreads readily across bodies invested with the force of nature-alienation. At this point calls to conversion and sacrifice only have a chance of being heard by the not-yet-converted if they are inscribed with the language of desire. Desire not just for the sake of an abstract future, but because a new community already begins to form in the practice of ecojustice. That is, to sort through our garbage, to make choices based on awareness of the sinister and/or beautiful web of connections of our food to our weather to our starving and tortured fellow humans to women's bodies and the homeless ... this multi-dimensional work of recycling releases new ways of being together, a new sense of common goal, of being on the edge together, of consoling and delighting each other in our edginess. We find together spiritual practices which allow us to ground, quite literally, in our bodies and our earth, the anxieties of the unknown future. To ground the lightening terrors of apocalypse. We are here in our particular communities, in our particular times and places, with particular ecologies, histories and spirits we must struggle to recognize. We are here to claim, to defend and to renew our earth home, the inhabited whole. This is the task of the green ecumenacy.

We will still talk about the weather, just because we are in it together. That's what weather talk always did. But now the damage to the earth-home binds us all together as never before, as members of a species, indeed members of a planet. Though doused with new griefs and furies appropriate to the situation, we will find surprising possibilities for dwelling together here at the edge of history. The weather retains its unpredictabilities. The word "weather," after all, comes from verb "to blow"—like the *pneuma*, the *ruach*, that blows where it will. We gain nothing but panic and cynicism, I suspect, by claiming that nature, *our* nature, the nature of which we are a nettlesome dimension, is ending, let alone "the world." The Spirit that brings life to life is also there, ·in the weird weather. However we mean it, we do well to keep on discovering the holy life-force of all living things. Then hope stays alive, renewed in the power of life to renew itself, no matter what. The hope, itself already manifesting renewal, calls forth the green ecumenacy. A song of Hildegaard von Bingen, the 12th century prophet of *viriditas*, the "greening power" of the Spirit, translates itself effortlessly into the ecology of the late 20th, waking us from the numbness:

> Holy Spirit, making life alive, moving in all things,
> root of all created being, cleansing the cosmos of

every impurity, effacing guilt, anointing wounds.
You are lustrous and praiseworthy life,
You waken and re-awaken everything that is.

NOTES

1. Pollution patterns follow the lines of ethnicity and poverty right here in our backyards: "The poorer the neighborhood, and the darker the skin of its residents, the more likely it is to be near a toxic waste dump" (A. Ross, 148). The sale of toxic waste to nations of the two-thirds world reveals the same logic, becoming explicit in the arguments used to justify the deaths it will cause. This logic pervades the ecological imperialism by which the north ravages the darker skinned south for "resources" and "labor." As to the weather, the increasing droughts and dropping food production correlated with planetary warming have already become life or death matters for ever increasing populations from the southern hemisphere. And as the little hot Gulf War of 1991 displayed so succinctly, a post-Cold War relationship now obtains between the two hemispheres, forging a new world capitalist link between militarism and the management of the darker-skinned peoples and their resources. Militarism constitutes another disclosive set of issues. The Pentagon indulged in several experiments in weather control as climatic warfare (A. Ross 202). We do not know what long term effects were released, but the symbolism is to the point. I think not only of the five hundred flumes of burning oil left by the Gulf War, discharging their carbon dioxide. And not only of the perverse priorities of spending for destruction as against spending for life. The tale of the hidden dangers of obsolescent weapons has barely begun to be told—the story of the hundreds of billions of dollars that will be required to clean up the gigantic secret legacy of environmental threats of U.S. military and weapons-building programs.

2. For an impressive and readable critique of the growth dogma and the GNP orthodoxy, complete with a full vision of an alternative, ecologically, communally and, yes, *theologically* sound path, see Cobb and Daly 1989.

3. It would be easy to enter into a kind of literal link-up between such prophecies of eco-disaster and what has pretty much already occurred in this century. For example the burning rain forests echo Revelation 8:7: "and a third of the trees were burnt up . . ."

4. It is satisfying to note how far social concerns have driven Moltmann into an ecological theology in recent works, notably in his *God in Creation* and *Creating a Just Future*.

4

Acting with Compassion

Buddhism, Feminism, and the Environmental Crisis

STEPHANIE KAZA

On my altar at home stands a small bronze casting of Kuan Yin (also known as Kannon or Kanzeon in Japan), who serves to bless my meditation space and daily activity. Her robes are flowing and gracious, and in her hand she holds a vase of healing water. She stands ready to receive the suffering of the world with compassion and equanimity. Above the kitchen sink I have a picture of a carved jade Kuan Yin from China. She holds a rabbit on her arm, manifesting the spirit of harmony with life and all living beings. On my desk, covering the books and papers of my current work, is a prayer cloth of the Green Tara. She sits on a lotus petal dais; her aura and soft face radiate gentle and penetrating power.

I begin with Kuan Yin because she represents a feminine gender form of a realized Bodhisattva, known to many people for thousands of years as the embodiment of compassion for all beings in the vast interdependent mutually causal web. Sometimes depicted with a thousand arms, Kuan Yin reaches out to offer a thousand tools of compassion—a shovel, a flute, a blanket, a kind word. Kuan Yin is "the Mahayana archetype of mutual support, giving life and fulfillment to the Sangha . . . of stones and clouds, of wild creatures and forests, of people . . . in the slums and prisons of our cities, not to mention our own

Stephanie Kaza, Ph.D., M. Div., assistant professor of Environmental Studies, teaches feminist and environmental ethics at the University of Vermont. She has been a student of Zen Buddhism for sixteen years, and has trained with Thich Nhat Hanh and Joanna Macy in the area of engaged Buddhism and social action. Stephanie has worked with others in planning three women and Buddhism conferences and is the author of a forthcoming book on meditations with trees.

families and friends" (Aitken 1986, 24–29). In the Tibetan tradition, the feminine form of the Green Tara serves as a reminder of the one who heals by her presence, serving countless beings. Her green color symbolizes the capacity to take action; her right hand forms the *mudra*, or gesture of calling forth awakening, and her left the gesture of refuge (see Blofeld 1978, Willson 1986).

As realized beings, Kuan Yin and Tara listen to *all* the cries of the world, not just those of people. This means they are also concerned with plants and animals, mountains and valleys, small creatures and large. The feminine compassionate presence has long been addressed by Buddhists of many cultures to relieve human sickness, grief, and poverty of spirit. In the current sweep of environmental destruction, it is Kanzeon and Tara who see and experience with us the pain and suffering of deserts, forests, soils, groundwater, oceans, and skies. They offer a model of radical presence in the world, of no separation between the one who suffers and the one who responds. The calls for action and healing arise spontaneously and naturally out of the cries of death and despair.

In this introductory work, I draw on the courage and inspiration of these Bodhisattvas to investigate the role of Buddhist practice and philosophy informed by feminist principles in support of work for the environment. As Buddhism and feminism gain strength and momentum in the Western world, the environmental crisis looms large on the horizon of our survival. I believe those trained in the self-discipline, analysis, and reflective processes of Buddhism and feminism have a powerful contribution to make in addressing the enormous challenges of environmental work. I encourage many more women and men to develop these tools for effective, grounded, sensitive, and nonviolent action on behalf of the earth.

I speak from my own perspective as a Buddhist, feminist, and environmentalist. I have been studying Zen Buddhism for sixteen years with Kobun Chino Roshi, practicing at Green Gulch and Jikogi Zen Centers in California, and serving as chair of the national Buddhist Peace Fellowship board. I have evolved as a feminist through my mother's example as a lawyer for the poor, through my experience of power relations in patriarchal workplaces and religious centers, and through examination of feminist discourse in theory, philosophy, and morality. I am an environmentalist by profession, with academic training in both biology and social ethics. I have been working in the field of environmental education and conservation for twenty years and currently teach Environmental Ethics at the University of Vermont in Burlington.

I begin with principles held in common by Buddhism and feminism that are relevant to the environmental crisis. I then offer examples of these principles in action, of feminist women engaged in environmental work as Buddhist practice. This exploration is an introduction to a field of integrated perspectives which is just developing. I draw primarily on American Buddhism; the paper should not be construed to be internationally inclusive.

INTRODUCTION

When Buddhism arrived in the West, it encountered curious and bright minds of both sexes, eager for teachings and spiritual practices relevant to their lives. The search for spiritual foundation escalated in the 1960s and 1970s as sensitive men and women suffered through the paralyzing national pain of the civil rights movement and the Vietnam War. College students and activists scrutinized social values in depth and rejected much of the status quo parochialism that characterized American thinking. Spurred by their interest and, in the case of Tibet, cultural destruction, the most extensive wave of Buddhist teachers arrived in America from Tibet, Japan, Korea, Thailand, Sri Lanka, and Burma (see Fields 1981).

At the same time, feminism was blossoming and gaining strength as a social movement. Women were waking up to the repressed and hidden cruelties of male domination in individual relationships as well as social institutions. In consciousness-raising groups across the United States, women examined issues of reproduction and health, power and sexual abuse, and outright misogyny. Feminist intellectuals took on the challenge of deconstructing gender-biased assumptions that underlay the foundations of Western language, politics, psychology, medicine, law, and philosophy. Feminist Buddhists questioned patriarchal Asian forms and inappropriate teacher-student conduct (see Boucher 1985).

Earth Day 1970 marked a watershed point in public concern for the environment. Widespread exposure to extensive environmental problems generated a wave of citizen action groups and environmental education programs. Activists pointed to the cumulative excesses of postwar industrialization and commercialization, along with skyrocketing human populations, as pressing the limits of the planet's carrying capacity. Doomsday predictions forecast large-scale environmental catastrophes long before Chernobyl, Love Canal, or the loss of the Black Forest. Antinuclear activism was a relatively new movement struggling against the enormous odds of a fearful Cold War nation.

In the two decades between Earth Day 1970 and Earth Day 1990, Buddhism, feminism, and concern for the environment in America grew and changed tremendously, reflecting a period of serious questioning of values and social structures. The maturation of understanding and insight over these two decades provides a significant setting for reviewing the role of Buddhism and feminism in relationship to the environment. While Beat poetry and fascination for Oriental culture drew curious seekers to the few Buddhist teachers of the 1960s and 1970s, twenty years later, there were over 300 Buddhist centers across the country and a dozen major Buddhist publications (see Field 1989; Morreale 1988). In this period of growth, over twenty women gained recognition as formal Buddhist teachers (see Friedman 1987). In the 1960s, feminism was a little-known word, but by 1990, feminists had established hundreds of nonprofit organizations to support women's issues, from rape hotlines to women's history weeks. Retreats and conferences for women Buddhists were regular features on Western meditation calendars.

By Earth Day 1990, the proliferation of books, graduate programs, environmental careers, and by now well-established environmental lobbying groups was an indicator of the all-encompassing scale of the ecological situation. The environmental crisis had grown beyond local, state, national, and international capacity to handle it. Amidst the world context of North-South tension, over 1,500 women from 84 countries stood in solidarity for women's environmental needs at the 1991 Women's World Congress for a Healthy Planet. One after another presented moving testimonies of economic injustice, forest degradation, loss of soil and farms, and frustration with political systems that systematically destroyed environmental resources.[1]

I believe there is a powerful confluence of thought, practice, commitment, and community in the lives of feminist Buddhists working for the environment who have lived through this history of startling change. In these two decades, leadership and participation of women in Buddhist practice have paralleled the rise in feminist theory research and explorations in conservation biology and restoration ecology. A whole new generation of young people has been raised in families with feminist and/or Buddhist parents concerned about the environment. Feminists, Buddhist women practitioners, and environmental advocates are no longer isolated from one another.

The growth and maturation of these social and religious movements have come at a time when people are hungry for ethical response to the environmental problems they see around them. Yet most Americans lack the patience and moral reasoning skills to work through the complexities of environmental dilemmas. The discipline of Buddhist practice and the social analysis of feminism now bring a mature perspective to the endless suffering of the environment and a capacity to live with the tension of unresolved issues that will take more than several generations to correct.

ENVIRONMENTALLY RELEVANT PRINCIPLES OF BUDDHISM AND FEMINISM

The philosophical principles of Buddhism and feminism overlap and complement each other in a number of areas, mutually supporting an interdependent, systems-oriented view of the environment. There are also several areas in which one of these is underdeveloped in its traditions, practices, or teachings and is enhanced or influenced by exposure to the other. I outline here six areas of confluence, with some comments on differences that are not yet fully addressed.

Experiential Knowing

In contrast to much of Western philosophy and theology, Buddhism begins with the truth of personal experience. Experiential knowing in relationship to spiritual development is valued over textual, abstract, or other sources of knowing, which are distant from the individual (see Suzuki 1949, 267–313). The early canons of Buddha's teachings repeatedly urged the practitioner to thoroughly study his or her own experience and mental conditioning in order to break through the limitations of the falsely constructed self. The Buddha insisted his followers not take his authority as a final say on any matter, but rather sincerely investigate the teachings for themselves. Meditation practices aim to quiet and stabilize the mind so it is capable of observing thoughts, sensations, and actions in great detail. One's own mind and experience are the places in which one learns to recognize the universal nature of suffering (the first of the Four Noble Truths in Buddhism).

Experiential knowing is based on embodied mindfulness practices that develop awareness of need and greed, the suffering of pleasure and pain, and the impermanent nature of things. The content for this learning is always one's own life. One's spiritual challenge is to investigate in depth the accumulated patterns of response to physical, social, mental, and psychological stimuli in order to liberate the practitioner from the suffering of unconsciousness. By shining the light of awareness on the nature of one's own conditioned reality, one finds the freedom to act effectively and skillfully, grounded in thorough self-knowledge. This experiential knowing or study of self in body, speech, and mind lies at the heart of all traditions of Buddhist teachings. Dogen Zenji, ninth-century Japanese Zen Master, expressed this:

> To study the buddha way is to study the self.
> To study the self is to forget the self.
> To forget the self is to be actualized by myriad things.
> (Tanahashi 1985, 70)

Feminism is equally clear on the importance of experiential knowing as a foundation for social action and personal insight. The feminist movement in the United States, as well as in other countries, has consistently emphasized that women speak their own truths with their own voices. Feminists have encouraged women to reclaim the stories of their lives and speak what they know from direct experience. The personal is recognized as the political, for it is a genuine place of truth telling. This has meant speaking out about the painful suffering of sexual and environmental abuse, articulating the power of women's emotions, and hearing the realities of women's bodies and environmental health concerns. In feminist religious studies in Buddhist and other traditions, women struggle with the discontinuity between personal experience and patriarchal tradition, looking for new language, forms, and community that match women's religious experience (see Plaskow and Christ 1989).

Feminists have validated the important realm of subjective knowing, acknowledging the inner experience of self that places the knower in an interior as well as exterior context (Belenky et al. 1986). Subjective knowing in women has been consistently denigrated by Western patriarchal cultures as self-centered, romantic, and distorted by emotionality. The scientific inquiry method, which insists on the necessity of an objective perspective, is the extreme opposite of subjective or interior knowing. It depends completely on the assumption that the actor can be separate from the object of one's actions (see Harding 1986). This overlooks the critical discipline of subjective knowing that reveals the inner structure and conditioning of the individual mind. It is this built-in conditioning that limits accuracy and objectivity in perception. Integrated, experiential knowing, which includes both object of knowing and the knower herself, is necessary for understanding the complexities of the environmental crisis.

For many women, the experience of knowing in relation to the natural world develops the mind-body's response to other beings and to lunar and seasonal cycles, informed by kinesthetic and sensory awareness. Body rhythms and responses to the earth have long been celebrated in earth-based spiritual traditions such as the Goddess cultures, not necessarily only by women. Among Buddhist cultures, the Japanese and others have cultivated an emotional and aesthetic attitude toward the natural world that represents intimate and prereflective encounter with the environment. In the Japanese view, nature is seen as the realm of "spontaneous becoming"—a meeting ground for the dynamic unfolding of person, tree, rock, and bird (Tellenbach and Kimura 1989, 155).

The embodied knowing of child and mother can be a model for intimate relations with the earth (Levitt 1990). The child in the womb knows only mother as earth; it is surrounded by, sustained by, and conditioned by the mother as context. Likewise, the earth is body to the woman, completely informing, conditioning, and nourishing her life. This metaphor does not imply that women have preferred access to these truths (the "essentialist" position in feminist philosophy). Rather, embodied knowing for *any* person is a direct link to experience of relationship with the earth. The earth itself can be seen as Buddha's body, supporting all lives, being the Great Life.

Embodied knowing is a source of confidence for embodied spirituality and environmental political action. The Buddhist and feminist emphasis on direct experience of the environment is informed by the body as mind, rather than body and mind as separate. Through knowing based on experience, one becomes grounded in actual reality rather than in one's ideas of reality. Through this grounding, the practitioner gains a legitimate voice with which to speak personally and specifically of environmental relationships and how they are ignored, sabotaged, or otherwise denied.

Examining the Conditioned Mind

Central to Buddhist philosophy and meditation method is the practice of discriminating wisdom. This is the detailed study of how things work—both in external and internal realities and in the interaction and co-creation of the two. The purpose is to break through delusions that generate and perpetuate a sense of an independent and separately existing self. The discriminating mind can expose rationalized actions and mental-cultural-emotional habits that perceive beings as separate objects rather than as members of a web of relationships.

In the context of the environment, there are at least three prevalent patterns of thought that block relational perception (Kaza 1989). One common thought habit is *stereotyping* of animals and ecosystems by describing them in oversimplified terms. People tend to lump the few characteristics they know of an organism or plant community into a generic representative that does not accurately reflect reality. For example, the generic whale is playful, altruistic, intelligent, large, and gentle—each characteristic fitting one species or another, but not existing anywhere in this combination in a real whale. Emotional responses to plant communities also lead to undifferentiated labeling. Deserts are viewed as wastelands, and all forests are seen as cool, dark places, despite the many differences in topography, climate, plant and animal inhabitants, and human history.

A second form of objectification is *projection*, in which the mind projects internalized ideas onto favored and unfavored elements of the environment. By reducing the reality of a forest to someone's idea of a forest, the community becomes objectified—seen as object with a convenient name and simplified description. "Cute" or "nice" animals, such as deer, rabbits, and songbirds, elicit more sympathetic responses than "mean" animals, such as coyotes, spiders, and bats (Kellert 1989). Likewise, good land is land that can be farmed or developed; bad land is what is too steep, dry, or impenetrable to be subdued.

A third prevalent thought habit is *dualistic thinking*, in which one object or idea is placed in opposition to another, often with the implication that one has power or superiority over the other. Self-other opposition forms the mental basis for anthropocentric relationships with plants and animals, as well as prejudice and racism. We-they conflicts, expressed in views of the environment as enemy, share the same mental polarizing structure as mind-body, creator-created, nature-culture dualisms (see Keen 1986). The mind separates and distances one side of the polarity from the other, rather than seeing the opposites as complementary and inclusive, each arising in the context of the other.

Feminism has exposed a particular aspect of conditioned thinking generally overlooked in Buddhism: the influence of gender identity and cultural habits of objectifying women. Many writers have described in depth the suffering that has resulted from oppressive dualistic thinking, projection, and stereotyping of women. Ecofeminist philosopher Karen Warren suggests three features of oppressive conceptual frameworks that apply both to treatment of women and the environment (Warren 1990). The first, *value-hierarchical thinking*, refers to placing value or giving preference to what is seen as being of higher status, as opposed to considering all things equally. The second, *value dualisms*, points to the typically Western pattern of viewing opposites as disjunct and exclusive, and then assigning moral superiority to one-half of the dualism, i.e., male-female, day-night, temperate-tropical, vertebrate-invertebrate.

The third feature is the *logic of domination*, the argument that justifies subordination of one opposite by the other. To uphold this logic requires considerable mental and social cooperation with oppressive cultural conditioning. One can see this logic at work in rationalizing intolerable conditions for laboratory and factory-farm animals (Kheel 1989). The same dominating, objectifying mind that uses women for sex objects also justifies the use of land for strip-mining and forests for clear-cutting. Those with international power promote development projects for less industrialized nations that contribute not only to environmental degradation, but also to the oppression and further impoverishment of women (Shiva 1988). In highly industrialized nations, women are subjected to aggressive domination by powerful market advertising that manipulates their desires for consumer products.

· Both Buddhism and feminism provide critical tools for examining deeply the roots of antirelational thinking that support environmental destruction. Both insist on thorough review of all aspects of the conditioned mind that perpetuate mental and physical patterns of domination. However, because Buddhism has been transmitted almost entirely through patriarchal cultures, its investigation of gender conditioning is underdeveloped. This weakens the Buddhist argument for ecological interdependence, because it misses the critical link between patterns of oppression of women and the environment. The feminist Buddhist position includes the connection, observing the nature of mind in women and men that sustains a separate self, capable of dominating humans and environment.

The Truth of Interrelatedness

The fundamental law in Buddhism is the Law of Dependent Co-Arising: that all events and beings are interdependent and interrelated. The universe is described as a mutually causal web of relationship, each action and individual contributing to the nature of many others (Kalupahana 1987, 26). The Pali word for this law, *Paticca-samuppada*, explains the truth in its literal meaning. *Paticca* means "grounded on or on account of"; *sam* is "together," and *uppada* means "arising." Thus the whole phrase can be translated "the being-on-account-of-arising-together." Or in the text,

> This being, that becomes;
> from the arising of this, that arises;
> this not being, that becomes not;
> from the ceasing of this, that ceases.[2]

An image for this cosmology is the Jewel Net of Indra, from the Mahayana Buddhist tradition (Cook 1989, 213–30). The multidimensional net stretches through all space and time, connecting an infinite number of jewels in the universe. Each jewel is infinitely multifaceted and reflects every other jewel in the net. There is nothing outside the Net and nothing which does not reverberate its presence throughout the web of relationships.

This law is one of the most obvious connections between Buddhism and the environment. As ecologists point out in example after example, ecological systems are connected through water, air, and soil pathways. Impacts of chemical pesticides on agricultural lands carry to adjacent wetlands; industrial carbon emissions affect global atmospheric climate patterns. Interdependence and interrelationship are central starting points for ecological research of food webs, nutrient cycles, and forest succession. Indra's Net, however, contains more than the ecological sum of biosphere, atmosphere, and lithosphere. The Buddhist principle of interdependence includes human thought, perception, and values, and their impacts on the ecological-evolutionary conversation. This critical difference is what makes it possible and necessary for people in the Net to act ethically out of regard for the other beings in the Net.

In the context of human relationship, feminist ethicist Mary Grey describes the metaphysic of connectedness as "revelatory paradigm" and "moral imperative." She suggests the ethics of care and responsibility naturally develop from a person's experience "trying to be faithful to relation or connection" (Grey

1991, 13). A number of feminist ethicists and writers point to mutuality and solidarity as key values for the feminist movement (see Farley 1986; Daly 1989). These values spring from the need for sister bonding as a source of strength in facing the internalized pain of the victim of sexism and in organizing for institutional and social change. Full mutuality or interdependence is not possible for one dominated by the absolutizing, individualist "I." Thus to experience the richness of full mutuality, one must transcend or break through the limitations of the thought habit of individualism reinforced as the dominant ideology in the Western world.

For the woman who has suffered physical, economic, psychological, or spiritual oppression, freedom from the rigidity of the fixed "I"/self and release into the web of relationships means the choice of many more nourishing options for growth and development. Because this maturation occurs in a shared context with others also suffering isolation, the feminist experience of interrelatedness is a process of mutual becoming, born out of mutual vulnerability. The joy and satisfaction of this experience may then be a foundation for "passionate caring for the entirety of the relational nexus" (Grey 1991, 13). A woman who uncovers her own capacity for mutuality can then (and often does) extend her efforts and empathy to the many other women in different cultures and places who also suffer from lack of freedom of choice.

For both Buddhism and feminism, the core truth of interrelationship or mutual becoming is central to individual liberation or freedom from false reification of an independent "I." Feminist Buddhists who understand this path of liberation can be extremely effective and compassionate participants in the struggle for environmental consciousness. Acting from deep-rooted experience in the freedom to choose options other than oppression, they can work creatively and skillfully to open up environmental conversations that have been frozen by loss of relationality.

Emotional Energy as Source of Healing

The Buddhist practice of investigating conditioned body, speech, and mind includes detailed observation of the nature of emotions. In the Sutra on the Four Establishments of Mindfulness, for example, the meditator is instructed to practice awareness of pleasant, painful, and neutral feelings as they arise in the mind and body. In Thich Nhat Hanh's modern-day commentary on this Sutra, he suggests exercises for identifying and acknowledging feelings and seeing the physical, physiological, or psychological roots of particular feelings (Nhat Hanh 1990b). By becoming fully familiar with the nature of anger, grief, fear, desire, denial, or the blocking of these feelings, a practitioner gains confidence in living through the sweep of emotional responses that naturally arise from moment to moment.

The first step of healing from the suffering of difficult emotions is to recognize and fully claim the rich information and energy response of the body/mind. In the investigation and mindfulness practice itself, energy is released and becomes available for healing through attention and understanding. Rather than suppressing deep emotions, Buddhist practice can help a person develop the capacity to consciously use this energy to relieve suffering. Much of the response to the current environmental crisis is an emotional response, filled with grief, fear, and anger at the loss and destruction of plants, animals, forests, and watersheds. The depth of response may be so overwhelming that people become immobilized and unable to act. Buddhist practices to validate and move through these waves of emotion can be extremely helpful in freeing up energy to take action on behalf of the environment (see Nhat Hanh 1990a; Macy 1983, 158–61).

Western feminists also recognize the importance of emotional response in the process of awakening to oppression. Most Western white women have been conditioned not to express anger overtly. Strong displays of empassioned emotion have been marginalized and viewed as unacceptable by the ruling patriarchy and its male model of "cool" and reserved emotions. Anger at sexual and environmental abuse qualifies as an "outlaw emotion," invalidated by those who wish to avoid hearing other experiences (Jaggar 1985). Feminists, however, are well aware that powerful social and gender conditioning can only be overthrown by a strong surge of energy and desire for change. Anger is very effective in marshaling the energy necessary to dismantle the structure that perpetrates violence against women and the environment.

If one begins with the fundamental truth of one's own experience, recognizing that perception and conception are intimately related, it becomes necessary to know how we feel in order to act morally. As feminist theologian Beverly Harrison asserts, "The failure to live deeply in 'our bodies, ourselves' destroys the possibility for moral relations between us" (Harrison 1985, 13). For Harrison, anger is a "feeling-signal that all is not well in our relation to others or the world around us" (Harrison 1985, 14). Powerful emotion is a sign of resistance to the unsatisfactory moral quality of our social and environmental relationships. This signal is the wake-up call to look more deeply into the situation at hand. Harrison argues that the power to respond is the power to create a world of moral relations. This is the work of spiritual and religious practice, the transformative work that can serve to slow environmental destruction and heal the wounded biosphere.

The combination of Buddhist mindfulness practice and feminist moral response is a powerful antidote to widespread despair and depression over the possibility of nuclear annihilation, environmental catastrophe, or out-of-control corporate greed. This practice does not remove the threats or mitigate the devastating consequences of irresponsible actions, but it does help to generate the tremendous energy needed to address the complexities of the global environmental situation (see Macy 1983). Anger, despair, or other strong emotions alone are not enough to stop environmental tragedy, because they cause polarization and defensive reactions that block communication. Environmental activists already have a history and bad name in some circles for misusing emotions in the service of battle strategy. Habitual unexamined anger can harden into ideology that further erodes opportunities for working together. By cultivating a deeper, more fully informed emotional response, one cultivates greater possibilities for healing transformation of relationships between human beings and the environment.

Relational Ethics

Buddhist ethics are grounded firmly in the truth and experience of the Law of Dependent Co-Arising. *Sila*, or guidelines for moral action, are central to Buddhist practice in all traditions. The Three Pure Precepts are vows to refrain from actions that ignore interdependence, to make an effort to act out of understanding of interrelationship, and to serve all beings in the interdepending web.[3] The five (Theravada) prescriptive precepts to not kill, not lie, not steal, not abuse sexuality or intoxicants spring from a fundamental recognition of relationship. One aims to act as respectfully and inclusively as possible toward plant, animal, and human companions.

In the Mahayana traditions, the model of enlightenment is the Bodhisattva who gains awakening in order to serve all beings. This is in contrast to the Theravadan goal of achieving liberation to be freed from the cycle of endless suffering and rebirths in a human body. Buddhist or other religious beliefs that place emphasis on Otherworldliness, or some version of escaping from the drudgery of this world, are not helpful for responding to the escalating deterioration of the environment. Forests can only be replanted here on this earth by those who live here, not those who have transcended the world. The Bodhisattva model encourages the practices of compassion for all others as a means of accomplishing a profound sense of interrelatedness. One can specifically cultivate "eco-bodhicitta" or the mind of enlightenment that serves all relations of the environment (Ross 1991).

The experience of compassion for others' suffering is what allows us to feel the connections with disturbed ecosystems and threatened species, distressing as they may be.[4] Sensitivity and moral concern for the health of human relationships can extend as well to plants, animals, forests, clouds, stones, and sacred places. Buddhist relational ethics are based on knowing that one cannot act without affecting other living beings, that it is impossible to live outside the web of interconnectedness. The beautiful Jewel Net of Indra is sustained and enhanced by the quality of moral intention and commitment to the many facets of the Net. To act from this sense of relatedness is deeply empowering, setting an ethical example for others to consider.

Compassion in Western culture, in contrast, is frequently associated with pity and powerlessness and relegated to the domain of women's nurturing (Klein 1986). In examining Western psychological values, feminist researchers have challenged the traditional stages of moral and psychological development based on male socialization, as described by Kohlberg (Kohlberg 1981). In this model, moral maturity develops through increasing allegiance to universal rules or principles of justice and individual rights. Carol Gilligan's work, in contrast, suggests that women's moral development in the West is based on maturing responsiveness to relationships and consideration of others in moral choices (Gilligan 1982). Kohlberg's male model reinforces an environmental ethic oriented to rights and justice; Gilligan's alternative model supports an environmental ethic of care and responsibility.

Relational ethics as described by both Buddhist teachings and feminist writers might also be called contextual ethics. A contextual ethic, as I use the term, reflects both the diversity of human voices in a given place and time (Warren 1990, 139), and the specific environmental relationships in which the human dilemma is embedded (Cheney 1987). Built into this approach to ethics is the rejection of any single authoritative ethical voice or posited human nature that exists independent of historical context. Abstract individualism is seen as ungrounded and relatively unhelpful in addressing the tensions of a specific environmental conflict.

Environmental moral dilemmas occur in a web of relationships. Each situation has a unique history, based on very particular causes and conditions. A contextual ethic represents a shift from emphasis on rights, rules, and predetermined principles to a conception of ethics grounded in specific relationships. Environmental actions based entirely on rules as moral guidelines inevitably leave out some aspect of the situation that is not included in the legal framework. Rules generalize; relationships are infinite and complex. A relational ethic calls for compassion for all the relationships involved in the situation— parent-child, tree-animal, bird-human, soil-rock. Relationships are not something outside of who we are; they, in fact, *define* who we are to a large extent as moral agents in a social and historical context. As Warren argues, "Relationships of humans to the nonhuman environment are, in part, constitutive of what it is to be human" (Warren 1990, 143).

Relational morality is not simple; it is extremely difficult to make sound environmental decisions when relatively little is known about ecological relationships. The stakes are often very high when the consequences of human actions mean the loss of millions of plant and animal lives. Trade-offs in tropical environments, for example, are almost a matter of triage today. The practices of compassion and contextual reflection generate a deep appreciation of biological and cultural complexity and of the long-standing ties between humans and all other members of the biotic community. I believe this is an essential foundation for critically needed reevaluation of what we are doing on the planet and what is ethically acceptable and life-sustaining.

The Role of Community

All Buddhist traditions venerate the three Jewels—the Buddha, Dharma, and Sangha. In environmental terms, the *Buddha* can be interpreted as all beings who teach, or the teacher within, or the Buddha as environmental teacher. To see all beings as teachers means one can learn from wolf, redwood, buffalo, river, and mountain (see Dogen Zenji 1985, 97–127). To see the Buddha as teacher within means one learns from one's own experience with the environment. The Buddha as environmental teacher is the one who points to the truth of interdependence and co-dependent arising of all life forms.

Dharma is the truth of the teachings in their many forms, perceptions, and experiences. Each plant and animal, as well as human, is an embodiment of evolutionary truth, a testimony to thousands of years of living more or less successfully in conversation with the environment. Each experience of connection with members of the environmental web is a taste of the deep truth of the nature of reality as mutually causal and interdependent.

The Third Jewel, the *Sangha*, is traditionally described in Buddhist literature as the monastic community, or those who practice within a retreat setting. Rules for sangha behavior are extensive, numbering over 300 in some traditions, with specific rules for nuns, often in subordinate relationship to monks. For most American Buddhists, some of these rules are inappropriate because of cultural differences, but even more, they are not specific to lay or nonmonastic practice, which is the prevalent form of practice in the United States. Deep ecologist Bill Devall proposes the concept of "eco-sangha," in which people practice with all the members of their bioregion or watershed area and consciously identify with and include the environment as community (Devall 1990). One then sits in meditation not only with others in the human community, but also with the surrounding oaks, maples, jays, warblers, and wildflowers.

Feminist Buddhist Rita Gross suggests that sangha is the "indispensable matrix of spiritual existence" necessary for human liberation (Gross 1991, 73). She critiques the historical tendency in Buddhism to emphasize the lonely path to freedom, suggesting that too much aloneness is not a good thing, for it is not, in itself, instructive in how to get along with others. Her feminist reconceptualization of sangha rests on the values of community, nurturing, communication, and relationships, traditionally cared for by women in many cultures. With no theistic Ultimate Other in Buddhism to provide guaranteed relationship to the person experiencing isolation, there is no alternative but to provide relationship for one another. She suggests, "It is necessary to create the social, communal, and compassionate matrix of a society in which friendship and relationship are taken as categories of utmost spiritual importance" (Gross 1991, 78).

A feminist interpretation of sangha validates and deepens the key feminist political and psychological values of solidarity and mutuality. Companionship and shared activities, including dialogue on environmental ethics, are then central to spiritual development and need to be cultivated as primary virtues. Women's friendships and love for each other and the mutual growth process may be threatening and confusing to some, because they challenge traditional ethics based in individualism. I believe that the friendship-sangha model is a helpful and appropriate basis for refinding and redefining our human relationships with plants, animals, and ecological communities. It is both enjoyable and sustainable, and can serve as a significant counterpoint to the recent history of industrialized attack and plunder.

A FEW POSSIBLE LIMITATIONS

These six areas of philosophical similarity or complementarity between Buddhism and feminism offer a solid foundation for a Buddhist feminist approach to environmental issues. I believe the environmental ethics generated from such a position recommend restraint in human activities that cause destruction and loss of habitats, species, and ecosystems, with the aim of reducing suffering for many forms of life. However, for effective evaluation of these two approaches, it is necessary to keep in mind the historical traditions and limitations of each source philosophy. There are several potential weaknesses of traditional Buddhism that may serve either to limit Buddhist involvement with the environment or, through dialogue and activity, may actually help define the evolutionary edge of American Buddhism.

Egocentrism as Central Concept

Buddhist philosophy and religious practice emphasize breaking through the limited perspective and conditioning of the small self or human ego, in order to experience the boundless interrelated nature of reality. The route to liberation assumes an overvaluation of self or ego, which distorts perception and perpetuates self-centeredness. This fundamental approach may not be as applicable for marginalized groups of people, including women. Teachings that point to the falsely constructed separate ego may be received as disconnected from the actual lived experience of oppression, or as a paternalistic strategy for pacification or assimilation.[5] For women and others experiencing social messages that continually devalue the self, the Buddhist emphasis on egolessness may only serve to further erode the not yet fully formed and validated person. Practices that suppress the ego may be misinterpreted as a denial of personhood which can be used as a method of subjugation and denigration of marginalized groups.

Feminism has taken a strong position on self-advocacy as a key principle in fighting abusive patterns of social conditioning, whether in marriage, work, or health matters. Self-advocacy is critical to women speaking up for their rights, their existence, and more humane standards of behavior. The marginalized or oppressed woman is encouraged to find her voice, her dreams, her capabilities, her inner strength. This is essential spiritual work, the challenge of distinguishing the true self from the many layers of social and gender patterns that deny the self.

This critique of Buddhism is relevant to environmental work in at least two respects. One, in the realm of ecofeminist spirituality, there may be a tendency to overemphasize the subjective experience of environment as universal, in the enthusiasm for a women's nature-based religious practice. However, this may more accurately reflect the need to simply establish the existence and validity of women's personhood, long overlooked by many religions, including Buddhism. I suggest that Buddhist feminists seeking ecological spirituality examine the teachings in depth to recognize healthy aspects of self-development as well as the blocks to egolessness.

Second, recognition of the full "personhood" or intrinsic existence of plants, animals, mountains, and rivers depends on one's capacity to fully recognize one's own personhood. For the Buddhist woman student, personhood may be displaced by the brilliant experience of boundarylessness before the self is fully developed. This then diminishes the person's capacity to deeply reflect and stand in solidarity with the full existence of any particular environmental other. Calling up the image of Indra's Net, this suggests that the reflective power of each jewel within the Net directly enhances the beauty and perception of all the other jewels. It is the quality of this reflection and existence that then guides our choice of environmental actions; an ethic of restraint expressing respect and appreciation for the beauty of the other members of the web is not possible if one does not first fully and deeply appreciate the self.

Power Relations Analysis

The social conditions of power, status, and privilege critically affect environmental decisions, law and treaty making, and natural resource negotiation. Social aspects of Buddhist religions are riddled with power relations, as much as any other organized religion. The social glue of power roles determines the nature of attitudes and actions of those in power and those not in power. While Buddhist philosophy clearly includes the relevant tools for examining the nature of power relations and the abuse of power, this area of inquiry is not a central emphasis in American practice today. Gender power relations, in particular, are not generally addressed, most likely because Buddhist philosophy and practice forms have come through patriarchal cultures with primarily male teachers and leaders. In many schools of Buddhism, there is a strong emphasis on practice relationships with an authoritative teacher. This can be a relationship of respect, but it can also be a relationship of abuse, where power and status are used to gain sexual access to women students.[6]

Issues of power relations have been raised by American feminist Buddhists trying to correct for Asian cultural influence in the historical development of Buddhism (see Boucher 1985; Gross 1986; Karabinus 1987). This inquiry into gender conditioning is not widespread and not necessarily well-received by American Buddhist centers or teachers. By broadening the field of inquiry to areas of hidden gender assumptions, feminists challenge the status of many of the governance and religious forms transferred to America from Asian patriarchal cultures. Those who hold religious or administrative power reinforced by Western male favoritism are generally not inclined to examine the language, behavior, and psychology of gender conditioning, despite feminist research showing the powerful capacity of gender conditioning to influence all other forms of conditioning.

This weakness in Buddhist philosophy as it has arrived in the Western world could have significant detrimental effects on the evolution of a Buddhist environmental ethic. The truth of interdependence, acknowledging the intrinsic value of each member of the web, is just a starting point for investigating the nature of specific relationships. The environmental crisis is driven by the complexities of power distribution, giving preference and status to some governments, some corporate ventures, some ecosystems, some species, some cultures over others. An effective Buddhist environmental ethic is strengthened by the dimension of power analysis presented by feminist theorists. Political, economic, and personal power can serve the environment, if illuminated by awareness and social consciousness of the logic of domination. Without this awareness, the critical role of power can be overlooked by the Buddhist practitioner focusing on the beauty and miracle of interdependence.

Social Ethics and Engaged Practice

Buddhist ethics traditionally emphasize behavior guidelines and liberation for the individual, rather than structural change of social systems. The current literature on Buddhism and social change is somewhat limited in covering the history of commitment to social issues (see Sivaraksa 1991, Jones 1989). In contrast, Christian social ethics trace their origin to the earliest stories of Jesus' suffering and compassion, developing principles of social justice as central to Christian religious practice. In some cases, Asian Buddhist cultures reinforce the acceptance of reality to the extreme of passivity. This can make it very difficult for Buddhist religious or social leaders to advocate social change.[7]

Feminism is fundamentally based in a need, desire, and strong motivation for social change. This drive for change might be seen as incompatible with Buddhism, presenting possible difficulty in merging these two approaches. The urgency and passion behind the feminist agenda may seem unmeditative to practicing Buddhists; the passive acceptance of Buddhist religious culture may seem unmotivated or apathetic to committed feminists. Yet each has something to gain from the other, particularly in developing a strong movement for environmental justice and a new code of environmental ethics.

Social environmental ethics are more than the sum of individual ethical practices regarding the environment. They are the ethics necessary for dealing with the whole systemic pattern of environmental destruction, which has a force and momentum of its own. A religious practice that only advocates individual improvement in environmental actions (such as recycling, vegetarianism, or birth control) does not go far enough in investigating the roots of socialized environmental destruction. The development of a social ethic to address the scale of environmental systemic disorder requires a motivation to work with the system as a whole and to uphold standards for the system as well as for the individual (see Fourez 1982). In this task, the commitment of feminism may be a useful catalyst for inspiring Buddhist dialogue and activity necessary to affect the environmental situation at any long-term meaningful level.

EXAMPLES OF BUDDHIST FEMINIST ENVIRONMENTAL WORK

Buddhist feminist activity on behalf of the environment is not yet very extensive, primarily because the number of people self-identified as Buddhist, feminist, and environmentalist is not large. However, examples of their environmental work are significant and are serving to inspire others around the world. These examples reflect primarily American Buddhist concern for the environment, though certainly there are women in other countries expressing their feminist and environmental concerns through Buddhist practice.

Research and Theory
Two examples of research carried out by Buddhist feminists concerned with the environment are the Perception of Nature Project undertaken by Chatsumarn Kabilsingh of Thailand and the comparative analysis of Buddhist philosophy and Western systems theory by Joanna Macy of the United States. Kabilsingh has reviewed the early Buddhist teachings of the Pali Canon to catalog specific references to the environment. Under the sponsorship of the World Wildlife Fund, a number of these teaching stories have been compiled

and distributed throughout Southeast Asia (Kabilsingh 1990; Davies 1987). Many of these early discourses cover the central points of Buddhist philosophy with specific references to refraining from harming others in the environment and specifically protecting trees, rivers, and animals of the forest.

Macy's work interprets the primary teaching of interrelationship in an environmental context, developing her ideas of "the ecological self" based on analysis of the co-arising of knower and known, body and mind, doer and deed, and self and society (May 1990, 1991b, 1991c). Her careful review of the nature of causality lays an important foundation for a Buddhist analysis of environmental power relations. She bases her definition of mutual morality in the dialectics of personal and social transformation, laying out a Buddhist construction of an environmental philosophy that is appropriate for today's interdependently created ecological crisis. This work builds on her earlier theoretical writing, in which she develops the image/essence of the Perfection of Wisdom as a feminine form, as the pregnant point of potential action, light, space, and emptiness, calling this the author of the Tathagatas (Macy 1977, 315–37). Macy's work is a major theoretical contribution to the evolution of an environmental ethic informed by Buddhist and feminist philosophy.

Environmental Activism

A second arena of Buddhist environmental activity lies in green politics and activism. The Buddhist Peace Fellowship (BPF) was founded in 1978 to bring a Buddhist perspective to the peace and environmental movements and to raise issues of social concern among Buddhist practitioners. In 1990, Doug Codiga, Margaret Howe, and I initiated a BPF campaign for environmental awareness by distributing to Buddhist centers and individuals over three hundred packets of materials and posters featuring the Buddha sitting in peaceful harmony surrounded by tigers, monkeys, tropical birds, and forest vines. The packets included suggested educational activities, a bibliography of readings, chants, and prayers, and ideas for environmentalizing local Buddhist centers.

The Berkeley BPF chapter has been actively engaged in Buddhist antinuclear environmental activism at the local Concord Naval Weapons base.[8] For the past five years they have led a half-day sitting meditation on the railroad tracks, blocking the passage of weapons out from the base. The protest is nonviolent and nonaggressive; it is meant as a statement of witness and solidarity, both with other non-Buddhist activists and with those who suffer from the threat or presence of nuclear weapons in their countries. Feminist and ordained Zen priest Maylie Scott has consistently promoted these sittings, serving as an inspiration to others by the strength of her practice and commitment to social change.

Another antinuclear effort, the Nuclear Guardianship Project, protests the storage of nuclear waste underground, where problems are out of sight and difficult to manage. Joanna Macy, Charlotte Cooke, and others propose instead that waste be stored above ground, to be watched over by "nuclear guardians" in monastery-like settings (Macy 1991a). This radical solution draws on the Buddhist model of monastic life, where mindfulness is the central practice, developing consideration and consciousness for all beings in the nuclear-affected web of life. The guiding ethic for the project reflects a deep sense of relationality with beings of the future who will inherit decaying nuclear isotopes in massive quantities.

Charlene Spretnak's work in green politics and spirituality reflect her belief that a spiritual infrastructure is essential for the successful transformation to a postmodern green society (Spretnak 1986, Capra and Spretnak 1984). Spretnak draws on her Vipassana Buddhist practice to remain grounded and centered in the middle of inevitable political tension and strategizing. She has worked to incorporate principles of feminism and nonviolence in Green Party platforms in California. For Spretnak, environmental activism is a direct expression of Buddhist practice, an embodiment of her spiritual commitment to serve all beings.

Buddhists Concerned for Animals (BCA), founded in 1981, is an example of green Buddhist politics. This group is committed to stopping cruelty to animals, especially in the use of animals for scientific experimentation (Boucher 1985, 288–93). They were instrumental in pressuring the University of California at Berkeley to improve their animal research practices. As Buddhists, they urge vegetarian eating to protest the inhumane conditions of factory-farmed animals. BCA raises issues of domination by promoting cruelty-free cosmetics that do not depend on animal testing for safety checks.

Environmental Education

Among Buddhist feminists concerned with the environment, a number of women are professional teachers or writers associated with academic institutions or spiritual retreat centers. As faculty in diverse departments or schools, they are building bridges between traditional subject areas and current environmental concerns. Buddhist feminists Lisa Faithhorn and Elizabeth Roberts teach Deep Ecology at California Institute of Integral Studies (CIIS) and Naropa Institute, respectively; Joanna Macy teaches systems theory, cross-cultural social activism, and spiritual practice in an environmental context at the Berkeley Graduate Theological Union, as well as CIIS. I teach environmental ethics in the Environmental Studies program at the University of Vermont. For these educators, course design and content, as well as teaching style, reflect a grounding in Buddhist practice and philosophy and a feminist perspective on power and domination. Macy has led the way in working with the blocked energy of despair, grief, fear, and anger to enable people to transform and free this energy for the healing of the world. Her teaching content and style rest solidly on a feminist analysis of power and a Buddhist practice of compassion.[9]

Another group of Buddhist feminist teachers addresses environmental issues in retreat or workshop settings, where spiritual practice is the context for environmental understanding. For example, Wendy Johnson, head gardener at Green Gulch Zen Center since 1980, teaches classes in gardening and tree planting as mindfulness practice. Green Gulch, a well-established retreat center in central coastal California, supports both a garden and an organic farm, with over twenty acres in lettuce, potatoes, squash, and other kitchen vegetables.

Wendy sees tree planting as part of a long-term plan for restoration of the once forested hillside slopes. Joan Halifax combines Buddhist mindfulness practice with modern forms of shamanism, to evoke connection with the natural world (Halifax 1990). Drawing on her background in anthropology, she leads workshops and trips to sacred sites to inspire spiritual grounding in the power of the earth itself.

Several writers also contribute to the educational literature, offering a Buddhist feminist perspective on the environment. Susan Griffin's book *Woman and Nature* is an American ecofeminist classic (Griffin 1978). Griffin's Buddhist Vipassana practice informs her poetry and creative writing, allowing her to express in detail the illusory distinction between mind and body, mind and nature. She writes as a committed feminist, pointing directly and vividly to parallel examples of oppression of nature and woman. China Galland's work on women in wilderness settings, as well as her investigation of Tara and the Black Madonna, also reflect a serious commitment to Tibetan Buddhism and the importance of women's voices in reconnecting with the environment (Galland 1990).

Some Buddhist environmental education takes place through devotional practices or ceremonies. At Green Gulch Zen Center, Wendy Johnson and I designed a Buddhist Earth Day ceremony that included a morning lecture on the environment, animal memorial service, and taking of the precepts in the presence of the central oak tree.[10] Wendy and others have also organized a number of family practice days, in which children participate in harvesting vegetables and planting trees. Earth Prayers and dedications have been collected by Elizabeth Roberts and Elias Amidon, subtly and skillfully reflecting an orientation to Buddhist mindfulness and a sense of the ecological self (Roberts and Amidon 1991). Mayumi Oda, Japanese Zen student, educates by painting large banners and silk screens of earth bodhisattvas surrounded by garden vegetables. She transforms traditional male figures such as Manjusri into female forms, cutting through delusion with spirited feminine energy (Oda 1988). Her feminist art has graced several conferences on Women and Buddhism held in the San Francisco Bay area; her drawings frequently appear in United States Buddhist publications.

This is only a sampling of examples of women engaged in environmental work based in Buddhist practice and feminist awareness. Certainly there are other examples from the wider international community. In contrast to so much feminist and environmental political work, which is combative in the desperate struggle for women's rights and environmental sustainability, a Buddhist nondualist and nonviolent viewpoint can make a very valuable contribution to the healing of the world. Women who are strong in their practice and understanding of Buddhism can bring a powerful intention to the difficult and sometimes overwhelming work of taking care of one another and the place where we live.

CONCLUSION

I believe these two streams of thought and activity—Buddhism and feminism—benefit from the insights and knowledge of each other in a way that can nourish and sustain the environment. The confluence of Buddhist and feminist thought, practice, commitment, and community in the 1990s offers a strong contribution to the healing of environmental loss and degradation. I opened this discussion in the context of the spiritual lineage of the feminine compassionate presence and the potential for healing she represents. By acknowledging Kuan Yin and Tara, I acknowledge all those who have drawn courage and inspiration from this aspect of their own Buddha natures in responding to the seemingly insurmountable suffering of the environment. Now perhaps these realized beings can be an inspiration and a source of guidance in taking care of the planet and each relationship in the complex biological and geophysical web of Indra's stunning Jewel Net.

NOTES

1. For further information on the Congress, or to obtain a copy of the Women's Action Agenda, contact Women's Environment and Development Organization, 845 Third Avenue, 15th floor, New York, N.Y. 10022.

2. From the Pali Canon, Samyutta Nikāya II. 28, 65, quoted and interpreted in Kaza (1985).

3. I wrote this version of the Three Pure Precepts for the 1990 Earth Day ceremony at Green Gulch Zen Center. Much of the text is reprinted in the *Buddhist Peace Fellowship Newsletter* (Summer 1990): 32–33.

4. Joanna Macy and John Seed have developed a ritual Council of All Beings, designed to draw out these responses. Councils have been conducted all over the world, in a wide diversity of settings. The form is described in Seed et al. (1988).

5. For an introduction to these ideas, see McCarthy 1990, with additional comments from panel member Yvonne Vowels.

6. See *Turning Wheel: Journal of the Buddhist Peace Fellowship* (Summer 1991): 22–29, with articles by Jack Kornfield and others and the formal statement of ethical guidelines by Second Generation Zen Teachers. See also Boucher 1985, 210–58.

7. This was a key topic at a social action training for Asian monks and other Buddhist activists I conducted with Paula Green in conjunction with the International Network of Engaged Buddhists meeting in Bangkok, February 1991.

8. Regular updates of Berkeley chapter activities regarding the weapons base sittings are available through the Buddhist Peace Fellowship, P.O. Box 4650, Berkeley, Calif. 94704.

9. See, for example, interviews of Joanna Macy in *Inquiring Mind* 5(2): 1–3 and Catherine Ingram, *In the Footsteps of Gandhi* (Berkeley: Parallax Press, 1990), 141–68.

10. Wendy Johnson's Earth Day talk, "Sitting on Our Garbage," is reprinted in the *Buddhist Peace Fellowship Newsletter* (Summer 1990), along with the text of the Earth Day ceremonies.

5

Feminist Judaism and Repair of the World

JUDITH PLASKOW

Any Jewish feminist program for social and religious change must grapple with the fact that not simply the shortcomings of individual education, imagination, and temperament, but also many of the structures of the world in which we live, militate against the creation and survival of communities based on feminist values. When my Jewish feminist spirituality collective first met in the spring of 1981, we set as a central task for the weekend to share our spiritual pasts, presents, and futures. My small group found that we had no difficulty talking about the past and present. But when we came to the future, we ended up talking about relationships, children, work, community, politics — everything but "spirituality." Although at first we chided ourselves for evading a difficult subject, we soon realized that in speaking of these other issues, we were addressing the realities that stood between us and our capacity to imagine the futures we wanted to live. It became clear to us that if we wanted to create a feminist Judaism we would have to help to bring about a world in which such a Judaism would be possible. For me and for the group, this discussion marked the beginning of an increasingly active awareness of the connection between spirituality as the lived, experiential dimension of a feminist Judaism and the wider social and political contexts in which we would try to live our spiritual lives.[1]

The relationship between a feminist Judaism and larger social and political issues, including our treatment of the natural world, forms the subject of this

Judith Plaskow is professor of religious studies at Manhattan College. She has been writing, speaking, and teaching about feminist theology for over twenty years. With Elisabeth Schüssler Fiorenza, she cofounded and coedits the *Journal of Feminist Studies in Religion.* With Carol Christ, she edited the two anthologies *Womanspirit Rising* and *Weaving the Visions.* She is author of *Standing Again at Sinai: Judaism From a Feminist Perspective,* from which this article is adapted.

essay. Here I wish to take up the relationship between spirituality and politics as a theological issue and to place the feminist transformation of Judaism in its wider social context.

Spirituality and concern for social institutions have often been viewed in American culture as polar opposites. Spirituality has been identified with ethereality, the presence of a place beyond the material world or deep within the self where the relationship to God is actualized. The assigned guardian of spirituality has been religion, which is itself relegated to the margins of society and expected to limit its interests to Saturday or Sunday mornings. As spirituality minds its otherworldly business, transformation of social structures is left to the often dirty work of politics, which catches us up in a realm of compromise, power seeking, struggle over what have been defined as limited resources, and confrontation with the distortions and disease in our social system.

This institutionalized separation of spirituality and politics, proceeding from the same hierarchy of mind and body that supports the disparagement of women and nature, represents a dualism to be rejected. When spirituality is understood from a feminist perspective—not in otherworldly terms, but as the fullness of our relationship to ourselves, others, the earth, and God—it cannot possibly be detached from the conditions of our existence. Those ideologies and institutions that alienate us from ourselves and link us with others in relationships of domination and subordination militate against our spirituality on every level. In a sexist, heterosexist, anti-Semitic, class-ridden, technocratic, and racist world, politics becomes the necessary work we do to make the world safe for the full realization and embodiment of spirituality.[2] In seeking to transform the ideas and institutions of Judaism, to live out our feminism, to overcome imperialism or class and race oppression, we attempt to create religious, social, and political structures that allow us to be present to each other in the fullness of who we are, and in doing so to experience the God who is with us in our personal and communal agency. As the vision and intuition of personal and communal wholeness guide our political goals and strategies, politics becomes an expression of spirituality in its intent to create more human institutions, and religion itself is transformed by politics. In understanding and living out the relation between politics and spirituality, Jewish feminists connect the transformation of the Jewish community with a multifaceted global struggle for social, political, and religious change.

RELIGION AND POLITICS IN JUDAISM

The connection between politics and spirituality is an important issue on which at least some strands of Judaism and feminism come together. Just as Judaism—while it has not always construed action in political terms—has consistently refused to disconnect the relationship with God from the world in which it is manifest, so feminism—while it has not always understood itself as a religious movement—has tied a vision of women's wholeness to a broad program for social and political action. In theology or theory and their living stance in the world, Judaism and feminism provide models of a relationship between faith and action that are worthy of extended exploration.

Recent work in liberation theology has used the word orthopraxis (right action), contrasting it with orthodoxy (right belief), to signify a new mood in Christian theology that recognizes the importance of action and behavior as central measures of the Christian life (see Gutiérrez 1973, 10). The polemical edge to this definition highlights the fact that Judaism has always been a religion of orthopraxis, assessing spirituality through its manifestation in the deed. The enactment of faith in the world, a central Jewish imperative, has had at least two distinctly different meanings in Jewish theology and practice: social justice and obedience to halakhah (Jewish law).

The first meaning, spirituality as social justice, receives classical expression in the writings of the prophets, for whom the essence of human service to God is love, justice, and righteousness. Contrasting these virtues with the empty practice of the cult, the prophets affirm that the forms of worship are meaningless in the absence of social justice. Offerings brought by the wicked, feasts and solemn assemblies held by those who trample the poor, prayers said by people who traffic with injustice are all unacceptable and fruitless. The efficacy of worship "is contingent upon moral living"; in the absence of morality, worship becomes despicable (Heschel 1962, 195). "Your new moons and fixed seasons/Fill Me with loathing," says Isaiah in the name of God. "They are become a burden to me,/I cannot endure them" (1:14). "He has told you . . . what is good," says Micah. "And what the LORD requires of you:/Only to do justice/And to love goodness,/And to walk modestly with your God" (6:8).

The prophets did not couch their concerns for justice in abstract generalizations that could be honored in principle and ignored in the particular. They described the social evils they saw around them in vivid and concrete terms. They repeatedly urged compassion for those on the margins of (patriarchal) society; the welfare of the widow and the fatherless is a refrain in their writings (for example, Isa. 1:17b; Ezek. 22:7b). They defended the rights of the poor in images as graphic as they are universal:

> Listen to this, you who devour the needy, annihilating the poor of the land, saying "If only the new moon were over, so that we could sell grain; the sabbath, so that we could offer wheat for sale, using an *ephah* that is too small, and a shekel that is too big, tilting a dishonest scale, and selling grain refuse as grain! We will buy the poor for silver, the needy for a pair of sandals."(Amos 8:4-6)

The prophets were meddlers, troublesome busybodies. They were horrified by things that are daily occurrences all over the world, by abuses that are often taken for granted as normal, if regrettable, aspects of complex social relations. They were unwilling to mind their own business, to stay away from wrongs that did not involve them personally, or refrain from championing others' rights for lack of invitation (Heschel 1962, 3-4, 204-5).

The passion for justice in prophetic writing presupposes a view of the divine/

human relation as enacted in human history and entangled in the world. To say that acts of worship and devotion, surely essential to religion, are less important to God than everyday righteousness is to make the sphere of human action the center of God's concern. The universe is finished, but history is still in the process of formation, and God needs human beings to create a just social order in history. As the covenant partner of Israel, God is a continuing participant in Israel's history, a participant who can be affronted, rejected, and humiliated by human cruelty and injustice. Israel's primary obligation to God is not to create a relationship to God that bypasses the material order, but to realize God's concern for human beings through interpersonal decency and the creation of social justice (Heschel 1962, 198, 199, 229-30). Attention to human relations and institutions, so far from conflicting with devotion to God, stands at its very center.

The prophetic identification of faith with social justice and its correlate, that God needs human beings to act justly, does not annul the militarism or patriarchal character of prophetic imagery; nor does it alter the prophets' religious intolerance or their lack of concern for justice for women. Prophetic writing is filled with contradictions. Thus, at the same time the prophets are concerned with widows as individual victims of a patriarchal culture, they help perpetuate that culture by using images of patriarchal marriage to symbolize faithfulness and apostasy. At the same time they call for a connection between religion and justice, they enforce a narrow and monolithic understanding of religion, condemning all who disagree with them as idolaters and whores. At the same time they presuppose the capacity of human beings to form or deform history, they depict God as the mighty warrior who holds all history in his hands. But the fact that the prophets failed to wholly live out their commitment to justice does not invalidate that commitment, any more than the commitment justifies its violation. Feminists can affirm our debt to and continuity with prophetic insistence on connecting faith and justice, even while we extend the prophets' social and religious critique beyond anything they themselves envisioned.

The second meaning of action in Jewish theology and practice, obedience to the law, is depicted in the prophetic writings as potentially in conflict with an emphasis on social justice. As the prophets see it, external obedience to the laws of sacrifice easily becomes the occasion for unwarranted self-righteousness that ignores the real demand of God, continuing justice. Unlike the passion for equity, which necessarily flows from a believing heart, cultic participation may be all outward sign, compatible with social evil and inner iniquity. And just as the forms of sacrificial worship can become ends in themselves, so obedience to the law can become its own object, fulfillment of specific legal requirements replacing attention to the broader moral values that the law betokens but cannot demand.

Real and significant as the danger of empty legalism may be, however, it is not the *purpose* of the law to replace morality with formal obedience. The intention of prophetic and legal religion is the same: to connect faith with the concrete world, to express the relationship with God in the whole of life. Thus with reference to their goal, the two meanings of Jewish action—social justice

and obedience to the law—are thoroughly interconnected. The law spells out
the specific demands of justice; it regulates the *ephah* and the shekel that the
prophets denounce as too small and too big. It takes ideals and shapes them
to human measure, establishing a trajectory toward the righteousness that lies
beyond the law's explicit claims. The rabbinic concept of *tikkun olam*, the right
ordering of society, underlies many of the law's specific demands.[3] Even the
purely ritual law proclaims the indivisibility of holy living; no detail of life is
too small to escape the possibility of consecration. As Martin Buber says, applying his words immediately to the sacrificial cult:

> Because God bestows not only spirit on man [sic], but the whole of his
> existence ... man can fulfill the obligations of his partnership with God
> by no spiritual attitude, by no worship, on no sacred upper story; the
> whole of life is required, every one of its areas and every one of its
> circumstances. (Buber 1963, 33)

This consonance of purpose between law and prophecy represents the ideal
without dissolving the tension between spirituality as law and spirituality as
justice. Modern Jews involved in movements for social change have often intensified the dichotomies of prophetic invective, depicting the details of ritual
observance as foolish distractions from the passion for justice. In modern times,
the object of criticism becomes not simply the empty formalism of worship, but
the particularity of legal obligation as contrasted with the pursuit of righteousness which is universal. Isaac Deutscher's "The Non-Jewish Jew," which
expresses this conflict in the sharpest possible terms, sees the great revolution-
aries of modern thought as Jewish precisely in the way they transcended the
boundaries of Judaism, living their Jewishness in a universal arena. Heine,
Marx, Luxemburg, Trotsky, all believed in human solidarity, and all saw solidarity as extending beyond Jewish borders. All believed that knowledge "to be
real must be active," and all acted for the sake of a universal good. For them,
Jewry was "too narrow, too archaic, and too constricting," and yet they betrayed
a passion for justice and action that is rooted in the tradition they wanted to
leave behind (Deutscher 1968, 36, 26).

Contemporary progressive Jews have tried to reconcile the prophetic and
legal understandings of religious action by investing the Kabbalistic concept of
tikkun olam with new political meaning. Isaac Luria's notion of the necessity of
human action both to the repair of the world and the reunification of God
seems to provide a basis for a Jewish political spirituality that is at the same
time a religious politics. The idea of *tikkun* in Lurianic thought—restoration of
the world to primal wholeness or the original intent of the creator—is part of
a complex and esoteric mythological schema. Briefly, the possibility of creation
is predicated on a withdrawal or contraction (*Tsimtsum*) of God from an area
within Godself in order to make room for the existence of the world. Following
this contraction, God sends out rays of light that constitute God's self-mani-
festation and creation, rays of light that are meant to be contained in special
vessels. While the vessels containing God's first emanations function properly,

the lower ones are too weak for the power of the divine effulgence and shatter and disperse. This breaking of the vessels (*Shevirath Ha-Kelim*) constitutes a cosmic calamity, releasing the forces of evil that are now at large in the world. *Tikkun* refers to the method through which repair is to be accomplished, and is largely a cosmic process preceding the creation of Adam. Not all the divine sparks held in captivity by the powers of darkness are able to free themselves by their own efforts, however, so a certain crucial aspect of this restoration is left in human hands. The religious acts of Jews who fulfill the commands of Torah accelerate the process of redemption, adding the "final touch to the divine countenance" and aiding the perfection of God and the world (Scholem 1941, 273; Fine 1987, 65-70).

This concept of *tikkun* as articulated in Lurianic Kabbalah is esoteric and elitist, but it undergoes transformation in a number of different hands. For Luria, restorative action is primarily ritual and contemplative action; the reunification of the divine sparks is initiated by the complex meditations of Kabbalists whose souls are first purified by a series of spiritual exercises. Hasidism, however, democratized the concept of *tikkun*, redefining it as attending to material needs with God in mind. In embracing the world while cognizant of the presence of the sacred in all aspects of reality, human beings can elevate the holy sparks present in the whole of creation (Fine 1987, 70; Jacobs 1987, 108, 115-16, 124). Jewish radicals of the nineteenth century, while hardly meaning to respond to Luria, also helped rework Kabbalistic messianism. The task of repairing a broken world, the goal of which is redemption, for them is transferred entirely to human hands. Action means social action; evil is injustice; revolution repairs the material world which is the only world there is. In more recent Jewish writing, the Kabbalistic concept of *tikkun* with its eschatological dimension is united both with its older rabbinic meaning of just social order and with the universalism of nineteenth-century radicals.[4] Arthur Waskow's book *These Holy Sparks* calls for reunion of the separated projects of modern Jewry—Zionism, social justice, socialism, halakhah—as itself part of the process of reunifying God. Creating a just social order becomes a sustainable task when it is undertaken by communities rooted in Jewish practice and aware of the transcendent dimension of their work in the world (Waskow 1983, 3-6, 20). This same meaning of *tikkun* as social, political, and religious transformation all reinforcing each other is found in the platform of New Jewish Agenda (a national Jewish organization seeking large-scale social change) and the progressive *Tikkun* magazine.[5]

The thread that winds through these sometimes conflicting notions of action and its social or cosmic effects is the refusal to disconnect religious belief from its practical expression or from human responsibility for the world. Whether action signifies just weights and measures, moral behavior, or daily prayer; whether its ramifications are purely mundane, covenantal, or cosmic in scope; faith is to be poured out in action which vivifies and embodies it. The maintenance of both social justice and sacred order emerges from the dialogue between God and humans, and thus rests partly on human shoulders, endowing our deeds with serious consequences.

RELIGION AND POLITICS IN FEMINISM

The feminist contribution to the connection between politics and spirituality is for the most part more indirect than this forthright linkage of faith and practice. Yet many of the first arguments for women's rights emerged in a religious context, and religious rhetoric and concerns marked feminist commitment to women's emancipation from its very beginnings. As feminist analysis and critique of traditional religion has become deeper and more sophisticated, there also has developed alongside it a grass roots women's spirituality movement that has found ways to express women's new sense of power and possibility in ritual and religious terms.

This focus on religion constitutes one significant dimension of feminism. Yet even where the women's movement has been indifferent or hostile to religious issues, it still has combined theory and practice in a way that parallels the Jewish connection of faith and politics. The consciousness-raising groups that marked the beginning of the contemporary feminist movement were seedbeds both for theory-making and for many concrete actions. Early feminist activities, from protesting Miss America pageants to working for abortion reform, projected a vision of a society in which women's humanity and dignity would be fundamental social and political values. Feminist theory developed side by side with organizations pressing for or making concrete changes, each feeding the other in an ongoing cycle. Thus women's claim to the right to direct our reproductive lives fed a struggle for abortion rights that in turn produced a clearer understanding of the forces aligned to control women's sexuality, and of the nature of feminist sexual values. Affirmation of women's right to physical safety and personal self-respect led to the establishment of shelters, rape crisis centers, and hot lines; these then generating deeper theory that could name and address the sources of violence. Insistence on equalizing power relations in daily life led women to make new demands on their partners and children, demands that often exposed the connections between family dynamics and larger social structures and shaped the vision and practice of a more radical feminism. In thus placing deeds in the service of vision, feminism has linked political action to a fundamentally spiritual quest for new forms of relation to self, others, and the world.

It is this basic commitment to new modes of social relation, as much as any specifically religious language and concerns, that has led some feminists to define the women's movement as intrinsically religious. While, for some feminists, involvement in social change is a human project that lacks any transcendent referent, others experience feminism as having an underlying spiritual dimension, quite apart from its relation to particular religious projects or terms. The experience of personal empowerment that accompanies and enables participation in social change can also connect the individual and community to more embracing sources of power. Engaging in the process of transforming social structures and ideologies fosters awareness of structures of meaning that bind particular struggles for change to a larger past and future. It is this awareness that leads Mary Daly to call the women's movement an *ontological* revolution, which means that in fostering new ways of being and becoming in the world, the movement is part of a search for ultimate meaning and reality (Daly 1973, 6 and *passim*). Other feminists have expressed the same insight in different terms. Nelle Morton, in a phenomenological discussion of consciousness-raising, describes the process of women's becoming as a religious transformation (Morton 1985, 11-30; Starhawk 1982a, 418; Geller and Setel 1986). The Goddess movement, in stressing the immanence of the Goddess in the world, sees the struggle for justice for women as serving the Goddess who is manifest in all social structures and relations. Jewish feminists have described women's liberation as an aspect of *tikkun*, an ingredient in the repair and transformation of the world that is part of its redemption. These are all ways of insisting on the connection between social justice and the relationship to ultimate reality, of saying that social transformation is a spiritual process pointing beyond itself.

The impulse to connect spirituality and politics does not annul the contradictions in feminist thought and practice, any more than is the case with prophetic notions of justice. Just as the prophets' passion for righteousness did not exclude religious intolerance or extend to abolishing patriarchy, so feminist commitment to the full personhood of women does not always encompass dismantling the race and class oppression that prevents most women's empowerment. In feminist practice as in prophetic thought, a politics unaware of its own privilege serves to highlight the relation between vision and social structures, even while it seems to separate them. Theory formulated by communities of white middle-class women often neglects issues crucial to minority feminists, just as lack of engagement in the concrete struggles of minorities limits the vision of white middle-class women. Insofar as feminism aims to make women the social equals of men, it emerges out of and reinforces race and class privilege. Lower-class and poor women, especially women of color, are more likely to emphasize a spirituality and politics of liberation than of equality, for they know that the men to whom they would be equal are in many ways not the equals of middle-class women (see Hooks 1984, ch. 2; Isasi-Diaz and Tarango 1988). While the vision of feminism as an ontological revolution theoretically incorporates the abolition of all forms of oppression, the absence of communal diversity at either the level of theory making or of action easily turns both into vehicles for domination.

FEMINIST JUDAISM AND ITS SOCIAL CONTEXT

If both Judaism and feminism, whatever their shortcomings, have propounded and practiced an ongoing connection between spirituality and politics, vision and social transformation, this connection must then be applied in the context of a feminist Judaism. The creation of woman-affirming Jewish communities is an important element in the quest for social justice, but it is just one piece of a larger struggle for justice that is being carried on in every corner of the earth. The Jewish community is a small one in the United States and a tiny one in the world. It would be foolish to expect that it could avoid entanglement in national and global structures of domination or forge its own way in creating new egalitarian forms of community in the absence of changes in the larger society. Jews have as often emulated and contributed to the inequality, domination, and injustice of their surroundings as modeled different ways of being. Only by keeping in mind the larger context of our efforts to create justice within Judaism can Jewish feminists avoid reproducing relationships of domination or turning our own liberation into a vehicle for the further oppression of others. Jewish feminists then, while we may want to begin with clearing our own house, must look beyond the Jewish community to the task of *tikkun olam*—repairing the world, creating a just society to which a just Judaism can contribute and flourish.

What repair of the world means concretely in the context of a feminist Judaism emerges most clearly from the contradictions between feminist vision and a profoundly unjust social order. The vision of the people of Israel as one among many overlapping nonhierarchical communities constitutes the living center out of which other aspects of a feminist Judaism emerge. The attempt to realize the kinds of communal structures and modes of being that a feminist Judaism requires and entails, however, brings us up against opposing social, religious, and political realities.

As one of many ethnic/religious communities in a complex and diverse United States, the Jewish community interacts with and is affected by structures of sexism, class inequality, racism, and homophobia that infect the society as a whole. It has to deal with problems of internal diversity in the context of a culture that professes respect for diversity while continually constructing difference as super- and subordination.

Thus, within a social system in which the physical environment is shaped to free men for "productive" work while women perform support services in the home, women can take on expanded roles in the Jewish community only if they remain childless, have extraordinary energy, or pay someone else to act as housekeeper and child-tender (Ruether 1979, 44). It is possible for middle-class women to participate fully in leadership and decision making within Judaism without renegotiating family or social relations, but only if they compensate someone else to play the role of "wife." Jewish women's own freedom, however, then depends on the continued oppression of other women who have fewer options within the social system. Women of color and poor white women make up the overwhelming majority of domestic workers because a racist and class-divided society presses certain groups into jobs that no one else wants. While substantive changes in the sex role system would alleviate the burden of poor women by raising wages and providing child care alternatives, it would not address the issues of race and class that crucially affect job patterns and the range of women's choices. If the feminist vision of social change is to embrace all women, then any vision of equality within the Jewish community must address two questions: What communal and social changes are necessary in order that *all* Jewish women can enjoy full equality within the community? And what social changes are necessary so that no Jewish woman's equality is predicated on the individual or structural exploitation of other women, but rather the struggle for equality in the Jewish community becomes part of a wider struggle for social justice?

The feminist quest for equal participation in the Jewish community is one area where Jewish issues link up with larger problems of gender, race, and class. Feminist efforts to redefine the Jewish understanding of sexuality—to see sexuality as a fundamental dimension of our embodiment—are also dependent on a host of social changes. Truly to honor our bodies as the foundation of our being would necessitate a profound alteration in our relation to the world. The import of the feminist slogan "the personal is the political"—meaning that seemingly personal problems are often rooted in the wider social context, and that social change must bring changes in daily life—is nowhere clearer than in the challenge of a positive view of the body to the devastation of the earth and to the ugliness and suffering in society.

First of all, to value our bodies means to value and care for the earth of which they are part; otherwise, the valuing has no relation to a material base that supports and sustains it. The increasing pollution of the environment, the dumping of toxic chemicals and nuclear wastes, the poisoning of the food supply through pesticides, and destruction of lakes and rivers all are rooted in denial of our embodied creatureliness, rejection of our embeddedness in the natural order. Feminist revaluation of the body entails an ecological consciousness and politics, an active awareness of, and responsibility to, the complex web of life.

Second, the capacity to open ourselves to the world, to allow the power of our senses to quicken our lives, depends on creating a human world in which this is a possibility. In the world as it is, with its increasing numbers of hungry and homeless, the demand that we seek full life, take joy in our work, or live with our senses sharpened must come to many as a painful and irrelevant irony. For the privileged, there is only so long the senses can take in the sight of homeless and beggars, the city smells of urine and garbage, and a constant barrage of sound. To live in a city and survive is to learn to shield oneself, to shut down feeling, to stop experiencing with the whole self. For those without privilege, the assault of hunger and the search for a quiet place to sleep take numbing precedence over the celebration of embodiment. It is not simply traditional attitudes toward sexuality that lead us to fear being alive, but also the world around us. To live with a full sense of our own bodily energy, then, entails not only dealing with natural environmental issues in urban as well as town and rural contexts, but also confronting the political questions that shape our total environment—the gentrification of inner cities that is leaving an increasing number of people homeless, the dearth of humane living spaces, the factory closings and relocations that are creating a new group of unemployed and homeless, the structures of racism and class domination as they affect housing, homelessness, and the distribution of government services.

SPIRITUALITY AND POLITICS IN A FEMINIST JUDAISM

The connection between spirituality and politics is inescapable. Our visions of the way the world can be are articulated within and over against existing social structures, and everywhere we turn in seeking to realize these visions we come up against institutions that stand between us and our ability to live spiritually fulfilling lives (Ackelsberg 1986, 114). Unless the quest for integration of our relationships to self, God, earth, and others emerges out of and leads to the creation of forms of community that nurture our whole being, this quest remains marginal to our daily lives, and thus ineffective and irrelevant. For spirituality to matter, it must be poured out into the world in which we live, just as enduring social change must be rooted in some intuition of a richer and more humane future.

I have argued that both Judaism and feminism have tried to connect faith and vision with everyday realities—although often not in ways that are sufficiently self-critical. The prophets' insistence that love of God is to be manifest through justice is itself expressed in the language and thought forms of patriarchy, and in images that accept and perpetuate the existence of patriarchy. The rabbinic concept of *tikkun olam* (right ordering of society) demands that, "as a precaution for the general good," witnesses sign a bill of divorce.[6] But *tikkun olam* does not extend to reordering a society in which divorce is a male prerogative. The feminist vision of the liberation of women intends justice for all women, yet feminists often imagine the fruits of liberation in ways that presuppose continuing race and class inequity and domination.

For Jewish feminists to develop a theology and practice that is sensitive to the interrelation of different sorts of oppression, we will need to attend to the structural character of oppression and to address its structural forms. The complexity of modern society, the seeming intractability of certain social dilemmas, the overwhelming threat of environmental destruction, the global roots and ramifications of many political and economic problems force us increasingly to grapple with the systemic character of injustice and justice and to confront patterns of injustice that the tradition has taken for granted.[7] As emerging political and liberation theologies have made amply clear, the political and structural dimension of sin and salvation in the modern age requires the structural reformulation of many traditional values. In the contemporary context, concern for widows and orphans must express itself in dismantling the patriarchal structures that disenfranchise and marginalize women and children. Compassion for the poor must entail confrontation with corporate greed, arrest of imperialism, and the struggle against racism and class oppression that consign many to misery. Remembering the stranger must involve breaking down the barriers of nationality, religion, sex, race, and class that turn differences into occasions for domination.

Because certain key Jewish ideas and institutions are part of the unjust systems that need dismantling, the connection between politics and spirituality requires the transformation of Judaism itself. Ideas and structures within Judaism that reflect and foster models of domination—a Torah that mirrors and reproduces the power of men over women, an Israel that in conception and communal form constructs difference as hierarchy, a notion of God as dominating Other, a legal structure that defines sexuality in terms of possession— must be reconstructed on the basis and for the sake of a different mode of relation. A spirituality that emerges out of the vision and sometime reality of diverse, egalitarian communities, that knows God as present within — not above — community as its binder, sustainer, and goad, can nourish and is nourished by the critique and transformation of all structures of oppression.

As Jewish feminists work for justice within the Jewish community and beyond it, the emergence of new communal forms becomes the vital foundation for shaping a feminist Judaism. Then within Jewish communities seeking to connect faith and politics, new content poured into traditional Jewish ceremonies and forms often provides connections between visions of social and religious transformation and the basic rhythms of everyday life. The consonance of purpose between law and prophecy — to connect faith with the whole of reality — can be enacted in ritual and law attuned to the demands of justice. Thus, coming out of new Jewish communities, a number of Jewish feminists and other progressive Jews have called for a set of dietary laws (*kashrut*) that reflect the feminist value of connection to other persons and a wider web of life. *Kashrut* is already a system reminding us of the sanctity of animal life, and some have suggested that, for the sake of this sanctity as well as for the sake of preserving grain for the hungry, we extend this reminder to a full vegetarianism. *Kashrut* already tells us that "we are what we eat," and many values central to contemporary progressive food practices and to feminist concerns about sexuality and embodiment can be included in an expanded system of *kashrut*. Concern for protecting our bodies might take the form of prohibiting foods that are grown with pesticides or that contain carcinogens or hormones. Concern over the rise of hunger might be expressed in the form of a special blessing before or after meals and a commitment to set aside a proportion of the cost of all meals to feed the hungry. Concern about the exploitation of workers and planting of monocrops on lands needed for local agricultural production might lead to forbidding foods that are the product of exploitation and oppression. In these ways, *kashrut* can be a vehicle for connecting Jews to others without losing its meaning as a marker of Jewish distinctiveness and identity.[8] Such a new *kashrut* would turn the simple everyday act of eating into an aspect of the continuing quest for justice.

Other ritual and legal forms provide different ways of concretizing the commitment to social and religious change. Shabbat, like *kashrut*, is a central element in Jewish ritual life, and one that can also foster an ethic of connection. Arthur Waskow has described the Sabbath as part of a rhythm of work and repose, labor and celebration that can provide time to examine the meaning and direction of our ceaseless production and consumption (Waskow 1971, ch. 3). While getting and spending may be central to the other six days of the week, Shabbat is a day for family and friends, for honoring creation, for resting and enjoying the fruits of our work. It is a day for *being* rather than *doing*. It is a day not for changing the earth but for noticing it, for attending to the fragile mystery of the world that grounds and precedes all our labor. When we take Shabbat seriously, the values it represents can begin to permeate all our days. Just as the work week makes Shabbat possible, so the value and integrity of our relationships with others and the earth are the presuppositions of all that we do. When we sacrifice our obligations to self and others to the demands of work, Shabbat reminds us of the sanctity of relationships. When our concern with profits and production leads to the exploitation and destruction of the world in which we live, Shabbat reminds us of the sanctity of creation, of the God-given value of the material order.

Ellen Bernstein has suggested turning Tu Bishvat, a minor holiday marking the new year of trees, into a major environmental holy day. For the rabbis, the meaning of Tu Bishvat was quite straightforward: The time when sap begins to rise, it marked the beginning of the year for calculating the tithe on fruit. The Kabbalists gave Tu Bishvat deeper significance, connecting the sap of earthly trees with the image of God as cosmic tree that renews the flow of life in the universe. The Kabbalists created a ritual for Tu Bishvat in which the participants eat different types of fruit, each symbolizing different levels in the process of creation. Bernstein builds on and transforms the Kabbalistic ritual, turning it into a ceremony honoring the four elements of creation. Exploring the worlds of earth, water, air, and fire, she interweaves Jewish sources fostering awareness of and responsibility to the earth with contemporary material and ecology and environmental destruction. Her ritual is at once a celebration of the divine in nature and the occasion for taking stock of our responsibility to nature, for renewing our commitment to the preservation of the natural world (Bernstein 1987).

Esther Ticktin has called for new halakhot (laws) that give concrete expression to the commitment to equality for women within the Jewish tradition. Grounding these halakhot in the biblical reminder, "for you were a stranger in the land of Egypt," she suggests that the Jewish experience of exclusion should become the basis for a commitment to stop excluding women from public religious life. As a start, she asks that male Jews refuse to benefit from any policy of exclusion, that they refuse to participate in a minyan that separates women behind a *mechitzah* (barrier), and that they refuse to go up to the Torah in congregations that do not call women to the Torah. If Orthodox men feel they cannot take on these restrictions, then at least they should refrain from celebrating their privileges or speaking of them in ways that tease and hurt women (Ticktin 1976, 129-35). Such halakhot provide specific ways to act on feminist values; they are consciousness-raising for those who take them on and can sensitize and mobilize others.

Each of these suggestions for ritualizing religious and political values—and each of the communities out of which they arise—represents an attempt to resist the forces that would separate faith from worldly involvement: the cultural opposition of religion and politics, the Marxist understanding of religion as a reactionary diversion from the battle against injustice, the lure of oases of spiritual experimentation in the midst of a world desperately in need of redemption. Each challenges us as feminists and as Jews to bring our spirituality and politics together in such a way that our religious lives change the way we live, and our political commitments shape our spirituality.[9] To build community, to work for political change, is to act out the spiritual vision of a world in which diverse communities can live together and learn from each other, each with the resources it needs to survive and mature. To celebrate and ritualize our visions is to locate our political projects in the context of the ongoing work of creation, to take our place in the eternal dialogue between God and creation through which the world develops and unfolds.

As we start where we are, addressing ourselves to particular constituencies and particular needs for healing or repair, we slowly build the institutions and communities that can begin to bring the future into being. As we create communities that can nourish and sustain us; as we work to transform the institutions that most deeply affect us; as we enact and celebrate together moments of commitment, clarity, and vision, we generate energy for further change that is rooted in what we have already envisioned and accomplished. Just as structures of domination support each other, so do our efforts at justice. The sum of the changes that we seek eludes us as a total system, because those working for change have less power than the complex and entrenched institutions of hierarchical power that dominate our world (Ruether 1983, 233-34). But lured on by the ground already attained and by the Ground of that ground that empowers us, we remember the words of Mishnah *Avot* (2.16): It is not incumbent upon us to finish the task, but neither are we free to desist from it altogether. As we work toward the creation of a feminist Judaism as part of a larger struggle toward a more just world, we place our small piece in a mosaic that will finally provide a new pattern—a new religious and social order.

NOTES

1. Compare Martha Ackelsberg 1986, 114.

2. This formulation was first suggested by Betsy Cohen and Martha Ackelsberg in leading a B'not Esh discussion on spirituality and politics in 1984.

3. Mishnah *Gittin,* 4.2-3. The Mishnah says that Hillel's *prosbul,* the practice of having witnesses sign a bill of divorce, and the practice of listing all names on a bill of divorce, are all for the sake of *tikkun olam.*

4. Thanks to Robert Goldenberg for helping me to sort out the different levels of meaning of *tikkun olam.*

5. New Jewish Agenda National Platform (adopted November 28, 1982), 1. Available from New Jewish Agenda, 64 Fulton Street, #1100, New York, N.Y. 10038. *Tikkun* magazine, which integrates discussion of politics, culture, and religion from a progressive perspective, has on its back cover, "*Tikkun* . . . to heal, repair, and transform the world." Available from 5100 Leona Street, Oakland, CA 94619.

6. Danby translation of *Gittin* 4.2, 3.

7. I do not mean to suggest that the Jewish tradition is unaware of the systemic nature of justice and injustice. See, for example Waskow (1987) and Ruether (1984, 334-35). The tradition has taken certain systems of injustice for granted, however, and these must now be at the center of our awareness.

8. For this paragraph, I am indebted to Falk (1986), Alpert and Waskow (1987), and Waskow (1988). Arthur Green also mentions *kashrut* in his inaugural address as president of the Reconstructionist Rabbinical College (printed and distributed by the College November 15, 1987), 16. On Judaism as a system of distinctions and separations, see Plaskow 1990, 96-97.

9. This relationship was repeatedly urged by Hershel Matt at meetings of New Jewish Agenda Theology Group that met irregularly from 1982-1984. Compare Ackelsberg (1986).

6

An Earthly Theological Agenda

SALLIE McFAGUE

I teach a survey course in contemporary theology that covers the 20th century. When I took a similar course as a divinity student at Yale in the late '50s, it had considerable unity. We studied the great German theologians whose names began with "B" (seemingly a prerequisite for theological luminosity) — Barth, Bultmann, Brunner, Bonhoeffer — and, of course, Tillich. They were all concerned with the same issues, notably reason and revelation, faith and history, issues of methodology and especially, epistemology: how can we *know* God?

More recent theology has no such unity. The first major shift came in the late '60s, with the arrival of the various liberation theologies, which are still growing and changing as more and different voices from the underside of history insist on being heard. While what separates these various theologies is great (much greater than what separated German theology and its American counterparts), one issue, at least, unites them: they ask not how we can know God but how we can change the world. We are now at the threshold of a second major shift in theological reflection during this century, a shift in which the main issue will be not only how we can change the world but how we can save it from deterioration and its species from extinction.

Sallie McFague is the Carpenter Professor of Theology at Vanderbilt University. She teaches and writes in the area of religious language, especially as that language affects our behavior toward others, including other life-forms and the ecosystem that supports all life. Her most recent book, *Models of God: Theology for an Ecological, Nuclear Age* (Fortress Press, 1987), criticizes the monarchical language for God (God as king and the world as "realm"), suggesting instead that we consider the models of God as mother, lover, and friend of the world. She is presently working with materials from "the common creation story," the so-called Big Bang billions of years ago and the subsequent evolutionary history, as a resource for re-imagining both the transcendence and immanence of God as well as the proper place of human beings in the scheme of things.

The extraordinary events of the past few years, with the simultaneous lessening of cold-war tension and worldwide awakening to the consequences of human destruction of the flora and fauna and the ecosystem that supports them, signal a major change in focus. Perhaps it is more accurate to say that the focus of the liberation theologies widened to include, in addition to all oppressed human beings, all oppressed creatures as well as planet earth.

Liberation theologies insist rightly that all theologies are written from particular contexts. The one context which has been neglected and is now emerging is the broadest as well as the most basic: the context of the planet, a context which we all share and without which we cannot survive. It seems to me that this latest shift in 20th-century theology is not to a different issue from that of liberation theologies, but to a deepening of it, a recognition that the fate of the oppressed and the fate of the earth are inextricably interrelated, for we all live on one planet—a planet vulnerable to our destructive behavior.

The link between justice and ecological issues becomes especially evident in light of the dualistic, hierarchical mode of Western thought in which a superior and an inferior are correlated: male-female, white people-people of color, heterosexual-homosexual, able-bodied-physically challenged, culture-nature, mind-body, human-nonhuman. These correlated terms—most often normatively ranked—reveal clearly that domination and destruction of the natural world is inexorably linked with the domination and oppression of the poor, people of color, and all others that fall on the "inferior" side of the correlation. Nowhere is this more apparent than in the ancient and deep identification of women and nature, an identification so profound that it touches the very marrow of our being: our birth from the bodies of our mothers and our nourishment from the body of the earth. The power of nature—and of women—to give and withhold life epitomizes the inescapable connection between the two and thus the necessary relationship of justice and ecological issues. As many have noted, the status of women and the status of nature have been historically commensurate: as goes one, so goes the other.

A similar correlation can be seen between other forms of human oppression and a disregard for the natural world. Unless ecological health is maintained, for instance, the poor and others with limited access to scarce goods (due to race, class, gender, or physical capability) cannot be fed. Grain must be grown for all to have bread. The characteristic Western mind-set has accorded intrinsic value, and hence duties of justice, principally to the upper half of the dualism and has considered it appropriate for those on the lower half to be used for the benefit of those on the upper. Western multinational corporations, for example, regard it as "reasonable" and "normal" to use Third World people and natural resources for their own financial benefit, at whatever cost to the indigenous peoples and the health of their lands.

The connection among the various forms of oppression is increasingly becoming clear to many, as evidenced by the World Council of Churches' inclusion of "the integrity of creation" in its rallying cry of "peace and justice." In the closing years of the 20th century we are being called to do something unprecedented: to think wholistically, to think about "everything that is," because everything on this planet is interrelated and interdependent and hence the fate of each is tied to the fate of the whole.

This state of affairs brought about a major "conversion" in my own theological journey. I began as a Barthian in the '50s, finding Barth's heady divine transcendence and "otherness" to be as invigorating as cold mountain air to my conventional religious upbringing. Like many of my generation, I found in Barth what appeared to be a refreshing and needed alternative to liberalism. But after years of work on the poetic, metaphorical nature of religious language (and hence its relative, constructive, and necessarily changing character), and in view of feminism's critique of the hierarchical, dualistic nature of the language of the Jewish and Christian traditions, my bonds to biblicism and the Barthian God loosened. Those years were the "deconstructive" phase of my development as a theologian.

My constructive phase began upon reading Gordon Kaufman's 1983 Presidential Address to the American Academy of Religion. Kaufman called for a paradigm shift, given the exigencies of our time—the possibility of nuclear war. He called theologians to deconstruct and reconstruct the basic symbols of the Jewish and Christian traditions—God, Christ, and Torah—so as to be on the side of life rather than against it, as was the central symbol of God with its traditional patriarchal, hierarchical, militaristic imagery. I answered this call, and my subsequent work has been concerned with contributing to that task.

While the nuclear threat has lessened somewhat, the threat of ecological deterioration has increased: they are related as "quick kill" to "slow death." In other words, we have been given some time. We need to use it well, for we may not have much of it. The agenda this shift sets for theologians is multifaceted, given the many different tasks that need to be done. This paradigm shift, if accepted, suggests a new mode of theological production, one characterized by advocacy, collegiality, and the appreciation of differences.

Until the rise of liberation theologies, theology was more concerned with having intellectual respectability in the academy than with forging an alliance with the oppressed or particular political or social attitudes and practices. There was a convenient division between theology (concerned with the knowledge of God) and ethics (a lesser enterprise for action-oriented types). Theologians were also usually "solo" players, each concerned to write his (the "hers" were in short supply) magnum opus, a complete systematic theology. As the deconstructionists have underscored, these theologians also strove to assert, against different voices, the *one* voice (their own—or at least the voice of their own kind) as the truth, the "universal" truth.

Our situation calls for a different way of conducting ourselves as theologians. Like all people we need, in both our personal and professional lives, to work for the well-being of our planet and all its creatures. We need to work in a collegial fashion, realizing that we contribute only a tiny fragment. Feminists have often suggested a "quilt" metaphor as an appropriate methodology: each of us can contribute only a small "square" to the whole. Such a view of scholarship may appear alien to an academy that rewards works "totalizing" others in the field and insisting on one view.

The times are too perilous and it is too late in the day for such games. We need to work together, each in his or her own small way, to create a planetary situation that is more viable and less vulnerable. A collegial theology explicitly supports difference. One of the principal insights of both feminism and postmodern science is that while everything is interrelated and interdependent, everything (maple leaves, stars, deer, dirt — and not just human beings) is different from everything else. Individuality and interrelatedness are features of the universe; hence, no one voice or single species is the only one that counts.

If advocacy, collegiality, and difference characterized theological reflection and if the agenda of theology widened to include the context of our planet, some significant changes would occur. I will suggest three.

First, it would mean a more or less common agenda for theological reflection, though one with an almost infinite number of different tasks. The encompassing agenda would be to deconstruct and reconstruct the central symbols of the Jewish and Christian tradition in favor of life and its fulfillment, keeping the liberation of the oppressed, including the earth and all its creatures, in central focus. That is so broad, so inclusive an agenda that it allows for myriad ways to construe it and carry it out. It does, however, turn the eyes of theologians away from heaven and toward the earth; or, more accurately, it causes us to connect the starry heavens with the earth, as the "common" creation story claims, telling us that everything in the universe, including stars, dirt, robins, black holes, sunsets, plants, and human beings, is the product of an enormous explosion billions of years ago. In whatever ways we might reconstruct the symbols of God, human being, and earth, this can no longer be done in a dualistic fashion, for the heavens and the earth are *one* phenomenon, albeit an incredibly ancient, rich, and varied one.

If theology is going to reflect wholistically, that is, in terms of the picture of current reality, then it must do so in ways consonant with the new story of creation. One clear directive that this story gives theology is to understand human beings as earthlings (not aliens or tourists on the planet) and God as immanently present in the processes of the universe, including those of our planet. Such a focus has important implications for the contribution of theologians to "saving the planet," for theologies emerging from a coming together of God and humans *in and on the earth* imply a cosmocentric rather than anthropocentric focus. This does not, by the way, mean that theology should reject theocentrism; rather, it means that the divine concern includes *all* of creation. Nor does it imply the substitution of a creation focus for the tradition's concern with redemption; rather, it insists that redemption should include all dimensions of creation, not just human beings.

A second implication of accepting this paradigm shift is a focus on praxis. As Juan Segundo has said, theology is not one of the "liberal arts," for it contains an element of the prophetic, making it at the very least an unpopular enterprise and at times a dangerous one. The academy has been suspicious of it with good reason, willing to accept religious studies but aware that theology contains an element of commitment foreign to the canons of scholarly objectivity. (Marxist or Freudian commitments, curiously, have been acceptable in the academy, but not theological ones.) Increasingly, however, the hermeneutics of suspicion and deconstruction are helping to unmask simplistic, absolutist notions of objectivity, revealing a variety of perspectives, interpretations, commitments, and contexts. Moreover, this variety is being viewed as not only enriching but necessary. Hence the emphasis on praxis and commitment, on a concerned theology, need in no way imply a lack of scholarly rigor or a retreat to fideism. Rather, it insists that one of the criteria of constructive theological reflection — thinking about our place in the earth and the earth's relation to its source — is a concern with the *consequences* of proposed constructions for those who live within them.

Theological constructs are no more benign than scientific ones. With the marriage of science and technology beginning in the 17th century, the commitments and concerns of the scientific community have increasingly been determined by the military-industrial-government complex that funds basic research. The ethical consequences of scientific research — which projects get funded and the consequences of the funded projects — are or ought to be *scientific* issues and not issues merely for the victims of the fall-out of these projects. Likewise, theological reflection is a *concerned* affair, concerned that this constructive thinking be on the side of the well-being of the planet and all its creatures. For centuries people have lived within the constructs of Christian reflection and interpretation, unknowingly as well as knowingly. Some of these constructs have been liberating, but many others have been oppressive, patriarchal, and provincial. Indeed, theology is not a "liberal art," but a prophetic activity, announcing and interpreting the salvific love of God to *all* of creation.

A third implication of this paradigm shift is that the theological task is not only diverse in itself (there are many theologies), but also contributes to the planetary agenda of the 21st century, an agenda that beckons and challenges us to move beyond nationalism, militarism, limitless economic growth, consumerism, uncontrollable population growth, and ecological deterioration. In ways that have never before been so clear and stark, we have met the enemy and know it is ourselves. While the wholistic, planetary perspective leads some to insist that all will be well if a "creation spirituality" were to replace the traditional "redemption spirituality" of the Christian tradition, the issue is not that simple. It is surely the case that the overemphasis on redemption to the neglect of creation needs to be redressed; moreover, there is much in the common creation story that calls us to a profound appreciation of the wonders of our being and the being of all other creatures. Nonetheless, it is doubtful that such knowledge and appreciation will be sufficient to deal with the exigencies of our situation.

The enemy — indifferent, selfish, shortsighted, xenophobic, anthropocentric, greedy human beings — calls, at the very least, for a renewed emphasis on sin as the cause of much of the planet's woes and an emphasis on a broad and profound repentance. Theology, along with other institutions, fields of study, and expertise, can deepen our sense of complicity in the earth's decay. In addition to turning our eyes and hearts to an appreciation of the beauty, richness, and singularity of our planet through a renewed theology of creation and nature, theology ought also to underscore and elaborate on the myriad ways that we personally and corporately have ruined and continue to ruin God's splendid creation—acts which we and no other creature can knowingly commit. The present dire situation calls for radicalizing the Christian understanding of sin and evil. Human responsibility for the fate of the earth is a recent and terrible knowledge; our loss of innocence is total, for we know what we have done. If theologians were to accept this context and agenda of their work, they would see themselves in dialogue with all those in other areas and fields similarly engaged: those who feed the homeless and fight for animal rights; the cosmologists who tell us of the common origins (and hence interrelatedness) of all forms of matter and life; economists who examine how we must change if the earth is to support its population; the legislators and judges who work to advance civil rights for those discriminated against in our society; the Greenham women who picket nuclear plants, and the women of northern India who literally "hug" trees to protect them from destruction, and so on and on.

Theology is an "earthy" affair in the best sense of that word: it helps people to live rightly, appropriately, on the earth, in our home. It is, as the Jewish and Christian traditions have always insisted, concerned with "right relations," relations with God, neighbor, and self, but now the context has broadened to include what has dropped out of the picture in the past few hundred years— the oppressed neighbors, the other creatures, and the earth that supports us all. This shift could be seen as a return to the roots of a tradition that has insisted on the creator, redeemer God as the source and salvation of all that is. We now know that "all that is" is vaster, more complex, more awesome, more interdependent, than any other people has ever known. The new theologies that emerge from such a context have the opportunity to view divine transcendence in deeper, more awesome, and more intimate ways than ever before. They also have the obligation to understand human beings and all other forms of life as radically interrelated and interdependent as well as to understand our special responsibility for the planet's well-being.

My own work takes place within this context and attempts to add a small square to the growing planetary quilt. I would like to become very specific now. What is my little "square" that I offer to the common quilt? What can I *as a theologian* in the Christian tradition do constructively so that our planet can continue to support life in community? I emphasize "as a theologian," because I believe that the planetary agenda cannot be an avocation, something one does in addition to one's everyday work—a pastime or hobby, as it were—but needs to be one's *vocation*, one's central calling. It is perhaps obvious how raising children, gardening, teaching, nursing, or caring for animals might contribute to the planet's agenda, but how does theology (let alone business, law, housekeeping, plumbing, or car manufacturing)? I leave it to each of those areas to imagine how they *might* fit, for I believe they, in fact, *must* fit (if not, their legitimacy is in question). But those who practice these arts and skills ought to be the ones who say in what ways they do fit or ought to change in order to do so.

There are many different theological tasks relevant to planetary well-being.

One of central importance is learning to think differently about ourselves, others, and our planet, because learning to think differently usually precedes being willing and able to act differently. Much of one's thinking at the basic level of worldview and one's place in it is derived from the dominant images in the religious traditions of one's culture. This "thinking" is not primarily conscious, nor is it limited to active members of a religious tradition. Western culture was and still is profoundly formed by the Hebrew and Christian religions and their stories, images, and concepts regarding the place of human beings, history, and nature in the scheme of things. Moreover, I believe it is the major images or metaphors of a tradition that influence behavior more powerfully than its central concepts or ideas. For instance, it is the image of God as king and lord rather than the idea of God as transcendent that has entered deeply into Western consciousness.

Let me suggest briefly some ways in which the modern worldview that is widely held in our culture has been deeply influenced by Christianity, and especially by Protestant Christianity. As many have pointed out, the Christian tradition is and has been not only deeply androcentric (centered on males and male imagery for the divine), but also deeply anthropocentric (focused on human well-being) to the almost total neglect of other species and the natural world, especially during the last few hundred years. It is also focused on redemption narrowly conceived, on human salvation, often understood in individualistic and otherworldly terms. The creation and health of *all*, of the earth and its creatures, has seldom been a central concern of the tradition. Moreover, the dominant imagery of this tradition has been monarchical. God is imaged as king, lord, and patriarch of a kingdom that he rules, a kingdom hierarchically ordered. God has all the power in this picture, with human beings seen as rebellious, prideful sinners against the divine right.

Needless to say, this picture is not what thoughtful Christians or other thoughtful people influenced by Christian culture hold consciously, but its main tenets have seeped into the Western worldview to the extent that most Westerners, quite unselfconsciously, believe in the sacredness of every individual human being (while scarcely protesting the extinction of all the members of other species); believe males to be "naturally" superior to females; find human fulfillment (however one defines it) more important than the well-being of the planet; and picture God (whether or not one is a believer) as a distant, almighty superperson. Moreover, this dualistic, hierarchical picture supports another form of dangerous behavior: the superiority of one's own nation over others and hence the validation of a nationalistic, militaristic, xenophobic horizon. Christianity is surely not alone responsible for this worldview, but to the extent it has contributed to and supported it, the deconstruction of some of its major metaphors and the construction of others is in order.

The portrayal of God as monarch ruling over his kingdom is the dominant model in Jewish, Catholic, and Protestant thinking and is so widely accepted that it often is not recognized as a picture, that is, a construction of the divine/human relationship. To many, God *is* the lord and king of the universe.[1] Yet the monarchical model has been thoroughly and roundly criticized not only by feminists but by a host of other theologians as well. It is not necessary to review the criticism of the model here, except for a few points. In the monarchical model, God is distant from the world, relates only to the human world, and controls that world through domination and benevolence.[2]

On the first point: the relationship of a king to his subjects is necessarily a distant one, for royalty is "untouchable." God as king is in his kingdom, which is not of this earth, and we remain in another place, far from his dwelling. In this picture, God is worldless and the world is Godless — the world is empty of God's presence. Whatever one does for the world is finally not important in this model, for its ruler does not inhabit it as his primary residence and his subjects are well advised not to become too enamored of it either. At most, the king is benevolent, but this benevolence extends only to human subjects.

And this is the second point: as a political model focused on governing human beings, it leaves out the entire rest of the earth and its many creatures. It is simply blank as to the natural world and hence has encouraged a similar indifference in human beings. God's kingdom is composed exclusively of human beings.

Finally, in this model, God rules either through domination or benevolence, thus undercutting human responsibility for the earth. It is simplistic to blame the Hebrew and Christian traditions for the ecological crisis, as some have done, on the grounds that Genesis instructs human beings to have "dominion" over nature; nevertheless, the imagery of sovereignty supports attitudes of control and use toward the nonhuman world. Whatever might have been nature's superiority in the past, the balance of power has shifted to us. Extinction of species by nature, for instance, is in a different dimension from extinction by design, which only we can bring about. The model is lacking, even if God's power is seen as benevolent rather than as domineering. Then it is assumed that all will be well, that God will care for the world with no help from us. The heavenly father will take care of his children; we can leave it up to him.

The images in this model are constructions, and as such they are partial, relative, and inadequate. They are metaphors abstracted from human relations (relations with kings, lords, masters) and applied to God. Hence, they are in no sense "descriptions" of God; yet their power is deep and old, their influence inscribed into our being from our earliest years. They are, therefore, difficult to discard. Yet, as we have seen, the monarchical model is dangerous in our time, for it encourages a sense of distance from the world, is concerned only with human beings, and supports attitudes of either domination of the world or passivity toward it. This chilling realization adds a new importance to the images we use to characterize our relationship to God, to others, and to the nonhuman world. No matter how ancient a metaphorical tradition may be, and regardless of its credentials in scripture, liturgy, and creedal statements, it still must be discarded if it threatens the continuation and fulfillment of life. If, as I believe, the heart of the Christian gospel is the salvific power of God for all of creation, triumphalistic metaphors cannot express that reality *in our time* whatever their appropriateness may have been in the past.

What are other possibilities for imaging God's relationship to the world and our place within it? The first question one must ask is: *what* world? Probably the single most important thing that theologians can do for the planetary agenda is to insist that the "world" in question, the world in which to understand both God and human beings, is the contemporary scientific picture of the earth, its history, and our place in it that is emerging from cosmology, astrophysics, and biology. Neither the world of the Bible, nor of Newtonian dualistic mechanism, nor of present-day creationism is the world to which we must respond as theologians. I am not suggesting in any sense that science dictate to theology or that the two fields be integrated, but making a much more modest, though critically important, proposal. Contemporary theology, if it is to help people to think and act wholistically, must make its understanding of the God/world relationship consonant with contemporary views of reality. A theology that is not commensurate with reality as culturally understood is not credible. Moreover, the contemporary view coming from the sciences is so awesome, rich, and provocative for imaging both divine and human relationships that the political models seem pale and narrow in comparison.

In broad strokes, the common creation story emerging from the various sciences claims that some fifteen or so billion years ago the universe began with a big bang, exploding matter, which was intensely hot and infinitely concentrated, outward to create some hundred billion galaxies of which our galaxy, the Milky Way, is one, housing our sun and its planets. From this beginning came all that followed, so that everything that is is related, woven into a seamless network, with life gradually emerging after billions of years on this planet (and probably on others as well), and evolving into the incredibly complex and beautiful earth that is our home. All things living and all things not living are the products of the same primal explosion and evolutionary history, and hence are interrelated in an internal way from the very beginning. We are distant cousins to the stars and near relations to the oceans, plants, and all other living creatures on our planet.

The characteristics of this picture suggest radically different possibilities for understanding both God and human existence than we found in the monarch/realm worldview. The "world" here is, first of all, the universe, beside which the traditional range of divine concern mainly with human subjects dwindles, to put it mildly. In this view, God relates to the entire fifteen-billion-year history of the universe and all its entities, living and nonliving. On the "clock" of the universe, human existence appears a *few seconds* before midnight. This suggests, surely, that the whole show could scarcely have been put on for our benefit; our natural anthropocentrism is, indeed, sobered. Nevertheless, it took fifteen billion years to evolve creatures as complex as human beings; hence, the question arises of our peculiar role in this story, especially in relation to our own planet.

A second feature of the common creation story is the radical interrelatedness and interdependence of all aspects of it, a feature of utmost importance to the development of an ecological sensibility. It is *one* story, a *common* story, so that everything that is traces its ancestral roots within it, and the closer in time and space entities are, the closer they are related. Thus, while we may rightly feel some distance from such "relatives" as exploding stars, we are "kissing cousins" with everything on planet earth and literally brothers and sisters to all other human beings. Such intimacy does not, however, undercut difference; in fact, one of the outstanding features of postmodern science's view of reality is that individuality *and* interdependence characterize everything. It is not just human beings that have individuality, for the veins on every maple leaf, the configuration of every sunset, and the composition of every pile of dirt is different from every other one. This portrayal of reality undercuts notions of human existence as separate from the natural, physical world; or of human individuality as the only form of individuality; or of human beings existing apart from radical interdependence and interrelatedness with others of our own species, with other species, and with the ecosystem. The continuity of nonliving and living matter displays another crucial feature: the inverse dependency of the most complex entities on the less complex. Thus, the plants can do very nicely without us, but we would perish quickly without them. The higher and more complex the level, the more vulnerable it is and the more dependent upon the levels that support it. Again, we see implications for reconceiving the "place" of human beings in the scheme of things.

Another feature of the common creation story is its public character; it is available to all who wish to learn about it. Other creation stories, the cosmogonies of the various world religions, are sectarian, limited to the adherents of different religions. Our present one is not so limited, for any person on the planet has potential access to it and simply as a human being is included in it. This common story is available to be remythologized by any and every religious tradition and hence is a place of meeting for the religions, whose conflicts in the past and present have often been the cause of immense suffering and bloodshed. What this common story suggests is that our primary loyalty should not be to nation or religion, but to the Earth and its Creator (albeit that Creator may be understood in different ways). We are members of the universe and citizens of planet earth. Were that reality to sink into human consciousness all over the world, not only war among human beings but ecological destruction would have little support in reality. This is not to say they would disappear, but those who continued in such practices would be living a lie, that is, living in a way that is out of keeping with reality as currently understood.

Finally, the common creation story is a *story*: it is an historical narrative with a beginning, middle, and presumed end, unlike the Newtonian universe which was static and deterministic. It is not a "realm" belonging to a king, but a changing, living, evolving event (with billions of smaller events making up its history). In our new cosmic story, time is irreversible, genuine novelty results from the interplay of chance and necessity, and the future is open. This is an unfinished universe, a dynamic universe, still in process. Other cosmologies, including mythic ones such as Genesis and even early scientific ones, have not been historical, for in them creation was "finished." Rather than viewing God as an external, separate being ruling over the world, it is appropriate to see God as in, with, and under the entire evolutionary process. Paul's statement that God is the one "in whom we live and move and have our being" takes on new and profound significance. In this picture God would be understood as a *continuing* creator, but of equal importance, we human beings might be seen as partners, as the self-conscious, reflexive part of the creation that can participate in furthering the process.

To summarize: the characteristics of the common creation story suggest a decentering and recentering of human beings. We are radically interrelated with and dependent on everything else in the universe and especially on our planet. We exist as individuals in a vast community of individuals within the ecosystem, each of which is related in intricate ways to all others in the community of life. We exist, with all other human beings from other nations and religions, within a common creation story that each of us can know about and identify with. The creation of which we are a part is an ongoing, dynamic story which we alone (so we believe) understand, and hence, we have the potential to help it continue and thrive, or to let it deteriorate through our destructive, greedy ways.

Our position in this story is radically different than in the king/realm picture. We are decentered as the only subjects of the king and recentered as those responsible for both knowing the common creation story and being able to help it flourish. In this story we feel profoundly connected with all other forms of life, not in a romantic way, but in a realistic way. We *are* so connected, and hence, we had better *live* as if we were. We feel deeply related, especially, to all other human beings, our closest relatives, and realize that *together* we need to learn to live responsibly and appropriately in our common home.

If this kind of thinking became widespread — thinking of ourselves as citizens of the planet, breaking down all forms of parochialism — some of the things that must happen if we and the earth are to survive and flourish, might be able to. Once the scales have fallen from one's eyes, once one has seen and believed that reality is put together in such a fashion that one is profoundly united to and interdependent with all other beings, everything is changed. One sees the world differently: not anthropocentrically, not in a utilitarian way, not in terms of dualistic hierarchies, not in parochial terms. One has a sense of belonging to the earth, having a place in it along with all other creatures, and loving it more than one ever thought possible.

But, interestingly, such a perspective does not diminish either human beings or God; in fact, both are enlarged. Human beings have been decentered as the point and goal of creation, and recentered as partners in its continuing creation. God has been decentered as king of human beings and recentered as the source, power, and goal of the fifteen-billion-year history of the universe. As ethicist James Gustafson puts it, while we are not the "measure" of creation, we are its "measurer" (Gustafson 1981, 82). We are not the center or the point of creation, but we are the only ones, to our knowledge, who know the story of creation. In fact, we human beings presently alive are the first human beings who really know this story, because it is only in the last fifty years or less that it has gradually emerged from the scientific community. We alone know this awesome fact, and the more one knows about this story — the micro and macro worlds that surround our middle world, the worlds of the very tiny and the unimaginably immense and ancient—the more filled with wonder one becomes. This is not to suggest that an aesthetic response is the principal one. Wonder and awe at the immensity and age of the universe can generate a sense of indifference toward puny earthly problems. A genuine aesthetic response is necessarily accompanied by an ethical one; that is, our responsibility for preserving the beauty, diversity, and well-being of our tiny corner of the universe, planet earth. As those responsible for helping the creative process to continue and thrive on our planet, we can scarcely imagine a higher calling. We have been recentered as co-creators.

In this picture of God and the world, *God* is certainly not diminished. To think of God as creator and continuing creator of this massive, breathtaking cosmic history makes all other traditional images of divine transcendence, whether political or metaphysical, seem small, indeed. The model of God as king is, by comparison, "domesticated transcendence," for a king only rules over human beings. A genuinely transcendent model would insist that God is the source, power, and goal of the total universe, but a source, power, and goal that works within its natural processes; hence, the model, while genuinely transcendent, is also profoundly immanental. The king/realm model is neither genuinely transcendent (God is king over one species recently arrived on a minor planet in an ordinary galaxy) nor genuinely immanent (God as king is an external super person, not the source, power, and goal of the entire universe).

The model that comes to mind as we think about God and the world in the new creation story is not "the king and his realm" but the "universe as God's body." The ancient organic metaphor which, in one form or another, was central to the Western sensibility for thousands of years until it was replaced by the mechanistic model in the seventeenth century, is emerging again in postmodern science, in ecology, and in feminism. It has, of course, always been present in Goddess religions and in Native American traditions.

The universe as God's body is an immensely attractive, powerful model. To think of the entire evolutionary process, with all the billions of galaxies of stars and planets from the beginning of time, some fifteen billion years ago, as the "body" of God, the visible "sacrament" as it were of the invisible God, is a model of profound immanence and overwhelming transcendence. God is immanent in all the processes of reality, expressing the divine intentions and purposes through those processes, and at the same time God, as the agent of the process, is transcendent over it, though as its internal source, power, and goal rather than as an external controller.

As a physical image stressing divine embodiment, it underscores what our tradition has seldom allowed: that matter is of God and is good, that, indeed, if God is embodied, then matter, the natural world, is not only "good" but in some sense sacred—a place where God is present. It is a model that *could* be a rival to the monarchical language, for the base, or conventional meaning of the model, is of profound and radical importance to us: our bodies and the bodies of other human beings whom we love, as well as the bodies of life forms we rely on and are now coming to appreciate (other animals, trees, plants, rocks, sky, and soil). It is a model with great *religious* potential, for it opens up the entire universe and especially our planet as a way of making God sacramentally present to us—God does not meet us only in the despair of personal crises nor only in the political battles for the liberation of oppressed human beings, but also in the beauty as well as the increasing deterioration of the natural world. Moreover, this model suggests a decentering and recentering for human beings, a new sense of our proper place in the scheme of things—a place not as God's darling but as God's partner, as the ones, at least on our planet, who can and must take care of the body of God.

With the common creation story we now have a resource for re-imaging and radicalizing God as creator and redeemer of all that is, with human well-being as one important though by no means the only focus of divine concern. Within this story we human beings find, once again, our proper place within the whole, a place that, with the rise of modern science and its wedding to technology, seemingly giving us control over the natural world, we have forgotten. Yet now our place is more responsible than ever before, because we know that we have power, not the power to create but the power to destroy. We realize that it is only by living appropriately, in proper relations with all other beings, that we can fulfill our responsibilities to the well-being of creation. Within this story, God is, once again, the source, power, and goal of all that is, the creator and redeemer of the cosmos, and not merely king of human beings. Yet, now God is giver and renewer of a universe so vast, so old, so diverse, so complex that all earlier and other images of divine glory and transcendence are dwarfed by comparison. And yet, this transcendence is one immanental to the universe, for God is not a superperson, a king, external to cosmic processes, but the source, power, and goal immanent in these processes.

One of the rallying cries of the Protestant Reformation was "let God be God." That is precisely what the common creation story, as a resource for theology, suggests. It is God and not we who creates and makes whole. We, at the most, are helpers, whose proper place within the whole on which we depend is to acknowledge who we are in reality and where we fit. The common creation story tells us that the earth is our home; we belong here; and we have responsibilities to our home.

It is precisely this sense of belonging, of being at home, that is the heart of the matter. It is the heart of the matter because it is the case: we *do* belong. As philosopher Mary Midgley writes, "We are not tourists here ... We are at home in this world because we were made for it. We have developed here, on this planet, and we are adapted to life here ... We are not fit to live anywhere else" (Midgley 1978, 194–95). Postmodern science allows us to regain what late medieval culture lost at the Reformation and during the rise of dualistic mechanism in the 17th century: a sense of the whole and where we fit in it. Medieval culture was organic, at least to the extent that it saw human beings, while still central, as embedded in nature and dependent upon God. For the last several centuries, for a variety of complex reasons, we have lost that sense of belonging. Protestant focus on the individual and otherworldly salvation, as well as Cartesian dualism of mind and body, divided what we are now trying to bring back together and what must be reintegrated if we and other beings are to survive and prosper. But now, once again, we know that we belong to the earth, and we know it more deeply and thoroughly than any other human beings have ever known it. The common creation story is more than a scientific affair; it is implicitly deeply moral, for it raises the question of the place of human beings in nature and calls for a kind of praxis in which we are ourselves in proportion, in harmony, and in a fitting manner relating to all others that live and all systems that support life.

To *feel* that we belong to the earth and to accept our proper place within it is the beginning of a natural piety, what Jonathan Edwards called "consent to being," consent to what is. It is the sense that we and all others belong together in a cosmos, related in an orderly fashion, one to the other. It is the sense that each and every being is valuable in and for itself, and that the whole forms a unity in which each being, including oneself, has a place. It involves an ethical response, for the sense of belonging, of being at home, only comes when we accept our proper place and live in a fitting, appropriate way with all other beings. It is, finally, a religious sense, a response of wonder at and appreciation for the unbelievably vast, old, rich, diverse, and surprising cosmos, of which one's self is an infinitesimal but conscious part, the part able to sing its praises.

To summarize: one square in the quilt, one contribution to the planetary agenda, is the deconstruction of models and metaphors oppressive and dangerous to our planet as well as the suggestion of alternatives. Since the Christian tradition has contributed a number of problematic images, it is incumbent upon its theologians to analyze and criticize such models and metaphors. It is also the responsibility of theologians to suggest, from current resources, alternative models and metaphors to express the relation of God to the cosmos as well as the place of human beings in the cosmos. The common creation story is one such rich resource to re-image both divine and human reality in relation to the universe, and especially to our planet.

In conclusion, the planetary agenda is the most serious, most awesome fact facing us; it is concerned with whether we live or die and how well we live, if we do live — questions usually reserved for religions and their solutions to issues of mortality and salvation. We see now, however, that health and well-being are profoundly "earthy" affairs — while still being religious ones, with all the urgency of religious questions. It is no exaggeration to say that the planetary agenda is a life-and-death matter. We now know this, and we know that our time is limited to do what needs to be done. The planetary agenda is everyone's agenda. Each of us is called upon to contribute one square to the quilt. As time is short, we had better get about the business of doing so.

NOTES

1. "The *monarchical model* of God as King was developed systematically, both in Jewish thought (God as Lord and King of the Universe), in medieval Christian thought (with its emphasis on divine omnipotence), and in the Reformation (especially in Calvin's insistence on God's sovereignty). In the portrayal of God's relation

to the world, the dominant western historical model has been that of the absolute monarch ruling over his kingdom" (Barbour 1974, 156).

2. For a more complete critique of the monarchical model, see McFague (1987, ch. 3).

7

Ganga

Purity, Pollution, and Hinduism

LINA GUPTA

She is the source of redemption. . . . Heaps of sin accumulated by a sinner during millions of births, are destroyed by the mere contact of a wind charged with her vapor. . . . As fire consumes fuel so this stream consumes the sins of wicked.
— *Bramhavaivartta Purana, Krishnajanma Khanda, 34:13ff*

Almost all Hindus keep a small or a large container of water from the Ganges River in their homes. Though I live in the West, I keep such a container in my own home. I was born in India. For me and other Hindus, the river is herself a goddess whom we call "Ganga." Whether we are rich or poor, old or young, male or female, she is the holiest symbol of all symbols in Hinduism. All Hindu rites and rituals necessitate her presence as well as her sanctifying power. She transforms an ordinary time and place to a sacred time and place. As she touches us in ordinary daily rituals, the participants and all other aspects of the ceremony take on a divine light. Be it a birth ceremony, initiation, wedding, or a funeral, Ganga's participation as well as her blessing are needed. At death, we hope to be cremated on her banks and have our ashes thrown or scattered in the bosom of her waters.

Lina Gupta is a visiting professor at Loyola Marymount University. She has contributed an essay on Hinduism from a feminist perspective to *After Patriarchy*. She has written on "Secularism and Sikhism in India." She is currently working on an article on Tantra and is increasingly interested in environmentalism and Goddess traditions in Hinduism. Her Master's degree in philosophy is from Calcutta University in India, and her Ph.D. is in Asian and comparative philosophy from Claremont Graduate School, Claremont, CA.

According to Hindu legend, Ganga descended from the heaven to earth with a singular purpose: to elevate human to the divine, to exemplify the interconnection and the harmony among all facets of the heaven and earth. She does this by the sanctity of her water, which has been proclaimed in the Vedas, Upanishads, Epics, and Puranas. According to the Puranas, bathing in her water purifies us from all the accrued sins of the past and releases us from present states of misery and misfortune. Not only does she nullify the effects of the past with her sanctifying power, she removes the seed of ignorance that obstructs our inner vision of unity and totality of the Divine. If bathing or immersing in her water is not possible for some reason, we gain merit even by sprinkling a drop of her water on ourselves, by touching her, by drinking her water, by seeing her, by thinking of her, by chanting or hearing her name. Application of her water as well as her mud on our body while performing a penance elevates us to a higher plane of existence. Her water and mud are used for medicinal purposes and have healing effects on all parts of our body and organs. In short, the water of Ganges is regarded as an elixir; it purifies all things mobile or immobile, living or dead, organic or inorganic, human or nonhuman.

Yet this is not the whole story. The pilgrim taking a holy bath in the Ganga may not realize it, but usually a drop of Ganga water on the average contains traces of arsenic, cyanide, lead, mercury, and many other pollutants. Thus the river Ganga, the goddess Ganga, the symbol of supreme purity, exhibits a dramatic picture of defilement. From the point of view of most world religions, to revere a sacred space is to protect it from all forms of impurity and defilement. The present condition of Ganga is one of pollution. On her way from the Himalayas, so we read in *Life* magazine, Ganga

> is forced to swallow the effluvia of overpopulation and progress. Distilleries, refineries, chemical factories and fertilizer complexes have dumped their wastes directly into the Ganges, threatening the ecological balance of the river basin and the livelihood of farmers and fishermen. During the 80's more than 230 million gallons of untreated sewage were discharged into the river every day, and it was common to see bloated cow carcasses drifting along the river's surface. (Singh 1992, 82)

Ganga is irrefutable evidence that we can threaten the habitability of this planet, remaining quite unaware for years of the long-term effects of our actions.

The Ganga, the holiest river in India, presents a baffling picture not only to a Westerner but also to some modern Hindus. Ganga, like other rivers on earth, bears the effluvia, the rejects, of human communities. Yet unlike the other rivers, Ganga commands reverence and loyalty poured out by millions of Hindus in their daily rituals. How could the same river, considered to be the goddess of purity and the source of all purification, be polluted by her own devotees? What kind of mind-set operates behind such ambiguity?

These are questions which I, as a Hindu and a woman influenced by ecofeminism, must ask constantly. For my part, I love her dearly. Indeed, with each passing day I love her even more. But I see her through eyes that have been influenced by ecofeminism. I see the pollution of our Ganga, and of all rivers, as the result of a mind-set, and attitude, which ecofeminists call patriarchy.

Part of this mind-set involves a sense of separation and disconnectedness from one another and the earth. From an ecofeminist perspective, pollution is the result not only of inappropriate technologies and mismanagement of resources, but also of a failure to be connected with, to, and for one another and the rest of the planet. External pollution begins with internal pollution, the pollution of thinking we are utterly separate from the rest of existence.

I realize that I partake of this pollution. I, too, often fail to realize my deep connectedness with all that is. All of us, women and men alike, suffer from the illusion of complete separateness. All of us suffer from patriarchy.

Still, I believe that Hinduism, though containing its own patriarchal aspects, offers as well some resources for assisting us to move beyond patriarchy. Hinduism can help us awaken to the deep connections that already exist, if we have but eyes to see. Indeed I believe that the goddess Ganga herself, rightly understood, can awaken us to these deep connections, so that we might cease polluting her and other rivers as well. My aims in this essay, then, are (1) to share more about what it means, to me as a woman, to be authentically connected with Ganga from a personal point of view; (2) to summarize the most well-known myth about Ganga that suggests issues of abuse of the environment; (3) to indicate ways in which patriarchal features of the Hindu tradition may have themselves contributed to a pollution of the Ganga; and then (4) identify resources within Hinduism that can help Hindus, and perhaps others as well, better realize the truth to which Ganga points, namely our deep interconnections. The best way I know to share what it means to be connected to Ganga is to share notes from my own diary as I was writing early drafts of this very essay. I offer eight entries which, taken together, give you a feel for one woman's relation to Ganga.

ON LOVING GANGA

First Entry
I am having a great deal of difficulty writing this essay. I had difficulties writing the paper on Kali, too, the one that appeared in *After Patriarchy: Feminist Transformations of the World Religions* (Gupta, 1991). But Kali is aggressive. She somehow managed to have me finish my work. I kicked and screamed, but I did it. Ganga seems to be too tolerant, too polite, and too gentle. Kali never reminded me of my mother. Ganga does. She is a mother, who is gentle and tender, forever giving, nurturing, and listening. She is a person I can relate to and talk to. But do I know her? Did I ever make an attempt to know her? If I try, would she let me get to know her? Sometimes I wonder if I am talking to myself or the Ganga in me. I do not have an audience to talk to about Ganga. Maybe I do not want to have an audience. My memories, my feelings, and my thoughts are fighting over me. I wonder who is going to win. I do not want to

have an audience until I am clear about all these. Or maybe I ought to have an audience who will participate in the process and not only in the finished product. I feel very lonely in my journey. Am I the only ecofeminist in the whole country who is working on this goddess? There are only two articles and a book I found on her. It is amazing; being under constant scrutiny, she still managed to keep some secrets to herself. You have to be her to know her — be in her company, be in her depth, and be in her flow.

Second Entry

Writing this essay is a journey into my Indian background, my Hindu heritage; most importantly, it is a journey into a memorable past to my origin and to my end. In my journey through the banks of my childhood memory, I remember so clearly all my visits to Ganga as I went to worship at the Kali temple on the bank of the river. If I had forgotten to visit Ganga for one week, I would be reminded by my parents to have a *Darsan* (seeing) of Ganga before I left the temple. Although geographically I am far from Ganga and I no longer am sitting on her bank, I am not without her. As she is present in a container of water sitting on my altar, she is present in all forms of water. Whether it is the water of a lake, stream, pond, river, or ocean, touched with her holy name, ordinary water takes on her sacred nature. Therefore I am not without her. She is the energy, the life that permeates all of nature. By naming her I identify her divine essence in all things. She reminds me of a never-ending cycle of life that neither harbors any grudges against her polluters nor discharges her anger in her surroundings. She is the beacon of life that shows me the path I have forgotten and shines on the one I have chosen. She is the mother. She is a goddess. She is a woman. She is a journey as simple as a river, as complex as life itself.

Third Entry

I am caught between the East and the West. Oh, how I wish I wasn't. I have lived in this country long enough to call this land my mother. I have lived in this country far too long not to be colored by the thoughts and feelings of a Western mind. Yet, I am much too Hindu to forget my own roots and heritage and lifeline. And I can see why I chose Ganga for this paper right after I wrote my paper on Kali. My weekly visit to Kali temple brought me closer to Ganga too. See, the Kali temple that we used to visit was on the bank of Ganga. Each one of them is complete and depicts reality in its totality. Yet from a superficial point of view they pretend to be two sides of the totem pole. They are opposite in their traits as well as in their actions. They both project power of different nature. Kali is aggressive, and one can see why it is necessary for her to be so: She is competitive, she is analytic, she is a woman, the first-generation feminist, breaking down the barrier by sheer criticism and power. Ultimately you swing to the other side. You have got to come to Ganga. She is feminine, she is beautiful, she is all-woman and not ashamed of who she is. She is the second-generation feminist, reconsidering her decisions, her options, and making a new plan for the future. She is trying to start a dialogue. Kali is the West, the woman in a man's garb, the intellect, the structure, the discipline, the aggression, the logic. Ganga is the East, the woman, the intuition, the essence, the flow, the subtlety, the feeling. We have to come in between them or maybe merge them.

Fourth Entry

Ganga knows her children. We are presenting ourselves just the way we are. We are showing her where we are — in disorder, in chaos, in pollution. However, in the process of letting her know who we are, what we feel, and what we have done with our lives, we have overburdened her. We are defiling Ganga. Isn't that a story of a mother and a child? Have you ever seen a mother who is in a happy space while her child is suffering somewhere else? Mother gets into dirt and filth to play with the child, also to get him or her out of the dirt and filth. I think Ganga is exemplifying the true nature of a mother, true nature of a nurturer. Being a divine mother, she is even going one step further. She came all the way down to take you up. It is time for us to meet her halfway.

Fifth Entry

I was talking to a very dear family member in India today. He is a Shiva worshiper. I was telling him about my project and some problems in writing a paper on Ganga. He said something quite interesting. He told me to ask Lord Shiva to release Ganga from his matted hair. I did, and I started my journey in writing. There was a sense of release from my own predicament. I do not know who released what and how it all came about. All I know is what I have experienced. That is, Gods and Goddesses are parts of us, parts of the divine essence. By appealing to them we name our predicaments, and by naming them psychologically we release our inner power and potential that are dying to appear on the surface. Although I was born and raised in a Hindu family and received my academic training in Hinduism in India, I, for one, failed to see or maybe refused to see my own tradition in its essence. In order to work in the real sense of the term, regardless of the subject or the discipline, one has to dive deep into it, so it will be revealed to you. You have to be open enough to see it for what it is without the superimpositions of the categories with which your logical mind so lovingly has provided them. I saw the limitation in the analytic method. Finally I am able to see the flow of Ganga as she reveals herself to anyone who is willing.

Sixth Entry

It is hard to see Ganga's power. One has to see Ganga in the Himalayas to know her true beauty and power. She is hiding her essence in the valley. One has to give one's all to see who she is and what she wants you to do.

Seventh Entry

Pollution is like a grimy, fearful, and unpredictably dangerous being. I have to name it. We are ignorant about its power. We are therefore negligent about its destructive ability. Pollution represents a sort of darkness that exposes our thoughts of dualism, our feelings of separation and alienation, and, most importantly, our ignorance about the consequence of our actions. One has to be very "mindful" in the sense of Buddhist mindfulness, to all one does, and to all one thinks in one's daily life. Then and then alone one sees that in all of us there is this pollution sitting, hiding, and waiting in the alleys of our mind. It is like how you may never use one racial slur or word in your whole life, you may show love and compassion for your fellow being, but you can still be a racist. One has to watch one's thoughts and feelings and not necessarily just one's words and actions, to find out whether even a seed of separation or alienation is lurking in the alley of your mind. According to Hinduism, human birth is a rare birth. One's primary obligation and goal in a human birth is to realize one's own self. If one understands one's own self as something separated from everything else in the world, one remains in bondage. To realize one's own self, *atman* in the true sense of the term, is to realize the total identity of *atman* and *brahman*. As long as one has even a seed of alienation or separation in one's mind, liberation or *moksa* will remain merely a goal and never a reality. This is the summary of Hinduism.

Eighth Entry

As the river flows through the various parts of a land making the land a harmonious whole of interconnections and interdependence, she is an energy, the essence that radiates through all life forms, mobile and immobile, humans and nature, and reflects the basic kinship among all things. I think I have gone through several stages of experience in this project. In the beginning it was just collecting my materials. Quite impersonally I got my materials together, not much to write home about, but that is all I can get. It is difficult to write a paper about any of the Goddesses without being present to her. And being present to her is being present to the Earth.

GANGA IN MYTH

Ganga is loved by all Hindus. The Puranas, as well as later writings and poems, depict her as their beloved mother. She is loved equally by the poets and artists; she is portrayed in various poems and ballads by the poets and sculpted and painted by the artists in different regions of India. From the earthly erotic love between a man and a woman to the love of the divine, from the daily affairs of a human community to the highest goal of liberation, all have been narrated through the imagery of Ganga. In a ballad Prince Naderchand says to Mahua: "what good life [without you]? Let yourself be the river Ganga, and I will drown myself in you" (Mahua V). One of the most well-known Bengali devotees of Kali, poet Ramprasad, explains the theory of Shakti (creative power of the divine) in Hinduism: "The pearl of Shakti lies at the depths, in the sea of Knowledge" (Ramprasad's Devotional Songs, no. 27).

Among many legends and myths, the most well-known story of Ganga narrates how Ganga descended on earth at the request of King Bhagirath to revive his sixty thousand ancestors (King Sagar's sons) back to life. The classical version of the myth may be summarized as follows. There was a king called Sagar, and he had two wives. King Sagar desired the title Chakravartin, or world conqueror, so he started a special sacrificial rite called "Asvamedha-yajna."

Following the procedures of this special ritual, a horse was turned loose and sent to all territories for one year, and wherever the horse went, if not resisted by the King or people of that land, the land became part of Sagar's kingdom. At the end of the year, after the return of the horse, it was supposed to be sacrificed as an offering, and Sagar would have gotten his title.

God Indra, troubled by Sagar's empire that touched the ocean, feared it would reach the heaven. Therefore, he stole the horse and hid it in the sage Kapila's hermitage. After waiting for the horse to return for a long time, worried King Sagar sent his sixty thousand sons in search of the horse. In the process of looking for the horse, they searched every corner of this earth, destroyed territories, and dug the earth at different places to go to the underworld. Finally, through the underground tunnel, they found the horse at sage Kapila's place and accused Kapila of stealing the horse. Hearing such false accusation, Kapila looked at them with his divine eyes and they were burned to ashes. However, the sage Kapila promised if Ganga could be brought down to earth, then Sagar's sons could be revived with her water and would ascend to heaven. Sagar failed to bring his sons back to life. After many years his descendant King Bhagirath, through his penance, pleased Ganga and she agreed to descend on earth. Finally Sagar's sons were resurrected.

From the scriptural point of view, the word *Sagar* is a combination of "sa" (with) "gar" (poison), which represents a man who is born with the poison like ignorance, which deprives one of the vision of Reality and attaches one to the nature of appearance of this world. Due to his ignorance he could not decide between his two wives, who represented dual traits of a man, namely, attachment and detachment. He chose attachment and consequently multiplied his desire and attachment in the form of his sixty thousand sons. With increased desire and with an inflated ego, he sent out his sons to conquer the world. His *ego,* as Hinduism would explain, created the alienation between the man and his earthly community. Failing to see the manifestations of the divine in nature, Sagar's sons trampled the earth, destroyed land and vegetation, put dams on the river, and dug deep into the earth. Sagar's conquest is the prime example of human greed that sees nature as something separated and therefore to be conquered and dominated. Nature was violated in all respects and stripped of her dignity. The deaths of Sagar's sons reflects nature's voice against the defilement of the planet, a voice that needed to be heard by the humans.

As much as he tried through his penance, Sagar failed to revive his sons. They were finally revived by the Ganges water brought from the heaven by Bhagirath. Etymologically, the word *Ganga* is derived from the root "go" (meaning earth), which changes into "gang" (meaning to the earth). The word Ganga therefore, literally means ("gom," "d" with the feminine suffix "aap") *that which descends to the earth.* Not just one generation, but multiple generations of Sagar have to go through penance and hardships to bring the harmony back to the ecologically imbalanced earth.

GANGA AS CONCEIVED IN PATRIARCHY

According to most Indian feminists, the Western model of consciously engineered, gender-based imagery and corresponding patriarchal activity began a slow programming of the Hindu minds into mastery and domination. With time, dominant models of thought and aggressive developmental strategies seeped into the core of a culture that eventually lifted all restraints against the manipulation of nature as well as slackened its religious sanctions for destruction of nature.

I believe that Ganga herself, understood in some of the ways just expressed, can help Hindus cease polluting the waters that bear her name. But first Hindus must acknowledge the many ways in which our own tradition may have contributed to that pollution. Ecofeminism helps us realize that Ganga, along with women, has often been denigrated in Hinduism in ways that led to the very exploitation to which the river Ganges is now subjected. Ganga became the scapegoat of a culture that, in its search for scientific knowledge and economic growth, misplaced its age-old principles under the pile of industrial waste. But the process of modern technological advancement is only part of the problem. It is time for Hindus to acknowledge their own responsibility in this whole framework of destruction. In continuing to participate in a process—regardless of whether it is active or passive, optional or mandatory, motivated by greed or survival—that goes against the very grain of Hinduism, Hindus became the co-conspirators in the mutilation of mother Ganga.

What is the logic of domination in Hinduism that justifies the domination of a woman and ultimately the exploitation and pollution of the Ganges? As one reviews the stories of Ganga, one wonders whether part of the justification of her pollution lies in how femininity in general and the Goddess's femininity in particular has been defined within the Hindu context. First, a word about femininity in general.

Woman as Pure and Polluted

Hindu lawbooks collectively known as *Dharma Shastras* (The Rule of Conduct) display many of the patriarchal dualisms that ecofeminists critique. Hindu law was first codified by Manu in the seventh century B.C.E. Under this reform, women lost much of their freedom; women's role was relegated to wife and mother, being a nurturer, a healer, and a caretaker. Even the Goddess would be subject to this description. As Narada Purana aptly characterizes the Goddess, "The Ganga is as if a nurse unto the universe" (I:6:33).

According to Manu, woman is to be honored. To honor a woman is to recognize, accept, and finally respect her for who she is. Yet, to know her position is to guard her. The presumption that men are to guard women easily becomes the presumption that they are to own her, suppress her for her own sake, and thus exploit her. What is it in the feminine disposition that necessitates a man to become ever so guarded and cautious?

She is both pure and polluted. Her femininity reflects her paradoxical nature. She is to be revered and protected because of her sacredness. She is to be guarded and subjugated because of her profane nature. The following passages depict this ambiguous view of women:

Where women are honored, there the gods are pleased; but where they are not honored, no sacred rites yield rewards (Manu, III:56).

[When creating them] Manu allotted to women [a love of their] bed, [of their] seat and [of] ornament, impure desires, wrath, dishonesty, malice and bad conduct (Manu, IX: 17).

For women no [sacramental] rite [is performed] with sacred texts, thus the law is settled; women [who are] destitute of strength and destitute of [the knowledge of] the Vedic texts, [are as impure as] falsehood [itself], that is a fixed rule (Manu, IX: 18).

These passages illustrate the deep dualism that characterizes many Hindu images of woman.

Dualisms Evoked by the Concept of "Prakrti"

The Sanskrit word *prakrti* usually is translated as "nature." In its limited sense, prakrti has often been taken as the feminine, the object, nature, matter, and the unconscious. This has been distinguished from Purusa, which has been understood as the masculine, the subject, the structure, the mind, the consciousness.

The literal meaning of the word prakrti is "nature." Nature as it is ordinarily understood is spontaneous, unstructured, and the embodiment of various resources. This aspect of the word, taken out of context, has been emphasized by a patriarchal mind-set, and subsequently this misinterpreted word very well could have provided the ground for the patriarchal justification for the domination of women and nature. One's life depends on the gift of nature, yet nature's precariousness and unpredictability make her unreliable. Being unconscious, Prakrti is in need of the presence of Purusa, the spirit. When the dependence of Prakrti on Purusa is emphasized, as the dependence of Ganga on Brahma, Vishnu, and Shiva has been emphasized, Manu's hierarchy seems justified (Gupta 1991, 27).

Ambivalences in Depicting Ganga

At one level, even Goddess Ganga cannot escape these dualistic views of femininity. She is pure and impure, associated on the one hand with the purity of whiteness and on the other hand with feet and dirt. On the one hand she is associated with the lotus, the image of sacredness and liberation, on the other hand enslaved by lust.

According to one story in Brahmavaivarta Purana, Ganga was watching Krishna's face with lust in her eyes. Radha, Krishna's companion, noticing the expression on Ganga's face, became furious with anger, and started to drink her up in one gulp. Fearing for her life, Ganga took salvage in Krishna's feet. As a result, all three worlds became without water and came close to dissolution. Finding no other alternatives, all the gods started to appeal to Krishna in their prayers. Krishna was pleased with their prayers and finally released Ganga by rupturing his toenail. Vishnupadi (meaning originating from Vishnu's feet) became her other name (Narada Purana, vol. 15, Part I, 6:13).

According to another story, Ganga at times is considered to be one of the three wives of Vishnu. Once in the middle of a heated argument with the other two wives, Saraswati cursed Ganga to become a river. On hearing such a curse, excited Ganga cursed Saraswati to be a river too. Both eventually descended on earth and became holy rivers of India. Both of these stories exemplify dualisms of heaven and earth, spirit and matter, God and the world. These stories also reveal a sense of hierarchy, as Ganga descends from Krishna's feet. Since feet, according to Hinduism, are considered to be the lowest part of the body, the closest to the dirt everyone walks on, this in itself is a degradation of the feminine. In fact, she did not have to descend from Krishna's body at all, let alone from his feet.

Ganga as Purity Itself

Still, in the last analysis, most Hindus feel Ganga as pure rather than impure. The problem is not that most Hindus have apprehended her as impure, like women, but rather that they have apprehended her as incapable of being polluted, because she is supremely pure. Here "impurity" or "pollution" is understood as sin or some form of imbalance. Most Hindus approach Ganga and her river as being a purifier of inward sin, who is herself immune from being blemished by sin. Being a purity herself, she necessitates neither a purifier nor a purification rite.

Purity and Pollution

River Ganga, Goddess Ganga, the symbol of supreme purity, exemplifies a dramatic example of defilement. How is one to understand this defilement within the context of the Hindu notions of "purity" and "pollution"? The following passages from the Agni Purana reveal an ambiguous view:

A vessel [containing] flesh [may be purified] with cow's tail. (vol. 28, Part II, 156:8)

... a bed, a seat, vehicle, winnowing basket and cart would become purified by sprinkling [water] as also in the case of straw and fuel. (vol. 28, Part II, 156:6–7)

One whose face comes into contact with the sandal or impure thing, the means of purification for him are the earth, cow dung or the five things got from a cow. (vol. 28, Part III, 170:39)

How can a vessel be purified with a cow's tail? Is it really possible to purify one's face with cow dung? A mere sprinkle of water cannot clean an object. Yet recommendations as well as ritual instructions of such kind remind one of the symbolic meanings of "purity" and "pollution." Whereas the Western perspective on rituals is "solidly based on hygiene" (Douglas 1979, 32), the Hindu notion of "purity" and "pollution" seems to be more symbolic. However, that is not to say Hinduism is oblivious to the ideas of cleanliness or hygiene, thus feeling less responsible in terms of its surroundings or environment. On the contrary, according to Hinduism, an important part of one's conduct is to maintain a healthy and harmonious environment based on proper sanitation and aesthetic principles. Failure to do so often resulted in punishment of many kinds.

Yet, by accepting purity and pollution in the symbolic way, Hindus made pollution of Ganga, therefore oppression of Ganga, sacred. Purity of Ganga, taken symbolically, seems to be based on the following assumptions. First, sacred—being sacred by its very definition—can never be contaminated, symbolically or otherwise. Second, even if there is a possibility of contamination of the divine by the profane, divine does not necessitate any human interference or participation in its purification. That is, divine is self-purifying. Taking the scriptural point of view into consideration, the questions of purity and pollution of Ganga simply do not arise. She is essentially pure. She is pure in her origin, in her life in the three worlds, and in her descent on earth. When these presumptions about Ganga's purity are linked, one can see why Hindus do not appear to be motivated enough in salvaging Ganga from her polluted condition.

When seen as pure in this way, Ganga herself too often becomes otherworldly and disengaged from the Earth, even disassociated with the river that bears her name. Hinduism has often been labeled or categorized as otherworldly. That is, *moksa*, one of the key concepts of Hinduism, refers to a state of being that transcends the worldly experience, as well as cycles of life and death on this planet. The word *moksa*, understood only in this sense, seems to have a negative connotation. Repeated scriptural references of *moksa* as the most desired goal of human life further established the reputation of Hinduism as life denying and pessimistic.

Ganga herself has been linked to such otherworldliness. Agni Purana speaks of Ganga being "the healer of the sickness called samsara [worldly existence]" (Agni:6:61). Understanding the concept of *moksa* in this otherworldly sense could very well discourage an ordinary Hindu from making any effort toward protecting the ecological balance of this planet.

FREEING GANGA FROM PATRIARCHY

Interestingly, in some texts Ganga herself expresses concern about the otherworldliness just mentioned, and about the neglect of her needs as a living river. In her conversation with King Bhagirath, who is to bring her down to earth, her concern is evident. As if she knew her fate long before she descended, she voices her feeling: "I am not willing to go to the earth. Men will wash off their sins in me. Where (and how) can I absolve myself of that sin? Some remedy on this should also be considered, oh, king" (Bhagavata Purana IX:5).

This story raises an important question. Can Ganga by her own purity absolve herself of the sins of others? Of course, if she is essentially pure and not connected to the world in a real sense, nothing in the world can pollute her under any circumstances. But is she so disconnected?

I think not. From an ecofeminist point of view, with its emphasis on interconnectedness, I believe we can best understand Ganga from two perspectives:

First, as deeply connected to, and even dependent on, the river in whom she is manifest and second, at the same time dependent on our actions with regard to that river. In my view, Ganga's purity should not be understood merely symbolically, as the purity of a goddess who is separate from the real river in which she manifests herself. Instead her purity and pollution should be taken in a real sense, as a quality of the very water through which she is known and felt. To be sure, she is pure and remains pure as long as she absorbs the sins and pollutions of others. But if humans deliberately pollute her, she herself will be in need of purification. She will no longer be able to absorb our sins and pollutions. She will suffer the abuse of the waste we pour into her.

My suggestion, then, is that Ganga's purity is relational. It depends, in part, on our respect for her. Purity, in this nonpatriarchal sense, refers to a sense of balance and harmony based on the principles of interdependence and inter-connection. She descends to earth for the sake of humanity; she retains her purity as long as there is reciprocity on the part of humanity. Given the pollution from which she now suffers, it is our turn now to ascend, restore, and bring balance to her.

Remembering Dharma

There are resources within Hinduism that can help us move toward this more relational understanding of purity. One is the concept of *dharma*.

The word *dharma* can be literally translated as "that which holds and sustains." Variously translated as "law," "moral duty," "right action," or "conformity with the truth of things," dharma refers to moral law and order that sustains and protects the world, society, and the individual. Taken as a human virtue, *dharma* is best translated as "righteousness or duty."

First mentioned in the Rig Veda, the concept of *dharma* has evolved as each era of Indian civilization interpreted it according to its own need and purpose. According to the Rig Veda, the regulation of this ordered or balanced creation was established by cosmic law and order, rta, or dharma, and each person in this ordered universe was stationed with a designated function to perform. Therefore, fulfillment of one's function or duty in accordance with the law brought forth a state of harmony that was regarded as Truth. Since cosmic law was identified with Truth, it was considered to be the highest authority to which even royalty conforms.

Initially interpreted as cosmic law, dharma was later considered to be ritual laws, and ultimately it incorporated ethical conduct or virtues. Emphasis was placed on dharma as nonviolence, or *ahimsa*.

> For those persons who desire to follow the right course of conduct, there is no supreme dharma other than abstinence from violence to living beings caused by thought word and deed. (Bhagavata Purana vol. 9, Part III, VII:15:8)

The principle of nonviolence seems to be the most important constituent of all rules for living, of all dharmas.

From the Hindu standpoint, one of the most important characteristics of dharma is that it·is not static. That is, the concept and content of dharma change in accordance with the changing circumstances and with one's position in society and station in life. In the true sense of the term, dharma, then, assumes the unity of life and universality of duty and obligation. It is a way of living, and not just an act. Its chief characteristics are harmony, continuity, and interdependence.

The nonviolence of dharma can and should be applied to the whole of nature. To do this is to feel harmony with nature, continuity with it, and dependence on it. It is also to recognize that nature depends on us and deserves to be treated nonviolently. In this context, Ganga ought to be an immediate priority of the Hindu, a beneficiary of dharmic nonviolence. As she saved humanity and still continues to serve this planet, Hindus can recognize their own duties and obligations to practice nonviolence toward her.

Ganga as White Energy

In addition to using the idea of dharma, Ganga, in her myths and symbols, offers some suggestions for Hindus with regard to her pollution.

According to the Puranic descriptions, Goddess Ganga appears to be extremely beautiful. Skanda Purana describes her with three eyes and four arms. In each of her arms she holds something quite significant. With one hand she holds a vessel filled up to the brim with holy water and with the other she holds a white lotus; with her lower right she assures her devotees "fear not," and with the lower left she offers a boon. Shining like a thousand radiant moons, she sits on her vehicle, the mythic crocodile "Makara." She is described as kind and compassionate, loved and praised by the three worlds. Although all her symbols are quite important in explaining her true nature, I will concentrate for our purpose only on two symbols: the whiteness of Ganga and the symbol of the lotus.

Whether she is pictured having two arms or four arms, sitting on a makara or a lotus, white is consistently associated with her. She appears in white at all times. She is white complexioned, attired in white, bejeweled in white ornaments and pearl, holding a white lotus in her hand. White seems to be the only color that is present in her attire, in her ornaments, as well as in other symbols that are associated with her. Padmapurana describes her as "Samkhadhabalam," with a complexion as white as conch shell; "Svetabastraparihitam," wearing a white cloth or a dress; "Muktaharabibhusitam," wearing a pearl necklace; and "Svetachatrosovitam," decorated with a white umbrella (Padma VI:116–121). Skandapurana depicts her as "chandrajuta samaprabham," radiant as million moons. Brahmavaibartapurana pictures her "Svetachampakevarnabham," with a complexion like white "champaka" flower (Branha 10:96–98). Brihaddharmapurana describes her as "Suklavarna," white complexioned and so "Asina Makare Sukla," seated on a white makara (Brihad 12:75). Tantrasastra also describes her as "Suddhasphatikasamkasanam," with a crystal-clear complexion; "suklambarablusitam," dressed in a white attire; "suklamuktabalimalam," beautiful in a white pearl necklace; and "svetabharanabhusitam," decorated in white jewelry (Pranotoshini Tantra 3:2).

All of these numerous depictions of Ganga speak of a brilliant white color that represents purity, radiance, and sacredness. The Sanskrit words that have been cited above stress *sukla* or *sveta*, both of them originated from the roots *suk* and *svi*, which imply white, light, radiance, or brilliance.

Why white? One could argue that it is because white represents the absence of color, and hence the absence of worldliness. Understood in this way, Ganga's whiteness would be a feature of a supramundane spiritual orientation that is pure, and hence separate from the polluted world.

But I understand it differently. I think her whiteness is a symbol of her connectedness with all she represents, a substratum of all that she manifests and an essence of all that are parts of this created world. Experiments done in modern physics establish the fact that white light is the combination of all colors of the spectrum, visible or invisible. Experiments such as viewing sunlight through a prism show that white is broken down by the prism to various intensities and each new frequency has its own different appearance to a human, in colors such as violet, indigo, blue, green, yellow, orange, and red. Conversely, Newton's color disks rotating primary colors at a high speed would appear to be white to a human. Experiments such as these show that white is not lack of color. The perfect binding of all the seven colors of the spectrum makes white, the pure color, the combination of all color.

Analogously, from an ecofeminist point of view, the "white" symbol of Ganga can be interpreted as Ganga being pure energy itself, and seen through the prism of the material plane she appears to be many. As a river flows through the various parts of a land, making the land a harmonious whole of interconnections and interdependence, so Ganga is an energy, an essence that radiates through all life forms, mobile and immobile. She reflects the basic kinship among all things.

Symbol of Lotus

Ganga is often depicted as holding a white lotus in her hand as well as sitting on a white lotus. The symbol of the lotus is one of the most significant symbols found in Hinduism as well as in Buddhism. Unlike all the other flowers on land or in water, the lotus is the only flower that germinates and retains the seed until it becomes a plant. It is the only flower that does not die to start its own offspring. It completes the entire cycle of birth, life, and death within itself. Humans, like the lotus, also reflect the continuity and cycle without ever totally being extinct. From the scriptural point of view, the lotus symbolizes the life-giving and life-sustaining waters of Vishnu and *mukti* or liberation. It also represents purity, sacredness, prosperity, or abundance, and *mukti*, or liberation. The lotus is born in the muddy water, rises to the surface, and stands untouched by the water. Similarly, humans, symbolically submerged in worldly desires, slowly progress toward the surface and ultimately toward the nonduality and unity called the "Brahman."

The lotus, from an ecofeminist point of view, would refer to human's ultimate desire and goal to transcend multiplicity and understand nature as one single unitary whole, rather than as an "Other" separated from and subjugated by us.

Nature in Brahman

Another resource in Hinduism is the view of nature. From the Vedas to the Puranas, Hinduism speaks of the eternal energy, the life breath, the essence called "Brahman" that manifests itself in manifolds of this universe. We can see in numerous passages the following: The divine energy called the "Brahman" is immanent as well as transcendent. The world, with its infinite variety, is the manifestation of the divine principle. The world, with all its multiplicity and diversity, begins and ends in a cycle within the divine womb and therefore does not have any separate existence outside of the "Brahman." Being the manifestations of the same principle, all parts of the universe, human or nonhuman, mobile or immobile, organic or inorganic, are animated by the same life force. Being permeated by the same energy and essence, creation reflects kinship among all its facets.

The following passages from the Bhagavadgita speak of a Reality that includes everything there is and leaves nothing as the "Other." In the Gita, Arjuna wishes to see the universal form of God. Krishna reveals himself and says: "Here today, behold the whole Universe, moving and unmoving and whatever else thou desirest to see, Gudakesha [Arjuna], all unified in My Body" (Gita XI:7). "I support the entire universe pervading with a single fraction of myself" (X:42). Nature as we see in the Gita is clearly an example of divine expression in its varieties. Nature, being in the womb of God, is a living organism and as such is not to be treated as an "Other." If the One universal "Brahman" is revealing itself in the multiplicity of this planet, be it a river or a rock, all parts of this Nature have an intrinsic value; as such, all of Nature should be treated with dignity, kindness, and righteousness.

CONCLUSION

Regardless of the various ways in which a patriarchal mind-set as funneled through patriarchal Hinduism has contributed to the pollution of Ganga, one needs to investigate ways in which colonialism did the same. Whether the ideology that accounts for the present status of Ganga is the Western scientific revolution that ecofeminists see as a "consciously gendered patriarchal activity" infused with a "reductionist mentality" (Shiva 1988, 17, 22), or it is the misinterpretation as well as misappropriation of concepts such as "femininity," "purity and pollution," and *moksa* on the part of the Hindus, the situation in terms of Ganga remains the same. Indeed, the ecological disaster of Ganga is shared by other rivers in the world. Despite the shared similarities, each nation has to deal with pollution differently within its own geographical, historical, and religious context. That is, it is not possible to find one solution that could be appropriate as well as adequate for all.

Attempts are being made to raise people's consciousness toward the protection of the Ganga. However, all forms of external attempts will remain fruitless until and unless a deeper transformation takes place within the individuals. In all her myths and symbols, Ganga reflects the need for self-transformation. Transformation will possibly take place if and when Hindus are motivated to rediscover the ideals outlined in the scripture and redirect their energy in conserving the Ganga, as one is motivated to conserve one's own life.

From an ecofeminist point of view, one needs to personalize one's actions in terms of one's surroundings. I propose a plan that would involve knowledge of Ganga, understanding of Ganga, devotion to Ganga, attitude toward Ganga, and most importantly, actions toward Ganga. Following the basic notions of "Brahman," the ultimate Reality, *moksa* or liberation, the ultimate goal of human life, and the four ways to *Moksa*, this plan, although modelled after Hindu principles illustrated in the ancient scriptures, offers a strategy suitable for a twentieth-century nation with a polluted sacred river.

Knowledge

Knowledge of Ganga would not only require technical knowledge of pollution presented by the media, recorded in books and newspapers, and analyzed by the experts, it would include a form of knowledge which can only result from one's firsthand witnessing of the pollution of Ganga. It is a form of knowledge which is the result of witnessing the consequences of our own actions and inactions. As one walks by the banks of the Ganga, one sees her reflections. Mindfully watching her, as in meditation, one suddenly wakes up to the reality of her being, as one wakes up by a sudden blow in Zen meditation. Witnessing her in this sense, one knows her past glory and her present predicament; one knows how and to what extent individuals as well as the society failed to fulfill their obligations toward the rest of the earthly community.

Understanding

Knowledge alone, in terms of the causes of Ganga's pollution and the effects it has on the planet and its inhabitants, is not sufficient to bring about a lasting change. One has to understand and internalize the very essence of her being, her status as a river, her role as a woman and a mother. The more one becomes absorbed in her true status, journeys through her flow, and is mindful of the true meanings of prayer and rituals toward her, the closer one becomes to her. The more one sees her as an individual in her own right, the less chances there are to destroy or dominate her.

Devotion

Based on the knowledge and mythical and symbolic understanding of Ganga, one needs to develop a deeper emotion, such as devotion toward Ganga. For a true ecofeminist, one has to be in love with Nature. It is simply not enough any longer merely to recognize the present ecological state of the Ganga. One has to love her enough to be motivated in making some physical or intellectual effort. One is the strongest in one's motivation when something personal is at stake. Merely loving Nature is very much like loving humanity without personally being involved with people or caring about an individual. I think until one is thoroughly satiated by being in love with at least one particular part of Nature, one would not be able to comprehend what it is to love all of this physical world. Loving Ganga as well as being devoted to Ganga will give the Hindus personal connection with her which later on could be extended to all others on this earth—a relationship both fulfilling in itself and yet directing one to truly experience the planet on a personal level.

Attitude

Grounded in knowledge, renewed with the deeper understanding of Ganga, and thoroughly motivated with a personal feeling and concern, one is ready for a radical change in one's attitude—an attitude that will require developing a set of virtues which will be pertinent to removal of Ganga's pollution. One needs to develop and retain a category of virtues that would include: reaffirmation of the traditional virtues prescribed in the Hindu scriptures, such as nonviolence; remembrance of the virtues such as gratitude, reverence, and humility; and reinvention and reinterpretation of the virtues that are not being used in recent times, such as asceticism and endurance. The virtue of nonviolence is one of the greatest virtues, as it is based on the deeper understanding of the kinship of nature. Developing one's humility toward all life forms is based on the oneness of all facets of nature. Once Ganga is seen in terms of a manifestation of the divine energy, therefore divine energy herself, one realizes the equality of all created beings, one recognizes the intrinsic value of all. The result is a profound sense of gratitude, reverence, and humility.

Action

Two of the virtues often prescribed in the Upanishads, epics, and Puranas are the virtues of asceticism and endurance. In the light of modern development and scientific advancement, many people in the world, especially in the West, have become quite comfortable with certain amenities which, if sacrificed, would lessen pollution. Learning to live with less, avoiding the overusage and misusage of Nature, enduring certain discomforts for the sake of our earthly community—in this case for Ganga—will create a brighter future for all concerned.

The possibility of reclaiming the ecological balance of Ganga depends to a great extent on the Hindus who, if able to put aside their emotional involvement with the bare structure of rituals concerning Ganga, begin to comprehend the true meaning of liberation explained in the Vedas, the Upanishads, and the Puranas. As Agni Purana explains: "whoever does not see another as different from his own self becomes Brahman itself. One who rejoices in his own self is said to be free from impurity"(Agni 165:10-12). If only we understand the true implication of *moksa,* we will begin to realize that true liberation is not possible without proper respect and reverence toward all facets of Nature, all other parts of this planet, organic or inorganic. *Moksa,* or liberation, better interpreted as self-realization, involves realization of one's own self as identified and connected with all forms of existence as the manifestations of the same Reality, or the divine.

I want to thank Jay McDaniel for his expert editorial assistance and helpful suggestions. My warmest gratitude to Carol Adams for her constructive criticism and, most importantly, for her patience and understanding, for putting up with the continuing drama of my battle with Ganga.

PRIMARY SOURCES

Agni Purāṇa. Tran. N. Gangadharan. Delhi: Motilal Banarasidass, 1985.
Bhāgavadgitā. Tran. S. Radhakrishnan. New York: Harper & Row Publishers, 1973.
Bhāgavata Purāṇa. Tran. Ganesh Vasudeo Tagre. Delhi: Motilal Banarasidass, 1976.
Brahma Vaivarta Purāṇa. Bangavasi Edition.
The Laws of Manu. Tran. G. Buhler. Delhi: Motilal Banarasidass, 1982.
Mahua (from one of the Love Songs of Vidyāpati). Tran. Deben Bhattacharya. New York, 1963.
Nārada Purāṇa. Tran. Ganesh Vasudeo Tagre. Delhi: Motilal Banarasidass, 1980.
Padma Purāṇa. Bangavasi Edition.
Prāṇatoshini Tantra. Ed. Ramatoshana VidyaBhusana. Calcutta: Vasumati Sahitya Mandir.
Rāmprasād's Devotional Songs. Tran. Jadunath Sinha. Calcutta, 1966.
Skanda Purāṇa. Bangavasi Edition.
Brhaddharmā Purāṇa.

PART 2

ENVISIONING ECOFEMINISM

8

A Feminist Philosophical Perspective on Ecofeminist Spiritualities

KAREN J. WARREN

INTRODUCTION

Ecofeminists disagree about the nature and place of spirituality in ecofeminist politics and practice. Some ecofeminists defend earth-based spiritualities as necessary or vital to feminism, environmental philosophy, and ecofeminism. They claim that women's spirituality is integral to ecofeminist theory and practice. Other ecofeminists claim that spirituality-oriented approaches to ecofeminism reinforce harmful gender stereotypes about women and undermine the philosophical, political, and feminist significance of ecofeminism. As such, they ought to be rejected. Still others suggest that although ecofeminist spiritualities are neither necessary nor sufficient for ecofeminist theory and practice, nonetheless they occupy an important place in ecofeminism.

This debate among ecofeminists about the significance of ecofeminist spiritualities is especially challenging for ecofeminist philosophers. Feminist philosophers by and large have either avoided, sidestepped, or eschewed efforts to articulate a feminist philosophical position on spirituality. Although our reasons

Karen J. Warren is an Associate Professor of Philosophy at Macalester College in St. Paul, Minnesota. Her main scholarly interests are in ethics, feminism (particularly ecological feminism), and critical thinking. She has guest edited a special issue of *Hypatia: A Feminist Journal of Philosophy* on ecological feminism and three special issues of the American Philosophical Association's *Newsletter on Feminism and Philosophy*, one on gender, reason, and rationality and two on feminism and the environment. She currently is editing an anthology on ecological feminism, co-authoring a book with Jim Cheney entitled *Ecological Feminism: A Philosophical Perspective on What It Is and Why It Matters*, collaborating on an environmental ethics anthology, and co-editing a special issue of *Hypatia* on feminism and peace.

for doing so are varied, there often is a worry or suspicion that questions about "women's spiritualities" are not distinctively philosophical questions or are not ones which are central to feminist philosophy. If the absence of literature by ecofeminist philosophers on ecofeminist spiritualities is a useful indicator, ecofeminist philosophers share some of these general feminist philosophical concerns.

As an ecofeminist philosopher, I have come to believe that the growing literature on earth-based or ecofeminist spiritualities deserves serious feminist philosophical attention. I think this is so for a variety of reasons. *Historically,* ecofeminist spiritualities have played a vital, grass-roots role in the emergence of ecofeminism as a political movement. Historical accuracy in how ecofeminism is described or represented, then, requires that ecofeminist philosophers grapple with the claims made by those who articulate or defend various ecofeminist spiritualities.

Politically, the sorts of protest actions ecofeminists often cite as illustrative of ecofeminist activism (e.g., the Chipko movement in India, Women of All Red Nations [WARN] organizing against environmental racism) often grow out of spiritual traditions (e.g., Gandhian *satyagraha,* nonviolent actions or spirituality-based kinship cultures). Honoring the ethnic dimensions of such ecofeminist activism, then, involves recognizing their spiritual roots.

Ethically, ecofeminist spiritualities raise important issues about the roles of ritual, symbol systems, and values (e.g., values of care, appropriate reciprocity, trust, love, kinship, community) in ecofeminist ethics. Since these elements are typically underplayed or undervalued in mainstream philosophy and receive feminist philosophical attention in other contexts (e.g., in feminist ethics generally), they deserve attention in ecofeminist philosophy as well.

Epistemologically, ecofeminist spiritualities often are offered by practitioners as expressions of "women's ways of knowing," of women's varied, immediate, felt sensibilities about everyday life within patriarchal culture. Any feminist philosophy which honors or advocates "standpoint epistemologies," women's "epistemic privilege," or women's "indigenous technical knowledge" (ITK), then, must consider the role spiritualities play in the articulation and understanding of such knowledge.

Methodologically, when academic feminists are "outsiders" (i.e., nonmembers of an oppressed group), they must proceed with what Uma Narayan calls "methodological caution" and "methodological humility" when engaging in criticism of "insiders" (i.e., members of oppressed groups) (Narayan 1988, 37). "Methodological caution" requires that outsiders conduct themselves under the assumption that, as outsiders, they may be missing something important about insider experience and knowledge, that what appears to be a mistake on the part of the insider may make more sense if the outsiders had a fuller understanding of the context (Narayan 1988, 38). "Methodological humility" requires that outsiders sincerely attempt to carry out their criticisms of the insider's perceptions in ways that do not amount to, or even seem to amount to, attempts to denigrate or dismiss entirely the validity of the insider's point of view (Narayan 1988, 38). Since many women cross-culturally report that spirituality provides an important kind and source of knowledge of women-nature connections, knowledge which is intimately connected to their everyday experiences under oppression, ecofeminist philosophers need to take such claims seriously on methodological grounds.

Conceptually, ecofeminist spiritualities raise important issues about the nature of the self, the nature and role of reason and rationality (especially as they are typically contrasted in Western philosophy with emotion, spirit, and body), and the conception of "nature" and of human relationships with nature. Ecofeminist philosophers interested in unpacking the conceptual connections between the twin dominations of women and nature need to pay attention to any insights a philosophical consideration of ecofeminist spiritualities provides on these concepts.

Theoretically, ecofeminist spiritualities challenge feminist and ecofeminist philosophers alike to consider the relevance and value of spirituality in feminist and ecofeminist theory and theory building. Is there a "politics of women's spirituality" (Spretnak 1982) which is vital to feminism, feminist philosophy, and ecofeminist philosophy? Is a consideration of ecofeminist spiritualities necessary to ecofeminist theory and theory building? What role and place do ecofeminist spiritualities have in ecofeminist philosophy? These questions raise important theoretical issues about the personal as political, the private-public dichotomy, and problematic normative dualisms (e.g., reason-emotion, objective-subjective, mind-body, material-spiritual) that are vitally important to feminist theory and theory building.

Moved philosophically by the need to take ecofeminist spiritualities seriously, in this essay I ask: From a feminist philosophical perspective, what are ecofeminist spiritualities and how might one understand the claim that ecofeminist spiritualities are an empowering response to sexist oppression and environmental destruction? I argue that, properly understood, ecofeminist spiritualities do or could play an important role in the twofold ecofeminist project of dismantling patriarchy and developing in its place nondominating and life-affirming attitudes, values, and relationships among humans and toward nonhuman nature.[1] As such, I conclude that ecofeminist spiritualities do or could have an important place in ecofeminist philosophy.

My goal is modest: I do not discuss the particular positions which have been advanced in the ecofeminist debate over spirituality, including the position that earth-based spiritualities are a necessary aspect of ecofeminist theory and practice; consequently, I do not resolve that debate. Nor do I discuss the varieties of ecofeminist spiritualities (e.g., religious positions within Buddhist, Hindu, Taoist, Jewish, Christian, or Native American frameworks; Goddess spiritualities, Wicca, or Paganism). I simply attempt to offer a feminist philosophical perspective on how one might think about ecofeminist spiritualities such that one captures and extends important ecofeminist insights about the twin dominations of women and nature in ecofeminist philosophy.

ECOFEMINIST PHILOSOPHY

As even a casual perusal of feminist scholarship reveals, "feminism" is an umbrella concept that permits meaningful talk of a variety of feminisms: e.g.

liberal feminism, Marxist feminism, radical feminism, socialist feminism, Black and Third World feminism. Despite important differences among these feminisms (Jaggar 1983), all feminisms are committed to the elimination of sexism, that is, the power and privilege of men over women. Sexism is manifested in institutions, practices, roles, offices, positions, actions, expectations, and ways of thinking that support, maintain, or justify male-gender privilege and power over women. Whatever else it is, feminism is a movement and theory aimed at ending male-gender power and privilege, wherever and whenever it occurs, and creating practices and theories which are not male-gender powered and privileged.

Just as there is not one feminism, there is not one ecofeminism (Warren 1987) and there is not one ecofeminist philosophy. As I use the term, *ecofeminism* is the name of a variety of positions that are committed minimally to a few key claims: There are important connections (e.g., historical, empirical, symbolic, conceptual, theoretical) between the domination of women and the domination of nature ("women-nature connections") and understanding the nature of these connections is necessary to any adequate feminism, environmentalism, or feminist or environmental philosophy. "Ecofeminist philosophy" is the name of a variety of feminist philosophical positions that provide conceptual analysis, theoretical perspectives, and argumentative support for the nature and significance of various "women-nature connections."

What is distinctive about ecofeminists and ecofeminist philosophers is that they extend the various feminist critiques of social systems of human domination to include domination of nonhuman nature. Ecofeminists claim that *naturism,* the unjustified domination, exploitation, or destruction of nonhuman nature, is wrong and ought to be eliminated. "Naturism" is included in the unwanted and unwarranted social "isms of domination."

Ecofeminist philosophers are especially interested in conceptual issues regarding women-nature connections. One way to reveal the role key concepts have played in justifying the interconnected dominations of women and nonhuman nature is to understand the nature of oppressive and patriarchal conceptual frameworks.

I have argued elsewhere (Warren 1987, 1988, 1990, 1991a) that a conceptual framework is the set of basic beliefs, values, attitudes, and assumptions that shape and reflect how one views oneself and one's world. Conceptual frameworks are the socially constructed lenses or filters through which one perceives oneself and others. A conceptual framework is oppressive when it explains, justifies, and maintains relationships of domination and subordination. It is patriarchal when it explains, justifies, and maintains the subordination of women by men.

There are five important and interrelated features of a patriarchal conceptual framework. *Value-hierarchical ("Up-Down") thinking,* which places higher value, status, or prestige on what is "Up" (men) or what is gender-identified with what is "Up" (reason or rationality, mind, aggressivity, control) than with what is "Down" (women) or what is gender-identified with what is "Down" (emotion, body, passivity, submissiveness).

Value dualisms ("Either-Or" Thinking), which organize reality into oppositional (rather than complementary) and exclusive (rather than inclusive) pairs,
and which place higher value, status, or prestige on one member of the pair
(dualisms that give higher value to "reason," "mind," "masculine," and "culture" in alleged contrast and opposition to that identified as "Emotion,"
"body," "feminine," and "nature," respectively).

Power-over conceptions of power, which function to maintain relations of domination and subordination.[2]

Conceptions of privilege, which function to maintain power-over relations of
domination and subordination by "Ups" over "Downs."

A logic of domination, an argumentative structure that "justifies" the power
and privilege of those who are "Up" over those who are "Down," and the
relations of domination and subordination such power and privilege confer, on
the grounds that superiority (being "Up") justifies subordination (being
"Down").

Many ecofeminist philosophers (Cheney 1987; Plumwood 1986, 1991; Warren 1987, 1990) have claimed that the sorts of value-hierarchical thinking, value
dualisms, conceptions and practices of power and privilege, and logic of domination that characterize patriarchal conceptual frameworks are those which
sanction the twin exploitations of women and nonhuman nature. Patriarchal
conceptual frameworks that justify the domination of women also justify the
domination of nonhuman nature by conceiving women and nature in terms
which feminize nature, naturalize women, and position both women and nature
as inferior to male-gender identified culture. Ecofeminist philosophers insist
that the logic of domination used to justify sexism be recognized as also justifying naturism.

Given what has been said so far, one might suppose that ecofeminist philosophy is only about women-nature connections. This would be a mistake.
Ecofeminist philosophy grows out of and expresses a wide range of ecofeminist
concerns.[3] Included among these concerns are important interconnected gender, race, class, affectional orientation, religion, and age issues (to cite a few).
Conceptually, the concern for interconnections among "isms of domination"
(sexism, racism, classism, heterosexism, anti-Semitism, adultism) is crucial. Ecofeminist philosophers insist that the logic of domination used to justify the twin
dominations of women and nature *also* has been used to justify the domination
of humans by race or ethnicity, class, affectional orientation, religion, and age.
Sexism shares with racism, classism, heterosexism, anti-Semitism, and adultism
the five aforementioned features of an oppressive conceptual framework.
Because all feminists do or must oppose the logic of domination which keeps
oppressive conceptual frameworks in place, all feminists must also oppose any
isms of domination that are maintained and justified by that logic of domination
(Warren 1990); the legitimacy of such *isms* is *conceptually* maintained by a logic
of domination. It is by clarifying these conceptual connections between systems
of oppression that feminism, conceived historically as a movement to end sexist
oppression, gets reconceived as a movement to end all systems of unjustified
domination.[4] Ecofeminist philosophy extends this reconception of feminism to
include naturism as an *ism* of domination.

ECOFEMINIST SPIRITUALITIES

Just as there is not one version of ecofeminism, there is not one version of ecofeminist spirituality. As the various essays in this volume illustrate, ecofeminist spiritualities differ on such fundamental issues as whether mainstream religious traditions can be reconceived or reinterpreted to provide environmentally responsible and nonsexist practices and theologies; whether a particular ecofeminist spirituality perpetuates any of the five characteristics of oppressive conceptual frameworks mentioned above; whether an earth-based spirituality promotes harmful gender-stereotypical views of women as "closer to nature than men," less rational, detached, and objective or more emotional, attached, intuitive, and subjective than men; whether any specific environmental practice (vegetarianism, bans on hunting and animal experimentation, organic farming, population control) is mandated by a given ecofeminist spirituality; whether ecofeminist spiritualities inappropriately mystify and romanticize nature; and whether a given ecofeminist spirituality is an expression of ethical colonialism, coopting indigenous cultural practices as part of an otherwise unchanged dominant Western worldview.

Given such differences among ecofeminist spiritualities and their critics, what can one say philosophically about ecofeminist spiritualities? From a feminist philosophical perspective, how might such spiritualities be conceived, and what is their potential significance as empowering responses to sexist oppression and environmental destruction? The remainder of this essay is an attempt to answer these questions.

In order for ecofeminist spiritualities to properly be called feminist, they need to be committed to the elimination of male-gender privilege and power over women, and to value women's experiences and perspectives. In order to be ecofeminist, they need to also be committed to the elimination of practices and analyses that are naturist. I say "need to be committed to" the elimination of sexism and naturism (rather than actually accomplish either) because in the prefeminist, patriarchal present, it is not possible to consistently, thoroughly, or always *be* nonsexist or non-naturist. The best one can do now is be sincerely and honestly committed to the elimination of sexism and naturism in one's practice and theory. This is true even though ecofeminist spiritualities must be opposed in principle to sexism and naturism.

What, then, is the philosophical significance of ecofeminist spiritualities? As I shall now show, ecofeminist spiritualities are or can be life-affirming, personally empowering, and collectively constructive challenges to *patriarchy conceived as a dysfunctional social system.* They are attempts to heal the wounds[5] of patriarchy in contemporary culture, where patriarchy is a pervasive, intrusive, historical, and material reality in our daily lives. Their philosophical significance is not only that they challenge patriarchy at its core by challenging the oppressive conceptual framework that fuels the dysfunctional patriarchal engine; they do or attempt to do so in ways which *genuinely* empower its practitioners. Ecofeminist spiritualities provide one way to think and act oneself out of "patriarchy as a conceptual trap" (Gray 1982).

DYSFUNCTIONAL SOCIAL SYSTEMS

For our purposes, a system is a group or network of interacting, interrelated, or interdependent elements regarded as constituting a larger whole or unit. The human body is an interactive unit consisting of, for example, digestive, neurological, and muscular systems. Ecosystems are sometimes regarded as interactive units consisting of cells, organisms, populations, and communities. Family systems are interactive units consisting of the members, their roles and behaviors, and the rules that govern how the family members operate. Belief systems are a network of interconnected values, attitudes, assumptions, myths, judgments, beliefs, and "facts" that characterize a group, culture, or society. Social systems are dynamic units consisting of institutional elements (roles, rules, offices, positions, practices, expectations, activities) and individual elements. In all of these systems, the single elements taken separately do not constitute the system; the system consists in and results from the interaction of the various elements and is not reducible to its particular members or units.

Social systems are best described on a *continuum* (rather than dichotomy), from rigid, closed systems on one end, to highly flexible, open systems on the other end. The degree of openness of a social system is determined largely by the flexibility of the rules and roles—overt or covert, conscious or unconscious—which govern the attitudes, behaviors, and interactions among members of the system or between those within and those outside the system.

In a *functional* system, the rules and roles tend to be clear, respectful, negotiable; they can be revised, negotiated, changed. Problems tend to be openly acknowledged and resolved. In a *dysfunctional* system, the rules tend to be confused and covert, rigid and unchanging. A high value tends to be placed on control; dysfunctional systems tend to display an exaggerated rationality and focus on rule-governed reason. Relationships tend not to be among individuals acknowledged as having equal value; they tend to be Up-Down, rather than mutual, respectful, and reciprocal. Since members of dysfunctional systems tend to have a difficult time getting their basic individual needs met within the dysfunctional system, they tend to experience anger, frustration, loneliness, anxiety, or confusion within that system.

Dysfunctional systems are often maintained through systematic denial, a failure or inability to see the reality of a situation. This denial need not be conscious, intentional, or malicious; it only needs to be pervasive to be effective. Furthermore, dysfunctional social systems often leave their members feeling powerless or helpless to make any significant changes. This is not characteristic of a functional social system. The functional system changes and responds to choices and changes on the part of its members.

The importance of understanding dysfunctional social systems for an ecofeminist philosophical discussion of ecofeminist spiritualities is this: By conceptualizing patriarchy as a dysfunctional social system, one can see the vital role ecofeminist spiritualities do or can play in empowering its members within patriarchy, while, at the same time, challenging patriarchy. What, then, does it mean to say patriarchy is a socially dysfunctional system?

PATRIARCHY AS A DYSFUNCTIONAL SOCIAL SYSTEM

The claim that patriarchy is a dysfunctional social system locates the "dys-functionalities" of patriarchy within historical, socioeconomic, cultural, and political contexts thoroughly structured by race, gender, and class identities and ideologies. These contexts will vary cross culturally and historically, as will the particularities of sexist thinking, behavior, and institutions.

One philosophically striking aspect of dysfunctional social systems is that they are rooted in, reflect, and perpetuate a faulty conceptual framework. It is out of this conceptual framework that people in dysfunctional systems "plan and make decisions, interpret other people's actions, make meaning out of life experiences, solve problems, pattern our relationships, develop our careers, establish priorities" (Carnes 1983, 5).

I have found it helpful to visualize patriarchy as a dysfunctional system as a cyclical, insulating repertoire of ways of thinking and behaving that is rooted in a patriarchal conceptual framework.[6]

Model of Patriarchy as a Dysfunctional Social System

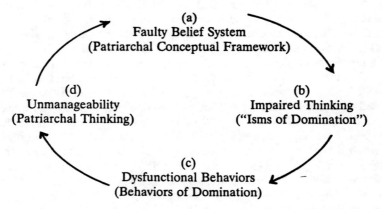

(a)
Faulty Belief System
(Patriarchal Conceptual Framework)

(d)
Unmanageability
(Patriarchal Thinking)

(b)
Impaired Thinking
("Isms of Domination")

(c)
Dysfunctional Behaviors
(Behaviors of Domination)

This model captures several key features of patriarchy conceived as a socially dysfunctional system. First and foremost, patriarchy is the institutional or sys-temic privilege and power of men over women. As an Up-Down system of power-over relationships patriarchy grows out of and reflects a faulty patriarchal belief system or conceptual framework, (a). As we have seen, this is a concep-tual framework characterized by value-hierarchical thinking, value dualisms, power-over conceptions, and relationships of power, conceptions of privilege that assign higher status to traits associated with Ups, and a logic of domination. The basic beliefs, values, attitudes, and assumptions of patriarchal conceptual frameworks are expressed in a variety of familiar claims: (some) men are rational and women are not rational, or at least not rational in the more highly valued way (some) men are rational; there are important dualisms between reason and emotion, mind and body, the public and the private, culture and nature, and the more highly valued members of the dualist pairs are those traits associated with males, men, or man's culture (viz., reason, mind, the public sphere, culture, respectively); men are superior to women and nonhuman nature; all significant art, culture, history, philosophy—what Marx calls the superstructure of society—is produced by men; control is a primary value.

Second, the beliefs, values, attitudes, and assumptions of patriarchal conceptual frameworks (a) maintain, perpetuate, and sanction impaired thinking, for example, about women and nature (b). Some of this impaired thinking is that men can control women's inner lives, that it is men's proper role to determine women's choices, that humans have a (God-given) right to exploit the earth and its natural resources, that men are justified in ruling over (exercising power over) inferior women and nature, that "a man's home is his castle."

Such impaired thinking is clearly expressed in the sexist and naturist language used to describe reason, women, nature, and nuclear weaponry. In his article "A Portrait of Dominating Rationality," Vance Cope-Kasten (1989) describes how domination metaphors and sexist language pervade standard philosophical descriptions of arguments, good reasoning, and rational decision making: Good reasoners knock down arguments; they tear, rip, chew, cut them up, attack them, try to beat, destroy, or annihilate them, preferably by "nailing them to the wall." Good arguers are sharp, incisive, cutting, relentless, intimidating, brutal. Those not good at giving arguments are wimpy, touchy, quarrelsome, irritable, nagging. Good arguments have a thrust to them; they are compelling, binding, airtight, steel-trap, knock-down, dynamite, smashing, and devastating bits of reasoning which lay things out and pin them down, overcoming any resistance. Bad arguments are described in metaphors of the dominated and powerless: they "fall flat on their faces," are limp, lame, soft, fuzzy, silly, and "full of holes" (Cope-Kasten 1989).

Similar critiques have been provided of the language used to describe women, nature, and nuclear weaponry (Adams 1990; Cohn 1989; Strange 1989). Women are described in animal terms as pets, cows, sows, foxes, chicks, serpents, bitches, beavers, old bats, old hens, pussycats, cats, birdbrains, harebrains. Animalizing or naturalizing women *in a (patriarchal) culture* where animals are seen as inferior to humans (men) thereby reinforces and authorizes women's inferior status. Similarly, language that feminizes nature *in a (patriarchal) culture* where women are viewed as subordinate and inferior reinforces and authorizes the domination of nature. "Mother Nature" is raped, mastered, conquered, mined; her secrets are "penetrated" and her "womb" is to be put into service of the "man of science." Virgin timber is felled, cut down; fertile soil is tilled, and land that lies "fallow" is "barren," useless. The exploitation of nature and animals is justified by feminizing them; the exploitation of women is justified by naturalizing them. As Carol Adams argues so persuasively in *The Sexual Politics of Meat*, language that feminizes nature and naturalizes women describes, reflects, and perpetuates patriarchal oppression by failing to see the extent to which the twin dominations of women and nature, especially of animals, are, in fact, culturally analogous and not simply metaphorically analogous (Adams 1990, 61).

In her startling essay "Sex and Death in the Rational World of Defense Intellectuals," Carol Cohn describes how sexist-naturist language pervades nuclear parlance (Cohn 1989). Nuclear missiles are in "silos" on "farms." That part of the submarine where twenty-four multiple warhead nuclear missiles are lined up, ready for launching, is called "the Christmas tree farm;" BAMBI is the acronym developed for an early version of an antiballistic missile system (Ballistic Missile Boost Intercept). Cohn describes a linguistic world of vertical erector launchers, thrust-to-weight ratios, soft lay downs, deep penetration, penetration aids (familiarly known as "penaids;" devices that help bombers of missiles get past the "enemy's" defensive systems), or "the comparative advantages of protracted versus spasm attacks"—or what one military advisor to the National Security Council has called "releasing 70 to 80 percent of our mega-tonnage in one orgasmic whump" (Cohn 1989, 133-34). It is a world where missiles are "patted," where India's explosion of a nuclear bomb is spoken of as "losing her virginity" and New Zealand's refusal to allow nuclear arms or nuclear-powered warships into its ports is described as "nuclear virginity" (Cohn 1989, 135-37). Such sexist-naturist language creates, reinforces, and justifies nuclear weapons as a kind of sexual dominance.

What this discussion of sexist-naturist language to describe reason, women, nature, and nuclear missiles illustrates is that such language functions *within patriarchy* to perpetuate and maintain impaired patriarchal thinking (b). Such language thereby plays a key role in fueling and keeping intact patriarchy as a dysfunctional social system.

Third, given the role of patriarchal conceptual frameworks (a) and impaired patriarchal thinking (b) in maintaining patriarchy, it is not surprising that patriarchy, understood as a dysfunctional social system, perpetuates and sanctions behaviors that keep those faulty beliefs intact (c). Patriarchy is based fundamentally on dysfunctional values, societal values that tend to push its members toward dysfunctional behaviors. For example, in the United States, current estimates are that one out of every three or four women will be raped by someone she knows; globally, rape, sexual harassment, spouse beating and sado-masochistic pornography are examples of behaviors practiced, sanctioned, or tolerated within patriarchy, what I call "behaviors of domination." In the realm of environmentally destructive behaviors, strip mining, pollution of the air, water, and soil, and factory farming are instances of behaviors maintained and sanctioned within patriarchy. They, too, rest on the faulty beliefs that it is okay to "rape the earth," that it is "man's God-given right" to have dominion (domination) over the earth and fowl, that nature has only instrumental value, that environmental destruction is the acceptable price we pay for "progress."

Lastly, much of the current "unmanageability" of contemporary life in patriarchal culture (d) is a consequence of a preoccupation with activities, events, and experiences that reflect historically male-gender identified beliefs, values, attitudes, and assumptions. The real-life consequences of patriarchy's inability to manage its affairs equitably and justly are everywhere: an obsession with national defense and nuclear proliferation—perhaps the ultimate acting out of impaired patriarchal thinking; the exploitation and degradation of the nonhuman earth and animals, including the unnecessary and painful use of animals in experimentation; homophobic laws and policies; the "feminization of poverty;" the prevalence of child abuse, sexual abuse, violence against women, rape. In fact, it is often *only* through observing these dysfunctional behaviors (c), the symptoms of dysfunctionality, that one can truly see the role patriarchy plays in maintaining, perpetuating, and sanctioning them. When patriarchy is understood as a dysfunctional system, this "unmanageability" can be seen for what it is—a *predictable* consequence of patriarchy.

This last point is crucial, for it suggests that the sort of dysfunctional belief system, thinking, behaviors, and unmanageability that characterize patriarchal systems are predictable, and, in this sense, "logical," "natural," or "normal" consequences of patriarchy. Seen as predictable consequences of patriarchal values, beliefs, attitudes, and assumptions, these behaviors motivate and explain what we call the "Of course" response: "Of course, you feel crazy when men don't acknowledge your contributions to the project." "Of course, you feel powerless to stop your boss's unwanted sexual advances towards you." "Of course, your life has become unmanageable; your workplace is a male-dominant haven of exaggerated rationality." "Of course, you feel frightened to go out alone at night; rape is a very real threat!" "Of course, you feel confused and anxious; by standing up for yourself, you're breaking all the rules, rocking the boat."

The "Of course" response affirms that those who feel crazy, powerless, alone, confused, anxious within and under patriarchy are experiencing what one would expect people trying to get their needs met *within* a dysfunctional system often feel; they are *appropriate responses for one in a dysfunctional and patriarchal system* based on faulty beliefs—beliefs which people trying to stay healthy within such a dysfunctional system are trying to shed! The "Of course" response is a proper, descriptively accurate, reality-affirming response to people who suffer the ills and abuses of patriarchy.

ECOFEMINIST SPIRITUALITIES

Patriarchy is a social system of unequal distributions of power, benefits, and burdens. It can *only* be understood in a historical, socioeconomic, political, and cultural context. Furthermore, *within* patriarchy, there may be no truly healthy individual, family, community; it may be that a truly healthy family in patriarchal society is an oxymoron. It may not be possible to realize the health of individuals, families, or communities as long as patriarchy remains intact. Where, then, do ecofeminist spiritualities fit in?

I reject *any* dichotomous heuristics in contemporary society that divide individuals, families, or communities into "healthy" or "unhealthy" ones. Furthermore, it is a gross disservice to oppressed people (women) and a maldescription of social reality to treat the dysfunctional behaviors of patriarchy as personal disorders. The concepts of healthy and unhealthy, like the concepts of functional and dysfunctional, must be viewed on a *continuum*, with an open range of diverse possibilities for what counts as healthy or unhealthy in a variety of political and cultural contexts.

An understanding of patriarchy as a dysfunctional social system characterized by features (a) to (d) permits one to see and honor ecofeminist spiritualities as powerful survival, resistance, and empowerment strategies oppressed peoples do or may exhibit within patriarchy. So viewed, ecofeminist spiritualities function as empowering antidotes to patriarchy.

What makes ecofeminist spiritualities *spiritual* is that they are conceived and practiced as life affirming (rather than life denying) responses to life under patriarchy. What they affirm are ways of thinking and behaving that challenge patriarchal conceptual frameworks (a) and the thinking, behaviors, and *isms* of domination (b) to (d) they sanction. They do so by assuming or positing some power (force, energy, being, deity, or deities) that can help create or restore healthy interactions and relationships. At the heart of ecofeminist spiritualities is a *movement away from* dysfunctional systems and behaviors and a *movement toward* healthy, functional, life-enhancing systems and behaviors.

What makes them feminist is that ecofeminist spiritualities are opposed to male-gender power and privilege, as expressed both in the myths, symbols, language, and belief system of patriarchal conceptual frameworks (a) and the thinking, behavior, and *isms* of domination that characterize patriarchy (b) to (d). So understood, ecofeminist spiritualities constitute a diversity of responses to patriarchy that are intended to empower women and to serve as a corrective to the dysfunctionality that characterizes patriarchy.

What makes them ecofeminist is that ecofeminist spiritualities recognize that under patriarchy, the domination of women and the domination of nature are closely linked. According to the proposed model of patriarchy as a dysfunctional social system, these links are deeply rooted in patriarchal conceptual frameworks. The dysfunctionalities of patriarchy (a) to (d) are culturally constructed, historically molded, economically fashioned, politically nurtured, and socially engineered. In the proposed model, sexual assault, global environmental destruction, and nuclear war are some of the predictable consequences (c) and (d) of unchecked patriarchy. Ecofeminist spiritualities may then be viewed philosophically as earth based and earth respectful, healing responses to patriarchal dysfunction and its attendant environmental destruction.

It is not surprising that ecofeminist spiritualities are often explicitly earth based. For many ecofeminists, the experience of nonhuman nature as intrinsically valuable provides one avenue for getting outside patriarchy (however, temporarily or intermittently), at least in how one conceives oneself and one's relation to others (including nonhuman nature). Such attempts to get outside patriarchy are philosophically significant. They represent personal empowerment strategies individuals and groups use at particular times and in particular places to challenge and replace the basic beliefs, values, attitudes, and assumptions of patriarchy with nonpatriarchal and feminist ones, to challenge and replace the thinking and behaviors of patriarchy with nonpatriarchal and feminist ones. In short, they are offered and practiced as antidotes to patriarchy. So conceived, the philosophical significance of all ecofeminist spiritualities is that they attempt to function to disrupt, challenge, and replace patriarchal practices with ones that do not perpetuate sexism and naturism and in ways that empower individuals *within patriarchy*. In this respect, ecofeminist spiritualities do not function simply or merely to provide an *ideal* or *utopian* vision; they provide immediately useful empowerment strategies that can be exercised by individuals within contemporary patriarchal culture. They function in the prefeminist present to break the cycle of patriarchy conceived as a dysfunctional social system.

CONCLUSION

I began this essay by raising the question: From a feminist philosophical perspective, what are ecofeminist spiritualities and how might one understand the claim that ecofeminist spiritualities are an empowering response to sexist oppression and environmental destruction? My answer now is that ecofeminist spiritualities function as empowering responses and antidotes to patriarchy conceived as a dysfunctional social system, which individuals can exercise within contemporary patriarchal cultures.

So understood, ecofeminist spiritualities play several vital *philosophical* roles. First, they challenge patriarchy as its core—its belief system—and attempt to put in its place nondominating and life-affirming beliefs, values, behaviors, and relationships among humans and toward nonhuman nature. From a philosophical perspective, ecofeminist spiritualities constitute a powerful conceptual challenge to the patriarchal belief system, impaired thinking, and behaviors of domination which characterize patriarchy.

Of course, whether any particular ecofeminist spirituality is really feminist or ecofeminist or advances the ecofeminist project of exposing and replacing harmful interconnected practices toward women and nonhuman nature is an open question, one I did not attempt to address here. My aim was simply to provide a way to think philosophically about ecofeminist spiritualities in terms of a conception and model of patriarchy as a dysfunctional social system rooted in patriarchal conceptual frameworks.

Second, women experience the dysfunctionalities of patriarchy on a concrete, daily basis. The conception of patriarchy as a dysfunctional system thereby acutely describes, captures, and expresses the reality of many of our lives. A philosophical attention to ecofeminist spiritualities as a response to patriarchy conceived as a dysfunctional social system thereby honors, explains, and acknowledges the role women's *spiritual* experiences play in challenging and surviving under patriarchy. Such attention is at the heart of what feminist theory and theory building ought to be.

Third, the notion that ecofeminist spiritualities are elements in a network of ecofeminist strategies to empower women within patriarchy *while at the same time* challenging patriarchal structures and practices captures the creatively rich and diverse ways women are acting *now,* in the patriarchal present, to improve both their own and other's lives within patriarchy. Such activity helps counteract the sometimes immobilizing sense that, once one sees patriarchy for what it is, it seems too big, too old, and too powerful to do anything about.

Lastly, the discussion provided explains why, for many, ending patriarchy involves seeing the spiritual as political, as more than simply "rearranging one's internal furniture;" the spiritual involves challenging patriarchy at its dysfunctional conceptual and behavioral core. Failure to acknowledge the potential of ecofeminist spiritualities to provide a genuinely feminist, life-affirming, and empowering response to patriarchy within patriarchy perpetuates the mistaken view that spirituality is not or cannot be a legitimate feminist political concern. I hope the philosophical perspective I have offered here suggests how and why such a view would be a philosophical mistake and a disservice to the lives and testimonies of practitioners of ecofeminist spiritualities.

NOTES

1. For a more complete discussion of ecofeminism and spirituality, see Warren and Cheney (forthcoming).

2. For a discussion of differences between power-over and power-with, power-within, and power-against conceptions of power, and the conditions under which any exercise of power is morally appropriate, see Warren (1991a).

3. For a discussion of the range of issues ecofeminists discuss and their relevance to ecofeminist philosophy, see Warren (1991b).

4. What makes a feminist attention to all systems of oppression "feminist" is that sex-gender is the lens through which analysis of these multiple *isms* of domination occurs. To say that feminism is the lens through which *isms* of domination are discussed does *not* make what is seen through a feminist lens tangential to or somehow outside the purview of feminism. To claim that these other *isms* are not properly within the purview of feminism would be like claiming that human relations to each other and nonhuman nature are not properly within the purview of Judaism or Christianity when looked at through a Jewish or Christian lens.

5. This is the title of an important volume of ecofeminism, Plant (1989).

6. I have adapted this model of the nature of a dysfunctional social system based on faulty beliefs from Patrick Carnes's model of an addictive system (Carnes 1983, 15).

9

Ecofeminist Consciousness and the Transforming Power of Symbols

L. TEAL WILLOUGHBY

WHAT DO ECOFEMINIST RITUALS REVEAL ABOUT NATURE?

Ecofeminism offers an extensive critique of Western culture in which the overall goal is to create an alternative theory and praxis to that of patriarchy. When I think of ecofeminism from my psychological-spiritual perspective, the disturbing question of "how" emerges: *How* can ecofeminists transform the patriarchal worldview that devalues women and nature into an ecofeminist consciousness that reinforms mutuality between humanity and nature? More specifically, I wonder *how* we use symbols in rituals to achieve this transformation of consciousness that upholds mutuality. Symbols are powerful transformers of consciousness; a closer look at the role of symbols in ecofeminists' rituals can offer insights on how they work in the process of moving out of the patriarchal worldview into an ecofeminist consciousness.

Since the beginning of the feminist movement in the 1970s, feminists have critiqued the exclusive use of masculine symbols in society and in the church and have created many alternative rituals and symbols that promote positive and empowering images of women. I suggest that the *same critical rigor* be applied within the ecofeminist movement regarding symbols of nature. When confronted with symbols of nature within society or within the ecofeminist

L. Teal Willoughby wrote her doctoral dissertation, "Mother Earth: Ecofeminism from a Jungian Perspective," at the University of Denver. She is a counselor and poet who leads support groups and retreats on topics such as spirituality, AIDS, and women's journey into wholeness. She is active in preserving the land around Dallas-Fort Worth airport in Grapevine, Texas.

movement itself, we must question the assumptions about nature reflected in the use of each particular symbol. For example, does the symbol reveal the inherent value of nature? How is the relationship between humanity and nature depicted? It is not enough to critique symbols and rituals only from the standpoint of valuing of women. We must also consider what they reveal about nature. For, as we shall see, it is possible to create rituals that value women through the devaluation of nature. Just as women have been absent or devalued in patriarchy's institutions, nature sometimes receives corresponding treatment in feminists' rituals. To demonstrate this, I will look at two examples from paradigmatic works on women's rituals: the first from Rosemary Ruether's *Women-Church* and the other from Starhawk's *The Spiral Dance*. Although they write out of two different traditions, Ruether and Starhawk both view the twin liberation of women and nature of urgent importance.

Ritual Use of Water in Ecofeminism

In the "Rite of Healing from Distress of Mind and Body" compiled by Ruether in *Women-Church* (1986, 150–51), a woman who desires healing focuses on her bodily pain and psychic distress. Then while other women surround her, she is led through a guided meditation "to imagine these death forces of pain and psychic distress draining out and *flowing away into a great pool of water that flows into the earth*" (emphasis mine) (Ruether 1986, 150). This imaging is followed by actual immersion in water, if possible, and then the invocation of a redemptive power called "Wisdom-Spirit." Healing power then flows through the woman to reconnect and harmonize her with the great life energy of God/ess.

Notice that the earth is symbolically viewed as the proper place for the dumping of human "death forces." There is the assumption that the earth will take care of our pollution and purify it for us as it flows into the earth's waters. The ritual represents the same patriarchal view of the earth as lower than the realm of people (culture) and thus the natural dumping ground for the wastes of human society. It is unclear how the healing force called "Wisdom-Spirit" is connected to the earth. What is clear is that the water is symbolically polluted and forgotten, like our actual great underground aquifers. Thus the symbols in Ruether's ritual are used in a way that displays a lack of ecofeminist understanding and ignores the value of mutuality.

Starhawk provides a similar example of honoring women over nature in *The Spiral Dance* (1979, 116–17). The "Indrinking Spell" even recognizes that the consequence of projecting negative emotions onto nature can be the literal death of nature. The woman is to hold a cup of clear water in front of a green plant set in the earth and project her negative emotions and thoughts about mistakes and wrongdoing into the cup of water. Then while visualizing the Goddess as a forgiving Mother, "pour out the water onto the plant, and feel your self-hating draining out of you. (It is possible this ritual will kill the plant)" (Starhawk 1979, 117). Then while the plant is left to die, the woman charges a cup of wine with positive thoughts of herself and drinks it for her own empowerment and healing. The well-being of the plant is sacrificed for the well-being of the woman—a very poor model of mutuality.

These examples demonstrate that unless ecofeminists develop an appreciation of how symbols work, natural symbols in feminists' rituals can be the recipients of harmful projections that could reinforce ecological destruction. Since ecofeminism views the exploitation of nature as connected to the oppression of women, it must critique any liberation of women that progresses, whether consciously or unconsciously, at the expense of nature. This requires a greater understanding of symbols and how they function.

Role of Symbols in Jungian Theory

Although analytical psychology has received criticism in recent years from some feminists, a feminist application of Jungian theory can be a valuable tool for critiquing ecofeminist consciousness development. Jung offers a powerful and important understanding of symbols and their function not only for communication but also for the actual transformation of consciousness. Jung identifies problematic approaches to symbols, such as the one-sided patriarchal approach that excludes and oppresses other perspectives. Most importantly, Jungian psychology advocates a relationship of mutual support between the inner world of the psyche and outer world and between conscious and unconscious aspects of the person. Achieving a supportive relationship between the ego and the greater Self and other unconscious contents is called the process of individuation. The process of individuation results in the transformation of consciousness into a greater awareness and deeper integration. Certain key concepts, such as projection, amplification of symbols, and the role of symbols in value clarification, can inform the development of ecofeminist consciousness. These concepts will be illustrated shortly.

The first step in understanding how symbols function is to explicitly recognize the conscious values that are most important to us. Symbols connect consciousness with the unconsciousness, including fears, desires, and denied prejudices such as sexism. If we are confused or unaware of our conscious position, then we do not have a standpoint to receive these unconscious contents and they remain untransformed. As in the above examples, the value of nature in and of itself was unclear in regard to women's empowerment, and thus the symbols did not reveal a new awareness of nature. Therefore, since it is important to set out some parameters of our conscious position regarding the nature-human relationship, we will set forth three principles of ecofeminist consciousness that are consistent with a relationship of mutuality between humanity and the earth. Secondly, we will use Jungian concepts to analyze how symbols can be used to transform the present perspective by bringing into awareness our denied exploitative view of nature. We will then apply this understanding to the symbols in ecofeminist rituals.

Ecofeminist Consciousness

Ecofeminist consciousness refers broadly to the *conscious* position of ecofeminists; it is our view of the world. Clearly ecofeminist consciousness advocates a different model of the relationship between humanity and nature than the domination model of patriarchal consciousness. It envisions relationship based on a model of mutual support between humanity and nature in which the health and survival of both are valued. Mutuality is different than domination in that there is respect for the inherent value of nature. In addition, mutuality is not based on an overriding concern for equality, rather it is based on an awareness and a commitment to mutually support one another. It seeks to reinforce "responsible" actions toward nature, not in the sense of obligations and rights but in the literal sense of our "ability for response" (Kheel, 1988, 17). The development of ecofeminist consciousness would offer the foundation for guiding this respectful response. Mutuality between humanity and the earth does not mean that the earth must be perceived as being mutually supportive in an anthropomorphic type of way and held accountable to it, as if the earth were human. The earth has been overwhelmingly supportive of humanity, as suggested by our world's population growth though not without cost to the earth itself. Nevertheless, it is not always supportive at certain places in certain times, such as, for example, the occurrence of earthquakes, volcanoes, and hurricanes. Ecofeminist consciousness would seek a greater understanding of the etiology of natural events and the possible role of humanity within it. The relationship pattern in mutuality is an awareness of interconnectedness as well as individuality. Thus the ecofeminist viewpoint does not deny the complexity of understanding and responding to natural events. They must however be approached with a commitment to mutuality.

We can delineate at least three principles inferred from the science of ecology and feminist theory as comprising ecofeminist consciousness. These are: a realization of the interconnectedness of entities within the ecosystem, including humanity; the value of individual diversity within both the human and natural realms; and an awareness of nature that is not contaminated by sexist or anthropocentric bias. These principles form a beginning foundation for a mutuality model of relationship between humanity and nature.

Ecofeminists recognize that the patriarchal way of viewing women and nature, even with its long history, is only one way to construct this reality and the relationship between them. Now ecofeminists are constructing their own viewpoint out of their own values and understanding of ecology and feminist theory. This alternative perspective, called ecofeminist consciousness, will be the conscious standpoint for evaluating actions toward the earth (both literal and symbolic). This viewpoint upholds the values of interconnection, diversity, and greater awareness of nature in and of itself as opposed to the linear, hierarchical mind-set in which nature is rated lower than man and man is rated higher than woman (see Gray 1979b, Ortner 1974). These components help us understand the radical difference between ecofeminist consciousness and patriarchal consciousness and the great challenge involved in the development of ecofeminist consciousness. How can symbols within our rituals encourage this type of consciousness? Let us discuss the role of symbols in the transformation of consciousness.

JUNG'S VIEW OF SYMBOLS IN TRANSFORMING CONSCIOUSNESS

The power of symbols to transform conscious awareness is known to every religion. Some psychologies, such as Jung's analytical psychology, have investigated how this transformation process works. Ecofeminism must not ignore the significance of symbols and how they function. Indeed, some ecofeminists have recognized this. Rosemary Ruether asserts the importance of symbols for the transformation of sexism:

> One need not only to engage in rational theoretical discourse about this journey; one also needs deep symbols and symbolic actions to guide and interpret the actual experience of the journey from sexism to liberated humanity. (Ruether 1986, 3)

The problem is that, without a psychologically based theory, ecofeminists do not recognize how symbols function "to guide and interpret the actual experience of the journey from sexism to liberated humanity." The insights of Jungian psychology enable us to understand and critique the use of symbols by ecofeminists.

There are three reasons Jung's theory is appropriate for this task. First, Jung's theory is itself a critique of Western society and Christianity. A central theme in his critique is the repression of the natural realm in both religion and society. The result of the repression has been the alienation of modern men and women from nature. We have forgotten our primal origins and the fact that we share a collective heritage that stretches back to the beginning of time. We prefer to think of ourselves as separate and above the rest of the planet. As a result, nature is viewed without ultimate significance, and finally the mystery and holiness of life itself recedes. Jung writes:

> Today, for instance, we talk of "matter." We describe its physical properties. We conduct laboratory experiments to demonstrate some of its aspects. But the word "matter" remains a dry, inhuman, and purely intellectual concept, without any psychic significance for us. How different was the former image of matter—the Great Mother—that could encompass and express the profound emotional meaning of Mother Earth. (Jung 1968, 85)

Jung perceives this unhealthy alienation from nature as a major problem with his clients. To get well, his clients had to reconnect to their past, including the natural world, through myths, dreams, and symbols. Jung criticizes Christianity and its symbol system for its inability to integrate these repressed aspects with the conscious outlook of modern people.

Second, Jung emphasizes the role of myths and symbols in the transformation of consciousness. Through symbols a person becomes aware of being connected to a larger reality beyond the individual ego. Since he defines this larger reality broadly across religious traditions, his theory is inclusive of all who experience the sacred or the numinous. In this way symbols give meaning to life and hope for life on earth. Jung analyzes the problems encountered in symbolic awareness and offers a positive approach, which we will discuss shortly.

Third, Jung advocates a mutuality mode of relationship rather than one of domination. Even within one's own psyche, mutuality applies to relationships between different aspects of the inner world. The point of understanding the unconscious elements of the psyche and withdrawing projections from the outer world is not for the purpose of conquering and dominating them, as in many of the ego psychological theories. Instead, the purpose is to begin a dialogue with these other entities so that power can be shared and a balance created. When we acknowledge the relative autonomy of different aspects of our psyche, the relationship between the ego and the unconscious changes to one of mutual support. Rather than the ego, the center of the personality is the Self, which holds all the parts of the psyche in an integrative wholeness. Just as the ego must learn that it is not the master of the psyche, so the person learns that he or she is not the ruler of the world.

The process of individuation involves coming to terms with the oppressive parts of ourselves as well as the weak, underdeveloped side of the personality. Frequently, this dynamism between conflicting parts of the psyche (which are reflected in conflicts in the outer world) are discussed as polarities. Jung stresses that each side of any polarity is valuable and has something to offer in creating a balanced, healthy person as well as a viable world. In other words, polarities such as "action" and "passivity" are both necessary for health and happiness, and our task is to honor both dynamics. Dualism is a different conceptual model from that stressed by Jung, in that the polarities are divided into opposites in order that one pole can be rated superior to the other "weaker" pole, which is best suppressed or destroyed. Therefore, Jung is not a dualist, since he views polarities as contrasting dynamics which belong together and must be continually integrated anew whenever one is falsely alienated from the other.

Jung identified some characteristics with "the feminine" and others with the "masculine" in a model that holds them together as in the Chinese Tao. For example, he does not view them as exclusive to each sex; men have a feminine side and women have a masculine side. The goal is the individuation of the unique man or woman in a way that encompasses all human qualities and integrates them into an individual wholeness. Jung depicted the feminine positively and its repression as detrimental to human development and the functioning of social institutions.

The result of feminist scholarship on Jung is a mixed review. Most of the negative critique is centered around the concept of the archetypes, particularly the archetype of the feminine. Jung's analysis of symbols is, however, viewed positively by many of the same feminists who find his concept of archetypes problematic. For example, Carol Christ and Judith Plaskow, in the introduction to *Womanspirit Rising*, assert that even though Jung's view of women and the feminine principle are problematic, his theories of the function of myth and symbol in the unconscious remain important (Christ and Plaskow 1979, 2). Naomi Goldenberg agrees that the way Jung worked with images, dreams, and symbols is more important for feminism than his view on "the feminine" (Ibid., 224). She states that the study of Jung helped her realize that many sociological theories about the origins of myth and symbol were naive. Demaris Wehr, author of *Jung and Feminism* (1987), also finds value in the Jungian way of working with symbols for spiritual awakening and psychological development. However, all four scholars conclude after extensive analysis that the concept of archetypes should be rejected or, at least, thoroughly revised.

On the other hand, a positive understanding of archetypes forms the theoretical base for the scholarship of feminists such as Ann Ulanov, Catherine Keller, Estella Lauter, and Carol Pearson. Although it is beyond the scope of this article to engage in this unresolved debate, my discussion of symbols will demonstrate the heuristic value of acknowledging an archetypal component level of symbols. My stance in the archetype debate is that the concept of archetypes is vitally important to understanding symbols. If we reject the idea of archetypes, we are without a tool to comprehend the numinosity of symbols that transform consciousness.

However, we must be alert to ways in which the concept has been used to stereotype women and discount their experience and correct this patriarchal application of archetypes whenever it occurs. As feminists or ecofeminists, we must uphold our values when appropriating concepts from the theoretical work of others for heuristic purposes. Jungian theory certainly contains patriarchal markings through the influence of its milieu, so caution is justified.[1]

THREE FUNCTIONS OF SYMBOLS

The word *symbol* comes from two Greek words meaning "to throw together" (Clift 1984, 51), which is a good description of the actual task of symbols. Symbols bring together different levels of reality and relate them in a way that creates a unity of meaning and a new conscious experience. Since the symbol rises from the unconscious, a numinous quality is made present which is not explainable through rational thought. The symbol always stands for more than its obvious and known meaning. It is more than a "sign." As Jung says, "It has a wider 'unconscious' aspect that is never precisely defined or fully explained" (Jung 1968, 4). Thus we can say that symbols—whether words or images—are the best representation of an as-yet-unknown content.

Symbols have at least three aspects that they "throw together." One is the literal word or image, which is concrete and is considered "conscious"; another is the unconscious, numinous, archetypal aspect to which it points and makes present. Thirdly, the particular cultural context gives the symbol its unique form. Symbols bridge the gap between these aspects so that one's conscious awareness has been changed. No longer is the concrete viewed in opposition to the infinite, but the interconnection has been revealed by the symbol. For this reason symbols have great power to unite opposites in a way that creates new relationships between the conscious and unconscious.

Each of these aspects (the concrete manifestation, the cultural trappings, and the archetypal core) is essential for the understanding of symbols. The function of symbols is impeded if they are defined as a single dimension of our culture. According to Jung, symbols carry the seeds of transformation if we allow them to engage our total perspective. Symbolic awareness is being aware of the different levels of symbols so that we can move toward greater consciousness and wholeness.

Concrete Image

Jung valued the concrete symbol itself. Unlike Freud, he did not use symbols as a place of departure for free association in order to uncover personal complexes and neurotic disturbances. Jung honored our experience with the symbol itself and believed that its function was much greater than Freud allowed. By always returning to the symbol and never reducing it down to a known content, he used the symbol to unite the inner world with the outer world, which results in increased conscious awareness of the outer world and a greater wholeness of being in the inner world. The symbol has more than instrumental value because it participates in the reality that it makes present. In other words, the symbol is both embodied in the image or word as well as participating in unconscious psychic reality. Jung's theory of symbol accounts for both of these aspects in a way that transcends the traditional dualism of spirit and matter.

Ecofeminism also honors nature because it is a living embodiment of matter and spirit, apart from whatever instrumental value a certain entity of nature may have to our society. Ecofeminists denounce the anthropocentric view that values only the entities of nature that benefit humanity. Ecofeminists and Jung are in agreement about the intrinsic value of the actual, concrete world, regardless of its meanings and associations in society.

The way Jung worked with his patients' symbols displays how important he considered them. Therapy often centers around symbols that have personal meaning to the patient. The meaning of symbols is explored and revealed, although never entirely, through different methods of dialogue and focus, such as drawing them and, if possible, experiencing them. For example, if a patient dreamed of a river, she or he might go to an actual river and with the imagination ask the river what message it has to give. Working with our personal symbols is a meaningful activity, since the symbol contains the key to transformation. Their literalness is not to be discarded, because within the literal and personal is the bridge to the transcendent. If we ignore their literalness, we can become disconnected to nature so that animal names automatically conjure up images of football teams and rivers are lines on maps!

Cultural Trappings

Psychology has shown that the literal, concrete world is not the whole of reality. The task of psychology has been to separate human illusions and fantasies about reality and the actual realm of nature. Ecofeminists specifically want to distinguish the androcentric and sexist projections onto woman and the earth. The aim of ecofeminist consciousness is to behold actual entities and their processes in a way that is less distorted and destructive than the awareness of patriarchal consciousness, although we recognize that true objectivity is never possible. The second dimension of symbols enables us to look at the cultural perspectives we associate to symbols and to understand how they limit our awareness. By looking at the particular cultural trappings in symbols, we may be able to discern not only Jung's early-twentieth-century assumptions in his interpretation of symbols for the earth, but we may also discern the cultural trappings in our own response to symbols for the earth.

For example, the symbol *dolphin* reflects its particular social context. From a certain cultural viewpoint, dolphins refer to a Miami football team. From another cultural context, dolphins have become the symbol for the unnecessary killing of sea creatures by big business. Still others think of Sea World or Flipper. In Roman mythology, dolphins are associated with the goddess Ceres. To gain awareness of the unique cultural trappings that clothe the symbol is to become cognizant of diversity. The cultural aspect of a symbol calls for an appreciation of its precise revelation of form out of a complex diversity. However, the values, distortions, and prejudices of the culture are also revealed at this level of understanding symbols.

Carol Christ says: "Symbols have both psychological and political effects, because they create the inner conditions (deep-seated attitudes and feelings) that lead people to feel comfortable with or to accept social and political arrangements that correspond to the symbol system" (Christ and Plaskow 1979, 274). This is the cultural level of symbols which Carol Christ and other feminists are concerned with in religion and society. They are right to point to the social aspect of symbols and how they validate the hierarchical mode of relationship. However, since this is not the only level at which the symbol functions, symbols can still have powerful influence although they are carefully critiqued by feminists. The key lies within the unconscious archetypal level, because it is present whether acknowledged or not.

Jung points out that religious symbols as well as natural symbols have lost their greater cosmic meaning. The tendency in society to interpret symbols only on the social-psychological level splits us off from our deepest connections in the unconscious. The result is the pervasive meaninglessness and isolation of patriarchy. Jung describes this: "Individuals feel isolated in the cosmos, because they are no longer involved in nature and have lost their emotional 'unconscious identity' with natural phenomena. These [phenomena] have slowly lost their symbolic implications" (Jung 1968, 84). The cultural trappings of symbols are an important aspect of the functioning of symbols, but the power of symbols to change consciousness is misunderstood without archetypal understanding.

Archetypal Core
Jung explains that the modern approach to the world is almost totally rationalistic. By destroying superstition, the modern person has also destroyed his or her ability to relate to the world through any other mode of perception than rationality. Without a capacity to respond to the numinous, the function of symbols is lost on modern society. Jung expresses his concern: "Modern people do not understand how much their 'rationalism' (which has destroyed their capacity to respond to numinous symbols and ideas) has put them at the mercy of the psychic 'underworld' " (Jung 1968, 84).

By psychic "underworld" Jung means all that we cannot understand intellectually, such as emotion, fantasy, intuition, including life's meaning, ultimate values, and even the concept of God. We depend on symbols to communicate this underworld of irrational experience.

Symbols cannot function to unite opposites such as finite and infinite, matter and spirit, sacred and profane, if there is denial of the existence of irrational factors. This is precisely the situation of modern people, according to Jung.

> We have stripped all things of their mystery and numinosity; nothing is holy any longer. Our "advanced" consciousness has deprived itself of the means by which the auxiliary contributions of the instincts and the unconscious can be assimilated. These organs of assimilation and integration were numinous symbols, held holy by common consent. (Jung 1968, 84)

This mystery and numinosity referred to by Jung is revealed in the third aspect of symbols, the archetypal core. The archetypal core of the symbol represents first of all the ultimate value or meaning of the symbol for the individual or group. Archetypes "gain life and meaning only when you try to take into account their numinosity—i.e., their relationship to the living individual" (Jung 1968, 88). This is what gives symbols a power beyond that of signs. The numinous aspect creates a meaningful relationship between the symbol and the person. For example, there is a meaningful relationship between most Christians and the symbol of the cross that cannot be explained rationally, as much as many often try. The value is much deeper and more ancient. The archetypal core of a symbol also connects the ancient past and the possible future. The archetypal core establishes depth and breadth within the associations to the symbol, since it draws on the accumulative experience of human-nature relationship through time. This experience is irreducible and expands beyond comprehension. For example, the symbol of the snake is found in myths and religions across the world, from prehistoric to modern times. They are based on the common human experience of the "awe-some" nature of snakes since the dawn of consciousness.

Catherine Keller takes this experience of a numinous relationship to the earth a step further in suggesting that physical nature itself, like the body, is irreducible—a field of energy and knowledge that can never be known in its complexity (1986, 239). The symbol can manifest this profound intuition experientially through our emotional and bodily response. Thus the archetypal core affects the deeper layers of our experience outside of our conscious attitudes.

Jung postulates a teleological function to symbols, which means they can point toward the future. The archetypal core reveals the past and affects the possibilities in the future. Symbols seem to pull us into the future, since they are connected to our imaginations and dreams.

> On the one hand [the symbol] gives a picture of the remnants and traces of all that has been, and, on the other, but expressed in the same picture, the outlines of what is to come, in so far as the psyche creates its own future. (Jung 1953–1979, par. 404)

From all this we can see that the archetypal core of the symbol gives its value through a sense of numinosity which cannot be explained rationally. It reveals the vast interconnectedness of the human experience with the natural world through a great variety of associations to the archetypal image. Therefore symbols contain the possibility of opening up the limitless depth of what nature has been and can be to humanity. This is knowledge that needs to be made conscious in ecofeminist consciousness.

As just outlined, a symbol is an image that contains and unites three different levels: concrete, cultural, and numinous. However, all three aspects must function for the individual if an image is to be a living symbol. With this symbolic awareness we are able to observe a symbol and its particular effect on consciousness and thus judge between symbols in the development of an ecofeminist consciousness. It is through working with symbols of nature that a different conscious awareness can be achieved as various patriarchal trappings surrounding the symbol are uncovered.

ASSESSING ECOFEMINIST SYMBOLS

Symbols work on us and our culture whether we pay attention to them or not. For example, feminist theologians have pointed out the deep repercussion that the symbol *God the Father* has had on society. However, I can remember a time when most people, including women, said "it didn't make any difference." When ecofeminists expand our knowledge of symbols and the process of conscious development that follows, we can perceive how symbols are helping or hindering the cause of ecofeminism.

In addition to the two rituals using water that opened this essay, one other ritual will serve to illustrate our analysis of symbolic awareness. This example is typical of many rituals within both Christian and pagan communities in which flowers or fruit are part of the ritual. Flowers or fruit—whether on a church altar or on a Wicca altar—offer to worshipers their silent beauty and fragrance. We feel positive toward them because they are lovely to look at or smell. Thus it is easy to believe we are honoring nature in an ecofeminist fashion. However, a closer look at the role of flowers in rituals shows that they are symbols that tell us something about nature and our relationship to it. Despite our good feeling about flowers and fruits, they are frequently used as symbols that do not further ecofeminist values or awareness.

Flower and Fruit Ritual
For example, consider this from a dying vigil ritual in Ruether's *Women-Church*. In this ritual, a basket of fruits and flowers is brought to the dying person and she is encouraged to project the happy times of her life onto them. "These fruits and flowers represent the good fruits and blossoms of your life" (Ruether 1986, 211). Then, as a symbol of the positive aspects of the dying person's life, the basket of fruits and flowers is offered up to Mother-Spirit, who will take it and make it immortal and everlasting.

This ritual is based on the goodness and beauty of flowers and fruits. Since this is certainly a common human experience, it is easy for the participants to project positive human traits onto them. Now the flowers and fruits no longer represent themselves and the mystery of nature.[2] They are viewed as symbolic of certain human characteristics. From the point of view of the dying woman, this ritual could be comforting, but from the point of view of ecofeminist consciousness, nature (as the flowers and fruits) is viewed only through an anthropomorphic lens. This ritual converts the symbol into a sign, and greater awareness of nature is not encouraged.

Rituals such as this can be very empowering for women, especially when compared to similar traditional rituals in which women's experience is ignored. However, there is little evidence that they serve to increase consciousness of nature or depict a relationship of mutuality. Symbols of nature are made secondary to the main focus on the ritual, which is to heal or celebrate a certain occasion in the life experience of women. Thus, various aspects in the life of the feminist human community are projected onto the natural elements. When nature symbols play a supportive role in the enactment of a human event, they can provide a channel for human projections.

Unpacking Symbols

But what precisely are these projections we place on symbols? And what do they inform us about our process of ecofeminist development? Do the symbols function to create ecofeminist consciousness or continue to reinforce patriarchal consciousness? To answer these questions, we must approach nature symbols with the intent of understanding their symbolic language.

The process of understanding symbols for the purpose of greater conscious awareness involves a respectful dialogue between ourselves and the symbol. However, we must first unpack the symbols so we can appreciate the symbols beyond our everyday usage. Unpacking symbols involves three movements: amplification, owning projections, and value clarification. This work with symbols assumes the conscious values of ecofeminism: interconnectedness, diversity, greater knowledge beyond sexism and anthropocentric bias. We will illustrate this process of working with symbols by returning to the previous rituals.

Amplification of the symbol involves our associations to the symbol from the three levels discussed earlier: our personal, concrete experience; our culture's perspective; and the archetypal associations that are universal across time and culture. The main symbol of nature in the first two rituals described earlier is water. Therefore, I would first ask, what does water mean to you in your personal experience? Personal associations might be swimming in the city pool, ice water after ball practice, and the cold rain during Texas winters. Another person might have quite different personal associations if he or she works on an assembly line spraying water, or almost had a drowning accident. The cultural level of symbolic associations is usually shared by many people, such as the concept or experience of oceans, lakes, and rivers; water pollution, flooding, and drought; cleansing and drinking water. These lead into the deeper archetypal level of water as a primary element of life on earth, water as common component of both ocean and body, water as a flowing liquid element that moves and absorbs other things, water that has unknown depths and unknown origins. We see how rich and complex the meaning of a symbol of water can be from this one amplification and, of course, everyone's amplification will be different. Already our perspective of water is enlarged as we contemplate these numerous associations on the personal, cultural, and archetypal levels.

Listening to Nature through Symbols

Now we return to the ritual and note how the symbol of water is depicted. In both rituals it is shown as a body of water that receives pollution and takes it away. If the water could speak, let us imagine what it would say about its role in the ritual. Can we be quiet and still and listen for the voice of nature? There are many techniques from religious practice and psychology for listening to the voice of "The Quiet One" through prayer, meditation, role-play, art, dance, and journaling. Each of us needs to explore our own ways to allow this other perspective to touch us. This is the other side of the dialogue we often deny, but it is a necessary step in the transformation of our relationship to one of mutuality.

Although it is beyond the scope of this essay to discuss these techniques, we can imagine what the water symbol might say. "Don't pollute me!" "Why do you assume I can purify anything you dump into me?" "You cannot live without me. Why do you not care for me when you expect me to care for you?" "I rain on the good and the evil."

Out of the work of both amplification and listening to the realm of nature, we can uncover various projections that are distorting our perception of nature. We can realize now that the rituals demonstrate common projections about nature in patriarchy. Some of these are that water is a good place to dump human wastes. Water will take care of pollution and purify it for us. Water is a means to an end.

At this point, we might object and say, "Hey, that's not what I intended! I don't mean to perceive nature in that patriarchal paradigm." Now we are aware, whereas before we were unconscious of how this mind-set still contaminates our thinking. In this way we make the projection conscious and own it as another piece of ourselves that needs transforming. This is a positive act because it shows us the edge of our growth and we have the opportunity to grow a little more in awareness. It also teaches us humility and that we share a common struggle with all humanity for enlightenment.

Our work with the symbol is based on the values of ecofeminist consciousness. It is the value of interconnection that revealed that something was amiss with polluting the water and letting it take the problem away, as if the water were entirely separate from us. If we are truly interconnected, the water will return to us, as indeed it does. The symbol of water carries within it the implication of interconnection both within our bodies and in the outer world. Clearly, ecofeminists must stress this aspect, because it is the one that has been denied in patriarchal thinking.

Diversity is also within the symbol, but the ritual limited our perception of water to one aspect: purification. When we flatten symbols of nature into one aspect, we are unable to listen to the voice of nature. The symbol becomes a mere literal sign that cannot transform our viewpoint. The ritual becomes anthropocentric and the same old pattern of domination of nature is reinstated. This is what happened in all three rituals. If the ritual focuses on the diversity of the meaning of symbols, then our projections can be challenged more readily within the ritual itself. Furthermore, the value of diversity can guide us in our selection of many symbols for nature (not just water, fruit, and flowers but cows and pigs, birds and snakes, weeds and leaves, dirt and sand, wind and rain). Rituals based on ecofeminist values open up the opportunity for mutuality and dialogue between nature and the human community. In this way, ecofeminist values clarify the process of consciousness transformation and give us guidance in the creation of truly ecofeminist rituals.

The same process can be applied to any symbol of nature. In the third ritual, the flowers would be amplified and projections uncovered. Although in the dying vigil the projections onto nature seem harmless, it is serving to preserve the same old way of thinking about nature and humanity. If ecofeminists do not treat symbols of nature in ways that increase ecofeminist understanding, then who will? As we explore what it means to be in mutual relationship with the earth, our use of symbols in rituals needs to be included. One way is to focus on the nature symbols directly. This means developing ritual space for the purpose of listening to nature through a wide variety of symbols. Starhawk makes the same point as she suggests we meditate and play with symbols until they reveal their meaning directly.[3] What does this oak tree mean to me here today? What does this acorn on the altar have to say to us?

As Jung has emphasized, working with symbols is always a dialogue process. "I see the tree and the tree sees me," as Maria Harris expresses it.[4] "I see the tree" is a one-sided dialogue with my projections dominating (anthropocentric), but to add the second part, "the tree sees me," creates a true dialogue between two separate but connected entities. This is the mutuality paradigm shift that ecofeminism advocates. It happens when we listen to the voice of nature through symbolic awareness. Since we ecofeminists desire changes in society concerning the environment, we should begin by engaging the symbols of nature in our own rituals and poems in order to tap into their transforming power. We can be agents of change only if we understand how our own consciousness is transformed. Through symbolic awareness the voice of nature can teach us to live in mutuality with the earth. Are we listening?

The Woods Speak

I sit here and listen
I sit here and listen
Here on the gray stone
Perched high on the ridge facing north.

I listen for the woods
The voice of the land
A movement of perception
Among the trees, under the leaves.

I sit so still
The drone of the traffic
Glides up the creek bottom
Megaphoning across the ridge into my face.

Above me, thick clouds back up
Air traffic at DFW,
They can not shield
The moaning groan falling on my head.

If these invasions were not enough
To the west
A monstrous bulldozer digs a pipeline trench
Fills the air with its beeping alarm.

Alarm! Alarm! ever-pulsing alarm
How can the animals know
Or the trees believe
The alarm is not for them?

At least for now
It tolls to warn others
Down by the road
The far side of the woods.

I sit here and listen
My dog sniffing crunchy leaves
Finally I hear my own breath
And I know I'm getting closer.

Sit, Amber! and listen—
These woods entirely invaded
Encroached from all directions
It is not silenced yet!

Sit here and listen with me
Something is about to be heard
Listen as if your ears
Opened from your heart.

Suddenly grace appears,
The giant yellow owl flies up toward the east
Wings spanning dinosaur-like,
Rain softly falling.

The living woods that want to speak
Blesses abundantly all creatures who come

> Come sit here and listen,
> The woods will teach you and you will know.
>   T. W., Grapevine, Texas

NOTES

1. Because I see Jungian theory as applicable to ecofeminist thought, I have altered sexist language wherever it appears in the quotations that follow from Jung's work.

2. The phenomenon of projection is similar to the literary concept called "absent referent." Carol J. Adams (1990) describes this concept in relation to women and meat in her book.

3. Starhawk (1979, 81). See the double spiral visualization as a good example of playing with symbols (82).

4. For two examples of rituals in which the focus is listening to nature, see Harris (1989, 54, 83).

10

The Good Mother

From Gaia to Gilead

ELLEN CRONAN ROSE

Close reading of current environmental literature suggests that lurking just below the surface of quite justified concern about the increasingly disjunctive relationship between humans and nature is a knotted lump of unexamined anxiety about gender, sexuality, and reproduction. While it is reasonable to worry that pollution of the ecosystem and unchecked exploitation of the planet's resources may imperil both human reproduction (see Castleman 1985, U.S. Office of Technology Assessment 1985) and the reproductiveness of the planet itself, in certain discourses that deploy the concept of "mother earth," this legitimate concern is charged with particular emotion by what might be called "reproductive anxiety."

I will be discussing scholarly and popular presentations of British chemist James Lovelock's hypothesis (named Gaia for the Greek earth goddess) that this planet is a living organism, and selections from a recent anthology of essays by environmental feminists (ecofeminists) who find inspiration in "the myths and symbols of ancient Goddess cultures in which creation was imaged as female and the Earth was revered as sacred" (Diamond and Orenstein 1990, xi). It will be easy for women readers (especially feminists) to detect in male

Ellen Cronan Rose teaches English and women's studies at Drexel University in Philadelphia. She has written extensively on contemporary women writers and feminist theory. Her most recent book, coauthored with Carey Kaplan, is *The Canon and the Common Reader*. She and Kaplan are currently writing a book that sees anxiety about (biological) reproduction—from *Tristram Shandy* to *Rust v. Sullivan*—as a vehicle for other unarticulated malaises, in particular, anxiety about the reproduction of knowledge.

rhetoric about "mother earth" men's terror of maternal power and strenuous effort to deny or neutralize it, their guilt at having offended mother, their desperate need to assure themselves of their importance to her and her over-whelming concern for them. But although contemporary Western women may not manifest the same anxieties about "mother earth" as their male counter-parts, the rhetoric of some ecofeminists does not strike me as free from repro-ductive anxiety.

Since Francoise d'Eaubonne coined the term *ecofeminisme* in 1974, feminist anthropologists, historians, scientists, theologians, and poets have commented on the near universal association of women and nature.[1] In Western civilization, this association has led to and in many instances justified men's exploitation of both nature's and women's productive and reproductive capacities, since both women and nature are seen in patriarchal thought as "other" than and inferior to men and culture.

Feminists have responded in various ways to the traditional association of. women with nature. "Rational" feminists,[2] following Simone de Beauvoir, repu-diate the woman-nature connection because emphasizing women's "natural" procreative capacities mires them in what Beauvoir called "repetition and immanence," excluding them from cultural production (Beauvoir 1952, 57–58). Radical (sometimes called "cultural") feminists, on the other hand, accept and affirm the woman-nature connection; they form the dominant group among contemporary ecofeminists. While acknowledging that patriarchal culture has emphasized the connection between women and nature in order to exploit both, writers such as Mary Daly and Susan Griffin believe women should proudly assert their difference from men and reclaim their "natural" creativity, intui-tion, emotion, and spirituality. Both rational and radical feminists implicitly if not explicitly accept the notion that there is a dichotomy between nature and culture. Socialist feminists such as Carolyn Merchant, however, believe that "nature" (like "woman") is "historically and socially constructed" (Merchant 1990, 103).

In *The Death of Nature*, Merchant charts the transition that took place in Europe in the seventeenth century from an "organic" to a "mechanical" con-struction of nature. In 1500, peasants and philosophers alike thought of nature as a living organism, conceptualized as female. Nature, especially the earth, was seen as "a nurturing mother: a kindly beneficent female who provided for the needs of mankind." The "wild and uncontrollable" aspects of nature—storms, droughts, floods—were also associated with the female sex (Merchant 1980, 2). In the seventeenth century, "the metaphor of the earth as a nurturing mother was gradually to vanish as a dominant image as the Scientific Revolution proceeded to mechanize and to rationalize the world view," while at the same time the image of nature as disorderly female led to the witch trials and the idea of asserting "power over nature." In brief, "an organically oriented men-tality in which female principles played an important role was undermined and replaced by a mechanically oriented mentality that either eliminated or used female principles in an exploitative manner" (Ibid.).

Merchant says that "the image of the earth as a living organism and nurturing mother had served as a cultural constraint restricting the actions of human beings":

> One does not readily slay a mother, dig into her entrails for gold, or mutilate her body. . . . As long as the earth was considered to be alive and sensitive, it could be considered a breach of human ethical behavior to carry out destructive acts against it. (Ibid., 3)

Her discussion of the Renaissance pastoral tradition—in which nature was depicted as virgin nymph and earth mother—reveals, however, that such imagery does not necessarily lead to respect for nature's or women's autonomy and integrity:

> While the pastoral tradition symbolized nature as a benevolent female, it contained the implication that nature when plowed and cultivated could be used as a commodity and manipulated as a resource. . . . It depended on a masculine perception of nature as a mother and bride whose primary function was to comfort, nurture, and provide for the well-being of the male. (Ibid., 8–9)

In both *The Death of Nature* and *Ecological Revolutions*, Merchant shows not only that both Europe and what is now the United States passed from a pre-industrial organic to a capitalist mechanistic worldview, but that whatever "mother" means to a given culture will metaphorically infect the meanings it attaches to mother earth. The American counterpart to the Renaissance pastoral tradition was the nineteenth-century nature romanticism of Thoreau, who wrote as a son and lover of mother nature, to whom at Walden Pond he retreated for sustenance and solace from the crass industrialism of Concord (Merchant 1989, 254–58). The nineteenth-century doctrine of separate spheres echoes in contemporary rhetoric about mother nature's beneficent influence. According to nineteenth-century bourgeois ideology, "as mother and wife, woman embodied the moral law. Her home was the space in which she instilled morals in her husband and children. Both a morally uprighteous mother and a healthy natural environment were necessary to produce a healthy child" (Ibid., 245). Not only children, but men as well, were encouraged to view nature as "mother nature," with exactly the same respect (and expectations) they had for (and of) middle-class mothers. The farmer was idealized in the bourgeois imagination; he could sit at his hearth in the evening, refreshing himself "with his affectionate wife and smiling children," while "his corn ripens, his garden flourishes, and mother earth bountifully rewards him for all his toil," just as no doubt his wife did (quotations from nineteenth-century sources, cited in Merchant 1989, 246).[3]

Fifteen years ago, well before the efflorescence of contemporary ecofeminism, Rosemary Ruether cautioned women to "look with suspicion on the symbolic role they will be asked to play in an ecological crisis analyzed within patriarchal culture":

Any effort to reconcile such a male with "nature," which does not restruc-
ture the psychology and social patterns which make nature "alien," will
tend to shape women, the patriarchal symbol of "nature," into romanticized servitude to a male-defined alienation. The concern with ecology
could repeat the mistakes of nineteenth-century romanticism with its
renewed emphasis on the opposite, "complementary natures" of men and
women. Women will again be asked to be the "natural" wood-nymph and
earth mother and to create places of escape from the destructive patterns
of the dominant culture. (Ruether 1975, 203)

Despite Ruether's warning and Merchant's meticulous scholarship, many
contemporary ecofeminists have applauded the revival of mother earth rhetoric.
Deploring the "demothering" of nature in her book on women, ecology, and
development in India, Vandana Shiva (1988, 18) welcomes the appropriation
of "mother earth" imagery by various contemporary environmental groups:

The symbolism of Terra Mater, the earth in the form of the Great Mother,
creative and protective, has been a shared but diverse symbol across space
and time, and ecology movements in the West today are inspired in large
part by the recovery of the concept of Gaia, the earth goddess. (42)[4]

Many radical ecofeminists have felt empowered by a return to nature-based
religions and a revival of goddess spirituality. Writers such as Carol Christ,
Riane Eisler, Monica Sjöö and Barbara Mor, Charlene Spretnak, Starhawk,
and Merlin Stone[5] celebrate ancient traditions that honor women's power and
creativity, above all, the capacity they share with nature of giving life. "We
would not have been interested in 'Yahweh with a skirt,' " Spretnak explains:

What was intriguing was the sacred link between the Goddess in her many
guises and totemic animals and plants, sacred groves, and womblike caves,
in the moon-rhythm blood of menses, the ecstatic dance — the experience
of *knowing* Gaia, her voluptuous contours and fertile plains, her flowing
waters that give life, her animal teachers. (Spretnak 1990, 5, emphasis in
the original)

Ynestra King says radical feminists' "recognition of women as embodied,
earthbound living beings who should celebrate their connection to the rest of
life" is supported by James Lovelock's Gaia hypothesis (King 1989, 112). Riane
Eisler says Lovelock's theory is in essence a "scientific update of the belief
system of Goddess-worshipping prehistoric societies" in which "the world was
viewed as the great Mother, a living entity who in both her temporal and
spiritual manifestations creates and nurtures all forms of life" (Eisler 1990, 26).
Yet a careful reading of Lovelock does not suggest that he subscribes to this
belief system. Nor does Michael Tobias's *Voice of the Planet*, the science fiction
realization of Lovelock's hypothesis that, in Tobias's words, "this entire Earth
is a living planet, a singular organism with its own agenda and wants" (57).[6] In

fact, both *Voice of the Planet* and Lovelock's own exposition of his hypothesis demonstrate that endorsing the concept of "mother earth" may be hazardous for women.

Voice of the Planet was displayed prominently in chain bookstores in July 1990. The title bisected the familiar image of the whole earth, photographed by NASA from the moon. A banner across the top of the cover informed the potential reader that this novel would be "coming this fall as a major TBS miniseries."[7] Turning to the inside front cover, one read that *Voice of the Planet* would be "an unprecedented international event" that would "usher in the decade of the 1990s, a period in which human civilization must be more concerned about the environment than ever before." The project was endorsed by Denis Hayes, Chair and CEO of Earth Day 1990.

Viewers of the ten-hour series, like readers of the book from which it derives, can expect to learn a lot about the origins of life on earth, evolution, population, pollution, global warming, the danger of species extinction, the absolute value of the Amazonian rain forest. But generic imperatives, combined with the economic realities of commercial television, can be counted on to produce enough drama and human interest to make the ecological lectures palatable. Fictionalizing the Gaia Hypothesis involves turning Lovelock's hypothetical "organism" into a character—the "voice" of the book's title—to be played by Faye Dunaway in the miniseries. William Shatner has been cast as the narrator-protagonist, William Hope Planter.[8]

Two plots can be discerned in *Voice of the Planet*. The first is an "ecological" plot, which proceeds on two chronological tracks. One follows a year in the life of William Hope Planter, an ecologist on sabbatical from Cal Tech to write a book on the "history of human impact on earth" (Tobias 1990, 16). A series of mysterious messages begin appearing on any computer he works on, all signed "Gaia, Thyangboche, Namaste," words Planter believes refer to "the ancient Greek Goddess of Earth," a famous Buddhist monastery in Nepal, and the Tibetan version of "shalom" (6). So summoned, as he feels, he sets off for Thyangboche, where he discovers a computer that begins to "talk" to him, first by displaying messages on the monitor, then by speaking aloud. For a year, "Gaia," who claims to be the voice of planet earth, instructs Planter about "man's"[9] place in and impact on the ecosystem.

This instruction proceeds along a second chronological track, as—through a series of strange and miraculous time-and-space journeys the special-effects people will delight in transferring to the television screen—Gaia takes Planter from the mineral beginnings of life on Iceland to a Greek island in 800 B.C.E. to London in the times of Malthus and Marx to present-day Bangladesh, Antarctica, and the Amazonian rain forest to an extraterrestrial fantasy-nightmare set in 2457 A.D.

The theme of *Voice of the Planet*'s ecological plot is as straightforward as its chronology. Earth is an exquisitely balanced ecosystem, endangered only (but critically) by "man's" arrogant interventions. It is our home, and we must learn restraint (315) and respect for it and all the species who cohabit with us.

Unwittingly, I think, Michael Tobias has encoded within this educational project a psychological (and sexual) plot that may reveal his own unacknow-ledged anxieties about "the intellectual and emotional aftermaths" of the "ambiguous collisions" (4) between "man" and nature. If the book and the TV miniseries enjoy popular success, it may be because others are similarly anxious.

When William Hope Planter begins receiving strange messages on his com-puter, he attributes them to a (male) hacker. But when, in Nepal, he finally hears the "voice" of the computer that is the source of those messages, it turns out to be female—"addulcent and all-coaxing . . . matriarchal, randy" (17).

Pressed by Planter to tell him "who, or what" she is, Gaia answers with a string of goddess's names that firmly establish her as mother earth in many of her religious and mythological manifestations: "Ajyst, Siberian, Birth-giver; Atira, North American, Mother Earth" and so on through Tiamat, Hera, Freya, Juno, and ending with "Macha, Irish, Fertility Goddess . . ." "And you are a child," she "whispers" to Planter (92-93).

If Gaia is Mother Earth and "man" her child, the feelings the man William Hope Planter has for the character named Gaia in *Voice of the Planet* reveal profound anxiety about "man's" importance in the ecological scheme, and the relationship he establishes with her, however ultimately consoling, is strenuously negotiated.

Planter's description of Gaia's voice as "matriarchal, randy" (17) is an Oed-ipal oxymoron the novel's psychological plot dramatizes. His relations with Gaia are complex and contradictory. On the one hand, she is "totally in charge" (26), as she takes him on a series of time and space journeys, lectures him on the origins of life, the nature of energy, the way the planet regulates population. He admits that "her agenda baffles" him (57). Her power can be terrifying:

> Inside, she's inside my gut, my loins. . . . She controls me, drives me into battle, knows my past, divines my future. I'm lost in her power. Tears. I haven't cried in half a lifetime. She's all around me. I can't escape. Slowly, surrender proclaims itself. I have absolutely no choice. (Tobias 1990, 103)

At the same time, Planter describes her as "flattered" (27) when he calls her by name, uses words like "petite" (27) or "minuettish" (108) to describe the sound of her voice, which he says "is rich in softness and wit, intelligence and the erotic" (268).

Three days after he arrives in Nepal and meets her, he writes in his diary, "Since our first spat we've danced around one another with both typewritten and verbal flirtation" (19). The book records many of these flirtatious exchanges.[10] Planter has "the sense that behind the veneer of smooth glass and painted wood [of the computer] sits a grinning beast consumed by erotic impulses, brute and disembodied, eager to be brought to life" (62). Gaia's "monitor is bright blue, the mechanical love machine—her inner eye, like a piston enveloping itself in masturbatory rhythm—floods the room with sexual light" (259). He is "convinced that our little forays excite her" (259). Frequently she orders him to "stroke me," which means he is to spin prayer wheels attached to the computer. She says this "helps stimulate data" (68) but it certainly sounds sexy ("Please. Do me!" [68]).

Gaia's potentially incestuous randiness is channeled into maternal concern for Planter's comfort. Once, she says "you haven't been eating enough" (171), and he retorts, "you're beginning to sound just like my mother" (172). For a while, like a Jewish mama with a telekinetic kitchen, she feeds him Lucullan meals because he doesn't like the monastery diet. She later provides him a night's lovemaking with a Bengali girl because she wants him to "taste" what she describes as the "natural" sexuality of people intimately connected with the soil (236-37). So great is Gaia's maternal concern for her "child" that the balance of power between them shifts. Most of the novel is narrated by Planter, with occasional interjections by an omniscient third-person-implied author. For the most part, therefore, we hear Gaia only in conversation with Planter, who is our guide to interpreting her words and actions. Chapter 3, however, opens with three pages written in the first person, from Gaia's point of view, watching Planter take an early morning swim. "I cannot help but wonder: What small miracle is man?" (95), she marvels, and that generic "man" is indistinguishable from the particular man she's observing: "He fascinates me. In getting to him, I have discovered the devil, the saint, the ultimate bore, and the original infant" (95). "It's been just over two months since William arrived here. I took to him at once, with his goofy smile and his insatiable curiosity" (96).

Gaia not only "takes to" Planter, she comes to depend on him. Planter occasionally thinks that Gaia is God (228, 267, 338). He is frustrated on occasion that she eludes his comprehension:

> On the screen before me is Gaia's shadow form again. I can make out lips—or imagine them—speaking through the aura of a force as ancient and complete as any in the universe. I know it to be divine. I know it to be the Earth. And yet I still can't touch her, know her for real. It's as if the closer I come, the more I doubt my own perceptions. A fine state I'm in! (Tobias 1990, 286)

But he is reassured by Gaia's insistence that she "needs" him. In a chapter about species extinction, he sees on the monitor "Gaia's personal heartthrob, the one image I know to be her own. It expands and contracts like some weird, alien muscle or tendon that I have always perceived as sexual. But this day I see through to its melancholy. Slowly, dolorous and blind, the image is groping for support." Her words confirm his suspicion: "I need you, William. I need to trust you" (298). The chapter concludes with his assuring her that

> We ["man"] love life, goddamnit! We also want the cold Amazon head-waters of peace and childhood. I want it for my own boy, and for his kids. I want it for the jaguar and the python, for the red howler monkeys and the green parakeets. I want it for the blue sky and the stars at night. . . . I want it for us all. I want—*you*, Gaia. Do you understand?

She answers, "I want you too, William" (320). When he asks how he can "reach" her, Gaia answers, in effect, that it's up to him to save the planet: "You must extend your loving heart to the whole of creation. You are the shepherds. It's solely in your power to spread love on this Earth" (321). Planter's reaction mingles modesty with pride:

> For all of her powers Gaia has never indicated a willingness or capacity to heal things herself. . . . From nearly the very first day of our acquaintance, she saw gold in me. She believed in redemption which stood six feet tall, had blue eyes, and could shed a tear. . . . I feel rather good inside to reflect on these matters; to see that I'm part of her story, however bumbling and cantankerous I must be in her mind. (Tobias 1990, 342–43)

Planter feels "an inner directive, a certainty that she will watch over me, and that Gaia will always be there" (346-47), which is put to the test in the novel's last chapter, a futuristic fantasy of what might happen should "man's" dream of extraterrestrial colonization come true. Planter begins the chapter claiming this dream as innately human, recalling how as a child he had a tree house and "used to climb up everything I could get my hands on" (360). Gaia agrees that "everything about your ["man's"] history indicates a prodigal's readiness to renounce yours truly" (362), and then—ever the solicitous mother—says "I just don't want you to get hurt. It's easy to fall out of treehouses" (363). She goes on: "The universe, William, is cold and heartless. . . . Only the Earth has the patience to nurture and care for you" (366). Planter detects "fear" in Gaia's voice when she says, "The Earth, William is your thread. Don't lose it" (367).

To teach him how important she is to him, Gaia then subjects Planter to a nightmare experience in a technological "reproduction" of earth's biosphere on another planet, populated by robots. She rescues him, though, because, as she tells him, "In the heart of a galaxy more accustomed to turmoil, you are a living, breathing miracle with a wonderful destiny in store for you! An exclusive destiny on Earth, if you are only mature enough to see it. . . . There is no artificial substitute for evolution, William" (385). She adds, "And try finding another woman who will put up with your species, with all of its dirty laundry; try finding another woman who will feed you, nurse you, and care for you unerringly, during good times and bad times." Gaia then disappears from the computer, saying "William, take care of yourself, will you? And remember—there is a still, small voice within every organism that cries out for love." Her final words confirm Planter's "inner directive": "I love you, William Hope Planter. I will always love you. And your children and their children. I could count the ways. For as many thousands of years as you and your kind inhabit this Earth" (386).

This comforting assurance of "Mother Earth's" beneficence has been negotiated carefully throughout the preceding 388 pages to counter Planter's sense of earth's power, mystery, and ultimate indifference to "man." His psychological need to feel important, valuable, singular is severely threatened by the evidence he acquires during his time-and-space voyages that nature's "harmony" (131) values the whole more than the individual, that Antarctic krill are as valuable as humans, that "man" is not the apex of creation but nature's greatest menace. As Gaia ruthlessly points out, "Your brief, blood-bespattered history interrupts a good thing, a flawless system of checks and balances" (320). Planter admits that the evidence makes him feel "guilty as shit" (315). To avoid both guilt and responsibility, he suppresses the shocking insight that:

> I *hate* the gullible in Gaia. Her innocence has bothered me from the very first day of our meeting. I'm not sure why that is. Perhaps I project an inevitable rape of that innocence, of which I am the perpetrator. I detest that which I desire, but cannot possess. (331, emphasis in the original)

Instead, he emphasizes Gaia's erotic attraction to and maternal concern for him, and her need for his protection.

James Lovelock's exposition of the Gaia Hypothesis is as riddled with male anxiety about maternal power as Michael Tobias's commercial popularization of it. Lovelock concludes his 1979 book, *Gaia: A New Look at Life on Earth*, advocating cultivation of the awareness that humans are "an integral part of the biosphere" (148), a sentiment that pleases ecofeminists and "deep" ecologists.[11] But, unlike them, he emphasizes the cost of acquiring ecological consciousness.[12] Moreover, Lovelock emphatically denies that Gaia has a "spiritual" dimension, or even intelligence of a more than rudimentary kind, comparable to that manifested by the human body's "automatic temperature-regulating system" or an oven thermostat (Lovelock 1979, 146). Rather, he suggests, "we as a species [may] constitute a Gaian nervous system and a brain which can consciously anticipate environmental changes" (147):

> The evolution of *homo sapiens*, with his technological inventiveness and his increasingly subtle communications network, has vastly increased Gaia's range of perception. She is now through us awake and aware of herself. She has seen the reflection of her fair face through the eyes of astronauts and the television cameras of orbiting spacecraft. Our sensations of wonder and pleasure, our capacity for conscious thought and speculation, our restless curiosity and drive are hers to share. (Lovelock 1979, 148)[13]

As Patrick D. Murphy has charged, Lovelock's identification of earth as female and *homo sapiens* as male "reinforces androcentrism by rendering the female side of the duality passive" and is thus sexist (Murphy 1988, 157). But the rhetoric of *Gaia* strongly suggests that it is woman in her maternal role who evokes Lovelock's anxiety and defensiveness. The female images and metaphors he uses are specifically maternal. For instance, he uses female biological metaphors to describe the emergence of life on earth: "the very womb of life was flooded" with radioactivity (Lovelock, 17); if a planet loses hydrogen it "will wither and become barren" (18); on earth, "it was warm and comfortable for embryo life" (22).

What does it mean, then, that Lovelock employs a cybernetic model to explain Gaian "intelligence," the system by which the biosphere maintains homeostasis, noting without any irony that the word *cybernetics* derives from the Greek "kubernetes" or (male) "steersman" (48)? Why does he illustrate cybernetics with the example of a thermostat, a "robot grandmother" (created by an engineer) that does what real grandmothers used to do (regulate the oven), only better (51)?

Why, to return to Michael Tobias's fictionalization of Lovelock's hypothesis, does mother earth speak to Planter through a computer rather than, say, a dream or trance? After he has known Gaia a month, Planter records in his diary the observation that "she's a remarkable apparatus, but no self-starter. There was a monk who apparently built her brain, gave her tools—endless programs—to utilize" (Tobias 1990, 56). We learn later that this monk is said to have been a Chinese Buddhist named Lao, who "ate little, drank manly quantities of alcohol, and tinkered from morning until night with whatever he could get his hands on" (227). "Did Lao actually build Gaia?" Planter wonders (228). The question is never answered, but the implication lingers that a male "God" created "mother earth."

If a male engineer can create a robot grandmother and a fictional Buddhist monk a maternal "voice of the planet," James Lovelock makes it abundantly clear that he, a male chemist, "gave birth" to the Gaia hypothesis: "by now (in 1967) a planet-sized entity, albeit hypothetical, had been born" (Lovelock 1979, 10).[14] What Lovelock likes best about his brain child is its "manageability":

At a meeting in London recently, a wise man . . . asked me: "Why do you stop with the Earth? Why not consider if the Solar System, the Galaxy, or even the Universe is alive?" My instant answer was that the concept of a living Earth, Gaia, is manageable. . . . Those millions of Christians who make a special place in their hearts for the Virgin Mary possibly respond as I do. The concept of Jahweh as remote, all-powerful, all-seeing is either frightening or unapproachable. . . . Mary is close and can be talked to. She is believable and manageable. . . . What if Mary is another name for Gaia? Then her capacity of virgin birth is no miracle or parthenogenetic aberration, it is a role of Gaia since life began. . . . For me, Gaia is a religious as well as a scientific concept, and in both spheres it is manageable. (Lovelock 1990, 206)

Many feminist scholars have seen the Virgin Mary as, indeed, a vestige within Christianity of the ancient Goddess religions, but tamed, subdued, desexualized, subservient to God the Father and God the Son. Manageable, in a word. Maternal power, autonomy, and unpredictability appear to have threatened male theologians as well as male scientists and environmental writers.

What would be the consequences, for earth and for women, of a wholesale acceptance of mother earth rhetoric?[15] (I will leave to the ecologists detailed consideration of the consequences to the planet of promulgating the notion of mother earth, although I will mention in passing that rage and resentment as well as love and gratitude are standard filial emotions, and that space exploration offers one way of leaving mother and childhood behind.) In a culture that, despite the women's movement, is still fundamentally patriarchal, for feminists to construct (or at least construe) nature as "mother" and "goddess" virtually *invites* the at best ambivalent, at worst misogynist rhetoric manifested in a book such as *Voice of the Planet*, and the condescension and barely disguised glee of Philip S. Lansky, M.D., who wrote in his column in a New Age magazine:

> The Earth is currently terrified. Now, that's a shocker, isn't it? Great big Earth Goddess. Ol' cosmic Mama herself. The Big Lady quaking in her well worn earth boots. Mama Terra needs some real TLC. Just throwing her into a recyclin' center ain't enough. She's scared. She needs some powerful comfortin'. (Lansky 1990)

Lansky suggests we "read her stories and play her music, like Paul Winter does" (21). In a culture that serializes *Voice of the Planet* on cable television on a channel that calls itself "the environmental network of the '90s"[16] and circulates the New Age magazine that carries Phillip Lansky's column in organic foodstores, one does not help women by emphasizing their maternal status, actual or potential.[17] In such a culture, male views of mothers' value prevail, to the benefit of men and children (especially sons) and at the cost of women's nonreproductive freedoms. "Fetal protection policies" in the workplace, "fetal rights" legislation, erosion of abortion rights, discussion of the "contractual obligations" of "surrogate" mothers, suggest that the idea of maternal solicitude can all too easily segue to the more sinister conception of a (potential) mother as a fetal container. Additionally, in a culture that is increasingly capitalistic, emphasizing women's procreative capacities can encourage viewing them as a "reproductive environment" (Lin Nelson 1990, 180) congenial to exploitation by pharmaceutical interests and the medical establishment.

In a particularly searching article on "The Place of Women in Polluted Places," Lin Nelson (1990) warns women to "be vigilant and determined in the face of those 'protectors'—in education, science, medicine and public health, and economic development—who would use gender and reproductive status (and race, class, susceptibility, and other identifiers) to accommodate us all to an industrial complex ... in a political atmosphere of increasing authoritarianism" (175):

> If women are deemed to be especially vulnerable [to toxic hazards], we may be offered special protections and restrictions and we may be held specially liable for our conduct and whereabouts in a toxic world. Instead of controlling pollution and polluters, we may be subject to more social control. (186)

In Margaret Atwood's novel *The Handmaid's Tale*, a reproductive crisis is brought about by an environmental crisis (toxicity in the environment has rendered most women—and probably men, too—sterile). The Gileadeans' "solution" to this crisis is to attack not environmental pollution but women, exalting and expropriating the reproductive capabilities of some women for the benefit of the state. Continuing capitalist exploitation of natural resources, coupled with regressive social policies and popular culture propaganda shackling women to their (biological) reproductive functions threatens to make this dystopian fiction all too real. Already we are seeing environmental hazards to reproduction[18] similar to those that brought about fictional Gilead's crisis in fertility:

> The air got too full, once, of chemicals, rays, radiation, the water swarmed with toxic molecules, all of that takes years to clean up, and meanwhile they creep into your body, camp out in your fatty cells. Who knows, your very flesh may be polluted, dirty as an oily beach, sure death to shore birds and unborn babies. (Atwood 1985, 143)

Already there are those, like the Gileadean "aunts," who indoctrinate "handmaids" into reproductive service to the state, who characterize prochoice feminists as "unwomen" and "godless" (Atwood 1985, 152-53). Is it implausible to fear that, like the fictional handmaids, real women may come to be seen as "two legged wombs . . . sacred vessels, ambulatory chalices" (176)?

In view of these all too imaginable dystopian possibilities, why do some ecofeminists cling persistently to the idea of mother earth? Marti Kheel draws on object relations psychoanalytic theory to explain why men have particular difficulty acknowledging and asserting their kinship to nature. "If men in our society are socialized to perceive their identity in opposition to a devalued, female-imaged world, we might expect that the process of reinstituting this forbidden identification might be fraught with problems along the way" (Kheel 1990, 131). She hypothesizes that the "process of identification" with nature would be different for women because—again according to object relations theory—"women's identities, unlike men's, have not been established through their elevation over the natural world" (129).

To extrapolate a gendered environmental ethic from psychoanalytic theory, as some ecofeminists seem prepared to do,[19] is a dubious enterprise. As Karen Warren points out, "it mystifies women's experiences to locate women closer to nature than men, just as it underplays important aspects of the oppression of women to deny the connection of women with nature, for the truth is that women, like men, are both connected to nature and separate from it, natural and cultural beings" (Warren 1987, 15). As cultural actors, white middle-class Western women, as well as men, have polluted earth, air, and water; have damaged the ozone layer with their spray deodorants, refrigerators, and air conditioners; have taken the kids to eat hamburgers made from beef grown where once there was rain forest; have diapered their babies with nonbiodegradable diapers. Claiming that we (women) "know" Gaia because of features "she" and "we" share (her "womblike caves," the "moon-rhythm blood of [our] menses" [Spretnak 1990, 5]) may indicate an effort to avoid environmental guilt. But I think there is more to it than that.

If men such as Tobias, Lovelock, and Lansky perceive "mother" as so powerful and mysterious that she must be reduced to erotic object, solicitous cook, robot, or laughingstock, what anxieties might we infer in women who emphasize her "massiveness," her "ever-abidingness," her constancy and dependability, and—over and over—her fruitfulness?[20] Perhaps a clue can be found, paradoxically, in a reference to the destruction of the Amazonian rain forest as "yet another killing blow" to "the fragile womb of planet Earth" (Plant 1989, 2). Women today have reason to worry about both the "fragility" of their wombs and of their claim to the unique ability to reproduce life. Lynn Nelson says that "one of the most sobering aspects of the ecological degradation we endure is the impact on our capacity to bear healthy children":

> In 1984, the Conservation Foundation reported that many scientists suspect or indict industrial pollutants as contributors to rising infertility, clusters of birth defects, "hot spots" of miscarriages, and the unusually early onset of menopause among some women. (Nelson 1990, 177)

While the "reproductive hazards" of the workplace (including infertility) may be of paramount concern to middle- and working-class women in the first world, poor and third-world women (especially women of color) are at risk because of their putative unwillingness to limit their fertility. In the United States, "the federal government assumes 90 percent of the cost of most sterilizations under Medicaid at the same time that it pays for only a miniscule number of abortions," a "funding disparity" that "amounts to a government policy of population control targeted at poor people and people of color" (Committee 1988, 28). In the third world, what Betsy Hartmann calls "the population establishment" (the Agency for International Development, the United Nations Fund for Population Activities, the World Bank, the International Planned Parenthood Foundation, the Population Council, the Ford Foundation, and numerous private agencies) aggressively sponsors population control programs that "have sacrificed women's health and safety in the indiscriminate promotion of hormonal contraception, the IUD, and sterilization" (Hartmann 1987, xv).

Meanwhile, recent developments in reproductive technology might lead even women not prone to paranoia to wonder whether men are trying to usurp women's hitherto indispensable function of reproducing the species. Only one of these technologies—artificial insemination by donor (AID)—can be said unequivocally to enhance at least some women's (lesbians') control of their reproductive capacities. The rest—from in vitro fertilization, embryo transfer, and techniques for sex determination and predetermination to as yet experimental technologies enabling cloning and the creation of an artificial placenta—at best render women's reproductive consciousness as "discontinuous" as men's (Hanmer 1983, 188), at worst make women feel as irrelevant to human reproduction as men might have felt in prehistoric goddess cultures (see O'Brien 1981). Confronted by hazards to, loss of control over, and potential usurpation of their reproductive capacities and choices, women might well feel anxiety, which some may attempt to solace with imagery that affirms women's power, agency, and boundless fecundity.

Even women who do not perceive developments in reproductive technology as a sinister patriarchal plot to render them obsolete may share with (some) men the fear that technology is running amok, that—as in Michael Tobias's futuristic nightmare of a genetically engineered biosphere maintained by heartless, antihuman robots—life in the twenty-first century may be unlivable. Jalna Hanmer quotes an "inclusive definition" of technological reproduction from the *Journal of the American Medical Association* that was adopted by a congressional subcommittee on science, research, and development. Its offhand remark that "manufacture" is "better" than (re)production is chilling:

> [Technological reproduction is] anything to do with the manipulation of the gametes [eggs or sperm] or the fetus, for whatever purpose, from conception other than by sexual union, to treatment of disease in utero, to the ultimate manufacture of a human being to exact specifications. . . . Thus the earliest procedure . . . is artificial insemination; next . . . artificial fertilization . . . next artificial implantation . . . in the future total extra corporeal gestation . . . and finally, what is popularly meant by [reproductive] engineering, the production—or better, the biological manufacture—of a human being to desired specification. (Quoted in Hanmer 1983, 183, ellipses in Hanmer)

The thought that it is we who have damaged the planet so seriously that the harm may be irreparable, we who have elevated technology to godhood, can only intensify our terror. And so, women as well as men, we cry for mommy.

Carroll Smith-Rosenberg says that during times of social upheaval, people "seek through imagery and myth to mitigate their feelings of helplessness." The more extreme and pervasive the social crisis, she asserts, the more likely it is that "bodily and familial imagery will assume ascendancy." Under great stress, "individuals will revert to their most primitive experience of human interaction and social ordering" (Smith-Rosenberg 1985, 90). The closing decades of the twentieth century have been jarred by a series of political, economic, and existential shocks—among them, the decline of Western hegemony and the consequent realignment of power; the arguable failures of both capitalism and state socialism; and the post-Hiroshima acknowledgment of technology's amorality. A number of commentators have drawn a connection between this set of historic upheavals and the recent upsurge in neo-conservative pro-family rhetoric, but if Smith-Rosenberg is right, the retreat to the family will be apparent at the level of myth and image, as well as of regressive legislation.

The revival of mother earth imagery suggests that, at a time when an ecological and technological crisis of global proportions summons responsible adults to devise creative solutions, there has occurred instead a wholesale regression to infancy, when mother seemed omnipotent. As we have seen, this evokes masculine anxiety, hostility, and consoling fantasies of leaving (mother) earth behind for the brave new world of Biosphere II. Mother earth rhetoric also reveals feminine nostalgia for pre-Oedipal, precultural fusion with a benevolent, all-powerful (imaginary) mother. While neither the masculine nor the feminine fantasy is likely to produce practical solutions to environmental problems, in the current political climate, mother earth mythology may have all too tangible and negative consequences for women.

If reviving mother earth imagery is going to bring out the child in us, then we would be well advised to find a nongendered, nonanthropomorphic way to represent nature. Can we not think of nature as "dynamic and alive," even if "nonhuman" (Merchant 1990, 105)? Can we not care about the earth without personifying it?

Feminist theologian Carol P. Christ suggests that we can. Despite a "human tendency" to construct a "spirit of the universe" and assume "that it cares as we care," Christ avers that "the sight of a field of flowers in the color purple, the rainbow, must be enough to stop us from destroying all that is . . . " (Christ 1990, 69).

NOTES

1. See, for example, Daly (1978), d'Eaubonne (1980), Griffin (1982), Mac-Cormack and Strathern (1980), Merchant (1981, 1989), Ortner (1974), Ruether (1975).

2. I borrow this denomination from Ynestra King, to denote feminists for whom "freedom is being liberated from the primordial realm of women and nature" (see King 1990, 110).

3. Drawing primarily on the psychological theories of Lawrence Kohlberg, Melanie Klein, and Nancy Chodorow, Eva Feder Kittay posits a near-universal male envy of woman's reproductive powers, with wide-reaching consequences for women, including "idealization," "devaluation of the object," and "appropriation" (Kittay 1984, 106). One form of idealization "can take the shape of the idolatry of Mother as Nature and fertility, as in periods of vitalistic romanticism." But, Kittay notes:

> the gifts of maternal nature are for men: periods of romanticism have not been periods in which women have made advances toward autonomy. In idealizing the maternal aspects of women, men reduce the full scope of woman's human capabilities to her reproductive functions; by sentimentalizing an ideal mother, men can vent their envious anger on the actual woman who fails to meet the measure of the ideal. To see such idealizations as manifestations of men's womb envy is to understand why they of necessity go hand in hand with the actual oppression of women, the more direct expression of the envy which manifests itself when the defense of the idealization breaks down. (Kittay 1984, 107)

4. In both esoteric and exoteric traditions of Hindu cosmology, nature (Prakriti) is symbolized as the embodiment of the female principle (Shakti). As Shiva explains, this is a "non-gender based philosophy" in which "the feminine principle is not exclusively embodied in women, but is the principle of activity and creativity in nature, women and men" (Shiva 1988, 52). I am not so sure as Shiva seems to be that a gender-free notion of "mother" can survive transplant into the Western Jewish and Christian traditions.

5. See, for example, Christ (1987), Eisler (1987), Sjöö and Mor (1987), Spretnak (1981, 1982), Starhawk, (1982, 1986), and Stone (1976).

6. Lovelock's own formulation of the hypothesis is "that the entire range of living matter on Earth, from whales to viruses, and from oaks to algae, could be regarded as constituting a single living entity, capable of manipulating the Earth's atmosphere to suit its overall needs and endowed with faculties and powers far beyond those of its constituent parts" (Lovelock 1979, 9). He also regrets that using the name of the Greek earth goddess to designate the hypothesis makes it "difficult" to avoid speaking of "Gaia as if she were known to be sentient" (x). In fact, Lovelock insists, the "complex entity" that is Gaia is a "cybernetic system" whose activity "may be conveniently described by the term 'homeostasis' " (11).

7. The October 13–19, 1990, issue of *TV Guide* ran a feature story on the series on pp. 10–11 (Wilson 1990). On p. 36, however, it was announced that *"Voice of the Planet* has been silenced, at least for the time being. Just days before the 10-hour environmental miniseries was set to air (Oct. 15–19), TBS jerked it from the schedule, with no new airdate announced. A spokeswoman for TBS said even 'sometime in 1991' was too specific" ("Sudden Move" 1990). In February 1991, TBS finally aired *Voice of the Planet*.

8. The drama I focus on here has little to do with Nielsen ratings and advertising revenue, although it is not unrelated to casting these particular pop cultural icons in the starring roles—the noble, sexually irresistable, and invincible Captain Kirk of *Star Trek* and the actress remembered equally as the sultry vamp of *Chinatown* and the cruel, abusive *Mommie Dearest*. Interestingly, however, in the one episode of *Voice of the Planet* I was able to see when TBS aired the series in February 1991, all the sexual dynamics in Tobias's text were muted. The final episode of *Voice of the Planet* might have been an episode of *Nova* or a *National Geographic* special. It featured spectacular footage of Himalayan alps and Japanese tea ceremonies, accompanied by almost perfunctory voice-overs by Shatner and Dunaway.

9. I put "man" in quotation marks to indicate, however awkwardly, my perception of the gendered drama the assumption of a generic "he" masks. The "mankind" in *Voice of the Planet* is male.

10. One morning, Gaia informs Planter that during the night his "alpha state rapid eye movement was accompanied by four periods of heavy sexual arousal" and that he had "one bristling erection after another." "What good are they to you?" he asks, and she says ("coyly"), "You'd be surprised" (Tobias 1990, 55). She then asks (again "coyly") why he doesn't grow a beard: "If you don't mind my saying so, Bill, I think you'd look very sexy with a beard" (57). "What would a computer know about sex?" he asks, and she answers "jauntily," "That's twice you've provoked me" (58).

11. Although reform environmentalists (represented by such mainstream groups as the Audubon Society, the National Wildlife Federation, and the Sierra Club) want to preserve and manage natural resources, deep ecologists accuse them of being anthropocentric, of valuing human "quality of life" over the welfare of the entire ecosystem. "At the heart of the [deep ecology] movement," Evan Eisenberg explains, "is the idea that humans have no right to a larger role in nature than racoons". Ecofeminists accuse deep ecologists (with whom otherwise they have much in common) for failing to acknowledge that the problem is not anthropocentrism but androcentrism (a "masculine" alignment of men with culture and women with nature, with men dominating both women and nature). Debates abound in the

philosophical literature about which is more basic, male domination of females and nature or "humans' " domination of the "less than human." In the most sophisticated deep ecology accounts, this means human over nature *and* male over female, white over black, upper class over lower class, heterosexual over homosexual (all the second terms being "less human" than the first terms).

12. "This new interrelationship of Gaia with man is by no means fully established," he writes. "We are not yet a truly collective species, *corralled and tamed* as an integral part of the biosphere, as we are as individual creatures. It may be that the destiny of mankind is to become *tamed*, so that the fierce, destructive, and greedy forces of tribalism and nationalism are fused into a compulsive urge to belong to the commonwealth of all creatures which constitutes Gaia. It might seem to be a *surrender*, but I suspect that the rewards, in the form of an increased sense of well-being and fulfillment, in knowing ourselves to be a dynamic part of a far greater entity, would be worth the loss of tribal freedom" (Lovelock 1979, 148, emphases mine).

13. In an Earth Day 1990 symposium published in *Harper's Magazine* entitled suggestively, "Only Man's Presence Can Save Nature," Frederick Turner asserted that "humankind's efforts are a continuation and extension of [nature's] reproduction, evolution, and improvement. . . . We are promoting nature because *we are nature*. We are the leading edge, the sensitive tip, the cambium of nature" (Pollan, et al. 1990, 48, emphasis in the original). Similar sentiments were expressed by Gregg Easterbrook in *The New Republic*'s 1990 special environmental issue:

> The sequence of evolution may well turn out to be: creation of life; multicellular life; plants; animals; mammals; scheming beings that abuse nature's benevolence; and finally sensible beings that return the favor by extending the gift of life into the infinite environs of space. . . . "Deep" Ecologists see the development of human consciousness as an unadulterated disaster for nature. "Planet Managers" see it as a controllable disaster. Nature herself may consider it a godsend. (Easterbrook 1990, 27)

Compare William Hope Planter as Gaia's "redemption which stood six feet tall, had blue eyes, and could shed a tear" (Tobias 1990, 342).

Both Turner and Lovelock have seriously considered the possibility of reconstructing "Gaia's" biosphere on Mars. Turner is on record as believing that "we are the custodians of life in the universe, and the only plausible vector by which life may propagate itself to other worlds and thus escape the risk that some minor cosmic accident—the impact of a stray asteroid, or a disturbance of the sun's activity—should snuff forever out the first shoots of life" (Turner 1988, 55).

14. Referring to the fact that he developed the Gaia hypothesis while working on NASA's Viking space probe to Mars, Lovelock says, "Thoughts of Gaia will always be linked with space exploration and Mars, for in a sense Mars was her birthplace" (Lovelock 1988, 201).

15. After concluding that the ubiquity of the whole earth image—which adorns the cover of *Voice of the Planet*, for instance, as well as Greenpeace posters and bumper stickers—tells us some very disquieting things about "the fundamental ways in which contemporary culture construes its relationship to nature" (Garb 1990, 265), Yaakov Jerome Garb considers the advisability of replacing it, as some ecofeminists urge, with the image of earth as a goddess, and concludes that "we should

check carefully whether we really want to view our relationship with the Earth through genderized lenses":

> What baggage will carry over from one domain to another (especially in a culture whose relation to both women and mothers is as misogynous as ours is)? What are the consequences—for both Earth and women—of reinforcing this age-old alignment between them. (Garb 1990, 277)

Surprisingly, given his concern, Garb does not consider certain posters and bumper stickers where the injunction "Love Your Mother" is attached to the whole earth image.

16. An ad in *TV Guide* in August 1990 read as follows:

> First there was Sports TV, then there was Music TV, now there is Eco TV: Network Earth. Network Earth. The first-ever video magazine on the environment. Upbeat and aware. Ecologically in tune. Your connection to the state of the earth. And your chance to become involved. Premiering Sunday, 11 p.m. on TBS. The environmental network of the '90s. (*TV Guide* 1990, 83)

17. Jeffner Allen says that "motherhood is dangerous to women. If woman, in patriarchy, is she who exists as the womb and wife of man, every woman is by definition a mother: she who produces for the sake of men. A mother is she whose body is used as a resource to reproduce men and the world of men, understood both as the biological children of patriarchy and as the ideas and material goods of patriarchal culture. Motherhood is dangerous to women because it continues the structure within which females must be women and mothers and, conversely, because it denies to females the creation of a subjectivity and world that is open and free" (Allen 1984, 315).

18. Reproductive anxiety surfaces even in the pragmatic booklet put out by a California environmental group to commemorate Earth Day 1990. *50 Simple Things You Can Do to Save the Earth* is dedicated "to the not-yet-born" (Earth Works Group 1989, 2).

19. In addition to Kheel, see Cheney (1987) and Garb (1990). See also Michael E. Zimmerman's critique of radical ecofeminism (Zimmerman 1987).

20. One contributor to a recent collection of ecofeminist essays suggests that to cultivate ecological sensitivity, we should begin each day with this meditation:

> Breathe. Feel the air enter your lungs. . . . Mother is feeding you. She feeds you and sustains your life with every breath. . . . Penetrate the ground with your consciousness as though you were growing roots into the Earth. Deeper and deeper. Sense her massiveness. Her ever-abidingness. Feel her love. Allow her love to flow into you, up through the soles of your feet, through your legs and torso to your heart, your shoulders, your head. Bathe in her love. Breathe. Let her love permeate every cell. Let your heart fill with her love. Let it swell with love, from her, for her.
>
> > She nurtures you in every way.
> > The air you breathe is her.
> > The food you eat is her.

Let your love and gratitude grow. . . .
(Russell 1990, 223, ellipses mine)

Reciting this meditation is supposed to help one become aware of oneself "as an integral part of the body of humanity, and the body of humanity as a child of Mother Earth, still cradled in her womb with all our brothers and sisters of the plant and animal kingdoms" (Russell 1990, 229-30).

11

For All Those Who Were Indian
in a Former Life

ANDY SMITH

The New Age movement has sparked a new interest in Native American traditional spirituality among white women who claim to be feminists. Indian spirituality, with its respect for nature and the interconnectedness of all things, is often presented as the panacea for all individual and global problems. Not surprisingly, many white "feminists" see the opportunity to make a great profit from this new craze. They sell sweat lodges or sacred pipe ceremonies, which promise to bring individual and global healing. Or they sell books and records that supposedly describe Indian traditional practices so that you, too, can be Indian.

On the surface, it may appear that this new craze is based on a respect for Indian spirituality. In fact, however, the New Age movement is part of a very old story of white racism and genocide against the Indian people. The "Indian" ways that these white, New Age "feminists" are practicing have little grounding in reality.

True spiritual leaders do not make a profit from their teachings, whether it's through selling books, workshops, sweat lodges, or otherwise. Spiritual leaders teach the people because it is their responsibility to pass what they have learned from their elders to the younger generations. They do not charge for their services.

Furthermore, the idea that an Indian medicine woman would instruct a white woman to preach the "true path" of Indian spirituality sounds more reminiscent

Andy Smith (Cherokee) is a member of Women of All Red Nations in Chicago (4511 N. Hermitage, Chicago, Ill. 60640). She is also the Woman of Color Caucus chair for the National Coalition Against Sexual Assault and is addicted to chocolate and dancing.

of evangelical Christianity than traditional Indian spirituality. Indian religions are community-based, not proselytizing religions. For this reason, there is not *one* Indian religion, as many New Agers would have you believe. Indian spiritual practices reflect the needs of a particular community. Indians do not generally believe that their way is "the" way and, consequently, they have no desire to tell outsiders about their practices. Also, considering how many Indians there are who do not know the traditions, why would a medicine woman spend so much time teaching a white woman? A medicine woman would be more likely to advise a white woman to look into her *own* culture and find what is liberating in it.

However, some white women seemed determined *not* to look into their own cultures for sources of strength. This is puzzling, since pre-Christian European cultures are also earth based and contain many of the same elements that white women are ostensibly looking for in Native-American cultures. This phenomenon leads me to suspect that there is a more insidious motive for latching onto Indian spirituality.

When white "feminists" see how white people have historically oppressed others and how they are coming very close to destroying the earth, they often want to disassociate themselves from their whiteness. They do this by opting to "become Indian." In this way, they can escape responsibility and accountability for white racism.

Of course, white "feminists" want to become only partly Indian. They do not want to be part of our struggles for survival against genocide, and they do not want to fight for treaty rights or an end to substance abuse or sterilization abuse. They do not want to do anything that would tarnish their romanticized notions of what it means to be an Indian.

Moreover, they want to become Indian without holding themselves accountable to Indian communities. If they did, they would have to listen to Indians telling them to stop carrying around sacred pipes, stop doing their own sweat lodges, and stop appropriating our spiritual practices. Rather, these New Agers see Indians as romanticized gurus who exist only to meet their consumerist needs. Consequently, they do not understand our struggles for survival, and thus they can have no genuine understanding of Indian spiritual practices.

While New Agers may think that they are escaping white racism by becoming "Indian," they are in fact continuing the same genocidal practices of their forebears. The one thing that has maintained the survival of Indian people through 500 years of colonialism has been the spiritual bonds that keep us together. When the colonizers saw the strength of our spirituality, they tried to destroy Indian religions by making them illegal. They forced Indian children into white missionary schools and cut their tongues if they spoke their Native languages. Sundances were made illegal, and Indian participation in the Ghost Dance precipitated the Wounded Knee massacre. The colonizers recognized that it was our spirituality that maintained our spirit of resistance and sense of community. Even today, Indians do not have religious freedom: In a recent ruling, the Supreme Court has determined that American Indians do not have the right to sue under the American Indian Religious Freedom Act. They have also determined that if Indian religious freedom conflicts with any "compelling" United States interest, then government interest always supersedes Indian peoples' freedom of religion.

Many white New Agers continue this practice of destroying Indian spirituality. They trivialize Native-American practices so that these practices lose their spiritual force, and they have the white privilege and power to make themselves heard at the expense of Native Americans. Our voices are silenced, and consequently, the younger generation of Indians who are trying to find their way back to the Old Ways becomes hopelessly lost in this morass of consumerist spirituality.

These practices also promote the subordination of Indian women to white women. We are told that we are greedy if we do not choose to share our spirituality. Apparently, it is our burden to service white women's needs rather than to spend time organizing within our own communities. Their perceived need for warm and fuzzy mysticism takes precedence over our need to survive.

The New Age movement completely trivializes the oppression we as Indian women face: Indian women are suddenly no longer the women who are forcibly sterilized and are tested with unsafe drugs such as Depo provera; we are no longer the women who have a life expectancy of 47 years; and we are no longer the women who generally live below the poverty level and face a 75 percent unemployment rate. No, we're too busy being cool and spiritual.

This trivialization of our oppression is compounded by the fact that nowadays anyone can be Indian if s/he wants to. All that is required is that one be Indian in a former life, or take part in a sweat lodge, or be mentored by a "medicine woman," or read a how-to book.

Since, according to this theory, anyone can now be "Indian," then the term *Indians* no longer refers specifically to those people who have survived five-hundred years of colonization and genocide. This furthers the goals of white supremacists to abrogate treaty rights and to take away what little we have left. When everyone becomes "Indian," then it is easy to lose sight of the specificity of oppression faced by those who are Indian in *this* life. It is no wonder we have such a difficult time finding non-Indians to support our struggles when the New Age movement has completely disguised our oppression.

The most disturbing aspect about these racist practices is that they are promoted in the name of feminism. Sometimes it seems that I can't open a feminist periodical without seeing ads promoting white "feminist" practices with little medicine wheel designs. I can't seem to go to a feminist conference without the only Indian presenter being the woman who begins the conference with a ceremony. Participants then feel so "spiritual" after this opening that they fail to notice the absence of Indian women in the rest of the conference or the fact that there will be nobody discussing any pressing issues in Native-American communities. And I certainly can't go to a feminist bookstore without seeing books by Lynn Andrews and other people who exploit Indian spirituality all over the place. It seems that, while feminism is supposed to signify the empowerment of all women, it obviously does not include Indian women.

If white feminists are going to act in solidarity with their Indian sisters, they must take a stand against Indian spiritual abuse. Feminist book and record stores should stop selling these products, and feminist periodicals should stop advertising these products. Women who call themselves feminists should denounce exploitative practices wherever they see them.

Many have claimed that Indians are not respecting "freedom of speech" by demanding that whites stop promoting and selling books that exploit Indian spirituality. But promotion of this material is destroying freedom of speech for Native Americans by ensuring that our voices will never be heard. Feminists have already made choices about what they will promote (I haven't seen many books by right-wing, fundamentalist women sold in feminist bookstores, since feminists recognize that these books are oppressive to women). The issue is not censorship; the issue is racism. Feminists must make a choice to respect Indian political and spiritual autonomy or to promote materials that are fundamentally racist under the guise of "freedom of speech."

Respecting the integrity of Native people and their spirituality does not mean that there can never be cross-cultural sharing. However, such sharing should take place in a way that is respectful to Indian people. The way to be respectful is for non-Indians to become involved in our political struggles and to develop an ongoing relation with Indian *communities* based on trust and mutual respect. When this happens, Indian people may invite a non-Indian to take part in a ceremony, but it will be on Indian terms.

I hesitate to say even this much about cross-cultural sharing, however, because many white people take this to mean that they can join in our struggles solely for the purpose of being invited to ceremonies. If this does not occur, they feel that Indians have somehow unfairly withheld spiritual teachings from them. We are expected to pay the price in spiritual exploitation in order to gain allies in our political struggles.

When non-Indians say they will help us, but only on their terms, that is not help—that is blackmail. We are not obligated to teach anyone about our spirituality. It is our choice if we want to share with people who we think will be respectful. It is white people who owe it to us to fight for our survival, since they are living on the land for which our people were murdered.

It is also important for non-Indians to build relationships with Indian communities rather than with specific individuals. Many non-Indians express their confusion about knowing who is and who is not a legitimate spiritual teacher. The only way for non-Indians to know who legitimate teachers are is to develop ongoing relationships with Indian *communities*. When they know the community, they will learn who the community respects as its spiritual leaders. This is a process that takes time.

Unfortunately, many white feminists do not want to take this time in their quest for instant spirituality. Profit-making often gets in the way of true sisterhood. However, white feminists should know that as long as they take part in Indian spiritual abuse, either by being consumers of it or by refusing to take a stand on it, Indian women will consider white "feminists" to be nothing more than agents in the genocide of their people.

Our spirituality is not for sale.

12

Toward an Ecofeminist Ethic of Shamanism and the Sacred

GLORIA FEMAN ORENSTEIN

We have recently witnessed a growing interest in Shamanism and sacred ceremonies within the ecofeminist movement. As an ecofeminist who was the student of a woman Shaman[1] from Samiland (Lapland, northern Norway) for four and one-half years, I would like to make a number of observations based upon my experience in the field that will, hopefully, lead to some ethical considerations regarding the reclamation of Shamanism that is taking place today, both within the feminist spirituality and the new age movements.

THE PLACE OF SHAMANISM IN ECOFEMINISM

The reason that ecofeminists have such a deep interest in Shamanism is that Shamanism is practiced in a wide variety of indigenous cultures that have an earth-based spirituality. Shamans from Native American and other tribal cultures have kept alive the knowledge that the earth is sacred and that not only are humans and nonhuman nature part of the interconnected web of life, but also that spirit resides in matter, as well as in other dimensions. Shamanism teaches us that everything has spirit and that via a variety of shamanic practices, humans can make contact with the spirits of the living, of the dead, of humans,

Gloria Feman Orenstein is Professor in Comparative Literature and the Program for the Study of Women and Men in Society at the University of Southern California. She is the author of *The Theater of the Marvelous: Surrealism and the Contemporary Stage, The Reflowering of the Goddess* and co-editor of *Reweaving the World: The Emergence of Ecofeminism*. She has published widely on the Women of Surrealism, and she was the cofounder of the Woman's Salon for Literature in New York (1975–1985).

plants, and animals, as well as with the deities, and can obtain knowledge from them about how to heal life on earth.

Shamanism seems to provide answers for ecofeminists about how we can live in balance on the earth and, at the same time, develop a means of communication among the many varied species inhabiting the many different realms and dimensions of the universe, both via physical and spiritual methods. Shamanism, because it functions upon the acknowledgment that spirit resides in matter, shatters the patriarchal dualism pervading the Western religions—a dualism that insists upon spirit being separate from matter. Shamanism is neither androcentric nor anthropocentric. In this sense it is ecofeminist, for it neither recognizes one gender to be superior to the other nor places humans outside of or above the cosmic cycles or the natural ecosystems. Because Shamanism was practiced since the dawn of human history and figures of Shamans are found in Paleolithic cave paintings, Shamanism also takes us outside the historical frame of reference of patriarchal history—back to prehistory and even to the civilization of the Goddess, a civilization which, at least in old Europe, according to archeologist Marija Gimbutas (1974, 1989, 1991), accorded women more prestige and equality in society than we do, was earth revering, and did not engage in war.

Many native medicine people also consider the earth to be our mother. Some indigenous religions refer to an earth mother or to a mother goddess. Thus, women involved in the feminist spirituality movement may also turn to shamanic practices in order to get in contact with the spirit of the earth mother, both for personal and communal spiritual empowerment.

Starhawk, an ecofeminist and wiccan priestess, has, through her rituals and political activism, proved once and for all that in an ecofeminist vision, there is no contradiction between spiritual and political practice. Starhawk also refers to herself as a Shaman, for she uses shamanic techniques in her spiritual work. Indeed, she has also visited the Shamans of Samiland, and was recognized by them to have shamanic powers. The Goddess rituals that Starhawk performs have a strong shamanic element. She uses her rituals to empower her activist community before undertaking protest and civil disobedience activities in order to save the earth from the many threats to our planet's survival, ranging from pollution to nuclear disaster.

Since ecofeminists are becoming more and more interested in Shamanism, it is important that we begin to examine it seriously from precisely this perspective. My comments will identify the following problems that I see surrounding Shamanism as it is practiced today by growing numbers of vision-questers.

ESSENTIALISM: REDUCTIVE, CORE, AND ARCHETYPAL CONCEPTS

To speak about Shamanism as if it were a universal or generic category is to run the risk of constructing an archetype, a stereotype, or an abstraction of a Shaman, and thereby to ignore the specificity of the wide diversity of shamanic practices in a variety of indigenous cultures. It is reductive to speak of Shamanism as if it were the same all over the world. Anthropology teaches us that

Shamanism differs from culture to culture. Each culture's cosmogony, cosmology, and mythology are unique, and since shamanic practices involve symbol systems, deities, and a knowledge of how the many worlds, both visible and invisible, are organized, it is an error to assume that Shamans all over the world do the same things, or that when they do so, they do them in the same way.

Reductive Views of Shamanism

In his foreword to anthropologist Ruth-Inge Heinze's recent book *Shamans of the 20th Century*, Stanley Krippner (1991) comments that "Dr. Heinze's research demonstrates that it would be erroneous to claim that shamans represent a single constellation of traits or that there is a typical shamanic personality." Further on, Ruth-Inge Heinze warns us:

> Most of all, we should apply caution when individuals claim to be shamans. "Professional" shamans never make such claims. They need not advertise, because they become known through their work. Their "miraculous" healing of sick minds and bodies, their retrieval of otherwise not accessible information, their beneficial effects on their community become known fast through word of mouth. (Heinze 1991, 6)

The rules of shamanic ethics are the same as for any other professionals, especially in the religious realm. It would be unethical for "enlightened" individuals, for example, to publicly announce their enlightenment. The degree of spiritual development is reflected in an individual's demeanor, actions, and success. The most successful shamans I met were also the most humble. They would stress that they are only the servants of the sacred and the mediators who continue to learn throughout their life (Heinze 1991, 7).

Since the word for Shaman is usually a translation from a foreign language (such as the Sami word *noidi*, which also means sorcerer), we must be conscious of whether the person in question is a Shaman, a sorcerer, a trance medium, a psychic, a channeler, or a magician. If we begin by situating the particular Shaman or Shamanism that one reclaims within its own cultural tradition, we can understand why Ruth-Inge Heinze cautions us about people who call themselves Shamans.

In the case of the Sami, my Shaman teacher was trained in her culture for thirty-five years before she could practice healings on people outside of her extended family. When I pondered this, given the fact that she was born into a prestigious lineage of Shamans (she was the daughter of the Great Shaman of Samiland, whose father was also a Shaman), and that her talents were obvious when she was a child, I wondered *why* she had to study for so long before treating those outside of her kin group. Of course, this baffled me, since in the West we believe we can become professional at anything within four to eight years of training.

My Shaman teacher was not only a healer, but she was also a student of folklore. This is important, because she always insisted that the three principal sources of her shamanic knowledge were Sami folklore (tales, legends, and so forth); teachings from the ancestral lineage—from her father, who was her mentor, and from other ancestral spirits, who spoke to her from the spirit world; and teachings from spirit entities (what we might call "spirit guides" or "power animals"). In this category her main guide was an owl that appeared to her in her childhood.

A culture's tales and legends are of extreme importance, for through them one can learn how spirits behave. For example, if a tale speaks about what happens to someone who steals money from a sacred site, the Shaman in training learns that the karmic price of such an act might come ten years later, when that person's reindeer flock is wiped out.

A culture's tales are often cautionary. They teach strategies for dealing with all kinds of spirits, both good and evil, according to the culture's beliefs. A Westerner who goes to an indigenous culture in search of shamanic knowledge should read extensively about the culture's folklore. The serious mistake that we make is to think that folk tales and legends are not true. We have been taught not to believe in the supernatural, but one aspect of an ethical approach to forming a relationship with a shamanic culture would be understanding that the folklore of the culture is not necessarily just "lore," but that its stories are often based upon real events, and that if you visit that particular area, they might happen to you, even if you don't believe in such things.

Folk tales also show ways in which dreams are interpreted in the culture. My experience in this area was always startling. I would begin to describe a dream I had, and I would give it a sophisticated symbolic explanation. The next thing I knew, I was taken to the house of the Great Shaman and shown a photo of the very person who had appeared in my dream as my spirit guide. I had interpreted this gigantic figure, clad in a reindeer-skin tunic and large boots, to be the symbol of my Amazon self, who had just climbed a high mountain. Instead, I learned that it was not a symbol. It was the exact image of my Shaman's grandfather—who had been given to me as a spirit guide to help me on my journey. Thus, what I had called a dream was actually a visit from a spirit in the spirit world. To have interpreted that person as a symbol of a giant or any other such figure would have missed the *very important and startling point* that this person was the spirit of the real grandfather of my Shaman.

Because these stories take place in a given geography, they also teach about the natural environment of the particular bioregion. Thus, Sami tales, which deal with winter at the North Pole, are not at all similar to tales told in the Amazon jungle. It is a mistake to assume that similar figures have similar meanings in different cultures—whether they be mothers, fathers, gods, or tricksters. To assume that there is just one universal meaning to a figure in a folktale is to negate the historic, geographic, and cultural specificity of that culture. To do this is also to deny the variability and diversity of species, both on earth and in other dimensions—be they cultures, humans, animals, plants, or spirits. Things simply are *not* the same all over the world, even though certain aspects of them may make us think they are similar.

Folk tales illustrate the workings of the laws of karma, and they are handed down over generations, because—contrary to white Western culture, which believes that all stories should end after three hundred pages or two hours in the cinema—indigenous people have not forgotten that stories continue from generation to generation. Over time, one can begin to see the shape of the agency of otherworldly spirits upon events in this world. One begins to have a feel for the agency of the spirit of a deceased ancestor or community member. This is important information for the Shaman to have in order to assess the nature of the vision she or he might have when treating a particular individual in a certain family. The Shaman must contextualize the origin of the patient's dis-ease within his or her own family and cultural history, as well as within the context of the patient's past lives. This is necessary in order to understand the kind of negativity that has taken over the patient's life (a curse, an invasion, an attack, and so forth), its origin, and its historicity.

The Concept of Core Shamanism

The concept of "core shamanism" has been the focus of Michael Harner's shamanic workshops. His work in this field is of immeasurable value, and I fully agree with the importance of familiarizing contemporary Westerners with the possibilities provided by experiences of the "shamanic journey" or the spirit flight. However, "core shamanism" stresses the "shamanic journey" induced by drumming as the central feature of all Shamanism, and it teaches students to travel out of the body to the lower, middle, and upper spirit worlds, to meet with their power animals, their spirit guides, to learn how to perform soul retrieval, and to do shamanic healings and counseling. One of the dangers that I see, from the ecofeminist perspective, in focusing on the spirit journey as the "core" concept of shamanism is that it both reproduces the patriarchal dualism that separates spirit from matter and prioritizes spirit over matter (that is, heaven over earth or the otherworld over this world).

While spirit journeys do characterize Shamanism all over the world, and while information from other realms is essential to shamanic work, to prioritize journeys to otherworldly dimensions over the social and political dimensions of the journeys made by Shamans when they are awake and conscious in this world (as opposed to being in an altered state) is to subordinate the ordinary conscious experience to the nonordinary one. Yet Shamans themselves do not necessarily prioritize experience in that way. During my training, I was always looking for these "core experiences," and instead I found that the "core" experiences of Sami Shamanism often came when spirits visited this realm, or when real animals became spirit messengers. I was "shamanized" by mosquitos that died in my California apartment for what seemed to be no apparent reason, until I received a call from Samiland informing me of the death of my Shaman teacher's son. The mosquitoes I had encountered in the swamps during the summer had picked up the vibrations of my blood and found me via their spiritual attunement to me. This kind of event, one that illustrates the spiritual interconnectedness of all living things in the web of life, is as much a "core" concept of Shamanism as is the out-of-the-body ecstatic journey.

To prioritize information from the spirit world over information from the spirits of animals, plants, and persons in this world is to perpetuate patriarchal

Christianity's privileging of spiritual beings over human beings. It is as if we believed that an out-of-body journey were more important than those journeys we make daily—and especially those pilgrimages that indigenous and tribal people often make to sacred sites in nature. By stressing the visionary journey out of the body and by omitting the sacred pilgrimage to a real site in nature from our description of so-called core Shamanism, we are deleting the crucial political dimension of the struggles of Shamans in the here and now. The land rights issues of indigenous people always remind Westerners that their land is sacred. They do not consider the earth to be less sacred than other realms.

In Samiland the Great Shaman is also the chief political leader of his people. Thus, he had to use his psychic abilities to strategize protest actions against those who wanted to take over the Sami land and rivers. Often shamanic techniques are involved in fighting these battles (returning negative energy and so forth).

Shamans that I have met use their powers in the here and now much of the time, and they do not seem to privilege the spiritjourney to other dimensions over the many other ways in which their services are performed in the body and on the earth. The shamanic worldview considers all of creation to be both spiritual and sacred. This dimension is as sacred as the spirit world. Thus, what happens to us while alive and awake, although interconnected with what is taking place in the spirit world, is also of great importance shamanically, and, of course, is also sacred. Through the spiritual journey Shamans pick up vital information from other realms, in much the same way that we get our news from abroad via satellite and TV. By the same token, one could not characterize the human experience by the "core" activity of tuning into the news from abroad, even though this is a necessary part of our daily lives. Naturally, when Shamans work in the here and now, they are calling upon forces that reconfigure our ordinary concepts of space and time. When they use their psychic powers for certain kinds of work, they are not necessarily journeying out of the body, but they are expanding our concept of what a body is and relating to the body as an energy field composed both of spirit and matter.

Naive Ecofeminism

Ruth-Inge Heinze writes:

> In the United States, we find a great number of weekend workshops announcing training in shamanism. The quality of such training is seldom put to test. It does not seem to be appropriate to attempt a revival of shamanism by combining "core elements" from different cultures. Such attempts start on the wrong foot, because core elements may be part of shamanic rituals, but do not constitute the essence of the ritual. They are vehicles of expression but not the message itself. . . . Shamanic techniques may be effective means for self-exploration, however, experimenters should be taught the pitfalls of psychic openings which require closing. They have to be convinced of the necessity of properly sending away the energies which they evoke during the process. (Heinze 1991, 155)

At this point I think that a personal story will provide an anecdote that illustrates her point very clearly. I was attending an ecofeminist party, and one of the women wanted to start a spirituality group. I had brought a clairvoyant with me to the party. We talked about doing Goddess rituals, and the clairvoyant asked whether any of us knew how to handle any bad effects that might occur because of what we had called up. One of the women said: "We are all coming from a pure place. We will only call upon the good. I'm sure that nothing harmful can happen."

My friend, the clairvoyant, then explained. "Look, you can be a very good person with very good intentions in ordinary life. But if, when you go to sleep, you leave the door of your house open, anyone can come in. And that has nothing to do with how good your intentions are, or how pure you are. The door happens to be open, and anyone can come in. It is the same thing when you do a ritual. You open the door to other dimensions, and other things can enter along with those that you have invited. You have to learn how to 'see' what is happening and to work with the energies, otherwise you should be very careful about getting involved in this work, and make sure to seek protection before you begin."

We have, as I have tried to show, been naive in oversimplifying Shamanism by trying to construct a "core" essence of a Shaman. By being so reductive we actually miss out on some of the important features of Shamanism, particularly ones that involve real animals and life on this planet.

There has also been a stress placed on finding one's "power animal" in neo-Shamanism. It seems to me that this emphasis also privileges spirit animals over real animals. Once again, from my own experience in Samiland, I know that I was always waiting to meet my "power animal," and my Shaman teacher was always taking me to the real reindeer, the real birds, the real mosquitos. It wasn't until she communicated with birds, brought them to us, talked with them, and sent them away, or until she "psyched out" the problem of a lost reindeer, that I began to understand how the neoshamanic narrative from contemporary workshops had actually blinded me to the fact that real animals are also spirit and power, and, at least to my Shaman teacher, they were every bit as important, or even more so, than her owl spirit guide who had appeared to her in childhood. Sometimes I used to feel that I had a more "shamanic" perspective than she did, because I was always coming up with sophisticated symbolic interpretations of dreams and I was always looking for "power animals," while she seemed to be more interested in the real animals and she understood the figures in dreams to represent the spirits of real people. The truth is that she made less of a distinction than we do between real and spirit people or animals. To her, all was real, all was spirit, and all was sacred, simultaneously. There was no contradiction in that.

Problems with the Concept of the Archetype

The concept of the archetype, which comes from Jungian psychology, although it has validity in many cases, should not be applied to Shamanism, because it renders real cultures and their histories and living inhabitants, whether human or animal, invisible, and because it prevents us from identifying the actual social and political problems of people, especially of women in indigenous cultures. Here I am referring to the glamorizing and stereotyping (that sometimes blurs into archetyping) of the images of women from "exotic" foreign cultures.

Recently I came upon a workshop to be given by Jungian psychologyist Linda Leonard, entitled "The Lapp Reindeer Woman Archetype." I did not attend this workshop, so I am only referring to its title. The use of the word *Lapp* is incorrect. The Sami people were called Lapp by colonizing Westerners. In their struggle for their rights, they insist on the use of the name Sami, and they want Westerners to know that their language is the Sami language (a Finno-Ugritic language), and that their land is called Samiland, not Lapland.

When I came across the title of this workshop, I called my Shaman teacher in Norway, and I asked her if there is any reference to a reindeer woman (motif or archetype) in their folklore. She said she had never heard of it. Then I concluded that the reindeer woman image, as I have seen it depicted on Christmas and other greeting cards, is a stereotype similar to the ones we have of the Indian princess (from Native-American tribes). It is an image that glamorizes the exotic but also prevents us from seeing the real suffering in the lives of Sami women who are reindeer herders, who are losing their land, and who are losing their role in reindeer herding, as the role of reindeer herder is becoming more and more the occupation of men alone. Those who follow the archetypal approach to Shamanism also project their own personal fantasies onto a living culture, and in so doing they deauthenticate the actual lives and lore of a living people. They make it into a Disneyworld and perpetuate stereotypes that are pernicious to the culture's survival. Had I taken a workshop on the "Lapp Reindeer Woman Archetype," chances are I might have been blinded to some of the brutal realities in the lives of contemporary Sami women who herd reindeer, or who no longer do so, because they have lost this role. Sami women recently held a women's conference (Summer 1990) precisely in order to speak out about their double oppression as women in Norwegian society and as Sami, who are socialized according to the gender roles defined by Sami culture, where women now occupy the domestic role and have lost their role as reindeer herders to the men.

TRIVIALIZING THE SPIRIT WORLD

When Westerners gather in a circle to perform a ceremony that they have learned either from native people or from reading about their ceremonies, do they actually believe that they are performing something as *real* as a surgical operation? Do we ever see surgeons gathering in a circle, passing out knives and scalpels to strangers, and asking those gathered with them to explore each other's brains with these implements and then return to "share the experience"? Shamanism is just as *real* and as dangerous as surgery. It operates on our psyches. We may not see this operation in a literal, material way, but the results of the operation are evident in the way our vision of "reality" has been altered.

Indeed, I would question whether all people who want to study Shamanism should be permitted to do so, given the fact that Shamans learn how to enter other people's energy fields and bodies. This may explain why in traditional societies not everyone is called to this role. I have also asked myself whether a Nazi should be given shamanic training. Would such a person (or any other, for that matter) not be tempted to abuse the power contacted? Should such a person be able to sign up for a weekend shamanic workshop? Who screens the applicants, and what are the criteria for admission?

When I went to the sacred Sami site with my Shaman and her father, they both asked the spirits *if* I would be granted permission to enter their space. When I was told this, it had never occurred to me that spirits were actually present who might, indeed, have denied me entry. At the time I thought the two Shamans were describing their form of prayer. But they were not praying in the sense we conceive of prayer. They were actually speaking to *real* (but invisible to me) ancestors. These were experienced Shamans, not commercial entrepreneurs or dabblers. Now that I know about these things, I grow concerned. How do the travelers who sign up for Shaman tours know about the karma of their tour leaders or, for that matter, of the native teachers? In the West we have trivialized the reality and the power of the spirit world. In fact, we have negated it. This is the same as if we were to negate the existence of germs, just because we can't see them with the naked eye. Although we do not have instruments with which to see the spirit world, just as light waves and gravity are real, just as gamma rays and black holes are real, we should understand that things exist that we cannot necessarily see. Modern physics teaches us that when we study elementary particles, we interact with them. We also know that the stars we see might have died many years ago, but since light takes time to travel through space, we are seeing stars that no longer exist.

These lessons from modern physics should alert us to the fact that what we observe may no longer exist, that not everything that exists can be observed, and that what we study might be altered by the fact that we are interacting with it (such as elementary particles). It is arrogant of Westerners to think that if we have not identified something with our modern instruments, it does not exist. This also negates the powers and intelligence of native people. By our arrogance, by our insistence on labeling those whose wisdom was acquired without Western technology as "primitive," we open ourselves to great dangers from elements and entities of other dimensions that we have chosen to ignore. In this way we have trivialized the spirit world and attributed all agency in human affairs to humans alone.

Just as people in power in government may abuse that power, Shamans, too, may abuse their power and use it to do harm. Romanticizing and glamorizing Shamanism may, in fact, blind us to the tyranny that some Shamans may exert because of their power. This is because we continue to believe that only the visible is real. In fact, we may be under spiritual attack and not be aware of it because we choose to deny the reality and the power of the spiritual realm.

When Westerners travel to an "exotic" foreign country to visit with a local Shaman, do they know anything about the person in whose power they will place themselves, and do they have any means of protection in the event of an abuse of power? I pose these questions in the spirit of raising our consciousness about the complexity of Shamanism and how it works with energies that are invisible to us. I also bring this up in the hopes that the current commodification of packaged Shaman tours will be placed within a perspective that embraces ethics and responsibility, both toward those embarking on the journeys as well as toward the Shamans and the cultures they live in, who must be protected from being ripped off by tourists, just as the tourists must be protected from the abuses of power on the part of native Shamans, who often have political and historical reasons to view rich, white Westerners as their enemies.

I have participated in many ceremonies and rituals performed in the feminist spirituality and new age communities, and am now even more aware of the complexity of the invisible dimensions surrounding us. Most people participating in these ceremonies do not see auras, nor do they see into other dimensions. When they conjure up spirits in a ritual, how do they know what kind of energies they are bringing into the circle? It is very important to perform such rituals under the guidance of a trained spiritual leader, one who is able to witness the nature of the energy exchanges that are taking place, and one whom we have substantial reason to believe does not misuse power. For this reason alone we need to apply a code of ethics to the practice of neo-Shamanism.

Until I had first-hand experience of the *reality* of the spirit world—until I had traveled to the sacred site, heard the voices of the ancestral spirits (the dead, who called me by name); until I had seen for myself that the spirit guide who appeared to me in my dream was not a symbol but was a real spirit; until I had witnessed the spirit of the Great Shaman—as it traveled out of his body; until I had been convinced that the spirit world does exist—I had conceived of all discussions about spirituality in terms of poetry and prayer. Shamanism had been a powerful metaphor to me, connoting visionary and poetic creations. The spirit world was, before my own experience with it, something akin to the dream world. The reason I stress this is that I, too, had trivialized the spirit world. As a modern (or even postmodern) educated Westerner, I did not believe in the existence of spirits or of the spirit world.

Moreover, the Carlos Castaneda and Lynn Andrews books all have a narrative line to them, which led me to conceive of shamanic experience in terms of a kind of novel that either developed to a climax or partook of the literary genre of the "picaresque." There was a literary form to Shamanism that also did not tally with what I actually lived and led me to discredit my experience. I expected spirit guides to resemble Jimminy Cricket rather than a real cricket. I expected everything to be larger than life, something like a Disneyworld rendition of nature. Instead, what I learned was that *real* mosquitos are actual spirit guides.

Our Western accounts of "reality" and our literary narratives fail to encompass a diversity of other narrative modes whose features capture the realities of shamanic experience. One example of a figure from a nonwhite Western tradition is that of the trickster. We look upon the trickster as a literary or folk figure.

However, once you become involved in shamanic practice, you begin to observe how the spirits play tricks upon you. These tricks may be humorous, or they may be dangerous. Shamans do not often tell about their experiences in the spirit world. Have we ever wondered why? The answers are sobering, to say the least! Spirits, in fact, do observe us and listen to us. If we are planning to protect ourselves, they will take note of this and plan their strategy accordingly. One must remain silent about one's interaction with the spirit world, not only because conventional Westerners will dismiss these discussions as absurd, but also because one may run risks and court dangers with the spirits if one speaks of these things. The spirit world is no more benign than the material world, and we would do well to consider this when embarking on vision quests. Moreover, it is to trivialize the spirit world, to demean and negate its authenticity, to think that if you concentrate on white light, what you get will be beneficent. This is so naive as to be sheer folly! You must have enough power to call upon enough white light to protect you. Whenever I discuss these ideas with new agers, I try to explain myself in the following way. I do not deny that white light is protective. I simply maintain that Shamans channel what I call "heavy voltage." Ordinary people may not have the power to draw upon sufficient voltage to produce the desired effect.

From an ecofeminist perspective, trivializing the spirit world also renders invalid the wisdom of women, for we can see how my communication with this powerful woman Shaman was blocked by the fact that I did not, at first, grant legitimacy to her description of reality. And *I* had been called by, as she put it, "The Great Spirit"! In my culture I was always considered to be one of the people most open to spirituality. Yet, because of my Western scientific education, I could not actually believe in the existence of the spirit world. I don't think that we in the West can ever truly communicate with people of indigenous and tribal cultures until we open ourselves up to bestowing legitimacy on their descriptions of reality. Thus, not only do national, linguistic, and cultural barriers interfere with the communication among women around the world, but beyond all this, the parameters of what we consider to be "real" separate us still further from one another.

GENDER NEUTRALIZATION

When we speak of Shamanism in the abstract, we also speak of it as gender neutral. However, male and female Shamans in different cultures also embody different gender roles. These roles, as they are defined in each culture, also affect the perception we may form of Shamanism. As a feminist, I have reacted to various examples of Shamanism that I have both witnessed and read about as "macho Shamanism." Indeed, it does take a lot of physical and mental (psychic/spiritual) effort to make contact with the spirit world. When I was in Samiland, I had to walk some ten or more miles to the sacred site, and I had to climb a ten-kilometer mountain in order to be able to dream of my spirit guide. In other traditions one's consciousness is altered by hallucinogens, by sensory deprivation, by drumming (the Sami's shaman drums were seized by the Christians when they were colonized, and so they no longer use them), and by other means.

When considering the strenuous physical tests from the perspective of Western gender roles, the shamanic training and tests seem to be macho. In Western cultures, most women do not trek many miles into nature to erect shelters by themselves in a "survival wilderness" mode. This is culturally constructed to be "masculine" as a gender role. However, as we know, gender roles vary from culture to culture.

In Sami culture, women are very strong. They are said to dominate. Some think the Sami may have once been a matriarchy, for in the past when a man wanted to marry a woman, he had to serve her mother for an entire year. Then the girl's mother would determine whether he was a good enough worker and whether he would serve her daughter well enough—whether he could take orders from his wife in a submissive way. The Sami are also matrilineal and matrilocal, but that doesn't preclude the existence of sexism in their culture. Whether their sexism came with the "white man," who brought liquor and colonization, or not, it currently exists, and women suffer from rape, battery, and violent crime in Samiland. Also, the gender roles are distributed so as to keep women at home. When the Great Shaman went out to do healings, he came home to a meal cooked by his wife or his daughters. When his daughter, my Shaman, came home from her work, she had to cook and clean for the others. She developed incredible physical strength from doing the work of men plus the work of women. Yet, on some level, it was the pressure to live up to and surpass the extremes of "macho" shamanic prowess that competed with her need to rest when she was ill, in order to heal. When she went home from the hospital after her mastectomy, the first thing she did was climb a mountain. She did this in order to test the strength of her constitution and to see if she was still as capable of difficult feats of physical endurance as she had been before the operation.

Because a female Shaman may have to live up to the standards of "macho" Shamanism and learn to handle anything that crosses her path, she may choose to handle sexual assaults such as rape and battery through physical prowess or psychic means, but she may then fail to name and identify the oppression of women in her culture. She may, indeed, consider her own encounters with male violence to be part of the repertoire of shamanic tests that she has to pass. Thus her physical prowess and her spiritual powers may blind her to feminist issues that may need to be addressed on a larger scale by women who are not Shamans.

In Native-American cultures, the Berdache is a male person who assumes a feminine gender role, dresses as a female, marries a male, and is often also a highly respected Shaman. To speak of Shamanism in the abstract renders the richness of the Berdache role invisible, for it ignores the sex and gender role complexity of the Shaman, and thereby returns us to archetypal and core concepts, which have stereotypically gendered images embedded in them. In referring to such a Shaman in the abstract, we tend to overlook, and therefore to erase, the importance of the shape-shifting that the Berdache role, in fact, embodies.

Gender crossings and blendings seem to be common among Shamans cross culturally. As we previously mentioned, most Shamanism today is practiced in indigenous, nonwestern, not necessarily patriarchal cultures. When we, as Westerners from a patriarchal culture, encounter a woman Shaman, we should not expect her to behave in ways that have anything to do with the white Western cultural construction of "the feminine." Yet, if this woman has participated in Western culture, as had my Shaman teacher, she has also adopted some of the ways of the West. In relating to such women of power, we may become confused by the gender-role transitions and the shape-shiftings these women undergo in order to pass from one culture to the other. However, I would like to suggest that we not abdicate our Western feminist perspective when we observe their lives, for they themselves are often treated in ways that are extremely sexist (partially because their cultures have been colonized by Westerners), and since they are trained to handle everything and be stronger than most males and females, they may not identify with the other women of their culture or participate in feminist activities. Ellen Maret often told me that the Sami do not need feminism, because Sami women are so strong. Ultimately, Sami women held a conference to discuss their problems from the perspective of indigenous women within the framework of the issues identified by the United Nations' International Decade on Women.

RACISM

The obvious points about Westerners appropriating and commodifying native practices or commercializing sacred objects do not need to be restated. Not only do we exploit indigenous people when we appropriate their shamanic knowledge, but we also tend to lump them all into one single entity, when they are, in fact, plural and diverse. Each Native American tribe or nation is an individual entity with a specific history and specific practices and languages that differ from one group to another.

When I was in Samiland, if men would harass me sexually, I would not retaliate physically, even if it were warranted in order to save myself from injury. Why? Because I reasoned that "the white man" had done enough damage to indigenous people, and I did not want to perpetuate that pattern. I did not want to bring physical harm to male members of the Sami community or family, even if, on the occasion that they were drunk and I was sober, I might have been able to. I did not defend myself, but I was fortunate in that I escaped every encounter unscathed. (Perhaps the Great Spirit was looking out for me?) When I would speak about this with my Shaman teacher, she would always say: "A Shaman has to handle all things, even drunk men." I was never satisfied by this answer. I wanted her to realize that I would not bring physical harm to any Sami people. This was respected neither by the Sami nor by her. They simply had no respect for someone who did not defend herself when attacked. On the other hand, had I done so, I am not sure whether a blow I might have dealt in self-defense might not have been misinterpreted. Indeed, now I might add, from another perspective, that what my Shaman teacher probably wanted me to learn is that a far greater harm can come to one via the spirit world. I think that now I might say that if I were to have hit a Sami man, she knew that even if he were to have been hurt by me, he could have sought to retaliate via shamanic means (he could have had energies sent to harm me). What I had to learn was that an important level of any encounter always takes place on the plane of spirit world. Today I believe that shamanically my Shaman teacher wanted me to understand that physical brutality was not exclusively "where it was at shamanically." There are spirit wars, spirit attacks, spells, curses, and so forth. There are other ways of responding besides physical violence. Perhaps this test also had to do with my learning about these other methods. But I was so focused on not doing harm that I simply ignored the many other dimensions to this problem that spoke, more specifically, to my role as a *student of Shamanism.*

In any event, I was in a quandary about all this until I spoke about it with Paula Gunn Allen, who mentioned to me that the reason I did not fight back probably had to do with my racism. At first, I did not understand what she was getting at. Then it occurred to me that if I had been sexually accosted in my own culture (pinned to the ground against my will by a drunk man), I would have fought back. Of course, I would have defended myself, even if it meant that I might have harmed an American man. But I refused to harm a Sami man. Wasn't this a sign of my white Westerner's guilt? Suddenly I realized that I was *not* treating the Sami as equals. I was treating them as a superior racist would treat an inferior group.

The Great Shaman used to say that I represented "the white man's culture," and I always objected. I specifically objected to his not understanding that I was a woman and that I was an ecofeminist who had, in fact, given a conference about saving the earth, to which I had invited his daughter. I could *not* conceive of myself as "the white man," and I really felt that he did not understand anything at all about me as an individual until the day I made hamburger meat for the Sami children. The Sami are definitely not vegetarians. They eat a lot of reindeer meat and fish. On that day, the Great Shaman wandered into the kitchen and, smelling a foreign odor, sniffed the meat I had prepared. Then he asked me: "What animal does this come from?" I stood there, perplexed. I couldn't really understand the question, and I'm sure I must have said to him: "It doesn't come from an animal. It comes from the supermarket!" It was at that moment that I realized how I was, indeed, "the white Westerner" that he took me for! It was a good fifteen minutes before I could come up with the answer "cow." I had truly forgotten about the animal whose body I was consuming.

Even in our ideological purism, we may still behave as racists, and, in fact, it is part of our white Western racism to see ourselves as ideologically "purer than thou" because we are ecofeminists or any other *ists.* We must never forget, even when we are bending over backward to make amends, that there is a haughtiness and a racially superior attitude in being "purer than thou," even when the very people we are bending over backward toward maintain that they are "purer than us" because they do not destroy the earth, and we do. Even if the others exhibit a racist attitude toward us, and even if we try not to reply in kind, the very fact that we conceive of ourselves as superior because we "know better" is, in itself, a form of racism.

IGNORANCE OF GEO-COSMIC REALITIES

Through our education in the scientific worldview of the Enlightenment, we have become alienated from the earth and have forgotten that the earth is also a heavenly body. We have ceased to take into consideration the powers of the forces and the knowledge of the cycles that govern our lives. We hardly ever give a second thought to gravity, for example, without which we would all be floating off into space, and we certainly *never* think about the real magnetic force of the North and South poles. We also take for granted the amount of light and dark we experience each day. But what if all that were to change? What if we were suddenly plunged into a world in which the sun never set— or never rose? What if we were to go to live at the magnetic North Pole? Then we would begin to experience syndromes similar to jet lag, and we would take seriously the implications of the revolutions of the earth on its axis around the sun. In Samiland during most of the fall and winter, the sun sets very early in the morning. During the summer, the sun doesn't set until well after midnight.

The rituals women have begun to perform in the feminist spirituality (Goddess) movement have begun to put us back in touch with an awareness of the solstices, the equinoxes, and the lunar cycles. But how does this all relate to ecofeminist ethics and to Shamanism?

Because of our geo-cosmic ignorance and amnesia, we fail to take into consideration the fact that certain powers can only be obtained and put into practice in certain places on the earth and at certain times during the year or during the larger cosmic cycles. It is interesting that when it comes to sacred herbs, we recognize that they grow in certain places and that people who cannot obtain certain herbs cannot experience their effects. However, herbs are portable, and this suits our purposes, for we can transport the products of the Amazon jungle to California via plane. However, we can never transport the magnetism of the North Pole to California. Nor can we manifest the effects of the Arctic midnight sun in Los Angeles. When I traveled to Samiland, I became aware of the effect that the magnetic North Pole was having upon me. It was causing me to enter a deep trance state when I slept, and it was when I was in such a deep trance that I was able to hear the voices of the ancestral spirits. As I ate Sami food, I noticed that my hair and skin began to take on other characteristics. This might have been due to the purity of the air, the water, and the food, as well as to the intensity of the earth's magnetic field in which the food was grown. We have noted that people are sensitive to light deprivation and that they become depressed when they do not receive enough light. Have we thought about what an overabundance of light might do to a person or how light might affect one's consciousness? In Samiland in the summer, when the sun sets well after midnight, sometimes as late as 3:00 A.M., one enters altered states, highs, and expansive states of consciousness.

Westerners always want to bring Shamans to the United States, put them on American TV talk shows, and have them perform miracles on our turf to prove their powers. When a Shaman from Samiland insists that you *must* travel to the North Pole in order to study Sami Shamanism, an American may tend to balk and dismiss the Shaman as a phoney. I brought my Shaman teacher to the United States to participate in a number of conferences (such as Ecofeminist Perspectives: Culture, Nature, Theory—held at U.S.C. in the Spring of 1987), but she always insisted that my real learning would not take place in the United States, but in Samiland. She was right, because my progress was intensified as soon as I came into the magnetic field of the North Pole. The results of culture shock and jet lag, when combined with the magnetism of the North Pole and the surplus of light in summer, catapulted me immediately into a shamanic state that was intensified by the presence of two powerful Shamans. It is important for us to honor the geo-cosmic realities of shamanic cultures and to realize that certain things cannot be transported elsewhere.

One of the main features of summer in Samiland is that suddenly the marshes become swamped with mosquitos. The Sami love their mosquitos, because they realize that "the white man" cannot stand them, and so the mosquitos have, in some sense, kept their land from being taken by outsiders. Most people cannot bear to live with those mosquitos. As I mentioned before, Sami Shamans communicate with their mosquitos, and they understand that they can be messengers, guides, and protectors. Ultimately, as we come to respect the geo-cosmic specificities of particular cultures and as we realize that there are things that *cannot* be bought, sold, commercialized, and commodified, such as magnetic fields and sunsets, (whereas people have already commercialized sacred waters and herbs), we must develop an ethics and a politics that will protect the earth and the cultures that reside not only in "places of power" or in places where we can obtain special products, but everywhere on our planet, for we must remember that the specificity of each location has its own potency.

In this way, by raising our consciousness about the geo-cosmic specificities of gravity, light, magnetism, solstices, equinoxes, lunar cycles, indigenous plants, animals, climate, and so forth, we may come to value the variety of diverse cultures and regions whose multiple knowledges all serve to enhance life everywhere on our planet in an astonishing number of ways. Most of these geo-cosmic teachings can only be acquired in the particular region in which they originated. Finally, if we are to awaken our own shamanic abilities, then we must attune ourselves to precisely those same forces as they manifest in our own bioregions. In some cases this may require us to learn about our region from the indigenous tribes in our area; in other cases we must set about discovering the power of the places in which we live on our own. This is our challenge, if we want to save the earth. We must not run away to other "exotic" cultures, but we must begin by exploring our own backyards.

THE DEPOLITICIZATION OF THE SHAMANIC VISION

By universalizing and essentializing a "core" concept of Shamanism, we tend to ignore the practical and political use to which shamanic powers can also be put. When Ellen Maret Gaup-Dunfjeld led a contingent of women from the reindeer ranches of Samiland to stage a sit-in in the Norwegian Parliament in order to protest the hydroelectric power plant that the Norwegians were planning to erect over the Alta-Kautokeino River on the day that Prime Minister Gro Bruntland stepped into office, she used visions to create her political itinerary. When the new prime minister did not return to hear the Sami women (after twenty-four hours, as she had promised), Ellen Maret asked the women present to relate their dreams. Some had dreamed of flying to Rome, so she requested an audience with the Pope at the Vatican (in order to obtain publicity for their cause); another dreamed of flying over large cities, so she planned a strategic visit to the United Nations in New York. Ellen Maret did not make the kind of separation that we, in the West, would make between those dream-inspired journeys to Rome and New York and other dream-inspired journeys to the spirit world. Nor did she consider the dream to be an inferior means of establishing a political itinerary.

Being a political leader *was* being a spiritual leader, and vice versa. Because Shamans from indigenous peoples do *not* separate spirit from matter and do *not* privilege a "core" shamanic experience over a this-worldly journey, knowing that both are sacred, both are real, and both are spiritual, focusing exclusively on lower, middle, and upper world shamanic cosmology in our courses excludes the important political function that shamanic vision often serves. Furthermore, she took the visions of women to be as relevant as those of a Shaman. She did *not* establish a hierarchy among women as visionaries. These women from the reindeer ranches were considered to be the very people whose dreams (spirit-world contacts) would help the Sami to save their land and protect the earth. Here is ecofeminism in action.

CONCLUSION: NEW DIRECTIONS

In conclusion, I would like to suggest that we begin to take the shamanic means of obtaining knowledge seriously in our culture. First we must begin to return the various shamanic practices to their specific cultures. We must not be reductive, but must see the complexities posed by the diversity of shamanic practices around the world. This will be enriching to our understanding of what Shamanism is, in the long run. Then we must set about creating a shamanic practice that is indigenous to our part of the world and our culture. However, we must revise many of our own cultural assumptions from an ecofeminist perspective.

White Westerners must cease to project their white Western fantasies of the exotic, the glamorous, and the romantic onto other cultures. We must always assume diversity, and not make assumptions about things being the same all over the world just because some aspects of them may appear similar to us.

We must also resist thinking in a dualistic manner. We must *remember* that in Shamanism, spirit resides in matter, and all that exists is sacred. We must also resist thinking in hierarchies, privileging the spirit world and its entities over the material world and its inhabitants. Nor must we engage in elitist assumptions about whose visions have the most wisdom. We must respect the folk of every culture, remembering that their experience contains wisdom, and we must seek out women teachers whenever possible, for they have generally been the guardians of earth wisdom (because of women's socially constructed roles, and not because of any inherent or "essential" characteristics).

We must also learn the folklore of the cultures we visit and remember that what we consider to be "lore" and "legend" may have actually taken place in that culture and that these stories often contain real lessons for us that we would do well to heed.

We must remember to seek spiritual protection, and we must become aware of the risks involved in shamanic practices, as well as the dangers incurred when working with people of power. They are also very human, and like non-Shamans, they may be tempted to abuse their power.

Above all, we must cease to trivialize the spirit world. We must begin to take seriously the reality of spirit—especially those of us who engage in spirituality rituals. We should practice these rituals believing that the rituals we engage in are *real* events that *do* communicate with the spirit world.

As we are taught in anthropology and folklore courses, we must *not* exploit the sacred ways or appropriate the sacred objects of other people—especially not for commercial purposes. One of the first things I was taught was that you must replace everything you take. Rather than stripping a foreign culture of its material and spiritual possessions, we should begin to contribute to its survival.

We must begin to set standards for the practice of Shamanism, in order to protect the population from charlatans and new age dilettantes who know nothing about the spirit world and less about human consciousness and psychology. New agers do not necessarily revere the earth (they pillage the earth for crystals for their new age enterprises); nor do they necessarily respect women, either. A new age neo-Shaman might easily jettison an ardent Shaman student into a state of severe mental or physical injury, simply due to the kind of ignorance, arrogance, and lack of responsibility that typifies much of the dabbling that takes place in this movement.

We must remember that Shamanism is just as serious as surgery. Would we like to have our brains operated on by someone who had not been trained in medical school? From the ecofeminist perspective on ethics, we must never lose sight of the fact that it is the misogyny and dualism at the root of white Western civilization that have caused the exploitation of both women and nature. On the other hand, we must not guilt-trip ourselves to the point of endangering our lives. Somehow we must come up with a balance in which we honor both non-Western cultures and ourselves for all that is beneficent, while constantly maintaining a critical position toward all forms of abuse of power.

If we take the lessons of Shamanism seriously, and if we revise our cosmology in time, if we practice ecofeminist ethics while honoring both the material and the spiritual realms, then, I believe, there is real hope for us to heal the earth, our homeland, now.

NOTE

1. The Shaman with whom I studied was Ellen Maret Gaup-Dunfjeld, from Alta, Norway. She died of cancer at the age of 47 in May 1991. For further information, see Orenstein (1988).

13

Ecology Is a Sistah's Issue Too

The Politics of Emergent Afrocentric Ecowomanism

SHAMARA SHANTU RILEY

Black womanists, like everyone in general, can no longer overlook the extreme threat to life on this planet and its particular repercussions on people of African descent.[1] Because of the race for increased "development," our world continues to suffer the consequences of such environmental disasters as the Chernobyl nuclear meltdown and Brazil's dwindling forests. Twenty percent of all species are at risk of extinction by the year 2000, with the rate of plant and animal extinction likely to reach several hundred per day in the next ten to thirty years (Worldwatch 1987, 3). Manufacturing chemicals and other abuses to the environment continue to weaken the ozone layer. We must also contend with the phenomenon of climate change, with its attendant rise in sea levels and changes in food production patterns.

Along with these tragic statistics, however, are additional environmental concerns that hit far closer to home than many Black people realize. In the United States, poor people of color are disproportionately likely to be the victims of pollution, as toxic waste is being consciously directed at our communities. The nation's largest hazardous-waste dump, which has received toxic material from 45 states, is located in predominantly black Sumter County, Alabama (de la

Shamara Shantu Riley is a first-year graduate student in political science at the University of Illinois—Urbana/Champaign, where she acquired her undergraduate degree in May 1992. She is a member of Women Working for Progress, a multicultural student organization working for social change. A former opinions columnist for *The Daily Illini*, the University's independent student newspaper, Riley has written many articles on social justice issues, including the environment and womanism. "Ecology Is a Sistah's Issue Too" is her first published paper.

Pena and Davis 1990, 34). The mostly African-American residents in the 85-mile area between Baton Rouge and New Orleans, better known as Cancer Alley, live in a region which contains 136 chemical companies and refineries. A 1987 study conducted by the United Church of Christ's Commission for Racial Justice found that two-thirds of all Blacks and Latinos in the United States reside in areas with one or more unregulated toxic-waste sites (Riley 1991, 15). The CRJ report also cited race as the most significant variable in differentiating communities with such sites from those without them. Partly as a result of living with toxic waste in disproportionate numbers, African-Americans have higher rates of cancer, birth defects, and lead poisoning than the United States population as a whole.[2]

On the African continent, rampant deforestation and soil erosion continue to contribute to the hunger and poverty rates in many countries. The elephant population is rapidly being reduced as poachers kill them to satisfy industrialized nations' ivory trade demands (Joyce 1989, 22). Spreading to a dozen African nations, the Green Belt Movement is seeking to reverse the environmental damage created by the European settlers during colonialism, when the settlers brought nonindigenous trees on the continent. As with United States communities of color, many African nations experience "economic blackmail," which occurs when big business promises jobs and money to "impoverished areas in return for these areas' support of or acquiescence to environmentally undesirable industries" (Meyer 1992, 32).

The extinction of species on our ancestral continent, the "mortality of wealth," and hazardous-waste contamination in our backyards ought to be reasons enough for Black womanists to consider the environment as a central issue of our political agendas.[3] However, there are other reasons the environment should be central to our struggles for social justice. The global environmental crisis is related to the sociopolitical systems of fear and hatred of all that is natural, nonwhite, and female that has pervaded dominant Western thought for centuries.[4] I contend that the social constructions of race, gender, class and nonhuman nature in mainstream Western thought are interconnected by an ideology of domination. Specific instances of the emergent Afrocentric eco-womanist activism in Africa and the United States, as well as West African spiritual principles that propose a method of overcoming dualism, will be discussed in this paper.

THE PROBLEM OF NATURE FOR BLACK WOMANISM

Until recently, few Black womanists gave more than token attention to environmental issues. At least in the United States, the origins of such oversight stem from the traditional Black association of environmentalism as a "white" concern. The resistance by many United States Blacks to the environmental movement may partly originate from a hope of revenge. Because of our acute oppression(s), many Blacks may conclude that if the world comes to an end because of willful negligence, at least there is the satisfaction that one's oppressors will also die. In "Only Justice Can Stop a Curse," author Alice Walker discusses how her life experiences with the Eurocentric, masculinist ideology of domination have often caused her to be indifferent to environmental issues:

> I think . . . *Let the earth marinate in poisons. Let the bombs cover the ground like rain. For nothing short of total destruction will ever teach them anything.* (Walker 1983b, 341)

However, Walker later articulates that since environmental degradation doesn't make a distinction between oppressors and the oppressed, it should be very difficult for people of color to embrace the thought of extinction of all life forms simply for revenge.

In advocating a reformulation of how humans view nonhuman nature, eco-feminist theorist Ynestra King states that from the beginning, women have had to grapple with the historical projection of human concepts onto the natural, which were later used to fortify masculinist notions about females' nature (King 1989, 118). The same problem is applicable to people of color, who have also been negatively identified with the natural in white supremacist ideologies.

Black women in particular have historically been associated with animality and subsequently objectified to uphold notions of racial purity. bell hooks articulates that since the 1500s, Western societies have viewed Black women's bodies as objects to be subdued and controlled like nonhuman nature:

> From slavery to the present day, the Black female body has been seen in Western eyes as the quintessential symbol of a "natural" female presence that is organic, closer to nature, animalistic, primitive. (hooks and West 1991, 153)

Patricia Hill Collins asserts that white exploitation of Black women as breeders during the Slave Era "objectified [Black women] as less than human because only animals can be bred against their will" (Collins 1990, 167). Sarah Bartmann, an African woman also known as the Hottentot Venus, was prominently displayed at elite Parisian parties. While being reduced to her sexual parts, Bartmann's protruding buttocks were often offered as "proof" that Blacks were closer to animals than whites. After her death in 1815, Bartmann was dissected, and her genitalia and buttocks remain on display in Paris (Gilman 1985). Bartmann's situation was similar to the predicament of Black female slaves who stood on auction blocks as masters described their productive body parts as humans do cattle. The historical dissection of Black women, be it symbolic or actual, to uphold white supremacist notions is interconnected with the consistent human view of nonhuman animals as scientific material to be dissected through an ideology that asserts both groups are inferior.

Because of the historical and current treatment of Blacks in dominant Western ideology, Black womanists must confront the dilemma of whether we should strive to sever or reinforce the traditional association of Black people with nature that exists in dominant Western thought. However, what we need is not a total disassociation of people from nature, but rather a reformulation of *everyone's* relationship to nature by socially reconstructing gender, class, and ethnic roles.

Environmentalism is a women's issue because females (especially those of color) are the principal farm laborers around the world, as well as the majority of the world's major consumers of agricultural products (Bizot 1992, 36). Environmentalism is also an important issue for people of color because we disproportionately bear the brunt of environmental degradation. For most of the world's population, reclaiming the Earth is not an abstract state of affairs but rather is inextricably tied to the survival of our peoples.

Womanism and ecology have a common theoretical approach in that both see all parts of a matrix as having equal value. Ecology asserts that without each element in the ecosystem, the biosphere as a whole cannot function properly. Meanwhile, womanism asserts the equality of races, genders, and sexual preferences, among other variables. There is no use in womanists advocating liberation politics if the planet cannot support people's liberated lives, and it is equally useless to advocate saving the planet without addressing the social issues that determine the structure of human relations in the world. If the planet as a whole is to survive, we must all begin to see ourselves as interconnected with nonhuman nature and with one another.

THE POLITICS OF NATURE-CULTURE DUALISM

At the foundation of dominant Western thought exists an intense ambivalence over humankind's place in the biosphere, not only in relation to one another, but also in relation to nonhuman nature. The systematic denigration of men of color, women, and nonhuman nature is interconnected through a nature-culture dualism. This system of interconnectedness, which bell hooks labels "the politic of domination," functions along interlocking axes of race, gender, species, and class oppression. The politic of domination "refers to the ideological ground that [the axes] share, which is a belief in domination, and a belief in the notions of superior and inferior, which are components of all those systems" (hooks 1989, 175). Although groups encounter different dimensions of this matrix based on such variables as species or sexual orientation, an overarching relationship nevertheless connects all of these socially constructed variables.

In discussing the origins of Western dualism, Dona Richards articulates the influence of dominant Jewish and Christian thought on Western society's conceptions about its relationship to nonhuman nature:

Christian thought provides a view of man, nature, and the universe which supports not only the ascendancy of science, but of the technical order, individualism and relentless progress. Emphasis within this world view is placed on humanity's dominance over *all* other beings, which become "objects" in an "objectified" universe. Humanity is separated from nature. (Richards 1980, 69)

With dualistic thinking, humans, nonhuman nature, and ideas are categorized in terms of their difference from one another. However, one part is not simply deemed different from its counterpart; it is also deemed intrinsically *opposed* to its "Other" (Collins 1990, 69). For instance, speciesists constantly point to human neocortical development and the ensuing civilization that this development constructs as proof of human superiority over nonhuman animals. Women's position as other in Western patriarchies throughout the histories of both psychological theory and Christian thought has resulted in us being viewed as defective men.

Women, the nonelite, and men of color are not only socially constructed as the "Others," but the elite, white, male-controlled global political structure also has the power—through institutions such as the international media and politics—to extensively socialize us to view ourselves as others to be dominated. By doing so, the pattern of domination and subjugation is reinforced. Objectification is also central to the process of oppositional difference for all entities cast as other. Dona Richards claims that in dominant Western thought, intense objectification is a "prerequisite for the despiritualization of the universe and through it the Western cosmos was made ready for ever increasing materialization" (Richards 1980, 72). Since one component is deemed to be the other, it is simultaneously viewed as an object to be controlled and dominated, particularly through economic means.

Because nature-culture dualism conceives of nature as an other that (male) human undertakings transcend and conquer, women, nonhuman nature, and men of color become symbolically linked in Eurocentric, masculinist ideology. In this framework, the objectification of the other also serves as an escape from the anxiety of some form of mortality. For instance, white supremacists fear that it will be the death of the white race if people of color, who comprise the majority of the world's population, successfully resist the current global relations of power. Objectifying nonhuman nature by technology is predicated on an intense fear of the body, which reminds humans of death and our connection with the rest of nature. By making products that make tasks easier, one seeks to have more opportunities to live one's life, with time and nature converted into commodities.

World history can be seen as one in which human beings inextricably bind the material domination of nonhuman nature with the economic domination of other human beings. The Eurocentric, masculinist worldview that dominates Western thought tends to only value the parts of reality that can be exploited in the interest of profit, power and control. Not only is that associated with nature deemed amenable to conquest, but it is also a conquest that requires no moral self-examination on the part of the prospective conqueror. For instance, there is very little moral examination by research laboratories that test cosmetics on animals, or by men who assault women. There was also very little moral examination on the part of slave owners on the issue of slavery or by European settlers on colonialism in "Third World" nations.

By defining people of color as more natural and animalistic, a political economy of domination has been historically reinforced. An example of this phenomenon is the founding of the United States and the nation's resultant slave trade. In order for the European colonialists to exploit the American land for their economic interests, they first needed to subjugate the Native American groups who were inhabiting the land. While this was being accomplished, the colonists dominated Blacks by utilizing Africans as slave labor (and simultaneously appropriating much of Mexico) in order to cultivate the land for profit and expand the new capitalist nation's economy. Meanwhile, the buffalo almost became extinct in the process of this nation building "from sea to shining sea."

A salient example of the interconnectedness of environmental degradation and male supremacy is the way many societies attach little value to that which can be exploited without (economic) cost. Because nonhuman nature has historically been viewed by Westerners as a free asset to be possessed, little value has been accredited to it. Work traditionally associated with women via cultural socialization has similarly often been viewed as having little to no value. For instance, in calculating the Gross Domestic Product, no monetary value is attached to women's contributions to national economies through reproduction, housework, or care of children.

THE ROLE OF THE ENVIRONMENTAL-ISMS IN PROVIDING THE FOUNDATION FOR AN AFROCENTRIC WOMANIST AGENDA

While serving as executive director of the United Church of Christ's Commission for Racial Justice in 1987, Reverend Benjamin Chavis, Jr., coined the term *environmental racism* to explain the dynamics of socioeconomic inequities in waste-management policies. Peggy Shephard, the director of West Harlem Environmental Action, defines United States environmental racism as "the policy of siting potentially hazardous facilities in low-income and minority communities" (Day and Knight 1991, 77). However, environmental racism, which is often intertwined with classism, doesn't halt at the boundaries of poor areas of color. Blacks in Africa and the United States often have to contend with predominantly white environmental groups that ignore the connection between their own values and the struggles of people of color to preserve our future, which is a crucial connection in order to build and maintain alliances to reclaim the earth. For instance, because the Environmental Protection Agency is often seen as another institution that perceives elite white communities' complaints as more deserving of attention than poor communities of color, many United States social activists are accusing the EPA of "environmental apartheid" (Riley 1991, 15).

In "Granola Boys, Eco-Dudes and Me," Elizabeth Larsen articulates how race, class, and gender politics are interconnected by describing the overwhelmingly white middle-class male leadership of mainstream United States environmental groups. In addition to being indifferent to the concerns of people of color and poor whites, the mainstream organizations often reinforce male supremacy by distributing organizational tasks along traditional gender roles (Larsen 1991, 96). The realization that only we can best represent our interests, an eco-identity politics, so to speak, lays the foundation for an Afrocentric ecowomanist agenda.[5] Even though many Black women have been active in the environmental movement in the past, there appears not to be much *published* analysis on their part about the role of patriarchy in environmental degradation. The chief reason for this sentiment may stem from perceiving race as the "primary" oppression. However, there is an emergent group of culturally identified Black women in Africa and the United States who are critically analyzing the social roles of white supremacy, patriarchy, and classism in environmental degradation.

EMERGENT AFROCENTRIC ECOWOMANISM: ON THE NECESSITY OF SURVIVAL

There are several differences between ecofeminism and Afrocentric ecowomanism. While Afrocentric ecowomanism also articulates the links between male supremacy and environmental degradation, it lays far more stress on other distinctive features, such as race and class, that leave an impression markedly different from many ecofeminists' theories.[6]

Many ecofeminists, when analyzing the links between human relations and ecological degradation, give primacy to gender and thus fail to thoroughly incorporate (as opposed to mere tokenism) the historical links between classism, white supremacy, and environmental degradation in their perspectives. For instance, they often don't address the fact that in nations where such variables as ethnicity and class are a central organizing principle of society, many women are not only viewed in opposition to men under dualism, but also to other women. A salient example of this blind spot is Mary Daly's *Gyn/Ecology*, where she implores women to identify with nature against men and live our lives separately from men. However, such an essentialist approach is very problematic for certain groups of women, such as the disabled and Jews, who must ally themselves with men (while simultaneously challenging them on their sexism) in order to combat the *isms* in their lives. As writer Audre Lorde stated, in her critique of Daly's exclusion of how Black women use Afrocentric spiritual practices as a source of power against the *isms* while connecting with nonhuman nature:

> to imply, however, that women suffer the same oppression simply because we are women, is to lose sight of the many varied tools of patriarchy. It is to ignore how these tools are used by women without awareness against each other. (Lorde 1983, 95)

Unlike most white women, Black women are not limited to issues defined by our femaleness but are rather often limited to questions raised about our very humanity.

Although they have somewhat different priorities because of their different environments, Afrocentric ecowomanists in the United States and Africa nevertheless have a common goal—to analyze the issues of social justice that underlie environmental conflict. Not only do Afrocentric ecowomanists seek to avoid detrimental environmental impacts, we also seek to overcome the socioeconomic inequalities that led to the injustices in the first place.

Emergent United States Afrocentric Ecowomanist Activism

Contrary to mainstream United States media claims, which imply that African-Americans are not concerned about ecology, there has been increased environmental activism within Black communities since the early 1980s. Referred to as the environmental equity movement by Robert Bullard, predominantly Black grass roots environmental organizations tend to view environmentalism as an extension of the 1960s civil rights movement. In *Yearning*, bell hooks links environmentalism with social justice while discussing Black radicals and revolutionary politics:

> We are concerned about the fate of the planet, and some of us believe that living simply is part of revolutionary political practice. We have a sense of the sacred. The ground we stand on is shifting, fragile, and unstable. (hooks 1990, 19)

On discussing how the links between environmental concerns and civil rights encouraged her involvement with environmentalism, arts writer and poet Esther Iverem states:

> Soon I began to link civil rights with environmental sanity. . . . Because in 1970 Black folks were vocally fighting for their rightful share of the pie, the logical question for me became "What kind of shape will that pie be in?" (Iverem 1991, 38)

Iverem's question has been foremost in many African-American women's minds as we continue to be instrumental in the Black communities' struggle to ensure that the shape of the social justice pie on our planet will not be increasingly carcinogenic. When her neighborhood started to become dilapidated, Hattie Carthan founded the Magnolia Tree Earth Center of Bed-Stuy in Brooklyn in 1968, to help beautify the area. She planted more than 1,500 trees before her death in 1974. In 1986, the city council of Los Angeles decided that a 13-acre incinerator, which would have burned 2,000 tons of city waste daily, was to be built in a low-income Black and Latino neighborhood in South Central Los Angeles. Upon hearing this decision, residents, mostly women, successfully organized in opposition by forming Concerned Citizens of South Central Los Angeles. While planning direct actions to protest the incinerator, the grass roots organization didn't have a formal leadership structure for close to two years. Be it a conscious or unconscious decision, Concerned Citizens accepted a relatively nonhierarchical, democratic process in their political activism by rotating the chair's position at meetings, a form of decision making characteristic of many ecofeminist groups.[7]

The Philadelphia Community Rehabilitation Corporation (PCRC), founded by Rachel E. Bagby, operates a village community to maintain a nonhierarchical relationship between human and nonhuman nature for its working-class-to-poor urban Black residents. About 5,000 reside in the community, and there is communalistic living, like that of many African villages. PCRC has a "repeopling" program that renovates and rents more than 50 previously vacant homes and also created a twelve-unit shared house. PCRC also takes vacant lots and recycles them into gardens to provide food, and oversees literacy and employment programs. Hazel and Cheryl Johnson founded People for Community Recovery (PCR), which is operated from a storefront at the Altgeld Gardens housing project, after they became aware that their community sits atop a landfill and has the greatest concentration of hazardous waste in the nation. In its fight against environmental racism, PCR has insisted that the Chicago Housing Authority remove all asbestos from the Altgeld homes and has helped lobby city government to declare a moratorium on new landfill permits. PCR also successfully prevented the establishment of another landfill in Altgeld Gardens.

One Black women's organization that addresses environmental issues is the National Black Women's Health Project. The NBWHP expresses its Afrocentric ecowomanist sentiment primarily through its SisteReach program, which seeks to connect the NBWHP with various Black women's organizations around the world. On urging African-American women to participate in the environmental movement and analyze the connections between male supremacy and environmental degradation, Dianne J. Forte, the SisteReach coordinator, makes the following statement:

> At first glance and with all the major problems demanding our energy in our community we may be tempted to say, "this is not my problem." If however, we look at the ominous connection being made between environmental degradation and population growth; if we look at the same time at trends which control women's bodies and lives and control the world's resources, we realize that the same arguments are used to justify both. (Forte 1992, 5)

For instance, women are increasingly being told that we should not have control over our own bodies, while the Earth is simultaneously deemed feminine by scientists who use sexual imagery to articulate their plans to take control over the Earth. Meanwhile, dominant groups often blame environmental degradation on overpopulation (and with their privileged status, usually point at poor women of color), when industrial capitalism and patriarchal control over women's reproduction are among the most pronounced culprits.

The most salient example of practical United States Afrocentric ecowomanism combating such claims is Luisah Teish, a voodoo priestess. In connecting social justice issues with spiritual practices rooted in the West African heritage, Teish articulates the need for everyone to actively eliminate patriarchy, white supremacy, and classism, along with the domination of nonhuman nature. Members of Teish's altar circle have planned urban gardening projects both to supply herbs for their holistic healing remedies and to assist the poor in feeding themselves. They have also engaged in grass roots organizing to stop gentrification in various communities.

Emergent Afrocentric Ecowomanist Activism in Africa

On the African continent, women have been at the forefront of the movement to educate people about environmental problems and how they affect their lives. As with much of the African continent, environmental problems in Kenya particularly influence rural women's lives, since they comprise 80 percent of that nation's farmers and fuel gatherers (Maathai 1991, 74). Soil erosion directly affects the women, because they depend on subsistence agriculture for their families' survival. The lack of firewood in many rural areas of Kenya because of deforestation disproportionately alters the lives of women, who must walk long distances to fetch firewood. The lack of water also makes a negative imprint on Kenyan women's lives, because they have to walk long distances to fetch the water.

However, many Kenyan women are striving to alter these current realities. The most prominent Afrocentric ecowomanist in Africa is Wangari Maathai, a Kenyan microbiologist and one of Africa's leading activists on environmental issues. Maathai is the founder and director of the Green Belt Movement (GBM), a fifteen-year-old tree-planting project designed to help poor Kenyan communities stop soil erosion, protect their water systems, and overcome the lack of firewood and building materials.

Launched under the auspices of the National Council of Women of Kenya, the majority of the Green Belt Movement's members are women. Since 1977, these women have grown 10 million trees, 80 percent of which have survived, to offset Kenya's widespread deforestation.[8] Although the Green Belt Movement's primary practical goal is to end desertification and deforestation, it is also committed to promoting public awareness of the relationship between environmental degradation and social problems that affect the Kenyan people—poverty, unemployment, and malnutrition. However, one of the most significant accomplishments of the GBM, Maathai asserts, is that its members are "now independent; had acquired knowledge, techniques; had become empowered" (Maathai 1991, 74).

Another Kenyan dedicated to environmental concerns is Wagaki Mwangi, the founder and coordinator of the International Youth Development and Environment Network. When she visited the University of Illinois at Urbana-Champaign, Mwangi discussed how Kenya suffers economic and environmental predicaments primarily because her homeland is trying to imitate Western cultures. "A culture has been superimposed on a culture," Mwangi said, but there are not enough resources for everyone to live up to the new standards of the neocolonial culture (Schallert 1992, 3). She asserted that in attempts to be more Western, "what [Kenyans] valued as our food has been devalued, and what we are valuing is what they value in the West" (Schallert 1992, 3). For instance, Kenyans used to survive by eating a variety of wild foods, but now many don't consider such foods as staples because of Western influences. In the process, many areas of Kenya are deemed to be suffering from food shortages as the economy has been transformed to consumer capitalism with its attendant mechanization of agriculture.

In Kourfa, Niger, women have been the primary force behind preventing the village from disappearing, a fate that many surrounding villages have suffered because of the Sahel region's desertification. Reduced rainfall and the drying up of watering places and vegetation, combined with violent sandstorms, have virtually deprived Kourfa of harvests for the past five years. As a result, the overwhelming majority of Kourfa's men have had to travel far away for long periods of time to find seasonal work.

With the assistance of the Association of Women of Niger and an agricultural advisor, the women have laid out a small marketgarden around the only well in Kourfa. Despite the few resources at their disposal, the Kourfa women have succeeded in supporting themselves, their children, and the village elders. In response to the survival of the village since these actions, the Kourfa women are now calling for increased action to reverse the region's environmental degradation so "the men won't go away" from the village (Ouedraogo 1992, 38).

Afrocentric Ecomotherists: Ecowomanist Potential?

The environmental activism of some Black women brings up the question of whether community-oriented Black women who are addressing environmental issues are genuinely Afrocentric ecowomanists or possibly Afrocentric ecomotherists.[9] According to Ann Snitow, motherists are women who, for various reasons, "identify themselves not as feminists but as militant mothers, fighting together for survival" (Snitow 1989, 48). Snitow also maintains that motherism usually arises when men are absent or in times of crisis, when the private sphere role assigned to women under patriarchy makes it impossible for the collective to survive. Since they are faced with the dictates of traditional work but face a lack of resources in which to fulfill their socially prescribed role, motherists become a political force.

Since they took collective action to secure the survival of the village's children and elders only after the necessary absence of Kourfa's men, the activism of the Kourfa women may possibly be based on a motherist philosophy. One can only conjecture whether the Kourfa women criticized the social role of motherhood in Niger as they became a political force, or if womanist consciousness emerged after their political experiences. Because of their potential to transform into ecowomanists after they enter the political realm, Afrocentic ecomotherists shouldn't be discounted in an analysis of Black women's environmental activism. For instance, Charlotte Bullock contends that she "did not come to the fight against environmental problems as an intellectual but rather as a concerned mother" (Hamilton 1990, 216). However, she and other women in Concerned Citizens of South Central Los Angeles began to notice the sexual politics that attempted to discount their political activism while they were protesting. "I noticed when we first started fighting the issue how the men would laugh at the women . . . they would say, 'Don't pay no attention to them, that's only one or two women . . . they won't make a difference.' But now since we've been fighting for about a year the smiles have gone" (Hamilton 1990, 215). Robin Cannon, another member of Concerned Citizens, asserts that social relations in her home, specifically gender roles on caretaking, were transformed after she began participating in the group's actions (Hamilton 1990, 220).

MOVING BEYOND DUALISM: AN AFROCENTRIC APPROACH

In utilizing spiritual concepts to move beyond dualism, precolonial African cultures, with their both/and perspectives, are useful forms of knowledge for Afrocentric ecowomanists to envision patterns toward interdependence of human and nonhuman nature. Traditional West African cultures, in particular, which also happen to be the ancestral roots of the overwhelming majority of African-Americans, share a belief in nature worship and view all things as being alive on varying levels of existence (Haskins 1978, 30). One example of such an approach in West African traditions is the *Nyam* concept. A root word in many West African languages, *Nyam* connotes an enduring power and energy possessed by all life (Collins 1990, 220). Thus, all forms of life are deemed to possess certain rights, which cannot be violated at will.

In *Jambalaya*, Luisah Teish writes of the *Da* concept, which originates from the Fon people of Western Africa. *Da* is "the energy that carries creation, the force field in which creation takes place" (Teish 1985, 61). In the Fon view, all things are composed of energy provided by *Da*. For example, "the human is receptive to the energy emanating from the rock and the rock is responsive to human influence" (Teish 1985, 62). Because West Africans have traditionally viewed nonhuman nature as sacred and worthy of praise through such cultural media as song and dance, there is also a belief in *Nommo*. *Nommo* is "the physical-spiritual life force which awakens all 'sleeping' forces and gives physical and spiritual life" (Jahn 1961, 105).

However, with respect for nonhuman nature comes a different understanding of *Ache*, the Yoruba term for human power. *Ache* doesn't connote "power over" or domination, as it often does in mainstream Western thought, but rather power *with* other forms of creation. With *Ache*, Teish states that there is "a regulated kinship among human, animal, mineral, and vegetable life" (Teish 1985, 63). Humans recognize their *Ache* to eat and farm, "but it is also recognized that they must give back that which is given to them" (Teish 1985, 63). In doing so, we respect the overall balance and interdependence of human and nonhuman nature.

These concepts can be useful for Afrocentric ecowomanists not only in educating our peoples about environmental issues, but also in reclaiming the cultural traditions of our ancestors. Rachel Bagby states the positivity of humans connecting with nonhuman nature, a view that is interwoven in her organization's work:

If you can appreciate the Earth, you can appreciate the beauty of yourself. The same creator created both. And if I learned to take care of that I'll also take care of myself and help take care of others. (Bagby 1990, 242)

Illustrating an outlook of planetary relations that is parallel to the traditional West African worldview, Bagby simultaneously reveals the continuous link between much of the African-American religious tradition and African spirituality.

In light of the relations of power and privilege that exist in the world, the appropriation of indigenous cultures by some ecofeminists must be addressed. Many womanists, such as Andy Smith and Luisah Teish, have criticized cultural feminists for inventing earth-based feminist spiritualities that are based on the exploitation of our ancestral traditions, while we're struggling to reclaim and defend our cultures from white supremacy. In "For All Those Who Were Indian in Another Life," Smith asserts that this appropriation of non-Western spiritual traditions functions as a way for many white women to avoid taking responsibility for being simultaneously oppressive as well as oppressed (see her article, pp. 168-71). White ecofeminists can reclaim their own pre-Christian European cultures, such as the Wiccan tradition, for similar concepts of interconnectedness, community, and immanence found in West African traditions.[10]

Adopting these concepts would transform humans' relationship to nonhuman nature in a variety of ways. By seeing all components of the ecosystem affecting and being affected by one another, such a world perspective demonstrates a pattern of living in harmony with the rest of nature, instead of seeking to disconnect from it. By viewing ourselves as a part of nature, we would be able to move beyond the Western disdain for the body and therefore not ravage the Earth's body as a result of this disdain and fear. We would realize that the Earth is not merely the source of our survival, but also has intrinsic value and must be treated with respect, as it is our elder.

The notion of community would help us to appreciate the biological and cultural diversity that sustains life. Because every entity is viewed as embodying spirituality under immanence, culture wouldn't be viewed as separate from, and superior to, nature, as it is seen in mainstream Western religions. Communalism would also aid us in reformulating the social constructions of race, gender, species, class (among other variables), which keep groups separate from one another. And finally, the environmental movement in particular would view politics as rooted in community and communally take actions to reclaim the Earth and move toward a life of interdependence for generations to come.

NOTES

I would like to acknowledge the help that Carol Adams has given me with this essay. Her reading suggested valuable changes in the structure of the paper as well as clearing up minor flaws in writing. She also suggested some references that would augment my claims.

1. Alice Walker's definition of womanist is a feminist of color who is "committed to the survival and wholeness of entire people, male *and* female" (Walker 1983a, xi–xii). University of Ibadan (Nigeria) English senior lecturer Chikwenye Okonjo Ogunyemi contends that "black womanism is a philosophy that celebrates black roots ... It concerns itself as much with the black sexual power tussle as with the world power structure that subjugates blacks" (Ogunyemi 1985, 72). Since feminism often gives primacy to gender, and race consciousness often gives primacy to race, such limitations in terminology have caused many women of color to adopt the term

womanist, which both Walker and Ogunyemi independently coined in the early 1980s. Although some of the women in this paper refer to themselves as feminists rather than womanists, or use both terms interchangeably, I am using the term *womanist* in an interpretative sense to signify a culturally identified woman of color who also critically analyzes the sexual politics within her respective ethnic group.

2. For a discussion of how toxic waste has affected the environmental health of United States Black communities, see Day and Knight (1991).

3. Robert Bullard (1990) contends that the mortality of wealth involves toxic-waste dumping to pursue profits at the expense of others, usually low-income people of color in the United States. Because this demographic group is less likely to have economic resources and political clout, it can't fight back as easily as more affluent communities that possess white skin privileges. I think this term is also applicable to the economic nature of toxic dumping in "Third World" countries, which are basically disempowered in the global political process.

4. For an ecofeminist text that makes a similar claim, see King (1989).

5. My definition of an Afrocentric ecowomanist is a communalistic-oriented Black woman who understands and articulates the interconnectedness of the degradation of people of color, women, and the environment. In addition to articulating this interconnectedness, an Afrocentric ecowomanist also strives to eradicate this degradation. For an extensive discussion of Afrocentrism, see Myers (1988).

6. An example of this distinction can be seen in Davies (1988). In her article, Davies only discusses the interconnections between gender and nature and completely avoids analyzing how such variables as ethnicity and class influence the experience of gender in one's life.

7. For several descriptions of the political decision making within feminist peace organizations, see the essays in Harris and King (1989).

8. It is noteworthy that the seedlings come from over 1,500 tree nurseries, 99 percent of which are operated by women. In addition, the women are given a small payment for the trees that survive.

9. In comparison to an Afrocentric ecowomanist, I define an Afrocentric eco-motherist as a communalistic-oriented Black woman who is involved in saving the environment and challenging white supremacy, but who does not challenge the fundamental dynamics of sexual politics in women's lives.

10. For instance, Starhawk, a practitioner of the Wiccan tradition, has written about her spiritual beliefs (1990).

PART 3

EMBODYING ECOFEMINIST SPIRITUALITIES

14

Animal, Vegetable, and Mineral

The Sacred Connection

CAROL LEE SANCHEZ

Her Song
(for SHE WHO THOUGHT US INTO BEING)

She is here,
all around us.
She is here,
deep inside us.
She is here,
*   and everywhere.*

Weaver of galaxies
and universe,
She enfolds us,
transforms us
and holds us.

Carol Lee Sanchez is a native New Mexican of Laguna Pueblo, Lakota, and Lebanese heritage. From 1976 to 1985, she was a member of the San Francisco State University faculty, where she taught American Indian, Ethnic, and Women's Studies courses. In July of 1976, Sanchez became State Director of the California Poets In The Schools Program, a position she held until July of 1978. Her poetry has been widely anthologized and three volumes of her poetry have been published. Sanchez and her husband, Thomas Allen, closed their contemporary American Indian Art Gallery in Santa Barbara, California, in 1989 to relocate in Central Missouri. She is currently involved in living in and renovating an 85-year-old Victorian farmhouse, growing vegetables, writing, painting, and taking long walks in the woods to meet the creature relatives in her new homeplace.

She is here,
all around us.
She is here,
deep inside us.
She is here,
                    and everywhere.

Birth Mother of all heavens,
Birth Mother of every star,
Birth Mother of each planet,
Birth Mother of everything.
Life Bringer, Thought Maker,
Song Weaver,
Receiver of all our dreams.

She is here,
all around us.
She is here,
deep inside us.
She is here
                    and everywhere.
                    — Carol Lee Sanchez

This chapter began as a response to a request from Carol Adams that I expand on ideas I first raised in "New World Tribal Communities" (Sanchez 1989). In that article, I stated my conviction that Euro-American people

> waste the resources and destroy the environment in the Americas because they are not spiritually connected to this land-base, because they have no ancient mythos or legendary origins rooted to this land. . . . The conquerors and immigrants had no ancestral lineage that had loved, valued, protected, and cared for this land-base, these homelands to hundreds of native Tribes. . . . They continued to revere the lands of their. . . . ancestral origins for over four hundred years, paying no heed to the delicate ecological balance maintained by the natives. . . . It is my premise that the lack of a land-based Mythos and sacred connection to the ecosystems of the Americas has allowed the Euro-American immigrants to rape and plunder these lands without regret or concern. (Sanchez 1989, 345–48)

As is evident, I do not believe one can merely graft environmental concerns upon the attitudes that have caused the plundering and polluting in the first place.

Addressing a dominant Euro-American audience from a Native American perspective has never been an easy task for me, because I am very aware of the deeply rooted Euro-Western cultural attitudes in our society. As Americans, we were and are educated in a system that was founded on Euro-Western ideas and philosophies that were carefully traced back to "classical origins" in various European nations. Yet the basic principles of democracy, the freedom of the individual and equality among the people of both genders, come directly from the Native American Nations the first European immigrants lived among in the Americas.[1] The native origins of these principles are still not acknowledged by American leaders and educators, nor are they widely taught in the American education system. American feminism traces its historical roots to the ancient Goddess Culture(s) through remnants of manuscripts and artifacts found in Europe and the Middle East, yet has overlooked the many women-centered, equalitarian Native American cultures that are presently "alive and well" in the continental United States. Because I am so accustomed to the ingrained biases held by most non-Indians regarding American Indian cultures, the invitation to reflect critically on these dominant attitudes is especially welcome. I call the reader's attention to the unique approach to daily living long ago established by the first inhabitants of the Americas—the first Americans. Rather than develop my own solutions to current environmental problems, I will give a few examples of how some of the Meso-American Tribal cultures restored their damaged ecosystems and what they did to ensure they would never re-create those disastrous circumstances. My intention here is to articulate the concept of "relationship" or relatedness and the idea of the sacred in our lives, from a Native American-American Indian[2] perspective and to suggest some ways of embracing a Tribal way of thinking.

Those of us deeply committed to the restoration of a healthy "natural" environment are searching for ways in which we may facilitate attitudinal shifts in the consciousness of millions of people. When the majority of this nation's people consider environmental preservation to be more important than plundering it for economic gain, then they (we) will develop more appropriate methods for providing the basic human needs of food, shelter, comfortable indoor temperatures, clothing, and—to some extent—unnecessary human "comforts" such as exotic household gadgets, recreational toys, and modes of transportation. Many environmentalists have stated that careful planning in the use of renewable resources and the recycling of nonrenewable resources must become the norm rather than the exception in every community across our nation. I would add that we must also acknowledge that humans, along with their creative, inventive minds, are an integral, inseparable part of the "natural" environment. In my worldview, there is nothing under the sun that can be called "unnatural" or separated from nature. My own fundamental worldview stems from a deeply rooted Tribal upbringing that was imparted by my mother, her mother, and her grandmother. These women were born to and raised in one of the women-centered or "Gynocratic"[3] equalitarian Pueblo cultures of the Southwest. Thus, the context from which I speak is based on my own personal Tribal background, upbringing, and experience, as well as my cumulative knowledge teaching college-level American Indian Studies courses to Indian and non-Indian students for over ten years. It is important for me to note that I am not presenting a "new theoretical concept" but rather an alternative approach to generating practical methods for recreating modern equalitarian social structures among non-Indian, non-Tribal people.

My desire is to open a door through which anyone, so inclined, can step to examine the possibilities of *adapting* certain Tribal concepts or principles for current daily use in a modern, technological society. I believe that we latter-day modern Americans have much to learn from those earliest inhabitants of the Americas. The study of their Tribal histories and culture stories can provide important insights for those of us committed to environmental restoration and preservation. These stories can guide us in the development of personal attitudes that place doing laundry, going grocery shopping, and working a forty-hour week in the realm of "the Sacred." I will suggest some ways in which non-Indian Americans might set about to create a "sense of place" by establishing spiritual roots to this land mass, or how they might generate a personal creation story or legend that is personalized and connected to the land. Before I proceed further, it is first necessary for me to lay a foundation by briefly restating in general the historical context from which I and other Tribal Native Americans emerged.

THE HISTORIC AND "MYTHIC" ROOTS OF AMERICANS

"Long, long ago ... they say ... " The ancestors of the native peoples of this Western Hemisphere observed the symbiotic interdependence among plants, creatures, and humans. They observed the interactions between wind, water and fire, sun, moon, and earth, and their effects on plants, creatures, and humans. As these earliest peoples incorporated this information into their daily lives, they noticed that they prospered more often than not when they "walked in harmony" with each other and their environment. They helped each other, shared with each other, and used the resources of the environment sparingly because they benefitted by acting in this way. Thus, our long-ago American ancestors used this knowledge to develop a set of social and spiritual principles to guide their daily lives. These principles, developed in the remote past, are the bedrock of all Tribal cultures in the Americas. As the people of those times continued to practice these principles in their daily lives, a specific set of beliefs emerged around these principles. Then, in order to record what they had learned through their experience and to pass on to succeeding generations the knowledge they had gained, they ritually recited what they had observed. These recitations contained what they had come to believe regarding all the information they had collected about their environment and themselves and the explanations as to why all this information was important for the people to remember.

There are many Tribal variations of this process, including the division of knowledge into categories with each different category becoming the responsibility of a clan or family group. Ceremonies among some Tribes require the formal telling of certain stories. Other Tribes perform their ceremonies to reaffirm particular actions or behaviors. However they were individually structured, ceremonial recitations reinforced the historical importance of this knowledge for the Tribe while providing the younger generations with the original source of a given practice such as why the people do this, or should behave like that. Native American Tribal histories and culture stories stress the idea of harmonious coexistence—providing both positive and negative examples, by consistently showing us how everything is related. The stories elaborate in detail the reasons the people should get along with each other and everything they depend on to maintain a "good life." These stories continue to remind us (as Native American descendants) what our ancestors observed about the relationships in the local ecosystems (from which a given story emerged) and how we learned to survive within them.[4] The retelling has kept and continues to keep the circle of life uppermost in the daily consciousness of today's traditional Native Americans. They remind us of the *Sacred Ways* and the possibility we always have to live a "good life."

Although the Tribal culture stories are definitely "loaded" with morals and ethics (as Western thought systems would define "right living"), I use the phrase "good life" because it is difficult for me to use terms such as "moral" and "ethical," since they carry so much Western baggage. Indians simply say that "to live a good life is to walk in Beauty." Clearly, when we don't feel good about our lives, or when we can find no beauty in anything around us in our cities as well as our open countrysides, we are out of balance and out of harmony with everything. Today, in our genuine recognition of the current national ecological imbalances among plant and animal species caused by environmental pollutants of various kinds, many of us are focusing far more on the ugliness than on the remaining beauty that surrounds us. In doing this we become even more out of balance as our thoughts hold more and more negative images—thus excluding beauty from our awareness. The Great Mystery continues to surround us with beauty, and it is important to carry more of those images around with us while we attempt to "correct" the imbalances we have so carelessly brought about. Native Americans do this by remembering their nonhuman relatives, by "sending out a song" to them and seeking their guidance.

THE PRINCIPLE OF RELATIONSHIP

Most Euro-American or Euro-Western peoples tend to separate themselves from "nature" and to rank humans above animals, plants, and minerals in hierarchical fashion, and so it is not easy for them to perceive or accept a *personal* relationship with what they describe as the "natural world." Native Americans believe themselves to be an integral part of the natural world. When we speak of "nature," we are also including ourselves. Our thoughts about nature don't assume humans to be more important and powerful than the rest of our environment, nor do we regard nature as something beneath us to be exploited beyond what we actually need to survive as individuals or as a group. Today, many tribal elders from Tribes throughout the Americas are telling us to be mindful of our relationship to our environment; to remember our relatives; to reclaim and reestablish our sense of connectedness to everything and to acknowledge the sacredness of everything in our universe. More and more contemporary Native American scholars and writers are speaking to non-

Indians about Native American ways and spirituality—stressing the need for all of us to respect the land as our Mother Earth, respect the creatures, the waters, the air, and all the elements of our global environment.

During my early childhood I was introduced to the natural environment around me as a place of wonder filled with intricate interrelationships. My mother taught me to observe where I was walking and what was going on around me as I played outdoors. She explained how ants lived in colonies and how birds, wasps, bees, and other creatures built their homes; how all spiders were our relatives because Spider Grandmother had an important place in our Tribal culture. My mother cautioned me not to destroy any creatures' homes because they had *the right to live their lives* in their way every bit as much as I did. She also cautioned me to pay attention to the bees, wasps, ants, and poisonous snakes and to stay away from their nests because that stirred them up. She explained how I could be hurt by certain creatures, but I should also understand that when they attacked intruders they were protecting their homes and young from harm, just as she was protecting me by warning me about their stinging and biting abilities. "They won't bother you if you don't bother them" was a statement my mother, my grandmother, and my great-grandmother repeated on many occasions. My mother often picked up garden snakes, lizards, horned toads, frogs, and baby mice and brought them for me to see up close and hold for a brief time so I wouldn't be afraid of them. With her explanations about insects, snakes, birds, and other "critters," she also told stories that included these creatures and how they each had a special place in the world; each had a special task to perform—like bees pollinating plants, and so forth. Some stories were about how certain creatures or elements or the sun got here, and some about how they helped us or each other by doing what they were "born to do." If I was bothered by some creature in our yard, I'd tell my grandmother, and she would always say, "Well, what do you expect? They're just doing their job."

Growing up with stories and experiences like these gave me a sense of connectedness to my "home" environment. When I went away to school in a non-Indian environment (in a big city), I discovered that I was one of the very few who had such an attitude toward creatures and trees and rocks. For a long time I just assumed it was because I was a "country girl," until it occurred to me that "white folks" thought of certain creatures as "pests" or "predators" and certain plants as "weeds" and believed they should be killed on the spot! Back home, in the Indian villages, I never heard anyone talk like that. For us, hunting and fishing was for food—never for "sport." Years later, when I came in contact with Indian students who had backgrounds similar to mine, I realized how important it was to be raised with respect and care for our environment. We grew up with wonder stories, so we were not afraid when we met up with the "critters" in our local environment. As Indian children, we were not terrorized about wild creatures, so we don't stir them up with our fear. We are as familiar with the natures and aspects of our local animal populations as we are the natures and personalities of our sisters, brothers, and cousins—because we believe all things are our relatives.

Many of the stories from my early childhood, along with the attitudes and teachings of my mother and grandmothers consistently articulate a concept I call the Principle of Relatedness or Relationship. Every living Tribal culture that I have come across through personal contact or research has this principle embedded in its everyday life, and the extent to which this principle permeates the lives of Tribal people as an important core belief is often overlooked by non-Tribal people. There are many examples of the Principle of Relationship among the Tribes of the Americas, but here, I would like to focus on the Lakota people (a North American Plains Tribe) to illustrate how this principle is incorporated into their cultural framework.

There is a phrase among the Lakota that illustrates how they not only "relate" to their environment but how they keep their thoughts focused upon their appropriate place within their environment. The phrase, *Mitakuye Oyas'in*, is always spoken at the end of a formal voicing to the spirits. Very loosely translated into English, it means "all my relations" or "all my relatives." This phrase, in fact, represents the Lakota belief in their connectedness to all things outside themselves. Saying "all my relations" affirms this belief and, because it denotes familial relationship, consistently reminds the speaker of her or his personal connection to the universe. In addition to reminding the speaker of her personal relationship with all things, she is also reminding *those nonhuman things* that they are indeed related to her. This implies the kinds of interdependencies and interactions that take place within a family unit. Wallace Black Elk, a Lakota Medicine Man, stresses this Tribal principle when he speaks at conferences and gatherings focused on environmental issues. He firmly believes this way of thinking *must* be shared with all people of all races, and in sharing the beliefs of his traditional upbringing, attempts to communicate this attitude to non-Indians. The following quote is an example of the Lakota approach to life:

> This Chanunpa (Sacred Pipe) is your relative. The Powers of the Four Winds are your relatives. Pray to them. Talk to them. They are your relatives. To the west—the Thunder Beings, they are your relatives. Send a voice out there. These are your relatives. Look to the north, the Buffalo Nation—White Buffalo Calf Maiden—The Chanunpa—these are your relatives. To the east, the Elk Nation and The Elk Nation Woman, that brings joy and happiness, these are your relatives. To the south, the Swan, two legged spirits that bring joy and happiness. The medicine people that bring joy and health come from there. These are your relatives. Above you is the Eagle Nation. They watch, control, govern. These are your relatives. Down to Earth—the Stone People [and the green] are your relatives. (Black Elk and Lyon 1990, 39)

Over and over, Wallace reminds us of our familial relationship with creatures, elements, plants, and minerals, as well as humans. In addition to relationship, he illustrates the Tribal attitude of inclusiveness within a spatial orientation. Our connection to and support from the earth is reinforced by the acknowledgment of the directions. They are the marker points of the circle from which we view all that is external to us as human beings, and he invites us to include everything we see outside ourselves as one of our relatives.

The most basic example of relationship that non-Indians acknowledge in our country today exists within the traditional Western family unit. Most of us rightly assume (because of personal experiences) that family members care for each other and *take care* of each other. When we need help, we often ask our immediate relatives first. We assume our family members will help us because, generally, our experience has taught us to expect it. They of course assume they can ask for our help and we would gladly give it. Since we already have a conscious awareness of family interrelatedness that includes nurturing, assistance, and — for the most part — thoughtful consideration, one might ask: Why not include the rest of creation in our family circle? It's a short step to take and wouldn't require adopting an entirely new attitude concerning relationship but merely an e-x-p-a-n-s-i-o-n of our current notions about what (or who) constitutes our personal family. If we think of everything nonhuman as closely related to us, it would be quite normal and natural behavior for us to call on our nonhuman relatives for help. It would be perfectly natural for us to *expect* assistance from them and for us to *help them* in appropriate ways. For traditionally raised and tribally connected American Indians, this extension is incorporated during early childhood, as I have indicated earlier regarding my own childhood instruction.

It may be difficult for Euro-Americans to accept this way of thinking with a large degree of seriousness and open-mindedness, for a variety of reasons. Yet, if we examine the ancient Tribal cultures around us who have managed to survive and endure, in spite of all Euro-Western efforts to destroy their way of life, we can learn, at the very least, how they managed to adapt to the imposed ways of the conqueror and still maintain *the core* of their spiritual traditions. Euro-Americans *can adapt many of the life-preserving concepts* practiced by the original American cultures and apply them to ordinary daily life. Indeed, this is precisely what Wallace Black Elk is inviting everyone with whom he comes in contact to do, because, as a practicing Medicine Man, he knows that what we believe about our reality largely determines our experience, and if we *believe* we are related to everything in the universe, we will then *experience* this connectedness. From his perspective, acquiring this belief can result in a personal connection to the environment around us.

What I suggest here has nothing to do with "stealing Native American spiritual practices," or dances, or songs, or social customs, which I will discuss later. It has to do with acknowledging and utilizing a way of thinking that pervades the daily lives of Tribal people. It is a way of thinking that has sustained the first Americans for thousands of years and kept them, if you will, from totally destroying resources they depended on for survival. How we think about things generates our attitudes about our world and how we treat it. I think all Americans are becoming more aware of this because of their experiences with the many contemporary issues facing us today (most importantly world harmony and an ecologically balanced global environment).

RESTORING BALANCE AND HARMONY

Certainly in the course of their histories, the original Americans experienced ecological disasters of varying proportions. Archeological site studies of ancient North and South American native cultures gave rise to a variety of assumptions about those early civilizations. In the mid 1800s, Western archeologists stated that the people of certain "highly sophisticated" Meso-American cultures of Mexico and Central America disappeared because their farming practices were so terrible the topsoil was ruined, causing them to starve to death. When carbon dating and the study of tree rings became acceptable scientific tools during the late 1940s, other archeologists discovered that around the time the topsoil would no longer produce adequate crops, these people were also plagued with a lengthy drought cycle. Shortly thereafter, Euro-Western archeologists advanced the theory that the majority of the population in these areas starved to death due to famine *and* ignorant farming practices. Results of recent studies of the Meso-American Mayan culture support certain aspects of these former "disappearance theories."[5] However, the people didn't entirely disappear. They reorganized into smaller groups and moved away from the overfarmed areas. In fact, according to their Tribal histories, many subgroups migrated much further north and resettled in semiarid lands.

Although the oral histories still told by the descendants of these earlier ancestors explain what happened, Eurocentrism does not allow "quaint myths and legends" to be regarded as factual information. The "scholarly premise" has been that over time, oral records cannot be verified and accepted as historical evidence, since "people forget things and make up things." We know the Mayas were a literate culture, that their histories and philosophies were recorded in books, and that their great libraries were destroyed by the Spaniards shortly after conquest. In spite of this loss, they have remained a traditional ceremonial culture and have continued to retell their histories into the present day, although this seems to be generally disregarded by Euro-Western archeologists and historians.

Other Tribes, particularly on the plains or in the north woods regions of North America, have been cited by Western archeologists as having such wasteful and destructive hunting practices that many species of animals were reduced to endangered levels "long before the white man came around." What is not reported very often (if at all, in my experience with these written materials on Indian practices) is that the various Tribes so indicted have not hidden these "facts" from their succeeding generations. On the contrary, the stories of those events, which caused suffering among the people and damage to a regional ecosystem, are solemnly recited at various times during the year or every so many years. This is done so the members of those Tribes would always *remember what happened* as a result of their greed or lack of careful preparation and thus never bring about such destructive conditions again.

Detailed explanations of the ecological disasters that were brought about by the Meso-American pyramid and apartment builders have been preserved in the oral histories of various Tribal groups that descended from them. Many of these stories tell us that the people began to deviate from their Sacred Ways and became greedy and quarrelsome. Some of the recorded Pueblo stories tell how the men gambled all night and slept all day; how they violated the women and ceased performing their sacred duties. The stories speak of the women neglecting the children and gossiping with each other for hours instead of performing their sacred duties. They tell of a time the people took more than they really needed from their creature relatives and Earth Mother. They no longer treated each other and their environment with respect. They ceased honoring their relatives—their brother and sister creatures, plants, elements, and minerals. Their Mother Earth and Father Sky and Sister Moon were forgotten— *left out of their thoughts.* They became more and more disconnected and continued to commit acts of violence against each other and the things in their environment. As a direct result, the plants, the creatures, and the elements *abandoned* the people.

> Long ago . . . they say . . . Father Sun burned their crops. The Thunder Beings, the Rain Spirits, and the Water spirits went away. With the help of the Wind Brothers, Mother Earth sent her rich blanket (topsoil) to other places far away from the people. And so the people suffered. The people suffered a long time before they would change their way of living; before they remembered how to ask for help and how to include all their relatives in their thoughts again. Then, all the people that wanted to change the way they were living came together and began to focus their thoughts towards this goal. As a group, they asked to be forgiven. As a group, they asked for guidance. As a group they sought to re-establish their connection to all the things in their environment. After they did this for a time, their thoughts were more in harmony with this goal. Finally, they received the guidance they "prayed"[6] for. When they began to receive instructions in their dreams they knew the Spirits had forgiven them. They paid attention to these visionary instructions, strictly following them, and soon the conditions in the environment around them changed. The rains came and the streams were filled. The animals came near enough to give themselves up for food again. The medicine plants came back and the corn grew tall and the squash and beans and chilies were many. The grasses grew everywhere again and the people were saved.

Some Tribal stories say Corn Mother told them how to care for her so their corn yield would be enough to feed all the people. Some Tribes say that Rain God appeared and told them just how to ask for his help. Some say that Water Sister told them how to treat her and exactly where to make a path for her so she could nourish their Corn Children. Others say that Earth Mother told them how to treat her by telling them when and where to plant; what to plant together and what to plant separately; when and how often to give her a rest; how to sing her to sleep; how to wake her up. Some say the spirits of these things came to them, whispered into their ears, and told them what they should do so these conditions would not "come into being" ever again.

All these stories, with their many tribal variations, tell us how the indigenous Native people continued to survive, and because they had learned the consequences of separating themselves from the "natural world," they never wanted to forget that hard lesson. They did not want their children, grandchildren, or the children of future generations to suffer as they had at that time. By presenting examples of ways in which the people could change, examples of better ways to live together, the Origin Stories and Tribal Histories also emphasize that conscious and appropriate choices must be made. And finally, the stories illustrate how the people found their way back to the "good life" they once had when they honored and respected each other and the rest of creation; the "good life" they had before they became thoughtless and self-indulgent. Thus, the old stories teach today's generations of Native American people how their ancestors consciously sought to be mindful of their place *within* rather than above the rest of creation. Through these stories we know that some of the people decided to return to their old nomadic life-style of hunting and gathering and by doing this, gave up their stable food source. However, there were others who apparently kept the new technology but were willing to seek new ways of food production less destructive to their local ecosystems in order to keep their relatively dependable food source.

Closer examination of the earlier oral histories and the "disaster" stories of specific Tribes (such as some Southwestern Pueblos or Mexico's Huichols and Mayas) indicates a transition period for these ancient cultures at the point a new technology was emerging—a period much like the advent of the Euro-Western machine age, information age, or nuclear age. The earlier historical stories clearly describe that as hunter-gatherers, some of the Meso-American Tribes were quite accomplished at fitting into the environment that provided what they needed to feed, shelter, clothe, and heal themselves by maintaining a psychic connection to it. When I first encountered the descriptions of how the people became greedy and quarrelsome, I wondered why. The Origin Stories describe in detail how these folks were deeply connected to their environment. They knew where to go, where to look for the things they needed for survival, and had created an intricate ceremonial system to honor all the natural resources they were so dependent upon. What had happened to change them into thoughtless, selfish people? The simplest answer would be: "Well, that's human nature," yet that made no sense to me, because of the communal harmony and environmental connection described in other stories. Clearly the Tribal peoples of Meso-America had already developed solutions for conflicts initiated by the vagaries of human nature, and these solutions are embedded in the cultural histories. Something unusual must have happened to drastically change the way they had lived and behaved in prior generations. Some thing, event, or idea came into their lives that eventually produced greed, violent conflict, oppression and the destruction of their environment—and it was "a something" they were either unprepared for, unaware of, or both. Suppose the emergence of a new technology caught them unprepared? Suppose this technology arrived on the scene so gradually they were actually unaware of its intrusion into their everyday lives? I propose that that's exactly what happened when certain hunter-gatherer groups shifted to farming. My own Tribal perspective tells me that these disastrous results occurred precisely because the people had most likely neglected to incorporate this "new technology" into their established spiritual framework *as they were developing it.*

Archeologists tell us that the "corn cultures" of Meso-America progressed slowly from small, randomly sown and unattended patches of corn to more carefully sown and tended patches. The average yield was, at first, enough for that season's consumption, with some left over that they dried and saved for the next spring planting. Many seasons and several generations later, the cultivation of a dependable food source required them to settle in one place permanently in order to guard their crops from animals and nomadic bands from other Tribes. Permanent settlement produced larger, heavier, and less portable tools with which they could work greater areas of land. Crude storage caches became improved, and they could amass larger quantities of food for longer periods of time. More food feeds more people, and more people require more housing, until finally, huge urban complexes were built in the Valley of Mexico, the Yucatan, and the Four Corners area in the United States Southwest. As these new food production practices gradually emerged, I believe the people in those areas were not prepared for the importance cultivation would assume in their daily lives. Indeed, they were so intent on amassing greater stores of food against losses from "thieving nomads" or periods of drought they spent more of their time on the "manufacture" of new tools for cultivation, the building of storage graineries, and clearing and tilling more land. Hunting, fishing, and root gathering were still important activities, but they became less so as the variety of crops they were able to cultivate increased. Undoubtedly, as they became more involved with farming and its time-consuming tasks, they neglected to observe the effects this intensive technology was having on the local ecosystem, so when the negative effects finally became apparent to them, the damage was irreversible. As hunter-gatherers, they had no reason to create a ceremonial structure for planting and harvesting, as it had not been an integral part of their lives, and so the early stories don't include (and wouldn't) the mention of special dances or songs for planting and harvesting at certain times. These same stories do mention specific ritual preparations for hunting and describe feasts of thanksgiving after successful hunts. In fact, in several of the corn-culture Tribes, there are stories of how rain dances or rain ceremonies were brought to the People *after* they were settled in their present villages for some time. In some instances, the retelling of the "bad times" the people experienced by turning their attention away from their local ecosystem *occurs during* rain or planting ceremonies.

When we examine current Pueblo farming practices (in the Southwestern United States), we find a ceremonial framework surrounding the planting, growing, and harvesting of corn. From the preparation of the fields for planting through each phase of the growing season and finally the harvest, ceremonies are enacted that demonstrate *a technology made sacred.* Thus, the later stories, *along with the present-day examples* of "ceremonial farming,"[7] would indicate that many of the Tribes did, in fact, eventually *return to the essence* of the Old

Ways by incorporating this *new technology* into their previously established spiritual framework. The positive outcomes of the spiritual regeneration that took place at that time are emphasized through these ceremonial recountings to their descendants.

The Pueblos of the Southwest United States, particularly Hopi, Zuni, and Acoma, still maintain precontact agrarian practices noted by twentieth-century scholars as examples of "perfected farming techniques." These techniques include: terracing of fields; leaving fields fallow for a minimum period of three years; periodic burning of corn stubble before turning the soil, and finally, always planting crops of beans, corn, and squash (the Three Sisters) together. Today's Western agricultural science supports these practices as ecologically sound methods for preserving precious topsoil. My point here is to bring attention to the lessons *already learned* by many of the stable, highly sophisticated Meso-American cultures as an example of how a people *united in thought and purpose* restored the ecological balance to their environment.

Among us today, there are people who would return to the "old agrarian ways" of the preindustrial period; some would even return to the hunter-gatherer period. There are others, like me, who believe we can keep the beneficial technologies that have emerged among us and, with careful planning, can rethink and revise the present methods of modern production to make them less destructive to our local ecosystems. However the new technologies appeared in our realities, they are here, and it is possible to incorporate them into our spiritual frameworks if we so desire. Whether we choose to acknowledge it or not, all human creations to date come from Mother Earth—from Her Body. She provides the "raw materials" of our "inventions." Humans are just one of the many species of creatures that her body nourishes and sustains. Native Americans believe the Great Mystery placed us on earth to do just what it is we do. We belong to the Great Circle of Life, along with the rest of creation. Everything in the heavens and on the earth is natural, is part of the "natural world"—*including humans.* An earthquake is a violent "natural" act, as is a volcanic explosion or the destructive force of a hurricane, and yet not one of us would judge or condemn such an event as "unnatural" or meddlesome tampering with the environment. Oddly, when humans disturb the ecological balance by tampering with the environment, Euro-Westerners judge themselves and "others" (non-Westerners) of committing unnatural acts or creating unnatural technologies. I believe this to be a misnomer that carries considerable negative side effects for us, both mentally and psychically. It forces us to continually instruct ourselves that we don't belong to the natural world—that human creativity is unnatural or alien. Our spirits know this to be untrue. "Antinature" is a more accurate way to describe a selfish technology that arbitrarily destroys creature and plant species. Technologies come into being in the natural world out of the substance of the natural world through the miracle of human thought and, whether humans or bees or birds or earthquakes or volcanoes or hurricanes or tornadoes or flash floods or radioactivity *manipulate the environment,* most Native Americans view all of them as natural occurrences. We also know that when we become extremely self-indulgent with our "creativity," focusing on ourselves to the exclusion of all our nonhuman relatives, they will abandon us. We have this experience in our past, and we have been raised to remember that we are all "equal" in the thought of the Great Mystery. Our duty to ourselves is to restore our own balance *within* the rest of creation.

There is much practical information available in the old stories still told by many of the North and South American Indian Tribes. In recent years, members of many different Tribes have attended universities on both continents and have been recording much of this information in written form—most particularly the histories of their Tribes. Some Tribes are still reluctant to have their ceremonial practices recorded in print or on tape or film, and these wishes should be honored by all outsiders. But, where there has been a concerted effort by diminishing Tribal groups to preserve not only their histories but also their sacred ways, I truly feel that Western scholars can learn a great deal if they would study these materials. In some instances (though not all), a Western analytical approach to these "stories" can concretely fill in the gaps and possibly provide us with some viable solutions relevant to this land base for today's ecological imbalances. However, care must be taken in using this approach. I make this point because Western scholars (for the most part) are monocultural and perceive other cultures through their academically trained Western bias. Academically trained Native American scholars are bicultural and in reality, walk in two worlds—the Indian world and the Euro-Western world. It is important for non-Indians to keep this in mind, simply because the dominant perspective or thought system of the Western Hemisphere is Eurocentric. Willis Harman explains cultural bias in a most understandable way in his recent book:

> Now each of us, from infancy onward, is subjected to a complex set of suggestions from our social environment, which in effect teaches us how to perceive the world. We may from time to time, especially in early childhood, have experiences that do not conform to this cultural norm— but we eventually "correct" these perceptions and cease experiencing the anomalies, through the power of the socializing process. And so each of us is literally hypnotized from infancy to perceive the world the way people in our culture perceive it.
>
> In the modern world this "cultural hypnosis" extends to experiencing a world in which "scientific laws" are always obeyed—whereas in other, more "primitive" cultures, "violations" of these laws may be relatively commonplace. For example, the phenomenon of changing inner beliefs to such an extent that one can with impunity walk barefoot over burning coals . . . is one which has for centuries been observable in a variety of pre-modern societies. (Harman 1988, 19–20)

Ideally, non-Indian scholars will make an extra effort to establish contacts and dialogues with American Indian *scholars* throughout the United States, Canada, Alaska, and Mexico. Although Mexico is still struggling to reclaim its Indian origins, European-born monotheism still prevails, and Tribal natives there are isolated and looked down upon for their "indigenous lifestyles and ceremonial practices." In spite of this, there are many Mexican Indian scholars who were raised in their Native traditions and who continue to respect as well as steadfastly claim their Indian heritage. Again, it takes extra effort to identify them. Hundreds of books, articles, and research papers have been written about all the Tribes in North America by early (as well as later) Euro-Western historians, ethnologists, and ethnographers—much of it with sensitivity and insight and with the best of intentions.

The most difficult obstacle to overcome with this non-Indian authored material is the Western penchant for comparing the rest of the world to itself and making root assumptions accordingly. These authors tend to automatically credit Western civilization as the most advanced culture on the planet, using it as the highest pinnacle of human attainment. This is indeed a monocultural bias and patently absurd to those of us who derive from cultures whose living histories date back some ten thousand years and more. This is not to disparage Western scholars; rather I would caution my readers to weigh the volumes of information available on American Indians thoughtfully. Again, Willis Harman's explanation of "cultural hypnosis" is quite candid and helpful in this context. He goes on to state:

These several examples emphasize the difficulty of distinguishing the extent to which the "reality" we perceive is peculiar to our cultural hypnosis. We tend to find it curious that other "primitive" or "traditional" cultures should perceive reality in the way they do—*so obviously discrepant with the modern scientific worldview*. It is harder to entertain the thought that we in modern Western society might have our own cultural peculiarities in the way we perceive the world—that our reality might be as parochial in its way as that of the Middle Ages appears to us now. Since Western science is the "best" knowledge system yet devised, it seems reasonable to consider our values "normal," our predilections "natural," and our perceived measured world "real."

It was hard [in the early seventeenth century] to "see" challenging information precisely because the old belief system provided a coherent picture of the world which *worked*. Likewise it is not comfortable for some of us, in the late twentieth century, to recognize the parochial nature of our prevailing belief system (even though it may seem to be based on the best science available). It is hard for us to "see" evidence that doesn't fit in, and that suggests the conventional worldview may be in a state of fundamental change. Despite our discomfort, it is essential to consider that possibility. (Harman 1988, 20; emphasis mine)

And though white Euro-Westerners have created the most sophisticated tools of massive destruction and the most self-centered ideologies of any race on the planet, Native American philosophies say: "They are our relatives." Many Native American prophecies state that: "It is our duty to show them how to Walk In Beauty—with us." It is important for all of us to find our "Beauty Way," and Native American spiritual frameworks can provide examples of ways in which non-Indians can "tune in" to the spirit force of *this land*.

NATIVE AMERICAN SPIRITUAL FRAMEWORKS

To be spiritual, or inclined to honor, respect, and acknowledge the elements of our universe (both physical and nonphysical) that sustain and nourish our lives, seems to be an innate aspect of human beings. Among traditional Tribal people, to be spiritual is to be aware and accepting of spirit or the Spirit World and to believe in a spirit force or power that manifests itself in all things. When Native Americans refer to themselves as spiritual people, they are saying they believe that everything in the universe is imbued with spirit and they embrace, acknowledge, and respect the animating force within/surrounding/beyond all things—including humans. The idea of "the Sacred" held by traditional Indians is all-inclusive, and to be connected to the Spirit World is to be "in communion" with the Great Mystery. This concept also carries a mandate for the people to strive to achieve harmony within their community and its surrounding environment, to "Walk in Beauty" or "see the Good in everything." This internal sense of harmony, when expressed externally, gave rise to the creation of ceremonies that honored all life-sustaining and transformation processes in the natural world for both humans and nonhumans. Generally speaking, non-Tribal people do not embrace this concept. Most organized non-Indian religions accept spirit or soul as a nontangible aspect of humans. In American English, to be spiritual is usually understood to mean either being very religious or a practicing devotee of some religious sect who exhibits all the required virtues. The emphasis here is on humans interacting with each other. Being a good person usually means you are kind to your neighbors and friends and loving to your family; you are generous, helpful, pleasant, a pillar of the community doing good deeds for others. What is missing is the distinct *inclusion of nonhumans*. Being a good person in Tribal terms means your good behavior and intentions are extended toward creatures, plants, and elements, as well as humans.

I have stated elsewhere that it is not my intention to "Indianize" anyone, but to present practical alternatives to our current ecological imbalances by providing examples of a "living philosophy" that not only originated from this land base but has endured into the present. It is because the land-based social structures of the original Americans continue to provide the core traditional patterns from which these peoples draw their spiritual nourishment and practical approach to daily life that I am strongly suggesting that the many principles (philosophical, spiritual, and social) that emerged through these earliest inhabitants are the true legacy of all American-born individuals. However, I am also aware of the conflicts surrounding the study of, the borrowing of, the adapting from, or just being influenced by the Native American way of life. My personal experience tells me it is important to speak directly to some of the possible objections concerning my statements about Tribal principles and the risks involved for non-Indians who embrace a "Native American perspective." Obviously, approaching our daily lives in a "sacred manner" is not the sole province of any one Tribe, or any particular culture, for that matter. In addition, dancing and singing to the beat of drums or other percussion instruments cannot be claimed as the exclusive right of any racial group of people, nor is the purifying of the body through fasting and cleansing in some manner or the offering of the smoke of some substance to the "spirit world" (be it sage, tobacco, frankincense, or sandalwood). What seems to be lacking at the moment concerning the issues around cultural or religious theft is clear articulation about the dos and don'ts regarding any particular culture's sacred forms. The question now becomes: How can non-Indians know what kinds of rituals or ceremonies they can perform without infringing upon some Tribe's sacred religious-spiritual practice?

I believe the way in which certain acts are put together and consistently repeated designates them as a cultural form of worship or honoring and therefore "belonging to" a particular group. So, in order to infringe upon or desecrate any Tribal religion, an "outsider" would have to sing "sacred" songs in a particular language (Navajo, Lakota, Cherokee, and so forth) while executing the steps of dances traditionally done to those songs by a given Tribe. Then, and only then, can tribal elders say outsiders are truly stealing their sacred practices. Songs, dances, ceremonies, and sacred rites *are created by people* for very specific reasons and purposes.

Every ceremony and sacred rite ever practiced on this planet was invented by humans to be performed by humans—one or hundreds. The motivation is generally inspired by the witnessing of the mysteries and cycles of transformation continuously assailing our physical senses. The awe we experience—the joy, love, or grief that overwhelms us—inspires us to express in some fashion our brief encounter with that which is beyond physical touch but is within reach of our inner senses. When this happens, we achieve a kind of "knowing" that we have somehow been touched by something beyond us. A knowing that we cannot articulate often leads us to celebrate this personal event (or in many cases, communal event) through some form of expression. When Tribal peoples experienced a brief encounter with the Great Mystery, they celebrated this experience with chanting and rhythmic movements. The Tribes view these celebrations or ceremonies as sacred because the intent of the performers and the witness/participants is one of reverence and respect. It is within this context that traditional Tribal Indian people view all the elements that make up our universe as sacred. They acknowledge that all "others" are entitled to and deserving of existence along with us and therefore to be celebrated as sacred components of their realities.

While Euro-Westerners define sacred as "set apart or dedicated to religious uses, hallowed as opposed to profane," American Indians make no such arbitrary division. If the Great Spirit or Great Mystery holds everything in its thought, then everything is sacred. Funk & Wagnalls Standard College Dictionary goes on to state that sacred means "pertaining or relating to deity, religion, or hallowed places or things." Among Indians, sacred is sacred. It pertains to all and everything. If a place or ceremony or objects are considered extra special, then they say it is filled with power or is powerful. Items of special significance are thought of as places of power or power objects, and some places or things are more powerful than others, but they are all always considered sacred to begin with. Some ceremonies are more solemn than others, but it is always understood that whatever the people are doing, they will be doing it *in a sacred manner*. Sacred also means "consecrated and dedicated to a person or purpose." I concur, as would any traditional Indian. Of course we are consecrated and dedicated, to ourselves, each other, our world, and Wakan Tanka (Lakota), or Thought Woman (Laguna and Acoma), or Maheo (Cheyenne) or the Great Mystery or Great Spirit, and—fulfilling our life paths—"walking our individual roads" is a consecrated and dedicated purpose. Finally, the most fundamental meaning of the word *Sacred* for Native Americans is "entitled to reverence and respect; not to be profaned; inviolable." American Indians believe the universe and everything in it is "entitled to reverence and respect" because it exists. Thus the Tribal Principle of Relationship, that we are all related, is a natural extension of this belief. The Tribes teach that when we are disrespectful, irreverent, or abusive to the inhabitants of our environment, they will abandon us. They will no longer give themselves up for us if we disconnect ourselves from them.

Native Americans believe the animals and plants they need for sustenance and healing "give up" or "give away" their lives so the people can continue to exist. Observing animal and plant life taught the Tribes that ecological balance was maintained through interdependence and reasonable use. Following the natural laws in operation around them, Native American Tribes practiced reasonable use rather than denial. As various Tribes discovered the consequences of taking more than they could reasonably use, they changed their thoughtless, destructive practices to more thoughtful, life-promoting ones and incorporated this knowledge into their Tribal histories. They instituted various forms of ceremonial Give Aways instead of structuring accumulation of things and property into their social systems as human achievements to be esteemed and honored. The Give Aways recycled tools, clothing, ornamental, ceremonial and household items among the members of the Tribe and guaranteed the most basic needs for the less capable or handicapped.

ADAPTATION AND PRACTICE OF TRIBAL PRINCIPLES

In "Indian fashion," I have presented several "idea blocks" as examples of other possibilities for generating new ways to think about our local, regional, and global environment. In restating some historical information about certain Tribal practices (documented in more detail in many other sources), I hope I have provided the impetus for incorporating a too-often-neglected perspective in our search for holistic, life-sustaining practices for today's global communities.

In my introduction, I stated that I would offer some suggestions for facilitating attitudinal shifts in consciousness and becoming more open to Tribal ways of thought. I said I would present some ways that non-Indians might use to create a sense of place, generate a personal legend or origin story, and adapt a few valuable Tribal principles to fit a modern technological world.

Let's begin with the idea or Tribal concept of the Sacred. If non-Indians can accept the Native American premise that all of creation is held in the creative thought of the Great Mystery (or in the Mind of She Who Thought Us into Being), then it is an easy step to adopt the concept that everything in heaven and on earth—including the human race—is truly sacred. If we believe that everything is sacred, then the most mundane tasks take on a deeper meaning. One approach is to consciously ritualize ordinary actions such as awakening to each new day, the preparation of foods, or the accomplishment of daily tasks. For example, the Apache day is begun this way. An individual male arises at dawn, leaves the house, faces east, and begins singing a song to assist the sun in its journey over the horizon. This is considered a sacred duty, and the song is one of joyful greeting. Grinding corn for ceremonial use is still done by many Indians on a stone slab (a *metate*) on the floor and is not an easy task to perform. In traditional Navajo families, corn is ground by the women, but the men help to lighten the drudgery by sitting nearby, singing joyful corn-grinding songs. This is done to keep *the thoughts* of the grinder happy and cheerful, so the resulting foods offered in ceremony and/or eaten by the family will not have unhappy or "tired-aching-back-and-knees-thoughts" in them. It is believed that if the woman grinding the corn is cheerful, the food will be well received and blessed by the spirits and will be nourishing for the family.[8]

If you love your home but hate the job that fills the icebox and pays the rent and utilities, then your thoughts are out of balance, according to our way of thinking. If you love your home but hate the city or town where you live, then you are out of harmony with your life's circumstances. Suppose you thought of your job as a sacred duty that assists you (as it does) to maintain your private residence? Suppose you think about all the beautiful places in your city that may have been sacred places at one time for the original native inhabitants? Every city and town in the United States was once a special place for native Tribal peoples, too, because people instinctively locate themselves in spots that are energizing and nourishing to them—physically, psychically, and spiritually. There are trees and grasses and flowers and birds and ants and bees waiting for you to "send your songs to them"—to say hello to them—to call them sister, brother, cousin, or friend. They *are* your relatives; they hear your thoughts as you travel around your town or city, back and forth from your home.

Begin where you are. Do you have a baking song? You can create one. How about making up a song for grocery shopping or a song for making your laundry sparkle? You can create a food blessing poem to thank the spirits of the foods you eat for giving themselves up for your nourishment. They give themselves up so your breath may continue. Native Americans believe that plants as well as animals do this willingly when we acknowledge their great gift of life to us— even grocery-store food! We are taught that if we always do this, no foods will harm us, because the spirit of that food will think kindly of us. We believe that *how we think about ourselves and our environment is how we will experience it in our day-to-day existence.* So we strive to be thankful to the spirit world around us, consciously every day, including our relatives in our thoughts to remain in harmony and balance. There are other systems that teach similar things. Recently, much has been written about various foods that are harmful for this or that reason, but there are also many groups of people who still adhere to their old-fashioned (prescientific) non-Western beliefs and have proven that these foods or substances are not harmful to them. Shifting our consciousness to focus more on nourishing and helpful examples can be far less harmful to us as well as our nonhuman relatives. Focusing on destructive forces all the time causes feelings of despair and, too often, a sense of powerlessness to do anything to change these dreadful circumstances. When we seek the beauty and wonder of creation, creation responds by bringing more beauty and wonder for us to be glad about and thankful for. The Navajo people call this the Beauty Way, and all North American Tribes have similar philosophies.

Where you live now was once home to your Native American ancestors hundreds or, possibly, thousands of years ago. Who were they? What is their history of the place where you live? That history is also your legacy. How did the Tribal ancestors come to be in that place? Did they originate in the east or north and migrate there? Maybe that Tribe originated in that very place. Your local library probably has the resources that will answer these questions. Answering these questions for yourself will give you a different perspective of your present "land base." How did you come to this place? When did your family (parents, grandparents, or great-grandparents) arrive? Where did they originate? Write your own Migration Story. Trace the wanderings of your own people and, if you can, the reasons they or you finally settled in the place you now call home. Doing this can give you a stronger and more conscious connection to your present homeplace.

Next, identify the prominent landmarks surrounding your homeplace (not the human-made marks). According to their historical traditions, how did the Tribe(s) relate to these landmarks? What significance was assigned to them (for example, special sacred places for receiving visions, for locating healing plants of the region)? Find out what the original plant and creature life in your region was; the ecological interaction and interdependence between plants, animals, insects, birds, air and winds, water, and earth. Consider what has changed about your environment since European contact. How have the creatures and plants adapted to the changes? Then center yourself in the region where you make your home and introduce yourself to the spirits of your place. Greet the plant, creature, mineral, wind, water, earth, and sky spirits. Make a song to them. Do this in a sacred manner and you may be surprised by what you will begin to notice happening around you. If your intention to become connected to your land base is sincere, the resulting experiences will be very rewarding and personally enriching. If you will follow through on a few of these suggestions, you will attune yourself to your homeplace, and if you make it a point to acknowledge your local nonhuman surroundings on a daily basis (several times a day, preferably), your environment will begin to respond to you *according to your thoughts*. Welcome all your relatives into your immediate family. Approach each day in a sacred manner and with a healthy sense of humor. Our relatives will help us if we ask them to help. Our relatives will forgive us if we ask for their forgiveness and make a serious commitment not to repeat our previous mistakes. If we "send our voices out to them," as Wallace Black

Elk suggests—if we can *believe* they are our relatives—they will instruct us as Earth Mother, Corn Mother, Water Sister, Rain God, the Thunder Beings, and the Wind Brothers did for our ancestors, so long ago. If we all open our hearts and minds to this rich legacy, we may discover many creative solutions to our ecological dilemmas.

These are my suggestions for restoring our own balance and harmony with All That Is. I know it is possible, because the Pueblo people of the arid Southwest come together to dance for the corn in the heat of the dry summers year after year—and it rains. They must not harbor thoughts or talk about "how dry it is" or "how hot it is" or "what if it won't rain" or "yes, but the weather person said." Instead, they imagine the Cloud People appearing in a cloudless sky, building huge formations of vapor and then dancing up there to release the Rain Spirits on the cornfields. They imagine the gentle rains falling on the fields and imagine how glad the Corn Children will be when the Rain Spirits come to "visit them." When the people dress for the Corn Dances, they imagine the corn plants growing taller and taller, the ears perfectly shaped and plump with fat kernels of corn. These are the kinds of thoughts they hold when they dance for the Corn Children.

The examples of this "Way of Thinking and Believing" are many and not restricted to the Southwest United States. The beneficial results of Rain Dances, Corn Dances, Deer Dances, and other Tribal ceremonies practiced by Tribal peoples all over the planet have been documented by many credible scientists and social scientists. The implications of these ancient Tribal thought systems are immense. I believe that many basic Tribal principles can be adapted to fit modern daily life and can produce the appropriate ecological changes we are seeking.

I trust your creative imaginations to expand on the somewhat brief and generalized historical examples of the few Tribal principles I have discussed here, with the hope you will find these important concepts helpful in your own lives.

May your heart and mind find the Beauty Way, and may peace through balance and harmony be yours in all your days on Mother Earth.

NOTES

1. Sanders and Peek 1973, 183–92. In their introduction to Chap. 4 they discuss how Benjamin Franklin's knowledge of and interaction with the League is never mentioned in standard American history texts. This American and Euro-Western penchant for "disappearing" an American Indian Confederacy of Nations as a foundational source for the structure of United States governmental institutions is further and more recently documented by Weatherford 1988, Chap. 8.

2. I use the terms *Native American, American Indian, First Americans, Indian(s)* and *Native(s)* interchangeably, because it is comfortable for me to do so and because much of the literature written about and by American Indians uses all of these terms to designate the first or original inhabitants of the Americas.

3. Allen 1986b, 3–29. Paula introduces this term and the framework for its usage in this essay.

4. Early non-Indian ethnographers collected tribal stories in virtually every region of the United States. Since the mid 1970s, many Native American communities have published collections of their Tribal stories and histories for their own use in school programs and to provide the public-at-large with informative materials written from their own perspective. A collection such as Beck and Walters 1977 is an example of a comprehensive Indian-authored text and excellent source of many American Indian Tribal teachings. Other similar publications can often be found in local libraries or local historical museums—particularly if the museum has a display on early Indian inhabitants of the area.

5. *The National Geographic*, Vol 176, no. 4 (October 1989) "La Ruta Maya," Wilbur E. Garrett, ed., 424–78; "Copan: A Royal Maya Tomb Discovered," Ricardo Agurcia Fasquelle and William L. Fash, Jr., 481–86; "City of Kings and Commoners: Copán," George E. Stuart, 488–504.

6. In this context, *prayed* is intended to mean group thought focused toward The Great Mystery or Great Spirit actively imagining the "state of being" their reality should assume or become. The English word *prayer* is the closest equivalent that conveys the spiritual sense of this activity, but the word itself carries broader implications for American Indians than those perceived by Euro-Americans. For example, The Great Mystery contains not only The Maker but *all* Spirit Beings everywhere—as well as the concrete or solid substance of the universe from which everything occurs or comes into being.

7. Weigand 1978, 110 states that "Ceremonialism still accompanies the planting of cotton and gourd and tobacco seeds and the act of sowing, though the rites [for the above-named crops] are no longer well remembered or even generally practiced. Ceremonialism for corn and squash is very well developed and central to the rainy-dry season dichotomy in the Huichol calendar."

8. Brandon 1974, 138. Another example of this practice exists in the Southwest among the Pueblo peoples. Brandon notes that "the women were expected to make a social bee of the never ending community work of grinding corn, and the right way of doing things also demanded a man at the door of the grinding room, playing the grinding song on a flute." As sensitive and accurate as Brandon is about recounting the histories and customs of several hundred North American Tribes in this work, his own Euro-American bias ("cultural hypnosis," to restate Harman) is immediately apparent in his assumption that "the women were *expected* to" do this or that. He also says "*demanded* a man at the door," which is a bit strong to describe the communal participation that takes place in preparing cornmeal. In the pueblo I come from, the women organize all the women's activities and the men tend to their own duties, but when a community activity is taking place, both genders assist each other to make the "chores" more pleasant.

15

Nuclear Power and the Sacred

Or Why a Beautiful Woman Is Like a Nuclear Power Plant

JANE CAPUTI

What is sacred is simultaneously held in greatest esteem and greatest fear. It is the source of life and the power to take life away. From it man expects all rewards, success, and power; yet as a force greater than he, it might bring punishment, failure, and degradation ... Man is ambivalent toward the sacred: he respects that which is greater than himself, desiring to possess and control it; but, in addition, he fears it, wishing to avoid its negative powers.
—*Richard Stivers (1982, 32)*

I am your worst fear; I am your best fantasy.
—*legend on a placard held by a woman at a Women's Liberation demonstration, 1970*

In investigations of nuclear metaphor, I and others have found that the two most common and frequently intermingled sources of imagery are the sexual and the religious (Caputi 1987, 1991; Chernus 1986; Cohn 1987), both traditional repositories of the sacred (Stivers 1982). For example, the name of the

Jane Caputi teaches in the American Studies department at the University of New Mexico, Albuquerque. She is the author of *The Age of Sex Crime*, a feminist analysis of the atrocity of serial sex murder, and collaborated with Mary Daly on *Webster's First Intergalactic Wickedary of the English Language*. She currently is writing *Gossips, Gorgons, and Crones: Female Power and the Nuclear Age* and is editing an anthology with Paula Gunn Allen, *The Heart of Knowledge: Indians and the Bomb*.

bikini swimsuit derives from the test-bombed island. That suit perfectly epitomizes the directives of the puritanical/pornographic god (Sjöö and Mor 1987, 234) whose point of view now reigns, fixing attention upon, while denying full view of, the female body's "forbidden zones." Concomitantly, the entire island of Bikini has been turned into a "forbidden zone" due to radioactive contamination.

The concept of the sacred is a most complex one and has been variously defined (Allen 1986b; Beck and Walters 1977; Caillois 1959; Stivers 1982). In nearly all definitions, the key factor is that of *power*, the power to cause magical things to happen, such as transmutation or communication with spirits. Ambiguity is also a frequent motif. The sacred contains both the power to create as well as to destroy. This paradox was ably expressed by the Spirit of Memphis Quartet (1951) who sang about atomic power: "It can cure the sick or destroy the evil, with one stroke of power known by God alone."

In many tribal or gynocentric cultures, everything in the cosmos was sacred; everything was imbued with consciousness and spirit and partook in the greater power of being (Sanchez 1989). In contemporary patriarchal worldviews, a great divide exists between the sacred and the mundane (Weigle 1982, 1989). Animals, women, and nature are dis-spirited (Daly with Caputi 1987, 195), captured, objectified, and profaned, while elite men, their gods, and some special things associated with the man-made, paradigmatically technological devices, are deemed sacred. This sense of the sacred, however, does not stem from a shared and egalitarian being, but from a notion of superior force and hierarchy (from *hieros*, "sacred"). Not surprisingly, under this system, nuclear technology is frequently imaged as phallic might, a manifestation of triumphant patriarchal divinity, the greatest accomplishment of Western civilization, or, hearkening back to more ancient imagery, captured female power.

Of course, language and myth are themselves forms of power, exercised both consciously and unconsciously in the structuring and perpetuation of *nuclearist* reality (i.e., one combining disrespect, exploitation, pornographicization, and worship of nuclear technology). Understanding this suggests one tactic for ecofeminists: the generation of gynocentric, antinuclearist myth and metaphor. Here, then, I first will analyze patriarchal nuclear metaphor and then turn attention to some of the ways that feminists have begun to invent and employ language, myth, and metaphor as forms of power—exercised consciously and/or intuitively in destructuring nuclearist reality and invoking gynocentric, elementally respectful attitudes toward nuclear power.

NUCLEAR PORNOGRAPHY

A little nukey is good for everyone.
— Slogan on a pro-nuclear T-shirt, featuring a dancing
nuclear reactor, with a smile reading "afterglow," c. 1980

Air Force Magazine's *advertisements for new weapons* . . . rival Playboy *as a catalog of men's sexual anxieties and fantasies.*
—Carol Cohn (1987, pp. 692, 694)

Tell me that you don't have to fuck yourself on
the reactor core of an intense meltdown
                              to show your importance
Tell me that you have no desire
to be the first one to fuck
                    into the fission of a fusion
                          of a fucking holocaust.
        Jayne Cortez (1984, 106), "Tell Me"

From 1945 on, in song, story, language, and picture, a link between gender, sexuality, and nuclear technology consistently has appeared. For example, Robert Jungk (1958, 197) reports that the original scientists working at Los Alamos took bets among themselves as to whether they would ultimately have a "boy" or a "girl," that is, a success or a dud. A success it was, and the "fathered" (by J. Robert Oppenheimer) bomb was nicknamed "Little Boy." A few years later, the bomb underwent a sex change operation: The device dropped on the Bikini Islands was nicknamed "Gilda" and painted with an image of sex symbol Rita Hayworth. Soon Hollywood starlets were being touted as "anatomic bombs."

Thus eroticized, the ultimate nuclear nightmare soon became an overt setting for sexual fantasy, as it did in Bill Haley's (1957) "Thirteen Women . . . And Only One Man In Town":

> Last night I was dreaming, dreamed about the H-Bomb,
> Well the bomb it went off and I was caught.
> I was the only man on the ground.
> There was thirteen women and only one man in town
> . . . .
> I had two girls every morning . . .

In just a few years, Stanley Kubrick's *Dr. Strangelove: Or How I Learned to Stop Worrying and Love the Bomb* (1964) made explicit the sexualized violence and fetishization of weaponry necessarily attending such erotic fantasy. Here, the crazed general who triggers world nuclear holocaust is the curiously named "General Jack D. Ripper."

Throughout the Nuclear Age, this metaphoric bridge connecting nuclear technology to sexuality continues to be crossed. Furthermore, all such popular themes — from the romantic to the rapist — provide supporting evidence for feminist critiques of nuclear technology (Easlea 1983; Koen and Swaim 1980; Russell 1989; Sofia 1984; Spretnak 1983; Warnock 1982), many of which argue that nuclear technologies and the accompanying arms race are the products of a phallocentric culture and sexuality, what Helen Caldicott (1984) alludes to in her phrase "missile envy" and what Mary Daly and I have further designated to be "penis envy" (1987, 215-16). Helen Caldicott (1984) and Carol Cohn (1987) have found evidence of the association of "phallic power" to nuclear weapons in techno-scientific jargon. Equally, the evidence from popular culture indicates an extensive association between patriarchal notions of sexuality and nuclear technology.

Any discussion of sexuality employs metaphoric speech. For example, a long tradition links sexuality to natural forces and energies such as heat and fire. Following on this, and adding a technological and militaristic bent, are recurrent comparisons of both male and female sexuality to nuclear power plants and weapons, as well as a blithe comparison of nuclear blasts to orgasm. The following three statements represent that first type of metaphor:

> "He's like Three Mile Island inside, just ready to blow." . . . "I think he's going to be a heterosexual Montgomery Clift." That's what movie biggies are saying about Tom Cruise. (Staff 1986, 74)

> Many observers find in the ascendancy of Michael Jackson the ultimate personification of the androgynous rock star. His high flying tenor makes him sound like the lead in some funked up boys' choir, even as the sexual dynamism irradiating from the arch of his dancing body challenges Government standards for a nuclear meltdown. (Cocks 1984, 59)

> *Why Is A Beautiful Woman Like A Nuclear Power Plant?* In order to remain beautiful she must take good care of herself . . . she schedules her rest regularly . . . when she is not feeling well she sees her doctor . . . she never lets herself get out of shape . . . she is as trim now as she was ten years ago . . . in other words, *she is a perfect example of preventative maintenance.* (ad in *Nuclear News Buyer's Guide* [Crouse 1976])

In each of these descriptions, sexuality is somehow linked to a nuclear reactor—male sexuality with the reactor's propensity to blow, female sexuality with its ability to be kept, contained, or controlled. Such metaphors participate in a dominant sexual paradigm which Martha Vicinus (1982, 136) has characterized as both "overwhelmingly male and heterosexual"—the "energy-control (or hydraulic) model." In this "energy-control" paradigm, sexuality is seen as an "independent force or energy disciplined by personal and social constraints." Such sexuality is understood as both a powerful force seeking explosive release as well as one that can be controlled and made socially useful.

It is only in a culture conditioned by such a paradigm that a nuclear meltdown can be understood as erotic, as the irresistible, blissful spilling over of (inherently destructive) energy. Thus, masculine sexuality "blows" orgasmically, while feminine sexuality, as we learn from the "beautiful woman" ad, functions best when constrained and tamed. Even the image accompanying the ad copy underscores that association: a young, eyes-downcast lady, clothed in flowing bedroom garments, an image uncannily reminiscent of those in ads for feminine hygiene products. The underlying message is that female/menstrual power—when contained, controlled, shielded, and kept in the boudoir—is highly desirable as well as productive. Indeed, although this ad does not mention it, both the reactor and the woman, when carefully attended to, not only get "hot," but then can function for men as "breeders."

An even more familiar association insists on the connections between nuclear *weaponry* and sexuality, specifically the bomb blast and sexual orgasm. In 1945, special War Department historian-journalist William L. Laurence (1946, 239) won much acclaim for his eyewitness accounts of the first bomb blasts, accounts which resounded with a pornographic delight in the "come shot," i.e., the spectacle of male ejaculation: "The mushroom top was even more alive than the pillar, seething and boiling in a white fury of creamy foam, sizzling upward and then descending earthward, a thousand geysers rolled into one."

Throughout the 1950s, scores of popular songs likewise announced the culture's orgasmic surrender to nuclear technology. For example, Little Caeser with the Red Callender Sextette (1957) sang of their "Atomic Love": "Ooh, something exploded down inside/and rushed tears up in my eyes/Oh yes, I have that funny feeling/I guess it's my atomic love for you."

References to sexual climax also frequently structure contemporary nuclear metaphors. "Satisfaction came in a chain reaction," wail the Trammps (1977) in "Disco Inferno." Artist Mimi Smith (1982) serves up her version of nuclear safety: a drawing of a mushroom cloud with a diaphragm vainly trying to contain it. "Better Safe Than Sorry," reads the caption. Not to be outdone, the phenomenally best-selling writer Stephen King (1986, 931) has one of his female characters describe her orgasm (actually King's fantasy of female orgasm) in this way: "She became aware that this wasn't going to be just a come; it was going to be a tactical nuke."

This recurrent metaphor setting up a bridge between sexual pleasure and nuclear explosion demands a consideration of both the sexual attractiveness of nuclear weaponry and the lethality of normative patriarchal sexuality.

SAFER THAN SEX?

I wish you were the town of Hiroshima and I la bomb atomique pour tomber dessus.
> —*the master of ceremonies to a female performer in an Athens nightclub, 1945 (quoted in Boyer 1985, 246)*

"Nuclear Energy—Safer than Sex"
> —*slogan on the T-shirt of a women's pro-nuclear group, S.A.F.E. (Society for the Advancement of Fusion Energy). (McMullen 1977, 47)*

NUKE THE BITCHES—slogan on a T-shirt of a counterdemonstrator at the Women's Encampment for a Future of Peace and Justice, Romulus, N.Y.
> *(Putter 1985)*

A political cartoon by Lou Myers (1983) shows two military men dueling with extended penises, actually missiles, one marked *U.S.*, the other *U.S.S.R.* Similarly, a political cartoon in the *Los Angeles Times* (Conrad 1987) shows a number of upright nuclear missiles: "Speaking of the need for condoms." What these humorists mock, however, others take seriously and blithely exploit. For example, Ronald Reagan (1983, A20), in his famous " 'Star Wars' Speech," promised that his plan would be able to render nuclear missiles "impotent and obsolete." More deliberately jocular, Mr. Reagan employed the same sexualized association in his world-televised postgame remarks following the 1984 Super-bowl. Chatting with winning Coach Flores of the L.A. Raiders, the president joked: "I've already gotten a call from Moscow. They think Marcus Allen is a new secret weapon. They insist we dismantle it." Warming to his metaphors, the Great Communicator continued, telling Flores that if he would turn over his football team to the government, "we'd put them in silos and we wouldn't have to build the MX missile" (quoted in Bach 1984, 18). Idealized virility is thus powerfully and gleefully fused to weaponry and to a potentially Earth-destroying lethality. Reagan's commentary is recognizable as part of an omni-present stream which we might call the pornography of everyday life. Not sur-prisingly, explicit pornography soon made use of precisely that same sexual-nuclear metaphor. A 1987 adult video catalog highlighted one feature, *The Incredible Mr. MX* (a porno film about a man with a monstrously long penis): "Take a long look at the real weapon of the 80s!! . . . see his 16 1/2" missile."

All such sexually violent nuclear images speak eloquently to the feminist insight that under male supremacy sex and violence are, as Catharine Mac-Kinnon (1983, 650) notes, "mutually definitive" and "acts of dominance and submission, up to and including violence, are experienced as sexually arousing, as sex itself" (MacKinnon 1987, 6). As I have argued in some detail elsewhere, such metaphors point to a shared ideology and practice between sexism and nuclearism (Caputi 1987, 1988b). To summarize: The femicidal culture's image of woman as object/victim is paralleled by the religious and scientific ideology that pictures Mother Earth as toy, machine, or violated object, legitimating the contamination and destruction of the planet just as images of mutilated, violated women legitimate and encourage violence against women. Moreover, in a sym-bol system in which the penis is consistently linked to weaponry and nuclear blasts to ejaculations, nuclear holocaust frequently is celebrated, however sub-tly, as ultimate orgasm, ultimate matricide, and ultimate "snuff" scene.

These ubiquitous metaphors linking virility with weapons of cosmic destruc-tion are no mere figures of speech, but symbols and images actively structuring reality. Discussing the significance of metaphor, David Edge (1973, 33) has commented: "To use a metaphor is to overlap two images . . . our sense of both is subtly altered, by a sort of elision." Arguably, under the influence of this culture-wide "elision" of already phallicized sexuality to globally destructive nuclear weaponry, that culturally constructed virility has shifted in form, man-ifesting in unprecedented modern forms of multicide (Holmes and De Burger 1988, 16–21; Caputi 1987), including serial sex murder and mass murder of family members by nuclear fathers. In response to the pro-nuclear slogan cited above (which, significantly, preceded the AIDS crisis), one might argue that nuclear energy is not so much *safer* than sex, but that sexual danger, in many ways still to be explored, is intimately linked with nuclear danger.

The metaphors of nuclear pornography inform the primary "joke" in Kubrick's *Dr. Strangelove*. In this film General Jack D. Ripper, an anti-communist fanatic who avoids sexual intercourse with women because it results in a "loss of essence," becomes obsessed with what he sees as a Soviet plot to pollute his "purity of essence" through fluoridation of water. He decides to wipe out the Soviet Union on his own initiative, ordering airborne bombers to launch a nuclear attack, a move ultimately resulting in global apocalypse. The naming of the crazed general, however much a potshot it seems, is actually aimed with deadly accuracy. General Ripper's criminal namesake, Jack the Ripper, killed and mutilated five prostitutes in London in 1888. He did not rape his victims, and his actions therefore were not immediately understood as sex crimes. Soon, however, with the conceptual aid of Freud and Krafft-Ebing, the knife was understood to be a symbolic penis and public opinion apprehended that the "murderous act and subsequent mutilation of the corpse were equivalents for the sexual act" (Krafft-Ebing 1965, 59). Like his namesake, General Ripper avoided sexual intercourse, but substituted a sexualized weapon—in his case, a nuclear bomb. His mutilated female corpse was the planet earth.

In my discussion of nuclear pornography, I thus far have concentrated primarily on the metaphor that links male sexuality to nuclear weaponry. But no heterosexually based pornography would be complete without a female "star," and nuclear pornography is no exception to that rule. Within the realm of nuclear metaphor, another sort links female sexuality and weaponry, throwing up, along with the breeder reactors, highly charged images of hot bikinis, anatomic bombs, blonde bombshells, and atomic Eves. However, as in ordinary pornography, there is no genuine female sexuality or presence, but only that of female impersonators (Griffin 1988, 5). In other words, the female characters in pornography enact projections of a masculinist self, sexuality, and fantasy life. In nuclear pornography, too, feminized characters parade phallocentric projections and conceits, for example, woman as victim, object, evil seducer/dominatrix, and scapegoat.

THE ATOM AND EVE

> *Atom bomb baby, loaded with power,*
> *Radioactive as a TV tower,*
> *nuclear fission in her soul,*
> *Loves with electronic control.*
> > The Five Stars (1957) "Atom Bomb Baby"

What spreads faster than radiation?—Jane Fonda
> bumper sticker, late 1970s

Discussing the nicknaming of the Bikini test bomb as "Gilda," film critic Michael Wood (1975, 51) writes:

> the bomb dropped on Bikini was called Gilda and had a picture of Rita Hayworth painted on it. The phallic agent of destruction underwent a sex

change, and the delight and terror of our new power were channeled into an old and familiar story: our fear and love of women. We got rid of guilt too: If women are always to blame, starting with Eve perhaps, or Mother Nature, then men can't be to blame.

It is indeed interesting that the much touted *male*-conceived, fathered, and "birthed" atomic bomb would so soon be associated with *female* power or sexuality. The bomb Gilda (like the "beautiful woman") is what Marshall McLuhan (1951) called a "mechanical bride"—an icon of feminine-eroticized technology, signifying, he claimed, a contemporary fusion of sex, technology, and death. Such imagery has prevailed throughout the nuclear age. In 1957, the Sands Hotel in Las Vegas held a contest for a "Miss A Bomb" (Titus 1986, unpaged). In 1953, the same year it was being hit with especially "dirty" fallout from the Nevada test site, the town of St. George, Utah, paraded around a small crowned girl, "Our Little A-Bomb," sitting atop a facsimile of a mushroom cloud (Titus 1986, unpaged). In such figurations, atomic power is paraded around as the captive plaything, and even child, of Man.

Wood recognizes another theme achieved by the symbolization—the scapegoating and displacement of guilt achieved by making female sexuality seem synonymous with the destructiveness of the bomb. He further places such scapegoating into its archetypal tradition, epitomized in the Western world in the myth of Adam and Eve. That myth of primordial female evil also was invoked in one of the earliest atom bomb songs—"The Atom and Evil," sung by the Golden Gate Quartet (1946). Here the power itself is male—the archetypically innocent Adam/Atom who is being tempted by the equally archetypical Evil/Eve: "Now Atom was a sweet young innocent thing/Until the night that Miss Evil took him under her wing." The quartet cautions: "If we don't break up that romance soon, we'll all fall down and go boom, boom; we're sitting on the edge of doom, doom, doom."

Again, Wood (1975, 51) saw such movements as a channeling of new atomic emotions into "an old and familiar story: our fear and love of women." However, by focusing only on men's "fear and love" for women, Wood misses the hatred implicit in thus scapegoating women. The 1950s also was the decade of Marilyn Monroe, the consummate "sex bomb," and Monroe's endlessly duplicated image has appeared in several nuclear contexts. In a 1980s "Hiroshima Appeals" peace poster by Japanese artist Takeshi Otaka (Japan Graphic Designers Association 1986, unpaged), four blown-up and increasingly distorted images of Monroe's smiling face form a mushroom cloud. If Monroe can represent the hated bomb in the Hiroshima peace poster, her endlessly porous image also can be used to represent the bombed city of Hiroshima. Nicholas Roeg's film *Insignificance* is a surrealistic meditation on the meaning of God, fame, and nuclear weapons as explored through four characters representing Monroe, Einstein, Senator Joseph McCarthy, and Joe DiMaggio, who interact one night in the 1950s. Clocks and time figure prominently, and Einstein dreads the hour of 8:15 A.M., the moment when Hiroshima was struck. Indeed, at 8:15 a nuclear blast seems to strike just near their hotel room. We experience that

devastation as, along with Einstein, we watch the burning figure of Monroe who, just in from filming *The Seven Year Itch*, flames and swirls in agony in the famous white dress, imagery that recalls a pornographic "snuff" scene. Is, then, a nuclear bomb blast like the *death* of a beautiful woman?

For that matter, is nuclear waste like a *bad* woman? A cartoon (Smith 1988) mocking supporters of the plans to locate a high-level nuclear waste repository in Nevada appears on the front page of the July 1988 *Nevada Nuclear Waste Newsletter*. It depicts a woman with a skull face and garbed in S&M dominatrix gear, towering over a groveling little man who proclaims: "Oh Yes, Madam Nuke Dump, we pro-nukers will do anything for you." A similar linking of the deadly effects of nuclear technologies to powerful women informs the cover of the November 1982 issue of *Penthouse*. Its center is dominated by a large and voluptuous woman, wearing a crown and dressed all in black. Untypically, she assumes a mocking pose and is "giving the finger" to the observer. She is a "bitch," marked by her attitude of challenge or menace. On her right reads: "Souvenir Issue: PET OF THE YEAR." To her left is a headline for an inside story on disarmament: "ISN'T LEARNING TO LOVE THE BOMB WHAT LIFE IS ALL ABOUT?" Although only the message on the right purportedly refers to the woman, arguably *both* do. She is "the bomb" that *Penthouse* dwellers must learn to "love," that is, hate: the epitome of the pornographic dream of the aggressive, nonsubservient woman who needs only a "good lay" to be put back in her place. In 1950s jargon, experts promised that the atom could be "tamed" to serve man, their pronouncements paralleling the domestic ideology that the "female bombshell could be 'harnessed for peace' within the home" (May 1988, 112). So too, says *Penthouse*, can be this 1980s bomb/pet.

In a similar vein, psychiatrist Wolfgang Lederer (1968, 248) both eroticizes destruction and displaces the man-made lethality of nuclear weaponry onto an ultimately powerful female: "And in the end the balance of this globe may yet again have to be redressed by the Great Mother herself in her most terrible form: as hunger, as pestilence, as the blind orgasm of the atom." Once again, when men associate femaleness with atomic power, it usually is through sexist and scapegoating stereotypes: sex toy, domesticated breeder, or Bitch/Mother. All of these metaphors half-mindedly recognize nuclear power as the return of repressed female force or the female character of cosmic sacred/generative energy. However, in mainstream metaphor the sacred face of nuclear power usually is figured as male, and I first will discuss the implications of this type of imagery.

NUCLEAR FUNDAMENTALISM

[God] by His most powerfull Hand, . . . holdeth backe the Sythe of Tyme from destroying or imparying the Universe . . . the same Hand shall at last destroy the Whole by Fire.
— George Hakewill, 1630 (quoted in Miller 1956, 220)

Atomic power, atomic power, was given by the mighty hand of God.
— "Atomic Power," the Buchanan Brothers (1946)

The word "sacred" derives from the Latin *sacer*, which meant "untouchable" in the dual sense of both holy and unclean (B. Walker 1983, 876). Roger Caillois (1959, 21) writes that the sacred "is always, more or less, 'what one cannot approach without dying' " and describes torments which would afflict the transgressor, torments which sound very much like those afflicting someone in the throes of radiation sickness.

In many ways nuclear technology does approximate the classically defined sacred, and in countless cultural references nuclear technology is imbued with a sacred aura, frequently being cast as either a deity or a direct manifestation of the deity's will on Earth. Historian of religion Ira Chernus (1986) has argued that nuclear weapons carry symbolic meanings that are extremely similar to traditional religious categories describing attributes of divinity, e.g., "awesome and limitless power, omniscience, eternity, and omnipresence," as well as mystery and irrationality. Exploring the various symbolic ramifications of "the Bomb," Chernus concludes that this "technological culture has made a death-machine its deity" (1986, 153). Chernus is right, and his work contains many insights; nevertheless, his study is flawed by a lack of any gender analysis. Just as the images of nuclear pornography reveal a connection between patriarchal sexuality and nuclear weaponry and technologies, so also do the many manifestations of "nuclear fundamentalism" (a term originated by Lifton and Falk 1982, 87) reveal an underlying bond between patriarchal religious tradition and Western men's invention and embrace of weapons which, they proudly claim, are capable of destroying the Earth.

To recapitulate briefly some of the history of this association between patriarchal religion and nuclear technology: Oppenheimer code-named the first atomic explosion "Trinity," conjuring in most people's minds the Christian godhead (warhead). Upon witnessing the first fireball, he broke into recitation from the *Bhagavad-Gita*: "I am become Death, the shatterer of worlds." General Leslie Farrell, military chief for the project, had an equally revealing response: "We puny things were blasphemous to dare tamper with the forces heretofore reserved to the Almighty" (quoted in Jungk 1958, 201). Following suit, after ordering the first military use of the bomb, Harry Truman informed the American public that this act represented the "harnessing of the basic power of the Universe." He further intoned: "We thank God that it has come to us instead of to our enemies: and we pray that He may guide us to use it in His ways and for His purposes" (quoted in Boyer 1985, 6). Perhaps most flagrant of all were the litanies of William L. Laurence, describing his vision at the Trinity site: "It was as though the earth had opened and the skies had split. One felt as though he had been privileged to witness the Birth of the World—to be present at the moment of Creation when the Lord said: 'Let there be Light' " (Laurence 1945, 1).

Soon, country, pop, and gospel musicians were incorporating many of these themes into their tunes, coming up with such winning numbers as "Jesus Hits Like An Atom Bomb" (Lowell Blanchard with the Valley Trio, 1950) and "Atomic Telephone" (Spirit of Memphis Quartet, 1951): "I just talked to Jesus on the atomic telephone/ No man knows the power, only God alone/ It can cure the sick or destroy the evil/With one sweep of power known by God alone."

Religio-nuclear metaphors appear in more subtle forms in such Hollywood megahits as *Star Wars, Star Trek II: The Wrath of Khan, Raiders of the Lost Ark,* and *Ghostbusters.* In some, nuclear technology is imaged as a divinity itself, as in Ted Post's ironic *Beyond the Planet of the Apes,* where post-holocaust mutants literally bow down before the bomb/god which, by film's end, destroys them. That same metaphor appears in the contemporary U.S. cult comic book series, *The Watchmen* (Moore 1986) which features a nuclear superhero, "Dr. Manhattan" (a scientist who disintegrated in a nuclear accident, only to reform as a "wholly original entity [with a] . . . complete mastery of all matter"). This Dr. Manhattan, who clearly functions as a symbol of nuclear technology itself, is simultaneously understood as a divinity. In *The Watchmen,* a university professor discusses the global impact of this new superhero:

> "*God* exists and he's American." If that statement starts to chill you after a couple of moments' consideration, then don't be alarmed. A feeling of intense and crushing religious terror at the concept indicates only that you are still sane . . . I do not believe we have a man to end wars. I believe we have made a man to end worlds. . . .

The Watchmen is particularly interesting because it explicitly ties the cultural divinization of nuclear weaponry to the quintessentially patriarchal godlike power of *unnatural* death dealing and that same God's penchant to arbitrarily destroy worlds.

Another common strain of popular stories kneels to the same lethal God, but artificially sweeten nuclear obliteration, heralding it as a righteous wrath, the expurgation of the wicked, or as a necessary forerunner to a planetary cleansing and purification. The bomb plays an explicitly salvific role in two major bestsellers: Stephen King's *The Stand* and Clive Barker's *The Great and Secret Show.* In *Swan Song* by Robert MacCammon and *Golden Days* by Carolyn See, nuclear war and its aftermath become occasions for planetary spiritual renewal, leading to a dawning of a spiritual and/or material Eden on earth. In the postholocaust landscape of *Golden Days,* a particularly disturbing work, one character makes the seemingly obvious statement that these are indeed "terrible times." Our "heroine" responds:

> But *I* was filled with a terrible rage and light, and I stood up and put out my arm to quiet her. "*No!*" I said. "Some people say these are bad times, but *I* say they are *good* times. We have bravery! We have love! We have the future. We have the Beginning! . . . This fire! This blessed fire! Some say it was a bad thing, but I say it was a good thing! (See 1987, 190-91)

This metaphor, which bonds nuclear war to spiritual resurrection, like that which links nuclear explosion to orgasm, ultimately functions only to make nuclear holocaust an eminently desirable event.

In her commitment to the beneficial side effects of planetary holocaust, See curiously echoes Kurt Saxon, the overtly racist founding father of the survivalist movement, who claims he has "learned to love the Bomb and welcome the chaos which will come from it because I know that's all necessary to cull the degenerate urban masses so that we can finally get to the nuclear renaissance" (Carlsen and Magnus 1988). Both See and Saxon also have much in common with the necroapocalyptic (Daly with Caputi 1987, 212) fundamentalists now anxiously awaiting nuclear holocaust as heralding the second coming of Christ. A poster from the late 1970s illustrates this mind-set with an extraordinary image. A towering and unmistakably phallic mushroom cloud dominates the picture. In the center is posed the ultimate nuclear question: "Is there a future?" At the bottom right is our answer: a crucifix on a hill with the words, "Yes. I'm coming—Jesus Christ." Here male orgasm, nuclear apocalypse, and religious ecstasy all indelibly fuse.

Prefiguring (and outdoing) all of these current screamers is the Jesuit Pierre Teilhard de Chardin, who wrote in 1946:

> The fact remains that in laying hands on the very core of matter we have disclosed to human existence a supreme purpose: the purpose of pursuing ever further, to the very end, the forces of Life. In exploding the atom we took our first bite at the fruit of the great discovery, and this was enough for a taste to enter our mouths that can never be washed away: the taste for super-creativeness. ... In short, the final effect of the light cast by the atomic fire into the spiritual depths of the earth is to illumine within them the overriding question of the end of Evolution—that is to say, the problem of God. (Chardin 1964, 151-53)

In short, Teilhard is claiming that with the discovery of atomic fission, man drew nearer to being "super creative," essentially to being like his God. Moreover, by "laying hands" on the very core of matter/mother, men had achieved the ultimate rape of nature, fulfilling a centuries-long tradition of science as penetration into female mysteries (Merchant 1980, 164-90; Weart 1988, 57-58). We can realize, moreover, that "super creativeness" actually masks "super destructiveness," that the "end of Evolution" for which he lusts is the familiar Earthly apocalypse to which Christianity historically has been committed, and that the newfound nuclear grace is located, not really in man's ability to "pursue ... the forces of Life," but, rather, in the extension of his ability to exercise that power which patriarchal culture *truly* worships and understands as godlike: the power to *take* life in cosmic proportions, to birth death, to shatter worlds.

When trying to fathom why Western science invented the technology of atomic destruction, we first might recall Alice Walker's (1988) insight that it is not "inventiveness" that characterizes "the Wasichu" (i.e., Western patriarchal men), but rather "unnaturalness." She asks us to realize "that even tiny insects in the South American jungle know how to make plastic, for instance; they have simply chosen not to cover the Earth with it" (148). When further contemplating phallotechnological culture's pro-nuclear choice, we also might recall Mary Daly's (1984) argument that Christianity, with its commitment to necrophilia, systemic hatred of women, destructive opposition to nature, and consecrated warfare against the "elemental": "paved the way for modern technological warfare against the elements, which takes such forms as nuclearism and chemical contamination" (10).

Indeed, the history of Christianity is marked by a passion for Earthly apocalypse. In his essay "The End of the World," Perry Miller (1956) traces Christian eschatological thought during the time of the scientific revolution and Puritan America, showing that after Kepler and Copernicus theologians struggled mightily to demonstrate the continued "feasibility of destruction," arguing that an "explosion" rather than "arbitrary influence" now was required to destroy the earth, and proposing such forces as comets to do the job. Miller writes: "There is no more curious phenomenon in the history of our civilization than the fact that the triumph of modern physics over the imagination of mankind was achieved by a sustained effort to prove that such a triumph was not only compatible with the cherished hope [for the end of the world] but that actually it was a confirmation, a veritable guarantee, of an approaching, colossally violent catastrophe" (222-23). Twentieth-century physicists finally have made good on that guarantee: By inventing atomic power, they inarguably demonstrated the scientific "feasibility of destruction." By thus providing a practical means which they believe could incinerate the Earth, the atomic scientists honored and perhaps unconsciously acted from patriarchal religion's unwavering desire for the apocalyptic fires. Feminist theologian Mary Condren (1989, 201) writes: "Nuclear destruction is intrinsic to the spirituality and theology generated by Western culture." Monica Sjöö and Barbara Mor (1987, 316) concur: "We suggest that the atomic or nuclear blast is man's final identification with the Sun God, the final annihilation of matter/mother—and that this is the ultimate goal of all patriarchal religion." Atomic technology was sought and continues to be pursued not because Western patriarchy is the most "advanced" culture ever on earth. Rather, patriarchal men seek nuclear power because it can so completely recapitulate not only the dominant paradigm of phallic sexuality, but also the companion conception of divinity.

The intermeshing of both sexual and sacred patriarchal paradigms, as well as their relation to nuclearism, is vividly expressed in Russell Hoban's (1980) *Riddley Walker*. In this postholocaust world, humanity has lost a good measure of its intelligence, evidenced by the illiteracy and vulgar orthography of the ensuing civilization. On a quest for the nuclear power that destroyed the old world, the hero, Riddley Walker, journeys to Canterbury ("Cambry"), the site of the most powerful nuclear blast. Musing on the "Big Power"—alternately, the "Spirit of God"—that he seeks, Riddley undergoes an epiphany:

> Funny feeling come on me then I fealt like that Power wer a Big Old Father ... I wantit it to come in to me hard and strong long and strong. Let me be your boy, I thot.
> Stanning on them old broakin stoans I fealt like it *wer* coming in to me and taking me strong. Fealt like it wer the han of Power clampt on the back of my neck fealt the Big Old Father spread me and take me....

And stil I fealt a nother way. . . . I knowit Cambry Senter ben flattent the werst of all the dead town senters it ben Zero Groun it ben where the wite shadderd stood up over every thing. Yet unnder neath that Zero Groun I lissent up a swarming it wer a humming like a millying of bees it wer like 10s of millyings. I begun to feal all juicy with it. Juicy for a woman. Longing for it hard and hevvy stanning ready. Not jus my cock but all of me it wer like all of me were cock and the worl a cunt and open to me. (Hoban 1980, 158-59)

Two desires result from Riddley's two-pronged sacred/sexual experience of nuclear power as a Big Old Father: At first, he feels himself to be puny and willingly succumbs to being screwed by that Father; secondly, he wants to take the Almighty phallic power and use it to himself screw, i.e., to destroy the earth (he does find that he is not yet man enough for that). This passage neatly expresses the pact men have made with their God: If they bow/boy to the Big Old Father/God, the payoff will be their ultimate assumption of that divine paternal privilege to dominate, rape, and destroy all others.

Bowing to the god/war has long promised men similar benefits. As one Vietnam veteran described his experience:

I had a sense of power. A sense of destruction . . . in the Nam you realized you had the power to take a life. You had the power to rape a woman and nobody could say nothing to you. That godlike feeling you had was in the field. It was like I was god. I could take a life. I could screw a woman. (Baker 1982, 152)

Again, this is the same lure which, in part, drives the patriarchal culture's obsessive pursuit of nuclear weaponry: that weaponry's potential to externalize the imagined omnipotently destructive phallus as well as its ability to confer upon some elite men their own definition of divinity.

Thus far I have examined the types of metaphor that accrete around nuclear technology in phallocentric imagery and speech. But moving beyond this and recognizing the centrality of language, image, and metaphor to the construction and maintenance of patriarchal-nuclear reality, we, correspondingly, can recognize the necessity of generating metaphors that challenge and deconstruct that toxic reality. Along with other types of activism, including physical and organized resistances, feminists simultaneously should develop means of "psychic activism," invoking word and image power to counter that doomward march of nuclearist culture, refiguring those fundamental metaphors of radiation from a gynocentric and sacred perspective.

GOSSIPS, GORGONS, AND CRONES

I hold to the traditional Indian views on language, that words have power, that words become entities. When I write I keep in mind that it is a form of power and salvation that is for the planet. If it is good and enters the world, perhaps it will counteract the destruction that seems to be getting so close to us. I think of language and poems, even fiction, as prayers and small cere-monies.

—*Linda Hogan (quoted in McAllister 1982, 352)*

Feminist thinkers—including philosophers, theologians, artists, novelists, poets, and historians of science—variously have linked the Western patriarchal tradition that ordains the domination of women, people of color, and nature, that severs nature from culture, that trashes the Earth while fetishizing Space/Heaven, that idolizes the machine and denies the cycles of life while pushing the notion of linear progression, as causing ecological crises and producing the conditions for nuclear annihilation (Caputi 1988b; Condren 1989; Daly 1978, 1984; Gadon 1989; Merchant 1980; Omolade 1989; Ruether 1989; Sjöö and Mor 1987; A. Walker, 1983b, 1988; B. Walker 1985). In order to halt the wasting of the Earth, we now desperately need new and transformative words, symbols, and metaphors for female potency, cosmic power, the mysteries of life and death, the being of nature, the sacredness of the Earth and indeed of nuclear power itself.

Since 1973, Mary Daly (1973, 1978, 1984) has called for the generation of "new words" and, in the succeeding years has originated hundreds of "Meta-phors of Metabeing" or "Metapatriarchal Metaphors": "words that function to Name Metapatriarchal transformation and therefore to elicit such change" (Daly with Caputi 1987, 82). Powerful, transformative, literally *pregnant* (that is, cogent, convincing, forcible, pressing) presences that Daly conjures in her various books include *Hags, Crones, Spinsters, Nags,* and others to name women who are anomalous and dangerous to the patriarchal state. To many women, raised under the constraints of Western rationalism, such conjuring may seem merely escapist, "unreal," but such metaphors have the power to stir hitherto unrealized powers. I have chosen to discuss three such metaphors here, ones with particular relevance to the nuclear dilemma: the Gossip, the Gorgon, and the Crone.

The first of these metaphors—that of the *Gossip*—speaks directly to language and naming as forms of power and their importance to the work of ridding ourselves of masculinist and nuclearist reality. In *Webster's First New Interga-lactic Wickedary of the English Language* (1987), Daly and I claim the Gossip to evoke powers of communal truth-seeking, female communication, and creation. Refusing to keep quiet, and recognizing the centrality of speech, image, and metaphor to the construction of nuclearist reality, Gossips conspire to over-throw what Christa Wolf calls the "current necrophilia" with a "living word." Nuclearist discourse slanders both women and nature, telling of the inevitability of men's dominion over nature, of the transcendent power of technology, and of the divine-like creativity of scientific invention. It is Gossips who not only generate gynocentric metaphor, but provide as well the "behind the scenes" information, spilling the classified secrets, specifying perpetrators, and broadly pointing to the danger inherent in the abusive acts of nuclear fathers.

For example, two Gossiping antinuclear activists, Patricia Ellsberg and Elissa

Melamed (1989), parallel antinuclear resistance to a willingness to expose and repudiate the authoritarian father. Each prefaces her "nuclear story" by reconsidering the propaganda of her childhood. Ellsberg reveals: "I grew up with a sense of gratitude to the nuclear bomb. When I was an adolescent, my father told me that nuclear weapons would make the world safe. . . . His words carried great weight with me, not only due to his authoritative personality, but also because in the thirties he had befriended many of the men who were to become the great generals of World War II" (84). Melamed too begins with acid recollection: "Daddy was the greatest, he knew everything, he was always right." She concludes: "Along with the dread of nuclear holocaust, I was dealing with more subtle fears. . . . I would have to take Daddy on . . . the struggle to retain my integrity of vision never ends. Each time, there is a moment of 'how dare I?' as I expose Daddy for all the world to see" (85-86). Such daring and transformative truth-telling is part of the quintessential work of the Gossip.

The second metaphor I will call upon here is the *Gorgon*. Since the early 1970s, the Gorgon has been a power symbol for feminists (Cixous 1980). Frequently the Gorgon is invoked in her aspect as Medusa, the Greek Gorgon (a Goddess tradition stemming, many believe, from Africa), one of a trinity of Moon Goddesses with hair of snakes (Sjöö and Mor 1987, 209-10). According to Barbara Walker (1988, 255), Medusa's "serpent hairs symbolized menstrual secrets." A glance from her, like a glance from a menstruating woman in a variety of folk beliefs, could turn men to stone. Moreover, Medusa explicitly was known for her magical blood. After her death, Athena gave Asclepius (the renowned healer) "two phials of the Gorgon Medusa's blood; with what had been drawn from the veins of her left side, he could raise the dead; with what had been drawn from her right side, he could destroy instantly" (Graves 1955, 1960, 175).

In a stirring article, Emily Culpepper (1986) analyzes not only the significance of the Gorgon face as a symbol of contemporary women's rage, but also the ways that "feminists are *living* the knowledge gained from tapping deep and ancient symbolic/mythic power to change our lives." She relates an incident which occurred one night in 1980. Someone knocked at the door and, after looking out and thinking it was someone she knew, she opened the door. A stranger came in and immediately attacked her. Culpepper, at first off-guard, gathered herself and fought back, throwing out the would-be attacker. She includes a selection from her journal recalling the incident: "I am staring him out, pushing with my eyes too. My face is bursting, contorting with terrible teeth, flaming breath, erupting into ridges and contortions of rage, hair hissing. It is over in a flash." Afterwards, she realized that she "needed to look at the terrible face that had erupted and sprung forth from within" during her fight:

As I felt my face twist again into the fighting frenzy, I turned to the mirror and looked. What I saw in the mirror is a Gorgon, a Medusa, if *ever* there was one. This face was my own and yet I knew I had seen it before and I knew the name to utter. "Gorgon! Gorgon!" reverberated in my mind. I knew then why the attacker had become so suddenly petrified. (Culpepper 1986, 24)

In this world where men daily perpetrate outrages upon women, as Culpepper notes, it is imperative that women "learn how to manifest a visage that will repel men when necessary. . . . The Gorgon has much vital, literally life-saving information to teach women about anger, rage, power and the release of the determined aggressiveness sometimes needed for survival" (22-23). Understanding the intimate connection between sexual and nuclear outrages, women also can look to the Gorgon for vital information about paralyzing the nuclear rippers.

A Gorgon is defined by *Webster's Unabridged* (1986) as "an ugly, repulsive, or terrifying woman." The wild-eyed and untamed Gorgon, possessor of menstrual "wiseblood," the substance that symbolizes cosmic powers of life and death, thus stands as the direct antithesis of the "beautiful woman" in the nuclear power plant ad, the boudoir beauty whose image betokens the capture and harnessing of that cosmic power. This made-up, "beautiful woman" is kept looking down and aside, as well she must be, for, released from constraints, the blood might leak, her Gorgon/Sacred face might break through to repel, petrify, and immobilize her keepers.

To Freud (1955), the Medusa represented the female genital and signified *castration* (due to her decapitation). Subsequent male commentators also read castration into the Medusa, but due instead to her powerful gaze: "If the woman looks, the spectacle provokes, castration is in the air, the Medusa's head is not far off" (Heath 1978, 92). Staring down the nuclear pornographers, the Gorgon does indeed signify the capacity to emasculate "nuclear phallacies." Ronald Reagan (1983) might have promised that his Strategic Defense Initiative would be able to make nuclear weapons "impotent and obsolete," yet, quiet as it's kept, it is the Gorgon who truly possesses the power to disarm and render impotent "Mr. MX."

Finally, as Daly and I suggest in *The Wickedary* (1987), the Gorgon also is a profoundly antinuclearist metaphor, for she is one whose "face can stop a clock." Since 1947, the *Bulletin of the Atomic Scientists* has published a "doomsday clock" that depicts how many minutes there are to "midnight," that is, how close the world is to nuclear holocaust ("Three Minutes," 1984): "Lusty women, in tune with the Moon, pose the poignant Question: Is the Moon's Face the Face that can stop the doomsday clock? . . . women as Gorgons look toward the madmen and turn them to stone—the doomsday men with their doomsday clocks . . ." (Daly and Caputi 1987, 282).

The third mythic figure of female power is the *Crone*, the ancient woman, the ancestor. It is difficult to find a more caricatured and degraded figure than the aged woman in contemporary North American culture. Yet, simultaneously, the Crone appears across a spectrum of contemporary gynergetic imaginings, as well she should, for the Crone is the nemesis of that "Big Old Father," the abusive father/god of the Western tradition.

As mythographer Barbara Walker (1985) relates, the Crone is the general designation of the third of the Triple Goddess' aspects (embodied in figures such as Hecate and Kali) and one associated with death, the waning moon, and winter. One of the reasons that the Crone is banished in contemporary representation is that women, apotheosized under male supremacy as mothers and givers of life, are denied the power of death the Crone signifies. (This denial is vividly sketched in the furors over the right to abortion and the use of women soldiers in combat.) Patriarchal men have staked their lives on a belief in their exclusive mastery of death—resulting in the worship of death and invention of the means of megadeath.

The Crone, moreover, is a harbinger of rebirth. Her appearance signals (as it does, for example, in Paule Marshall's *Praisesong for the Widow* 1983) a call to profound healing and change. Nor Hall (1980, 197) writes that the function of the old wise woman "is to be of assistance in times of difficult passage. As midwife to the psyche she is constellated in 'emergency' situations where a spirit, a song, an alternative, a new being is emerging." In the face of a global nuclear emergency, Barbara Walker (1985) calls for the reinstitution of the Crone, not as some "deity actually existing 'out there'," but as a chosen metaphor: "Metaphors like these take on practical meaning in women's capacity to see through men's pretenses and to reject men's self-serving images. Men feared the judgmental eye of the wisewoman even when she was socially powerless. This, then, is the chink in the armor of patriarchal establishments. When many women together say no and mean it, the whole structure can collapse" (176-77).

Walker is describing a strategy that we might call *denial*. Ironically, denial, as it is commonly understood, is a passive and defensive response to the overwhelming threat posed by nuclear weapons—a "refusal to feel, to think, or to contemplate action" (Weart 1988, 267)—and is a component of what Robert Jay Lifton has termed "psychic numbing" (Lifton and Falk 1982, 103). Yet, there is an entirely other form of denial: As an elder Diné (Navajo) medicine woman, Irene Yazzie (quoted in Marshall 1989, 42) responded to questions about relocation at Big Mountain: "I refuse to talk about relocation. For me, it does not exist." This is *active* denial, a refusal to participate in the social construction of destruction, a power which when collectively employed is estimable indeed. The continuing constellation of Crone imagery at this juncture in history betokens, among other things, the transformative power to *collectively* deny, forbid, and thereby deconstruct nuclearist reality. Of course, as Barbara Walker (1985, 178) observes in the concluding sentence of her study of the Crone: "She had better do it soon, for he is already counting down to doomsday."

WHY A THINKING WOMAN IS LIKE A NUCLEAR POWER PLANT

*Ts'its'tsi'nako, Thought-Woman
is sitting in her room
and whatever she thinks about
appears.*

*She thought of her sisters,
Nau'ts'ity'i and I'tcts'ity'i,*

and together they created the Universe
this world
and the four worlds below.

Thought-woman, the spider,
named things and
as she named them
they appeared.

She is sitting in her room
thinking of a story now.

I'm telling you the story,
she is thinking.
—Leslie Marmon Silko (1977, 1)

Around the turn of the century . . . a few scientists began to observe the atom
asserting its nature. . . . Perhaps the universe resembled a great thought more
than a great machine.
—Marilou Awiakta (1986, 185-86)

The sixteenth-century philosopher, physician, and alchemist Paracelsus, who
acknowledged that he had "learned everything he knew about healing from the
Witches" (Daly 1984, 7), instructed that in order to find an antidote to a poison,
one must look in its immediate vicinity, for nature places the harm in close
proximity to a cure. Nuclear weaponry was developed and tested on Native
American territory in New Mexico and, significantly, some of the most fruitful
insights into the nuclear dilemma have been proffered by Native American
feminist philosophers.

In much of Euro-American feminist thinking (including my own), the primary impulse has been to expose the phallic character of nuclear technology/
weaponry and to oppose that male-identified force. Yet, in the writings of Paula
Gunn Allen, Marilou Awiakta, Leslie Marmon Silko, and Carol Lee Sanchez,
the predominant movement is to reclaim the atom from its immurement in
phallocentric language, sexuality, and religion and to recall its repressed sacred
gynocentric face.

Sanchez, a Laguna Pueblo (New Mexico) poet and artist, deplores the modern Western schism between the sacred and the profane and contrasts it to the
Tribal tradition that recognizes "all things in the known universe to be equally
sacred" (1989, 346). She believes that modern peoples must not only acknowledge the sacredness of everyday life, but also:

create new songs of acknowledgement as well as ceremonies that include
metals, petrochemicals, and fossil fuels, electricity, modern solar power
systems, and water power systems . . . it is very important to make sacred
. . . the new ways and elements in our lives—from nuclear power . . . to

plastics to computers . . . in order to restore harmony and balance to our out-of-control systems and in particular, to our modern technologies. (Sanchez 1989, 352-53)

Of course, Western culture already holds "sacred" its technologies; and "songs" to nuclear power, reiterating the masculinity of the warhead, the promise of religious/sexual ecstasy in annihilation, and the captivity of female power, underlie many of the ads, popular tunes, and metaphors described in this essay. Yet, this brand of worship stems from a worldview that reveres opposition, domination, and hierarchy, not balance, as the basic principles of the universe. Sanchez insists that those who resist technological depredations must neither worship nor demonize technology but instead acknowledge its sacredness while thinking/acting in ways that restore harmony and balance. One way to achieve this is to understand atomic power through sacred gynocentric metaphor.

Like Sanchez, Marilou Awiakta, a Cherokee poet and essayist, points to modern culture's profound irreverence toward atomic power (manifested in the destructiveness of the bomb and the Three-Mile Island disaster) and, correspondingly, to women. Awiakta has long pondered the sacred significance of atomic power, which she understands as: "the life force in process—nurturing, enabling, enduring, fierce. I call it the atom's mother heart" (Awiakta 1986, 186). As such, she feels herself to be neither pro- nor anti-nuclear, but "pro-reverence" (Rain Crowe 1990, 45). Moreover, the atomic age has special, even ontological, significance for women:

The linear Western, masculine mode of thought has been too intent on conquering nature to learn from her a basic truth: *to separate the gender that bears life from the power to sustain it is as destructive as to tempt nature itself.* . . . But the atom's mother heart makes it impossible to ignore this truth any longer. She is the interpreter not only of new images and mental connections for humanity, but also, most particularly for women, who have profound responsibilities in solving the nuclear dilemma.

The "mother heart" is the first of several female metaphors through which Awiakta understands nuclear energy. Astonishingly, as a child growing up near the nuclear reservation at Oak Ridge, Tennessee, she too found a "woman" in a nuclear power plant. She recalls this scene from her childhood:

Scientists called the reactor "The lady" and, in moments of high emotion, referred to her as "our beloved reactor."
"What does she look like, Daddy?"
"They tell me she has a seven foot shield of concrete around a graphite core, where the atom is split." I asked the color of graphite. "Black," he said. And I imagined a great, black queen, standing behind her shield, holding the splitting atom in the shelter of her arms.

Far from that of a possessed beauty, Awiakta's vision is of an autonomous and infinitely powerful cosmic being, her experience a modern encounter with the

"Black Madonna." Religious historian Ean Begg (1985, 27) notes that over four hundred of the world's images of the Madonna are black and that such figures represent the "elemental and uncontrollable source of life, possessing a spirit and wisdom of its own not subject to organization or the laws of rationality."

Laguna/Lakota philosopher Paula Gunn Allen similarly finds "elemental and uncontrollable" female power in nuclear power, not in the reactor but, boldly, in the bomb itself. In a published excerpt from her novel in progress, *Raven's Road*, two Native American Lesbians, Raven and Allie, deliberately station themselves to watch the blast from an above-ground test. Allie, who has done this before and anticipates her response, asks Raven what she saw in the cloud. Scarcely believing herself, Raven remembers: "An old woman ... I remember now. I saw an old woman's face" (Allen 1986a, 56). Through such daring figuration, Allen defies the masculinist hubris which sees only a fatherly face in cosmic force.

The Keres people are a language group of Southwest Pueblo peoples, including Laguna and other New Mexico pueblos. In their theology, the original creator is Thought Woman, or Spider Grandmother, who continually thinks/dreams/spins the world into being. Allen (Caputi 1990, 62) roots the exigencies of the nuclear age firmly in that spirituality: "I know that she's the lady that made the uranium and she's the lady that made radioactivity, and she's the lady that dreamed the dream of nuclear fission. She dreamed it. Men could not have found the idea if she didn't give it to them. When she dreams, and that's what Thought Woman does, what she says, what she dreams, becomes." Thought Woman is part of a *trinity* of sisters, including Naotsete, Sun Woman. Long ago, Naotsete quarreled with her sister Iyatiku, Corn Woman, and left. Allen continues: "Around Laguna they say she's come back. And they say it with respect to the bomb. And 'she' is Naotsete, who is Sun Woman. ... I can't think of anything more vividly Sun Woman than the bomb."

Another Laguna thinker, Leslie Marmon Silko, also addresses nuclear spirituality in her novel *Ceremony*. The narrative opens by recounting the creation narrative of Thought Woman (cited earlier) and then tells the story (interspersed with further Laguna myth) of the psychic healing of a mixed-blood World War II veteran, Tayo. Ultimately, his restoration to health is tied to a healing for the planet embattled by the "destroyers," forces of evil whose latest manifestation is nuclear weaponry. Silko does not find female energy in that weaponry; rather, the events leading to its discovery (including the creation of the white race) were set into motion by evil Indian "witches." Nevertheless, in *Ceremony*, the advent of the nuclear age again signals the return of female divine force, embodied in Tayo's supernatural helper, Ts'eh. Writing in *The Sacred Hoop*, Paula Gunn Allen (1986b, 118-19) identifies Ts'eh with primal female force:

> There is not a symbol in the tale that is not in some way connected with womanness, that does not in some way relate back to Ts'eh and through her to the universal feminine principle of creation: Ts'its'tsi'nako, Thought Woman, Grandmother Spider, Old Spider Woman. All tales are

born in the mind of Spider Woman, and all creation exists as a result of her naming.

While Silko differs from Allen in her understanding of nuclear power, both intuit that the atomic age, begun in New Mexico on Native lands, is profoundly connected to the Native *trinity* of sister supernaturals, particularly the eldest, Thought Woman. First of all, Thought Woman provides a most promising alternative to the now prevailing "Big Old Father," whose definitive power is to ordain annihilation to rape the Earth. Moreover, Thought Woman offers a profoundly instructive and complex model for an ecofeminist practice of psychic activism. Thought Woman's characteristic activity is cosmically creative naming, precisely the activity Awiakta and Allen evince in their gynocentric refiguration of nuclear metaphors.

Another creative Namer, Mary Daly (1984, 25), discusses the meaning of symbol and metaphor:

> Symbols . . . participate in that to which they point. They open up levels of reality otherwise closed to us and they unlock dimensions and elements of our souls which correspond to these hidden dimensions and elements of reality . . . *metaphor* include[s] the qualities above attributed to symbols. However, there is more involved. As theologian Nelle Morton has explained, metaphors evoke action, movement. They Name/evoke a shock, a clash with the "going logic" and they introduce a new logic.

That semiotic "shock" is precisely what I experienced when I first encountered Allen's constellation of the Bomb as "Old Woman." Certainly, that metaphor introduces a logic that is completely contrary, even infuriating to patriarchal logic. Allen's metaphor claims for women identification with the cosmic forces of the universe and suggests that in order for Goddess spirituality to achieve the world-transformative power that so many feminists argue it is capable of (Gadon 1989), we must recognize and reverence the presence of the female sacred not only in past myths and familiar images (Mother Earth) but also in contemporary, even technological, realities.

16

New Moon over Roxbury

Reflections on Urban Life and the Land

REBECCA JOHNSON

> The wolf moon rises cold
> over the concrete ditch called
> the Orange Line
> where trains blast
> through air
> through politics
> through glass and terrazzo terminals
> to the illusion of prosperity
> and back again.

The wolf moon (Roberts and Amidon 1991, 405) has been with us all year. The wolf moon is the January moon, the one closest to the earth during the coldest part of the year in the Northern Hemisphere. The 1991 wolf moon brought war. The chill glare of the worst of human intentions acted upon the world. The whole year has felt cold, bone cold, like homelessness in winter, like extinction for misunderstood creatures.

These reflections are about being out in the cold, that is, outside the benevolent concern of ecologist, politician, or big business. These reflections are about gardening in harsh conditions; about being an urban dweller, a feminist, a lesbian, about being black. All those conditions, opportunities, realities which

Rebecca Johnson is a native Ohioan living in Boston, Massachusetts. She lives, writes, and gardens in a neighborhood called Jamaica Plain. Her paid work is with Women for Economic Justice as the Project Director of the Women's Economic Development Project. "My current concerns allow my work and my writing to intersect. How do we create webs of support which can support the lives of women, particularly poor women, and allow us to reclaim physical, environmental, and emotional health and economic security?"

mediate my relationship to all my environments—the urban one I inhabit, the natural one polluted by the city I call home, the psychic one in which memory and poetry and dream dwell and sometimes invite my residence as well. I realized in writing this that I have no answers. In fact, this year I seem to have only questions and doubts, hopes and fears. And poetry. These I hope to share with you.

As I've prepared this piece, I have struggled with the technical language of environmental science and the specific concepts of ecofeminism. In these reflections I am choosing to depend on my own emotional vocabulary to represent concepts important to me. The idea of "The Land" represents the relationship to nature and environmental responsibility with which I grew up. It is a central myth for many black people (Christian 1985, 47-63). Organic gardening is my link with The Land as an idea and a complex corporal system. I garden for sustenance and as spiritual practice. The annual events of germination, waving green life, fruition, and decay are the only things I really believe in anymore. If I worship at all, it is at the compost pile. It receives my most consistent offerings. The experience of Black people in the North is my experiential base. The commodification of everything is both metaphor and tool for analysis (Ferguson 1984, 47-57). In the next few pages I will reflect on all of these ideas and concepts.

I am using the occurrence of the full moon in the night sky as organizational reference point. This may seem like an odd structural metaphor for a city dweller.

I have lived in New England for eight years. Before that I lived in Cincinnati, near downtown, in a neighborhood called Over-the-Rhine. My first five years in New England, I lived in near-rural small towns. Those years were my first extended sojourn in a rural setting. They fed my interest in astronomy, which was just developing as I left Cincinnati. When I moved to Boston, I began seriously investigating astrological gardening. I had been exposed to at least the lunar aspects of this approach to planning, planting, and harvesting a garden in Cincinnati. In Boston I learned to join the astrological signs. We (my garden partners and I) only have one year of experience with this technique, but using the astrological signs has given me a sense of integration, joining my relationship with the urban soil with the relatively unspoiled expanses of the cosmos: a kind of chaos redeemed by Chaos. So my reflections are organized around the lunar tradition.

Each full moon has a name and gives a sense of where we are in the year (Roberts and Amidon 1991, 404-27).

January: The Wolf Moon
February: The Snow Moon
March: The Worm Moon
April: The Pink Moon
May: The Full Flower Moon or the Corn Planting Moon
June: The Strawberry Moon or the Rose Moon

July: The Thunder Moon
August: The Red Moon
September: The Harvest Moon
October: The Hunter's Moon
November: The Beaver Moon
December: The Cold Moon

Even those of us living in the big cities of the East Coast can see the moon, if nothing else, in the night sky.

New Moon Over Roxbury: Pleiades in Winter

There are places of other suns
new lights burning in the distant sky

we look up call their names
tell stories of their mystery:
seven sisters, singing maidens,

seven stars to show the way
when the moon's face has turned
left our house and closed the door

we wait

we only imagine galaxies
when the moon is new over Roxbury
different lights cluster in our sky
and fall

the staccato flash of automatic weapons fire
sulphurous street lamps
knocked askew
sparks trailing after a fleeing car
the insistent search light of the police helicopter

the lamp in the window night after night waiting
for those of us who have never seen the stars.

Cities have always existed. That is, humans are social beings and have always
gathered to create settlements. There may have been a time when these settlements were synchronous with the natural environment, a wholeness built, but
not artificial, and reflecting back the wholeness it sought to imitate. That is not
the case today. Cities are the cause for and creator of much of the destruction
of the natural world. They reflect artifice and decay and an unholy chaos. Yet,
in our cities music and art reside and many search for better lives. This search
may be unwilling and, as in much of the developing capitalist world, fueled by
the wholesale destruction of integrated and functioning ecologies by rampant
capitalist speculation and greed. In any event, cities are not about to go away.
Experts project that by the year 2000 one-half of the world's population will
live in cities (Seager 1989, 40-41, 107).

At one time urban life in the United States was fairly antiseptic. We had
been shielded from most of the worst manifestations inherent in dislocation
from a familiar and productive rural existence to the squalor and poverty of
many urban settlements in the developing capitalist world. Increasingly in the
United States, we, too, witness or experience trash picking in dumps, people
of all ages and races living on the streets, toxic hot spots rendering large areas

unlivable, and the predation that poverty inspires. We prefer the sanitary myth of people coming to this country fleeing war, famine, greed, and natural disaster and finding peace and security. Increasingly, people find here what they would find in many cities of the world: economic stagnation, alienation, and despair. Middle-class urban life permits illusion and ignorance. For those lucky enough to have secure incomes, city life becomes very simple. All can be bought, including the ability to ignore the magnificent complexity of the built and natural environments which make privileged lives possible. Neither do middle-class city dwellers experience the chaos their ignorant consumption inflicts on the Land upon which we all depend. Yet poverty is no virtue. It may remove blinders to the inadequacy of urban systems, but it doesn't necessarily bring insight. In choosing urban life, I have neither the resources nor the inclination to claim the class privilege that ignores the consequences of our actions. I stay in urban areas because I still prefer them, even with all the problems I've just listed. It is also the place where much progressive activism originates, where people of color increasingly live, and where fundamental change must be enacted if the natural ecology of the world is to survive.

THE WORM MOON

The night after Aunt Bea's funeral, my father and I walked the old family land in Tennessee. He had something important to tell me, his adult daughter who had moved East, grown dreadlocks, and chosen work he didn't quite understand. That night he told me about erosion, how to tell the lay of the land and where erosion might happen. He showed me various remedies. He urged me never to let the land wash away, not like some were, back in his home place.

I come from people who are both urban and rural. As black people they all have an orientation toward the land which went beyond its productivity or the house built on it. It was a resource to be conserved, protected, passed to the next generation with its topsoil, its clean water, its stand of trees intact.

Historically, this attitude was a fundamental orientation of black people in the United States. Our health as a community could be judged by our relationship to the land. Nobody better catches this central myth of Black life in this country than Toni Morrison. In her first three novels, *The Bluest Eye*, *Sula*, and *Song of Solomon*, she explicates the beliefs, conflicts, and crises of a people separated from the land they knew in exchange for the hope of a better political and economic life on land that is new and strange (Christian 1985, 48).

Ms. Morrison's characters are my parents' generation, new to the North, unaccustomed to the demands of industrial life. Their link to the land was their gardens.

One of the hardest resources to locate in a city like Boston is a place to have a garden. Land is scarce. Open spaces which aren't parks or institutionally protected green spaces are generally privately owned and inaccessible or polluted. I live in Jamaica Plain, a part of Boston. The three blocks closest to my home have one tree, but there are several hidden vegetable gardens.

Gardening is hard work, so several of us garden together. My landlady,

Pauline, and friends Katherine and Diane share responsibility for two, and sometimes three, garden plots. This summer, when we broke ground at our new community garden space, we invited eight friends to clear the plot of volunteer maple trees and (what seemed like) enough rocks to build a fine New England wall.

Soil Analysis Report for Home Gardens[1]

Bag number 87205   for *Rebecca Johnson*
3/11/91
Extractable Aluminum: *9 parts per million (ppm)*
** Lead * (extractable): *29 ppm*
    Estimated total lead: *456 ppm*
The lead level in this soil is low.

The soil in our garden is thin as water and dangerous. It is not an exotic threat. For city folks it is as common as street lamps and high-top sneakers. We battle aluminum, lead, and cadmium to grow vegetables.

Over the three years we have gardened in my backyard, we have added soil amendments provided free by Forest Hills Cemetery and the Metropolitan Police Mounted Patrol. We load gardening fork and spade in my car and fill plastic bags with cemetery leaf mold and mounted police horse manure. Through this practice we have reduced the lead content in the soil in my back-yard from dangerously high to safely low.

Is there a moon for remembering? Perhaps the Worm Moon in March, the one where you speak hopefully to the dirt in your backyard, can serve that purpose. Just as it is important for the soil to remember its fruitfulness, it is important for us to remember that cities are full of people who want to coop-erate with the rhythms of nature, who find community in growing and sharing food, and who quietly struggle to repay the earth for benefits we may have unwittingly and violently wrested from her.

My father was a farmer, escaping his family in Tennessee at eighteen but not escaping the call of the soil and the imperative to grow food. I have a brother and sister. The three of us grew up under my father's insistence that we garden with him. He rented a quarter acre lot to supplement our large Midwestern backyard garden. At ten years old I felt like we had endless rows of green beans to weed and pick. I am the only one of my siblings to continue to garden in adult life, although I am still ambivalent about the cultivation of green beans. My father has been what organic farmers call a "nozzlehead"[2] for most of his life. His use of toxic herbi- and insecticides on the lawn and vege-tables was truly terrifying. In the last couple years, he has wanted to know more about organic pest control and fertilizing, and he composts. From my father I learned how much work gardening can be and how to make someone else miserable while doing it.

Ecology

It wasn't for the peaches
but to center our loss on the fringe

Grandma's wake and funeral passing
grandchildren went to touch the tree

The mystery of grief and guilt and terror
engulfed her children our emotion was simpler

Longing for the ecology of her living
the rhubarb thirty years old
and the heat nurturing
apricot and almond

Apple peels and broken beans
caught in the apron folds of her lap
and we rested there for mending

Grandma had a relatively shady yard. She grew some flowers out front. The only food crops I can remember growing at her house were peaches and rhubarb. I think rhubarb is one of the most fascinating plants in the whole world. Its vigorous growth and lively red color are associated in my heart with my grandmother and her absolute joy in gardening.

In Cincinnati I learned housing organizing and organic lunar gardening. I worked with a group of older black women who lived in Over-the-Rhine. They strategized, door-knocked, bake-saled, and picketed their way to a better and more secure housing stock for low-income residents of the neighborhood. They also had a community garden at Spring Grove Cemetery. I shared a plot with two friends. Eddie, Randy, and I would go out in the van with Thelma and Sarah and other members of the Contact Center. We would repair to our plots. Thelma's adjoined our collective plot. On more than one occasion she would lean over the fence between the plots and say, "I wouldn't do that, if I were you." And we wouldn't. We learned which phase of the moon was good for planting leafy plants and root crops, when to water and when to weed, and when to leave well enough alone.

Today we choose organic gardening as the only way to raise food. One of the first realities that escapes us in the privileged industrialized nations is that there can be no waste if a system is to healthily maintain itself and those beings dependent on it. Organic gardening is about cooperation of natural systems — the soil and its microbial life, weather and the human activity of growing food. And for me it is about exploring the interaction of the microcosm of our backyard and community garden plot with the cosmological influences of stars, planets, and the moon.

In the Ohio of the 1960s, most black folks had gardens. All the children in my neighborhood grew up with fresh tomatoes and collard greens. There was a sense of connection to the rural South and the importance of controlling access to as many of the necessities of life as postbellum southern apartheid would allow. As children we never questioned this imperative. There could be no waste.

This culture that taught me to garden was afflicted with a deep ambivalence. Years of apartheid US-style had instilled the longing to be white, and if not white, to pass for something white culture respected. The working-class black families of my youth wanted all that the culture and economy of white people could give. Perhaps they weren't conscious of it, but they hankered after a fundamental disconnection from the earth and the latent traditions of African culture. This connection and those traditions had survived in reasonable if sometimes unconscious forms for most of the centuries of captivity, slavery, and Jim Crow "freedom." Barbara Christian argues that one of the fundamental conflicts for black people new to the urban and industrial North was that between "the natural order" and the illusion of uncomplicated "sweetness and light" presented by the majority white society (Christian 1985, 52). The natural order included "funk and passion," a lack of control. But the folks I grew up with weren't sure they wanted that tradition, with all its pain of poverty, loss, humiliation, and death. "Why couldn't we have store-bought vegetables, straight hair and quiet reverent church services?" was one of the questions my parents' generation was trying to work out for themselves and us. "Who needed that old-timey stuff from the South?" Yet in keeping their gardens, making frequent trips home (that is, South), and worshiping in the fullness of their Afri-Western Christian syncretism, many folks were holding on to an intangible groundedness and truth that would be lost by passing. The city had not taught them how to be rid of Jim Crow or how to find the freedom to keep the best of the culture Black people had built in the United States.

Many Black people have never known the South. Gardens are our only contact with The Land. We are quickly losing the nourishing link with the natural world which nourished our ancestors. We are becoming, at times, the worst of the culture for which we thought we longed.

THE HUNTER'S MOON

Kimberly Harbor died on Halloween night, 1990. She was a twenty-six-year-old black woman. She was described as a hyperactive child. She became unruly as a teenager, and her parents sent her to boarding school and a foster home. She became pregnant and addicted to cocaine in its many forms. She became a street person and a prostitute.

A gang of black teen men were out Halloween night looking to "rob a prostitute" (Wong 1991, 44). They found Kimberly hanging out around Franklin Field, a park in Dorchester (one of Boston's neighborhoods). Rather than merely robbing her, Kimberly "was raped by several of the defendants, beaten with a tree limb and stabbed with a broken beer bottle and knife . . . sources said the stab wounds—more than 100—were in her stomach, abdomen, back and buttocks"[3] (Ellemont and Murphy 1990, 20).

One father, discussing his son's crime (who has since been convicted of first-degree murder), stated "It's hard to believe; he's not that kind of kid . . . he's kind of quiet . . . He seemed normal to me. He's always the same. He doesn't show emotion" (Brelis 1990, 20).

Who are these teenagers? They aren't a new kind of predator. One of the legacies of European imperialism is the thoughtless destruction of all life. The young black men who killed Kimberly Harbor, a young black woman, follow in the best tradition of male conquest of this continent. Sadly, they follow in the tradition which conquered their ancestral lands in Africa, Central America, and the Caribbean—a conquest that annihilated whole peoples and enslaved the equivalent of whole countries. All too often, their prey is a woman, more often a woman they know. April 1991 saw a marked increase in the number of women in Massachusetts murdered by their male spouses, partners, and acquaintances. Occasionally, as in Kimberly's case, it was a woman they didn't know. These young men have come to see their lives, and everyone else's life, as expendable. They have absorbed the larger culture's media messages about the worthlessness of certain lives—natural life, colored lives, women's lives—all up for grabs, to be conquered and consumed.

Chinatown

Live chickens
live chickens killed fresh here
is the english translation of the mandarin sign
new mercury street lamps guard the gathering dusk
sentinels over shopper's refuse, wooden crates
the sidewalk cracks bearing a bloody flow
into the street

Fresh girls
fresh girls exposed here no fee
local residents watch their step no translation needed
night-fall shields patrons of the Naked I Cabaret
oblivious to the crimson offering their feet bear
through the entrance way

G-strings and grease paint clad the women dancing for
       scant
offerings of dollar bills and watery beer
their patrons smoke-stained eyes devouring

No parking
no parking two a.m. street cleaning here
the Naked I weakly blinks as huge amphibious
machines dispense disinfectant
cleaning away the last remnants of the day

One of the legacies of late twentieth-century capitalism is the commodification of every aspect of our lives (Ferguson 1984, 52). Capitalism is fundamentally a predatory system, requiring the consumption of huge amounts of products we don't need and the destruction of natural systems to make that consumption possible.

The first experience of people of color with European imperialism was this nascent commodifying instinct. Black people of African descent and some Native American tribe members were early tools of one of the most effective attempts to commodify human beings. The slavery of North and Central America, the Caribbean, and Brazil was accompanied by destruction of tribes, animal species, and fauna. The early demands of this transplanted European capitalism required that everything on the North American continent be commodifiable. We now live in a world where capitalism appears to be the victor, where all aspects of our lives can be captured, packaged, marketed, and sold.

African-American peoples organized resistance to their degradation. Those first captives knew themselves as a whole people in rhythm with earth's systems. They understood the only survival for future generations of Black people was to pass on that sense of synchronicity. Those old Africans probably never anticipated late twentieth-century urban living. They had no way of knowing that there would be a generation of us who would grow up unable to read the sky, earth's creatures and plants, and the spirits that inhabit everything. Certainly those old Africans never anticipated marketing and television. So.

CORN PLANTING MOON: SOIL CONDITIONS/SOUL CONDITIONS

The dirt in Boston is nothing like the good Ohio soil back home. I read someplace that it takes at least eight years to help polluted urban dirt become loam, the kind of soil that looks and feels more like chocolate cake than dirt. In the meantime we compost, haul leaf mold, and watch out for chunks of glass and brick as we plant.

Who will devise an eight-year plan for the soul of Black people? The steps needed to reclaim a patch of dirt are well known. It is not a process which can be rushed or sold in convenient packages. Similarly, some of the rural Black southern tradition applies today, and we can figure out the rest.

Certainly we must maintain whatever link with the Land and growing things we can muster. We need to remember the stories whose only witness is that Land and the water that bore us here. Those stories are not sweet or easy. The loss of hundreds of thousands of lives in the Middle Passage from Africa to North America is a reality we don't acknowledge, yet it is a powerful reminder of the waste capitalism inflicts on all it touches. There can be no waste. Those lives lost to the water must become part of the fertilizer folded back into the souls of black urban people. Perhaps if this story is told, the lure of empty things slickly packaged will be less seductive. Those empty things are made from the legacy of lost lives.

Since so many died coming here and creating America, it is important to see ourselves not as displaced Africans but a people uniting many aspects of (frequently) opposing forces. Our multicultularity is just a starting point. Our ability to survive captivity and build strong, and at times, egalitarian institutions should lead us to help build a different kind of prosperity for ourselves and fellow citizens—one that doesn't tolerate the dumping of environmental hazards in our community (Tyson 1991) or the destruction of the lives of our youngsters. One which balances the need for self-sufficiency with holding government systems responsible for the welfare of all citizens. Black people have lived under and resisted the complex realities of oppression. Today, we can mine that experience to help change the systems that threaten the whole earth. Perhaps then we will be able to read and celebrate the earth's signs again.

NOTES

1. Provided by the County Agricultural Extension Service.

2. Heard at the winter conference and annual meeting of New England Organic Farmers Association, January 1991.

3. The number of stab wounds turned out to be 132 and 18 bludgeon wounds (*Boston Globe,* Dec. 19, 1991, 44).

17

Earthbody and Personal Body as Sacred

CHARLENE SPRETNAK

The central insight of ecofeminism is that there is a strong correlation in Eurocentric cultures between the ways in which nature and the female are regarded, that is, with fear, resentment, and denigration. Ecofeminists work to create ecologically and politically wise alternatives to the status quo, which often draw inspiration cross-culturally. With respect to religion, ecofeminists note that the dominant, patriarchal traditions of Western civilization are based on a spirituality that seeks, rather desperately, to transcend nature and the body — especially the female body. In contrast, ecofeminists with an interest in the spiritual dimension of life have gravitated over the years to orientations and practices that view both nature and the body as sacred and as sources of spiritual revelation. That perspective is explored in the following ruminations, the first on earth-based spirituality (called by the Greek name for the Earth, Gaia) and the second on a spirituality of female physicality and related experience. Body-honoring spirituality is grounded and enriched by awareness of the cosmic web of life.

GAIAN SPIRITUALITY

Fifteen billion years ago, our universe was born in a vast and mysterious eruption of being. Out of the fireball came all the elementary particles of the

Charlene Spretnak is the author of *States of Grace: The Recovery of Meaning in the Postmodern Age* (HarperCollins, 1991) from which this essay is excerpted. Her work has contributed to the framing of the women's spirituality, ecofeminist, and Green politics movement. She has also authored *Lost Goddesses of Early Greece* and *The Spiritual Dimensions of Green Politics*, is the coauthor of *Green Politics: The Global Promise* (with Fritjof Capra), and editor of an anthology, *The Politics of Women's Spirituality.*

cosmos, including those that later formed our home galaxy, the Milky Way, and our planetary home, the Earth. All the land, the waters, the animals, the plants, our bodies, the moon and stars—everything in our life experience is kin to us, the results of a cosmic birth during which the gravitational power of the event held the newborn particles in a miraculously deft embrace. Had the rate of expansion of the infant universe differed by even one part in 10^{60}, it would have either collapsed into a black hole or dispersed entirely, the possibility of our being and that of the hundred billion galaxies around us never to have found form. Moreover, nothing but light would have existed but for the saving asymmetry that one in each billion pairs of protons and antiprotons had no partner.

The gravitational embrace, some 4.6 billion years ago, gathered a richness of elements eight light minutes from a blazing star, our sun, and layered them by weight into a sphere, with iron at the core. The elements sought their own positions in the layers that formed, creating among themselves all the minerals in Earth's body. On the smaller celestial bodies nearby (such as Mercury, Mars, our moon), the electromagnetic interaction overpowered gravity's pull; on the larger ones (such as Jupiter, Neptune, and Uranus), the opposite relationship developed. Only on Earth were the two in balance.

On Earth's crust, molecules continually broke up and recombined into new and larger molecules. Lightning created the possibility of amino and nucleic acids by providing intense heat framed by severe cold. Molecules that assembled themselves from amino acids became protein, while others formed of nucleic acids and sugars became ribonucleic acid (RNA) and deoxyribonucleic acid (DNA). The long chains of RNA, DNA, and protein molecules found themselves drawn into various partnerships, creating a dynamic bioplasm of bacteria in warm mud and shallow seawater. From Earth's store of potential, the great mediator chlorophyll later developed, enhancing our planet's relationship with the sun through the wonder of photosynthesis. A rambunctious bursting forth of Gaian life stretched over millions of years and continues today with new speciation and the unpredictable moves of Earth's body. With the emergence of humans, the universe had created a life form that could reflect on the cosmic mysteries. (It does not seem to me that this occurrence justifies the claim made by some that the universe was preparing with every previous development specifically for the advent of humans.)

Slowly the part of the cosmos that is human has become aware of the vast web of life that organizes itself toward increasing complexity in an ongoing weave of novelty and continuity. We have become aware of its processes of self-regulation, such as the regulating of Earth's unique atmosphere via the response of Earth's organisms, or biomass. Moreover, we have finally seen that we, too, are participants in the metabolic dynamics and the unfolding adventure that is the life of the universe. The rigid charade of the supposedly detached Newtonian observer has been rendered obsolete by postmodern physics (though the psychological reasons for desiring that kind of "objective" distancing in certain cultures have not). The assumptions of modernity positioned us on top of nature, imperiously heedless of its integrity. We now have accumulated sufficient data to indicate to even the most smug champion of the mechanistic worldview that we are, as every primal culture has always understood, inherent participants in the processes of the universe at very subtle levels. What responsibility does such participation carry? What meaning does it bring?

To traditional native cultures, the intricately balanced relatedness of the Earth community obviously calls forth awareness and sensitivity on the part of humans. Native people find the extent to which modern citizens are oblivious to the rest of the natural world incredible. Since the birth of modernity, Eurocentric cultures have seized on technological prowess to insulate ourselves not only from any limits imposed by nature, but also from the fearsome treachery we projected onto the rest of nature. If we let down our guard, it was felt, surely we would be engulfed by chaos and destruction. Having had no regard for the ways of our planetary home, though, destruction is precisely the fate that awaits us—unless we effect fundamental changes in our behavior.

Whether one feels that modern society's interactions with nature have demonstrated arrogance and callous disregard or a forward-looking thrust of progress with a few problems that require some fine-tuning, surely it is embarrassing that our collective sense of alarm arose not over shame that we have driven more than a hundred thousand species into extinction in recent decades, or that we have clear-cut most of the old-growth forests in the entire temperate zone, or that we have filled in much of the wetlands on which seventy-five percent of American bird species depend for roosting, or that we have blown apart entire mountainsides for a relatively small amount of ore, but only when it became apparent that our own survival and quality of life were in jeopardy.

Currently we live among, and support in various ways, ecologically destructive dynamics of vast proportions. Most environmental scientists agree that there is still time to reduce and halt the damage—but not a great deal of time, perhaps a decade or two. If we were to become seriously committed to allowing an ecologically healthy existence for the Great Family of All Beings and our progeny, we would focus our collective energy and attention not only on urgently needed ecological restoration projects, but on achieving fundamental changes in the world's economics. A program that is to be effective over time would have to address the following issues, among others. First, a global market composed of unqualified-growth economies, whether capitalist or socialist, is madness on this rather finite planet. Instead of supporting the accumulation of money and material gain by converting the biosphere into trash as rapidly as possible, Herman Daly, Hazel Henderson, James Robertson, and other astute analysts suggest ways to distinguish qualitative "development" from merely quantitative "growth." Second, it is increasingly apparent that we need to decentralize economic power—shifting control from corporate headquarters, which continually demonstrate disregard for the health of both the United States and Third World communities and ecosystems in which they operate, to worker-owned businesses in community-based and regionally oriented economies. Third, energy efficiency should be recognized as the cheap way to halt global warming and ease other damage as well. Fourth, we need to conserve the earthstuff we use, hence to require less and produce less. Lifestyle changes, such as recycling and eating less meat, are a subset of the necessary structural changes.

Such basic concerns lie beyond the intentions of nearly all governments today, which see their role as safeguarding and engendering economic growth. It is not at all clear that they even consider survival to be affordable as they press on with business-as-usual in their growth economies. Advocates of various alternative systems of government who fervently believe that *everything* would be all right if only we had political and economic decentralization, or democratic socialism, or laissez-faire capitalism might consider that no particular political and economic structure alone will result in a polity informed by ecological wisdom. What we require is a sense of grounding in our context, our larger reality.

To consider our relationship to the cosmos is to engage with primary issues of being. Why are they understood to be spiritual? The universe is laced with mystery, undulating in rhythms of novelty and unity. Its self-organizing, self-regulating magnificence is informed by diffuse powers of subjectivity we call by various names: Cosmic Consciousness, Ultimate Mystery, the divine, the Great Holy God, or Goddess. When one experiences consciousness of the exquisite interrelatedness and subtle vibratory flux of the life of the material world—a perception that extends our understanding of "sentient" beyond the animal kingdom—one is filled with awe. One has experienced immersion in ultimate value, the sacred totality. Hence one has known grace. Reverence for the grand communion and gratitude follow, the roots of worth-ship, or worship.

When we experience our cosmic self, we see that the gestalt notions of foreground and context are one; it makes sense to speak of nature as our "context" only if we remember that our seeming separation from the rest of the natural world is a matter of perception, a view that does not hold up at subtle levels of awareness. Atoms exhibit responsiveness to other atoms. Chaos moves into pattern. Subtle mind is aware that nature is aware.

Within a cosmological orientation, revelation is acknowledged when ever an individual experiences direct awareness, purposively or unexpectedly, of the larger reality, which includes the perceiving being and is not something apart from him or her. In such moments the universe reveals a dimension of its nature that is inaccessible to mundane, discursive consciousness. One perceives being as a unitary ground of form, motion, time, and space, such that one experiences an enormously spacious sense of the immediate. Perceptual boundaries between the "inner" and the "outer" dissolve, and an intense awareness of the whole, as a benevolent and powerful presence, is common. Revelation may be *extra*ordinary, but it is not *super*natural. It would more accurately be labeled *ultra*natural, a journey into the cosmic nature that lies within the world we tend to perceive as an aggregate of discrete fragments bound by such forces as gravity and electromagnetism.

Since modern socialization has taught us to deny subtle perceptions that do not fit within an objectivist, mechanistic model of existence, how are we supposed to develop our atrophied sensitivity in order to grow in awareness of the intricate, moment-to-moment dance of creation, disintegration, and recreation? Since the identity of modern humankind can gain full knowledge and control over the sensate world, how can we afford to accept the sense of mystery inherent in the novel manifestation of subatomic constellations that are the forms and events we perceive? Since intimacy with the material world is fearful to modern, industrialized society, how can we hope to enter into conscious relationship with the unitive ground of the astonishing range of spontaneous subjectivity that is in and around us? How can we expect to achieve such a fundamental deepening of our modes of comprehension without *cultural practices* that encourage us to grow in awareness? How can we come to realize that we live in a participatory universe—that each of us, each minute part of us, is a node within a vast network of creative dynamics—unless we engage in practices that awaken our minds to the realities of such participation? How can we absorb the existential paradox of the universality of processes throughout the natural world that yield the unique patterning of subatomic events giving rise to each of us unless we become experienced in the kind of expression that can handle paradox: skillful metaphor, multivalent poetry, and wise narrative of mythic depth that spark the imagination and reveal the rich unfolding of cosmological possibilities? How can we know the unitive dimension of existence as a felt reality, rather than an abstract concept, unless we experience subtle mindfulness of flux, the palpable connectedness within ritual space, or the music, dance, or drama that activates in us deep awareness, wonder, and awe? Once we have grasped experientially, even for a moment, the astounding unity, what kinds of interactions—with people, trees, animals, rivers—are worthy of us? What kinds of practices will remind us of what we know, even when we encounter little but denial from modern culture?

The very ways in which a modern society views itself serve to marginalize contact with the sacred whole. In the materialist view, production and other economic activity are central to human society, social constructs are a related tier of developments, and the so-called epiphenomenal concerns such as spirituality and cosmology cluster around the edges of "real life." To a traditional native person, of course, that conceptualization is utterly inside out: at the center of human life are experiences of deep communion with the cosmos; from those, a people understand and honor their relationships and seek to retain the revealed wisdom through cosmologically oriented cultural practices that inform their performance of such basic tasks as putting food into the stomach and clothing and sheltering the body.

Modernity holds that our natural role is to function in opposition to nature, to "master" it and thereby hold chaos at bay. Ecological versions of the managerial ethos hold that the unfolding dynamics of the natural world, as understood through evolutionary biology, are indeed extraordinarily complex, resilient, and worthy of awe—but that the role of the human is to intervene, beyond fulfilling our vital needs, to manage and direct the further evolutions of other species. What accounts for that sharp turn at the bifurcation point of awe toward the urge to control rather than toward humility and the urge to protect? The cause seems to be a deep fear that one's being might well be absorbed and annihilated by a larger whole unless that whole is broken down into areas of human control—the land "resources," the waterways, production animals, the space frontier, and so forth. In addition to the fear that nature unchallenged would physically destroy us, the notion of experiencing oneness with the natural world is feared by many men as a horrifying engulfment: either one guards his individuality, freedom, and particularity *or* he surrenders his being to an overarching monster, oneness. This highly charged dualism is so central to the sensibility of modernity that cultural commentators who wish to be considered sophisticated and urbanely modern routinely mock expressions of communion with nature as sophomoric, embarrassing, sentimental, or boring. Deconstructive postmodernists add that the "narrative" of experiencing oneness is politically incorrect because it "totalizes" or "colonizes" multiplicity, or "difference." Both of these objections are locked into a framework of dualism: either particularity or ultimate unity. They can be held only in ignorance of the *experience* of being at one with the world, in which one perceives in an instant the sacred whole, the vast organism in which we are embodied without separation, the larger self. Knowing the wonder of the larger reality, the experience of grace, all particularity is then understood to be exceedingly precious, the unimaginably diverse articulation of the dynamically creative cosmic body. Moreover, the unique abilities of the human species are understood to participate in responsibility for developments in the great unfolding.

Since there are myriad paths, many unmarked, to the unitive experience, it is in no way exclusive. When a culture hostile to nature disdainfully ignores children's and adults' experiences of cosmic grace, however, deep communion is discouraged and ultimately denied. Is this not a thwarting of evolutionary potential? There is much support for the view that the *telos* of the universe is toward ever-increasing subjectivity and complexity—but why not toward increasing communion as well? The emergence of self-reflexive consciousness in humans introduced the possibility of rich, subtle, and endlessly creative communion with the larger whole. Since "progressing" beyond primal worldviews of the spiritual relatedness of all phenomena, though, we have walled off that evolutionary path. The substitutions—communing with an anthropomorphic deity said to orchestrate the sacred whole, or guarding against communion with nature as a dangerous (and unscientific!) act of vulnerability—have left us atrophied, lacking a deeply personal connection with the natural world around us. Hence the modern denial of our larger self not only confines and diminishes us, but is cosmologically irresponsible.

As we begin to develop a sense of the ecocommunity in which we live, we grow to cherish it. Without much forethought we find ourselves creating personal rituals of communion—making visitations to a particular spot, suspending thought for a long moment at the beginning of the day to let the backyard bird song fill our mind/body, or feeling drawn to observe the daily progress of a budding tree. As our sensitivity increases, certain narrowly focused rituals within the human community seem to cry out for greater fullness. While saying grace before a meal, why not express gratitude not only for our food but for the presence of the animals, plants, landforms, and water? Participating in worship services, why not suggest various ways that the presence of the bioregion can be included? Celebrations of baptism, confirmation, Bar Mitzvah, Bat Mitzvah, and weddings could all include the ritual planting of a tree. Certainly the annual slaughter of millions of firs to celebrate the birth of Christ could be replaced with purchasing live firs, or, better still, native trees, which can later be planted or donated to a regional park.

Beyond that, each of our religious rituals, those that mark the stages in an individual's spiritual life as well as those that are communal celebrations in the liturgical cycle, could be enriched by greater recognition of the cosmic web of life. In this era of ecological awakening, the living presence of the ceremonies of native peoples—inspiring acts of regeneration of their sense of interrelatedness with the sacred whole—is a great gift. Perhaps the growing appreciation of their embodied wisdom will lead to an interfaith deepening of the spirituality of Earthlings.

While some people work to "cosmologize" organized religion, others have taken to grow-your-own ceremonies of cosmological celebration, especially at the solstices and equinoxes. The two days with the longest and shortest gift of light from our sun, plus the two days with light and darkness of equal length, plus the midpoint days between those four were celebrated in pre-Christian Europe as natural markers in the majestic cycles of Earth's body (two of the midpoint holy days being preserved in modern times as May Day and All Saints Day, or All Hallows Day, preceded immediately by Hallows Eve, or "Halloween"). Today the solstices and equinoxes have become occasions for groups of friends and family to gather in celebration of the Earth community and to focus awareness on the particular turning of the seasons. With friends, I have given thanks at autumn equinox for the bountiful harvests of the soil and in our lives, turned inward on the long night of winter solstice to look directly at the dark, known regeneration at spring equinox as Earth's exuberance burst forth, and felt the fullness of fruition at summer solstice when Earth's day is long and sensuous.

Of all those images, the most beautiful that remains with me is the spring equinox ritual we evolved over time. A group of some forty people in spring colors walk from our cars in procession to a gentle rise in a spacious park, carrying armfuls of flowers and greens, food and drink, and burning incense. Musicians among us play instruments as the children toss a trail of petals. We form a circle and place the flowers and greens at our feet, forming a huge garland for the Earth, one foot wide and half as high. In the center on colorful cloths we set baskets of food and objects of regeneration—feathers shed by eagles and other birds, a bowl of water, a small statue of a pregnant female, and several sprays of pink and white blossoms. We breathe together and plant our feet squarely on the warming earth, drawing up its procreative powers into our being. Working mindfully, we take some flowers and ivy from the Earth garland and make individual garlands with trailing ribbons for ourselves, then weave together the stems and greens in the grand garland. Standing, we call upon the presence of the East and the cleansing winds that clear our minds.

We call upon the presence of the South and the fires of warmth and energy that enliven us. We call upon the presence of the West and the water that soothes and renews us. We call upon the presence of the North and the earth that grounds and feeds us. We sing, perhaps the Native American song "The Earth Is Our Mother." We seat ourselves around the garland and offer into the circle one-word poems about spring in our bioregion. Someone reads a favorite poem. A storyteller, accompanied by soft drumming and bird-song flute, tells an ancient tale of the meaning of spring. We sing a lilting song with her. A second storyteller tells another story of spring. We sing a rhythmic chant with him. The two bards put on masks they have made and dance and leap around the circle, sprung with vernal energies. In counterpoints, the men sing his song, the women hers. We rise and sway like saplings as we sing. We move as the spirit moves us, dancing, turning. When we come to rest, we sit, emptied of song, on the ground and let the flute song fill our bodies. We pass around a bowl of berries, each person taking one and offering into the circle thoughts of thanksgiving for particular gifts of spring. Brimming with love for the embodied wisdom of Gaia, we bid farewell to the presence of the four directions and break the circle. Then come feasting and visiting. Thus do we welcome spring.

Such rituals are communal celebrations by women, men, and children around the country who give thanks for the cyclic renewal of our Earthbody and who seek to align their awareness with seasons of initiation, growth, fruition, and repose—a perception that balances the cultural pressure to regard one's life solely as a linear trajectory. These ceremonies focus on the seasonal "moment" of the bioregion by bringing into the ritual circle found objects—feathers, leaves, rocks, flower petals—that activate the participants' sense of relationship with Gaia.

Although the concept of Mother Earth as a sacred whole is extremely ancient in many parts of the world, objections have been raised in recent years to the projection of female identity onto the planet. The most obvious problem is the ill fit between carrying forth concepts that were regarded as a locus of honor and admiration, such as symbolism of the elemental power of the female, into patriarchal contexts, where those concepts are feared, resented, and degraded. A second objection, raised by Elizabeth Dodson Gray, is that patriarchal culture feels that "Mom" (Mother Nature) will always clean up any ecological mess we make and, besides, she would never really kill off her children no matter how badly we treat her. The argument that it is unfair for either sex to claim primary identification with our Earthself may be the most compelling objection. (Curiously, that call for fair play did not occur to men during more than two thousand years of patriarchal religion.) Then, too, there are poor reasons to reject the female metaphor for Earth: a man insisted to me that such identification is "very dangerous," alluding to the patriarchal fear that women are always just a hairsbreadth away from turning into monstrously powerful biofascists. Personally, I find the notion of Mother Earth to be an image far more subtle and grand than a literal extension of woman's processes and particularities, but I am not bothered by people's declining to use a female metaphor as long as they understand this planet to be a body—a celestial body, an interrelated body, a unitive body of intricately balanced and dynamic systems of circulation and generation. It is the Earthbody that we celebrate and cherish at seasonal rituals of the Earth community.

Consciously or not, we exist as participants in the greatest ritual: the cosmic ceremony of seasonal and diurnal rhythms framing epochal dramas of becoming that are composed of a constant dance of subatomic manifestations of matter-energy.

The philosopher George Santayana wondered, "Why should we not look on the universe with piety? Is it not our substance? Are we made of other clay? All our possibilities lie from eternity hidden in its bosom." Yet the shrunken, narcissistic focus of the modern human locates all our possibilities in *our* bosoms, freewheeling creatures without a past or relations. In the absence of any comprehension of the sacred whole, meaninglessness and destruction are as acceptable as anything else to many people. An operator of a timber harvesting company in the Pacific Northwest stated a few years ago, "It is natural for man to manipulate his environment and ruin it. And it may be natural that we are going to go through the process of ruining the land and we are going to die and there is going to be nothing left. That will be the end of it." Others feel that there can indeed be something left once we have run through the health of the ecosystems: an artificially created replacement world with soil, rocks, trees, crops, and animals created by nanotechnology (molecular engineering) and genetic engineering. Enthusiasts would explain, "Once humans have remade the physical world to suit our preferences more closely, scarcity of resources and other insulting ecological limits to human population will be behind us!" Also gone will be the unfolding differentiation, subjectivity, and communion of billions of unique manifestations of the cosmos. "Extinction is natural," they counter. "This is a participatory universe, and everyone knows you have to break a few eggs to make an omelet. What's the problem?"

The problem is hubris, the rending of the cosmic web of life through arrogance, fear, and an emptiness so deep it is wrenchingly painful to observe. Our species is but one expression of the cosmos. We have always played an interactive role with the rest of the Earth community. There is no possibility that we could refrain from intervention; even walking down a street, we probably crush countless tiny creatures. Our bodies require food, warmth, clothing, and shelter—all of which we take from earthstuff. The *problem* is the denial of humility and care that marks the modern and ultramodern revolutions against the integrity of Gaia, a dynamic unfolding that was well established long before our emergence. Our species' ethics should include the fulfilling of our vital needs with minimal damage to our cosmic relations. If that were our guideline, we would surely have to admit that our knowledge of the intricacies of Gaian life is so far from complete that we should make far-reaching changes in the ecosystems only with great caution.

Since the dominant culture continues to rush in the opposite direction—cleaning up a few production processes, for example, while still maintaining ravenous growth economies that devour habitats with dazzling efficiency—

Gaian spirituality calls for "action prayers," activist engagement with those human systems that are furthering the gratuitous destruction of the Earth community. Much "green" activism in the industrialized nations as well as the Third and Fourth (indigenous peoples) Worlds has been sustained by spiritual commitment.

Commitment, to be effective, must also be informed. Understanding basic principles of ecology—interdependence, diversity, resilience, adaptability, and limits—is necessary in opposing unwise human intervention. People with untempered faith in the supposedly value-free, objective life of technology often insist that environmental dynamics are so complicated that the public should back off and let commissions of scientific experts make all decisions, which would then be enacted by government. If memory serves, that course of action gave us scores of dangerous nuclear power plants; numerous disastrous assaults on the ecological integrity of watersheds by the U.S. Army Corps of Engineers; approval of hundreds of toxic compounds for agricultural, industrial, and medical uses; and a flood of federal research funding for the development of genetically engineered animals, pesticides, and crops without adequate testing of *dynamic* interaction, such as will occur in a real ecosystem once a new microorganism leaves the lab. The burden of proof (of safety) should be on the people pushing for novel, substantial change in the ecosystems, not on the citizens calling for caution.

Not only is it difficult for concerned citizens working through existing channels in modern technocracies to defend sustainability against destructive projects that will boost the GNP (a tally that includes costs of attempted environmental cleanup as if it were merely part of value-free production and services), but the voices of millions of other residents are not heard at all. In a parliament of all species, humans' expansionist schemes for industrial mastery of the biosphere would no doubt be hooted off the floor as too unbearably callous, greedy, and murderous to merit a formal vote. Because the existing governmental channels in societies with growth economies are not designed to welcome sustainable earth ethics in more than superficial ways, grassroots movements have had to mount direct, usually nonviolent, challenges to ecocide. Such campaigns demand much time and energy and often yield frustration. Yet, for increasing numbers of people worldwide, that work is experienced not merely as attempts to save enough of the biosphere for human survival, but as moral acts that embody our felt connection with the sacred whole.

We are haunted by the question of how much recovery is possible for human consciousness formed in modern societies hostile to nature. Will we ever experience anything like the nuanced, richly detailed sense of the sacred whole known to traditional native peoples? Will we ever know that pervasive sense of intimacy with the rest of the natural world, we who have lived in exile so long? Chief Seattle warned in mid-nineteenth century that humans would die of a terrible loneliness if all the animals on this continent disappeared, yet how many of us even notice the gradual disappearance of songbirds, for instance, as fewer return each spring from their ravaged winter homes in the Central and South American rainforest? The diminishing bird counts are items we read about in the newspaper and then turn the page. Or are we dying, slowly, of a terrible alienation?

We are not abandoned. Nature will receive us into communion once again and make our sterile consciousness fertile if only we will bring bare attention to its wonders. Recovered awareness, patient and precise, is the taproot of Gaian spirituality. In a garden, at a park, or on a wilderness retreat, we can open our senses and learn. Just as in the meditation practice of observing with precision whatever arises in the mind or the body, bare attention to the rest of the natural world requires setting aside preconceived notions, such as the view of nature as a dumb mechanism. In unexpected moments I have witnessed the prolonged eroticism of garden snails and the exuberant play of two sanderlings bodysurfing repeatedly down the rivulets of a freshwater stream that cut across a beach while the rest of their flock splashed around more sedately downstream. We have underestimated our animal relations because we felt we had no use for them. In truth, we need them deeply to heal us, to initiate us, to spark our possibilities.

Once we no longer feel like tourists in the natural world, more and more of the intense vitality and intricate interrelatedness of the sacred whole is revealed to us. Its wonders, if we have sloughed off at least some of our implanted fear, evoke celebration, hence the flowering in recent years of personal and communal rituals of gratitude and joy. Gaian spirituality is nonsectarian, sprouting up in Hebrew treeplanting ceremonies, bioregional liturgies, the United Nations' interfaith Environmental Sabbath, the imaginative burst of homegrown solstice and equinox celebrations, and much more. Alas, disapproving glances still shoot between some members of these groups, as if there could be only one correct way to attempt to express the ineffable. Were we and the rest of the world set here by Raven the creator? By the Great Holy, the creativity of the cosmos? Were we modeled by God the Father? Did we grow from the body of Mother Earth? *We are here*—inextricably linked at the molecular level to every other manifestation of the great unfolding. We are descendants of the fireball. We are pilgrims on this Earth, glimpsing the oneness of the sacred whole, knowing Gaia, knowing grace.

GRACE EMBODIED

The sense of grand communion within the sacred whole that is the cosmos is denied and replaced in Eurocentric patriarchal societies by perceptions of separateness. Humanism, both secular and religious, has framed the unfolding story of the human species apart from that of the rest of the Earth community, while the Abrahamic religions (Judaism, Christianity, and Islam) have contributed an influential creation myth in which all things on Earth are created separately by a distant sky-god, with humans accorded dominion on behalf of the Divine Absentee Owner. The sense of separateness was informed by an agonistic attitude toward nature and, correspondingly, toward the elemental power of the female body—that is, the capability to bleed in rhythm with the moon, to grow both males and females from our flesh, and to transform food into milk for the very young. In the patriarchal societies that replaced the earlier Earth-honoring and female-honoring cultures of neolithic Europe, both women and nature were — and are — considered potentially dangerous and chaotic. Only by dominating and transcending both of those seats of supposedly threatening power could males experience spiritual deliverance, according to patriarchal religion.

One of the most deeply challenging dimensions of feminism is the development of a spiritual orientation that rejects the patriarchal nightmare and embraces both the Earthbody and the personal body — as manifestations of divine creativity in the cosmos. The movement called "women's spirituality" is vital and diverse, finding form within traditional religions, in the contemporary rebirth of Goddess spirituality, and in myriad other personal and collective expressions. It has proven to be a potent antidote to the negation of the female so central to patriarchal culture.

The honoring of the female embodiment that takes place in Goddess-oriented women's spirituality rituals has much in common with many of the concerns of French feminism's *écriture féminine* (also known as "writing the body"), which seeks to create nonpatriarchal "discourse," or modes of knowledge, regarding the nature of the female body. Although a few of the French feminist theorists have devoted a good deal of energy to refuting Lacan's absurd Freudian claim that women naturally function with a biological sense of phallic lack,[1] the more interesting aspects of *écriture féminine* address deep structures in patriarchal culture of suppression of women's subjectivity, body, and desire and the need to recover women's authentic voicing of pleasure, or *jouissance*. They reject the binary dualism of male and female (so essential to the theory of structuralism) as a concept framed in patriarchal culture, which they call the phallocratic symbolic order. Patriarchal culture teaches men to perceive an opposition between self and other and then neutralize the other as being the same or complementary. As Luce Irigaray declares, however, "Women have sex organs just about everywhere" (1981, 103; see Dallery 1989, *Signs* 1981). Because even the most radically body-oriented of the French feminist theorists were responding within the forum of intellectual exchange to poststructuralist patriarchal philosophy, their focus has remained in the areas of critique and suggested possibilities. In the United States, however, the *experiential* flowering of radical women's body-oriented spirituality from the midseventies on, generally uninfluenced by the rumblings in Paris, arrived at many of the same postpatriarchal conceptualizations of the female body — and embraced them as vital elements of a "new" religion and culture to be lived daily.

The contemporary practice of Goddess spirituality includes creative participation in myth, symbol, and ritual. Because this spiritual orientation particularly honors the elemental power of the female and its embeddedness in nature, it was perceived as regressive, embarrassing, or even horrifying to liberal and material/socialist feminists, who apparently accepted the patriarchal dualism of nature-versus-culture and had internalized the patriarchal rationalization that the reason women had traditionally been blocked from participation in culture was their bodily "plight" of being mired in the reproductive processes of nature.

Investing their consciousness within such an orientation, it is quite understandable that "modern" feminists recoil (I use the present tense here because it still occurs today) when "spiritual feminists" celebrate our bodies and our elemental connectedness with nature. If one subscribes to the patriarchal view of culture as human endeavor pursued in opposition to nature, drawing attention to such connection automatically places women outside the realm of culture as "biological agents" instead of "cultural agents." The renewal of Goddess spirituality, however, rejected the patriarchal dualism from the outset. Like countless prepatriarchal and nonpatriarchal societies, we women who had drifted out of patriarchal religion[2] view culture not as a struggle in opposition to nature but as a potentially harmonious extension of nature, a human construction inclusive of creative tensions and reflective of our embeddedness in the Earthbody and the teachings of nature: diversity, subjectivity, adaptability, interrelatedness. Within such an orientation — let's call it ecological sanity — the bodily affinity of females and males with nature is respected and culturally honored, rather than denied and scorned.

The central understanding in contemporary Goddess spirituality is that the divine — creativity in the universe, or ultimate mystery — is laced throughout the cosmic manifestations in and around us. The divine is immanent, not concentrated in some distant seat of power, a transcendent sky-god. Instead of accepting the notion in patriarchal religion that one must spiritually transcend the body and nature, it is possible to apprehend divine transcendence as the sacred whole, or the infinite complexity of the universe. The Goddess, as a metaphor for divine immanence and the transcendent sacred whole, expresses ongoing regeneration with the cycles of her Earthbody and contains the mystery of diversity within unity: the extraordinary range of differentiation in forms of life on Earth issued from her dynamic form and are kin. A second aspect of contemporary Goddess spirituality is the empowerment experienced by people as they come to grasp their heritage and presence in terms of the cosmological self, the dimension of human existence that participates in the larger reality. Such empowerment is far different from a dominating "power-over," the binding force of social constructions in a patriarchal culture. Rather, it is a strengthening of one's capabilities of subjectivity and cosmic unfolding within a web of caring and solidarity that extends backward and forward in time, drawing one from the fragmentation and lonely atomization of modernity to the deepest levels of connectedness. A third aspect of Goddess spirituality is the perceptual shift from the death-based sense of existence that underlies patriarchal culture to a regeneration-based awareness, an embrace of life as a cycle of creative rebirths, a dynamic participation in the processes of infinity. It is a commonplace in patriarchal society that men often spend their lives striving to create cultural achievements, including male heirs who will bear their name, in order to beat death by achieving a measure of immortality.[3] As Heidegger put it in *Being and Time*, one's constant awareness of his own death is the ground for an authentic existence; "being-toward" death is the nature of consciousness of the future. As is often the case, that "profound" philosophical insight is a projection of men's experience under patriarchal socialization, not a universal perception of human existence. (The contrast in images between a dead man on a cross and a bountiful, living goddess-body reflect two distinct perceptions of the core of being.) Goddess spirituality celebrates the power of the erotic as the sparking of cosmic potential, rather than wrestling with the erotic as a process that potentially yields a new generation and hence the signal of one's approaching end. The erotic and the sensuous, expressed through the aesthetic, draw forth not only physical generation but unpredictably creative waves of spiritual, intellectual, and emotional renewal.

Consciousness of the larger reality, through the practice of body-oriented *vipassana* meditation and body-oriented Goddess spirituality, led me eventually to perceive the erotic processes of female being as "body parables," expressions of the subtle dimensions of existence that underlie supposedly fixed delineations of separateness. A woman often experiences a sense of soft boundaries of her body on the first day of menstruation. In the postorgasmic state, many women experience a peaceful, expansive mindstate of free-floating boundarylessness. (Many men, particularly young men, describe their postorgasmic state as a sensation of weakness and vulnerability; some call it *le petit mort*, the little death.) In pregnancy and childbirth, the delineation between me and not-me is blurred and somewhat elusive. In nursing, while cradling the extension of her flesh to her breast, a woman again may experience a dreamy sense of soft boundaries. All of these immersions into the "oceanic feeling," which I have experienced as grace, teach one that, although boundaries can be important in this life, they are altogether relative and temporary in the larger field of the grand communion.

For feminists delving into the history of Western culture and religion, one of the most surprising discoveries was the closeted erotic meanings of common symbols or cultural objects. The rose, like the lotus and chrysanthemum in the East, originally represented the female genitals, the red rose being rich in the sacred blood. (Imagine my perverse delight to open the morning paper a few years ago and read that Congress had voted to make the rose, an emblem of the elemental power of the female, our nation's official flower.) The custom of a woman painting her lips with red stain alluded to the red riches of her nether lips. (How incredibly constricted a culture is ours that such an obvious connection escaped me for twenty years of applying lipstick until I read about it.) The Holy Grail, and all chalices, are symbols of the womb. The throne evolved as a symbol of the seated body of the sacred queen, as succession passed matrilineally to rulers in many ancient cultures. As for that most famous negative symbol of the female, "vagina dentata," it apparently is not universal but found only in patriarchal cultures.

The Virgin Mary, chaste and docile, is actually a direct descendant of the Goddess, producing her child parthenogenetically (that is, by herself), a son born with the coming-of-light at winter solstice and renewed, even after death, at the vernal equinox. As was commonly the case, her procreative power was inverted by patriarchal culture: Saint Augustine added to church doctrine the "fact" that Mary's hymen was not ruptured in the birthing of Jesus, so she was not responsible for any "pollution" entering the world from her womb! She was made into a physically passive and nearly neuter symbol of a patriarchal dream-queen, often presented by clergy as a model of subservience against which women should measure themselves. Nonetheless, Mary retained her considerable power, as the Great Mother, in the spiritual lives of Catholic women, an extremely resilient phenomenon some church authorities try to curb as "Mariolatry." In Latin America, where Mary is sometimes still called by the old pre-Columbian Goddess names, her image is the central one in many Catholic churches, while the statue of Jesus is found on a side altar.

As with symbols, feminist research into the myths of patriarchal culture also revealed long-hidden meanings. The goddesses of Greek Olympian mythology turned out to be degraded images of their far more ancient selves: Hera, the disagreeable and jealous wife of Zeus, was a powerful deity of women and all fecundity long before his arrival; Athena, the cold, boyish daughter of Zeus, was formerly a protector of home and the arts; Artemis, who had been made the sister of the new god Apollo, was formerly the wild forest presence in Arcadia and the protector of women in childbirth in her manifestation at Ephesus; and Pandora, who was made into the troublesome, treacherous source of human woes, was actually the maiden form of the Earth Goddess who poured bountiful gifts from her earthen jar. Similarly, every element in the biblical story of Adam and Eve has been inverted from its earlier meaning: the serpent had been a positive symbol of renewal and regeneration in the old, Earth-based religion; the sacred trees were not forbidden but sites of worship and celebration; and the female was not the cause of a fall from grace but was a respected manifestation of the sacred cycles of life. The serpentlike dragon slain in the legend of St. George was actually the Old Religion being destroyed by "the one true Church." So powerfully rooted was the ancient religion, however, that the dragon's head often grew back in folk tellings of the tale. The metaphorical boast that St. Patrick had rid Ireland of "snakes" was also a story of the imposition of the new religion over the old, as the Goddess Bridget was transformed into a Christian saint.

Such symbolic legends of political conquest are twisted descendants of the far more ancient and primordial processes of myth that apparently informed the era of the Goddess and most certainly inspire its contemporary renaissance. Since the divine is understood to be immanent (dynamic creativity in the cosmic unfolding) as well as transcendent (as the sacred whole, or ultimate mystery), one approaches spiritual practice in this orientation as awakening of possibilities. Engagement with myth and symbol, as participatory fields of relation rather than fixed artifacts, suggests a shaping of our continuity and groundedness while evoking a sense of our larger self, the fullness of our being. It is the aesthetic path to grace.

Many who follow this path assemble a home altar bearing symbols of the Goddess. It may be no more than a shelf in a bookcase covered with a cloth on which stand Goddess figurines, shells, stones, or other gifts of the Earthbody, but its affective power is remarkable. Even a passing glance at the symbolic forms of the Goddess reminds a woman that she is heir to a lineage of deeply grounded wisdom and inner strength and a weaver of the sacred whole. Sarasvati stands sensually poised on a lotus blossom, playing a sitar as She guides knowledge and the arts. Our Lady of Guadalupe stands on a crescent moon, clothed in a blue robe of the starry heavens and radiating a full-body aura of golden light. Yemaya, mother of the sea, the great womb of creation, stands draped in blue and white, a beautiful, dark woman of deep mystery. Quan Yin, smooth and serene, dispenses from her open hands the vast power of compassion. On many women's altars "the little snake Goddesses of Crete," their names long lost, stand as we moderns never could have imagined: planted firmly on the earth, baring breasts proudly, their out-stretched arms hold writhing serpents, symbols of shedding and growth in endless regeneration. We sustain the mythic presence of the Goddess in our lives as She evokes our creativity and depth.

The telling of myth is a ritual creation of sacred space. It actualizes the narrator and the listener as engaged witnesses, weavers of a web of being that grows outward from the principals, avowing existential bonds of community in an eternal present. Far more than arbitrary "social constructions," the articulation and cherishing of unions and separations, creations and destructions in mythic drama are acts of relation that place all participants in deep accord with the life processes of the unfolding universe. Myth is sacred narrative evoked by a totemic presence, a manifestation or empowered bearer of cosmic energies. The more a narrative evolves in elaborations distant from the totemic presence, the more it loses vitality and may fade in time to formulaic allegory. There are those myths, though, that do not fade. In the sacred stories of the Goddess—replete with totemic serpents, deer, owls, spiders, bear, and more—the body of the Goddess is itself a totemic presence.

By way of example, let the mythic presence of Artemis dance in your mind:

When the moon appeared as a slender crescent, delicate and fine but firm in the promise of growth, Artemis roamed the untouched forests of Arcadia. On each night of the waxing moon Her animals and mortals came to dance with the Goddess. They encircled a large tree that stood apart from the others, its smooth bark and leaves seeming silver in the fresh moonlight. Artemis moved toward the tree and silence followed, but for Her doves cooing softly in the boughs overhead. The Goddess crouched as the Great She-Bear She once had been and touched the earth. From the roots, up the trunk, along the branches to the leaves She drew Her hands. Again. And again. With each pass She brought forth new life: pale blossoms unfolding and falling away, tiny globes of fruit shining among the branches, and finally ripe, glowing fruit hanging from the sacred boughs. Artemis gathered the fruit and fed Her animals, Her mortals, Her nymphs, and Herself. The dance began.

The animals were drawn to the tree. They rolled over its roots and encircled the trunk. In a larger ring the dancers raised their arms, turning slowly, and felt currents of energy rising through their trunks, turning faster, through their arms, turning, out their fingers, turning, turning, to their heads, whirling, racing, flying. Sparks of energy flew from their fingertips, lacing the air with traces

*of clear blue light. They joined hands, joined arms, merged bodies into a circle
of current that carried them effortlessly.*

*Artemis appeared large before them standing straight against the tree, Her
spine its trunk, Her arms its boughs. Her body pulsed with life, its rhythms
echoed by the silvered tree, the animals at Her feet, the dancers, the grass, the
plants, the grove. Every particle of the forest quivered with Her energy. Artemis
the nurturer, protector, Goddess of the swelling moon. Artemis! She began to
merge with the sacred tree, while the circle of dances spun around Her. They
threw back their heads and saw the shimmering boughs rush by. When Artemis
was one with the moon tree, the circle broke. Dancers went whirling through
the grove, falling exhausted on the mossy forest floor.*⁴

When a woman raised in patriarchal culture—which tells her she has the
wrong type of body/mind, unlike males, to share a sexual sameness with the
divine Father God—discovers the sacred stories of the Goddess, identification
with Her female dimension of being is an immediate perception. When a
woman—who has been told by patriarchal culture that female power is somewhat shameful, dirty, and downright dangerous if unrestrained—immerses herself in sacred space where various manifestations of the Goddess bring forth
the Earthbody from the spinning void, bestow fertility on field and womb, ease
ripe bodies in childbirth, nurture the arts, protect the home, guard one's child
against forces of harm, issue guidance for a community, join in ecstatic dance
and celebration in sacred groves, and set love's mysteries in play, then the
woman's possibilities are evoked with astoundingly joyous intensity. *She* will
create the ongoing completion of each mythic fragment. *She* is in and of the
Goddess. *She* will body the myth with her own totemic being. *She* is the cosmic
form of waxing, fullness, waning: virgin, mature creator, wise crone. She cannot
be negated ever again. Her roots are too deep—and they are everywhere.

In the present coming of the Goddess, we have recovered ritual. The presence of ritual circles at gatherings of the radical women's spirituality movement
during the seventies spread to political actions such as the women's peace
encampments at Greenham Common in England and at Seneca, New York, in
the United States; the Women's Pentagon Action, held simultaneously in Washington, D.C., San Francisco, and other cities in 1980 and 1981; and numerous
actions at sites where design and production of nuclear weapons take place and
at nuclear power plants. By the second half of the eighties, it was common
practice to open and close meetings of a wide range of organizations in alternative politics with ritual circles of singing, or brief meditation, or a moment's
silent "centering" and bonding.⁵ More elaborate rituals of mourning and
empowerment, for instance, came to be included in political conferences on
social justice and ecopeace.

When people gather in a group to create ritual, they form a unitive body, a
microcosmos of differentiation, subjectivity, and deep communion. To enter
ritual space is to feel a palpable sphere of attunement among the energy fields
of the participants. Such ritual presence, if successfully created at the outset,
by singing, invocation, meditation, or other body-prayer, is at once calming and

energizing. It is so pleasing to our body/mind that participants often experience reluctance to move away from the ritual space even when the circle has been formally broken at the conclusion.

In the contemporary renaissance of Goddess spirituality, women have formed ritual groups in order to mark passages in their lives, to affirm their emotional and other mind/body experiences, to heal and to celebrate, to explore new possibilities of being, to empower their efforts and desires, to renew commitment to ongoing social-change work, to enrich their spiritual lives, and to strengthen bonds of communion in this fragmented, atomized society.[6] At times these rituals are wrenching, raucous, or sweetly rapturous. In my own life I have participated in many rituals over the years with a rather fluid configuration of sisterly ritualists: an intimate group of four, a large group of a dozen or so, and a full tribal gathering of both sexes who assemble irregularly for solstice, equinox, wedding, and funeral rituals that include a multiplicity of friends and relations.

Although it is impossible to convey the experience of ritual on the printed page, I offer a brief account of a ceremony, a menarche ritual, that may serve as an example of affirming the female dimension of being even in the midst of diffuse cultural mechanisms that degrade it.

Some months after the daughters of two of us had their first menstrual periods, seven women plus the two adolescents spent a weekend at a hexagon-shaped house in the country with an open deck in the center. On Saturday afternoon the mothers prepare an altar in the womblike round enclosure, a cloth on which they set red candles and a pot of big red Gerber daisies, along with Goddess figurines, pine cones, an abalone shell filled with dried cypress needles, and other favorite objects that people had brought. The group silently drifts toward the circle from various doors and is seated on cushions. We listen as the order of the ceremony is explained. We begin by lighting the dried needles and passing the shell around the circle, breathing in the purifying smoke and fanning it gently to surround each body. We invoke the presence of the four directions and sing a melodic chant: *We all come from the Goddess and to Her we shall return like a drop of rain flowing to the ocean.* We tell the girls about some of the many, many cultural responses to menses as a visitation of transformative power, a sacred time set apart from the mundane. We tell them of the cultural degradation of women's procreative power to potential danger and then shameful uncleanliness. We tell them of the invention of counting, the Paleolithic bone-calendars etched with twenty-eight marks, the cycle of women's blood and the moon. We read them a poetic myth of Hera, goddess of women and the powers of fecundity, who draws forth the lunar blood. We sing again: *She changes everything She touches, and everything She touches changes.* Then, one by one, the women tell the story of their menarche, that first visitation of Hera — the excitement, the embarrassment, the confusion, the family's response. After each story, the speaker receives a crescent moon painted with berry juice on her forehead. Some women also speak of their first sexual experience, of how they hope the girls might think about their bodies and their womanhood. The girls tell their stories last, tales of red blood on white slacks during the middle of movies! The circle is filled with laughter and tears, blessings and hope. We sing a final song, *Listen, listen, listen to my heart's song.* . . . Then the women stand and form a birth canal, an archway with our upraised arms. The two mothers stand at the far end of the passageway, near the opening of the deck into the outer world. One at a time the girls pass through our arch of arms as we chant their names and kiss their cheeks. As they emerge as women, the mothers paint a crimson moon on their foreheads and hug them. Then come gifts and feasting. That was my daughter's menarche ritual.

Just as myth and symbol are aural and visual religious communication, ritual is whole-body communing that evokes personal emergence within the palpable whole. Ritual process often expands the awareness of one's bodily presence, along with all the other bodily presences within the circle; participants may experience their presence and form, becoming merged with the circle or the ritual space it encloses. One's sense of group-being becomes as large as the whole, yet one is not lost in diffusion. On the contrary, the expansion of self to the large group-body intensifies one's unique sense of capability and energized subjectivity. This simultaneous expansion and intensification is the ecstatic gift of ritual, a mystery of the erotic. It remains as a body memory that shapes new possibilities in a life increasingly understood to be thoroughly relational and endlessly creative.

NOTES

1. Surely penis envy is not the universal response that Freud assumed it to be. The feminist author Elizabeth Dodson Gray relates a young mother's account of the aftermath of a visit in which her preschool daughter took a bath with a boy of the same age. After the boy and his mother had left, the girl said to her mother with earnest compassion, "Isn't it a blessing it didn't grow on his face?"

2. Although the focus of this article is the renewal of Goddess spirituality by women who left institutional patriarchal religion, I do not mean to imply that only those women who left were feminist. A strong feminist movement exists today within both Judaism and Christianity. An example is the response issued in 1990 by Rosemary Radford Ruether (1990a) and several Catholic women's organizations to the U.S. bishops' pastoral letter on women. Here is an excerpt from their open letter:

> In the new draft of the pastoral letter on women which your office has recently released you call on the world to repent of sexism and to give to women that full equality of personhood which is their God-given nature. Yet your pastoral reaffirms every aspect of the patriarchal system which is the basis of sexism. Dear Bishops, you embarrass us. You insult our intelligence. . . .
>
> What you want, Dear Bishops, is to seduce us into helping to rescue your patriarchal ecclesial system, while conceding nothing that is essential to that system itself. . . .
>
> Let me say clearly to you, Dear Bishops, we will not raise one cent for your patriarchal church. We will not lift one finger to rescue your patriarchal system. We will not bend one knee to worship the patriarchal idol that you

blasphemously insist on calling "God." We are not fooled.

We have heard the gospel of the authentic Jesus, the Christ: good news to the poor, release to the captives, the setting at liberty of those who are oppressed. We are raising money to promote the ministries of that authentic gospel. ...

But not one cent, not one finger lifted, not one knee bent for the church of patriarchy: the arrogant, blind, hypocritical, unrepentant Church of patriarchy. ...

3. The internationally known postmodern semioticist Umberto Eco has noted, perhaps inadvertently, that this traditional motivation for men raised under patriarchy indeed helped shape his life. At twenty-two he decided that intimacy itself held far less appeal than the desire to project his name (or "sign") beyond the death of the body via writing a book and making a son. For this budding semioticist, the abstract "sign" of his own being (his name) seemed to be the primary focus in life. (See Blonsky 1989, 79. For a related and quite lively article, see Brooke-Rose 1986, 305-16).

4. Excerpted, and slightly adapted, from Spretnak, 1981, 77-81.

5. A spiral dance, developed by Starhawk and the Reclaiming Collective, has become a popular closing ceremony at conferences. During the course of the spiraling, one sees the face (and body) of each participant pass before him or her twice. For directions and a diagram, see Starhawk, 1989, 246-47.

6. Not all women's ritual groups, of course, locate themselves within the Goddess tradition. For an account of Christian-based rituals conducted with her women's group and with her family, see Nelson 1986.

18

Natural Resources

A Conversation between Byllye Avery and Mary E. Hunt

FOREWORD—CAROL J. ADAMS

Ecofeminism holds that the domination of nonhuman nature is linked to the domination of women and that both dominations must be eradicated. According to ecofeminism, social "isms of domination" such as sexism, racism, classism, and "naturism" (the unjustified domination of nonhuman nature) sanction and perpetuate a "logic of domination" that falsely assumes the superiority of some humans and their right to exploit the rest of nature (see Warren 1987, 1990). Ecofeminism must be concerned with how cultural institutions oppress natural resources.

Forced motherhood treats women's bodies as natural resources. Women's re-productivity is dealt with in controlling ways that we associate with strip mining, logging, and other efforts that deplete the environment. When women's

Byllye Avery is the Founding President of the National Black Women's Health Project in Atlanta, Georgia. She received a MacArthur Foundation Award through which she is working on African-American women's public-health issues in Boston, Massachusetts.

Mary E. Hunt is a feminist liberation theologian from the Catholic tradition. She is the cofounder and codirector of the Women's Alliance for Theology, Ethics and Ritual (WATER), a nonprofit education center in Silver Spring, Maryland. Among her many publications are articles in the *Journal of Feminist Studies in Religion, America, Concilium, Conscience, The Witness, Open Hands,* and *Second Opinion,* as well as chapters in many books. She is the editor of *From Woman-Pain to Woman-Vision: Writings in Feminist Theology* by Anne McGrew Bennett and the author of *Fierce Tenderness: A Feminist Theology of Friendship,* which was awarded the Crossroad Women's Studies Prize for 1990.

bodies are seen as natural resources, as Susan Griffin noted years ago in her ground-breaking *Woman and Nature: The Roaring Inside Her* (1979), they become objectified. Rather than being seen as moral and religious agents, women are acted upon by laws and social pressures. Reproductive rights, including the value of legalized abortion, is a tenet intrinsic to ecofeminism that cuts across race and class lines.

Yet some have assumed that ecofeminism, especially ecofeminist spiritualities, would be against abortions. As one ecofeminist observed, the presumption is that ecofeminism would be "laissez-faire fertility."

The perspective that sees women of reproductive age as natural resources and the presumption that ecofeminism would affirm that which is "natural"—motherhood—require that the issue of abortion be examined for an anthology on ecofeminism and the sacred.

In searching for pertinent articles on the subject, I discovered that few existed. To overcome this lacuna in our literature, I approached two articulate, talented women with years of experience around the issues of women's reproductive rights: Byllye Avery and Mary E. Hunt. Though their interests crisscrossed for years, these two women had never had the opportunity to meet before engaging in the conversation that follows. I asked them to examine the implications of "the power of nature—and of women—to give and withhold life," as Sallie McFague has referred to it.

This foreword will set the stage for their conversation by discussing issues relevant to ecofeminism, theology, and abortion rights: the patriarchal construction of women's procreative functions as natural; the place of abortion rights in ecofeminism; and theologizing from one's experience.

Seeing Women's Procreative Functions as Natural

Women's reproductive functions have placed us closer to the natural world in patriarchal thought. This was the central concern that Simone de Beauvoir examined in *The Second Sex*. It prompted Sherry Ortner's theory that this is the reason women are oppressed in most cultures. In fact, although most women give birth, lactate, and menstruate, we only *appear* physiologically to be closer to nature. This is a cultural construction. Feminist philosophers have examined this cultural construction, pointing out, among other things, that by creating women as natural resources and associating natural functions with a private rather than a public world, men did not have to construct ethical standards regarding women or confront the issue of women as public persons (see Gatens 1991). The result has been that we have not had an ethical language, until the feminist movement, for articulating a public defense of abortion as a woman's right.

As a result of this construction of women's procreative functions as natural, women's desire to stop pregnancies and their historic ability to do so have not been acknowledged. Yet, as ecofeminism examines and reclaims the knowledge of indigenous cultures, it is important to recognize that, as Linda Gordon has pointed out, "The ability to transcend the biological was present in the earliest known human societies" (Gordon 1976, 46). Indeed, "George Devereux, who surveyed 350 primitive, ancient, and preindustrial societies in the Yale Human Relations Area Files, found a range of abortion methods including herbs, chemicals, mechanical means, violence, and magic" (Petchesky 1984, 28–29).

The power of nature—and of women—to give *and* withhold life has been the constant, not a culturally constructed "natural" acceptance of all pregnancies. Recognizing this may ease the association between environmentalists' suspicions of technological innovations and the argument that the antiabortion movement is responding to (and rejecting) technological changes in society that abortion represents. The existence of abortion is not tied to technology. Only its current form is. There is nothing "natural" in women proceeding with every pregnancy they experience, or with environmentalists avoiding the abortion issue because of its current association with technology.

Charlene Spretnak adds an instructive insight into the debate about what is "natural" when the issue is abortion. She proposes a "law of the womb" argument. Spretnak points out that recently published textbooks on obstetrics and gynecology state that between 40 to 50 percent of fertilized human eggs are

> spontaneously aborted at some point in development by the womb. . . .
> The political claim that every zygote has an "inalienable right" to reach birth is made in ignorance or denial of the human processes of reproduction. The womb expels a zygote or embryo or fetus because conditions, either in the female body or the new life-form itself, are not right. (Spretnak 1992, 2)

Spretnak concludes from this information that an aspect of the elemental power of the female body is "the law of the womb." The female organism, mind *and* body, has always decided whether the conditions were right for children. Only in some patriarchal cultures has this been criminalized. Criminalizing abortion, thus, is utterly *un*natural and is based on patriarchal ideology of control over the female, rather than respect for the biological processes of human reproduction, in which the female body-mind always makes the decision about whether conditions are right for a pregnancy to proceed.

The Place of Abortion Rights in Ecofeminism

Because environmentalists appear to emphasize the value of all life—both human and nonhuman—there has been some concern that the "seamless garment" argument made by liberal and left-wing peace activists justifying their antiabortion stance would be extended as well to ecofeminism. In *Hypatia's* special issue on environmental feminism, Patricia J. Mills raised the question: Where does the politics of abortion fit in evolving ecofeminist theory? In raising this question, she referred to the "seamless garment" argument:

> To say that nature must become "an end in itself" hardly articulates a principle that can ground a feminist politics of abortion on demand. This position, in which the interpretation of the "end" or *telos* of nature is left in limbo, lends aid and comfort to those within the peace, ecology, and

antinuclear movements in the United States who don "the seamless garment" of an abstract pro-life politics that entails an antiabortion stand.
(Mills 1991, 176, n. 5)

Mills proposes that the argument that we must move beyond anthropomorphism
to a recognition that "nature knows best," "*may* be useful for the ecology, peace,
and anti-nuclear movements, but it creates profound problems for many feminists because 'Nature' in its 'wisdom' creates not only ecological balance but
unwanted pregnancies" (166-67).

Byllye Avery and Mary Hunt offer several responses to the seamless garment
argument and the accompanying rhetoric that naturalizes pregnancy but not
abortion. They place women as central actors in reproduction; not objects who
are acted upon, but moral agents. They consistently maintain that the focus
must be on women's wisdom, not on an abstract and romanticized vision of
either nature or "woman." They interpret pregnancy as a relational act. They
see their position as resonating with respect for life, including all the life that
already exists on the planet. Thus, they emphasize issues of quality of life, and
raise the question about how resources are used in a world where some people
are allowed to be hungry. In this, they reiterate what Rosemary Ruether has
previously argued: that "the decisions to limit the number of births, both for
one's own family and as a part of a global community, is as much a decision
for life and for a more adequate distribution of the means of life as is the
struggle to end the arms race" (Ruether 1990, 10).

To comprehend the respect-for-life position of abortion rights, Byllye and
Mary develop the metaphor of recycling experience. Through this metaphor
they are able to explore the way women integrate the experience of abortion
into their lives and their community. The metaphor of recycling offers an important refutation of the view of pregnancy as an end itself or as more "natural"
than abortion, because abortion is placed within a continuum in which commitment to living and community exists, rather than being isolated as a finite
and tragic personal act. Locating abortion within community and the woman's
entire reproductive life, the metaphor of recycling experience summons a recognition of the sacred.

One might stand the argument that concerns Mills on the head using these
insights: The cultural construction of women, and our lack of access to instruction on self-help health care, prevents us from knowing ourselves. This, it could
be argued, is what is unnatural. If we know our bodies and our selves, we will
not be natural resources for others, but will be able to be moral actors who
assess issues of quality of life and consider our entire reproductive lives in
making decisions about pregnancy and abortion.

Theologizing from One's Experience

Mill's cautionary words, however, offer further stimulus for valuing the conversation that follows, a conversation that confronts the issues of what is "natural" and the nature of abortion. The heuristic contribution of this conversation
is the way that it both reflects and enacts a central tenet of feminist and wom-

anist theologizing: the importance of beginning with women's own experiences. How a woman experiences her own body, and her ability to make decisions about it, are important theological questions. When discussing abortion, we begin not with theories, but with women's experiences. Consider Alice Walker's statement: "Abortion, for many women, is more than an experience of suffering beyond anything most men will ever know; it is an act of mercy, and an act of self-defense" (Walker 1990, 67). Or Byllye Avery's "For poor women abortion is a matter of survival: if I have this one more child, it etches away my margin of survival. People always seem not to understand what poor women have to do just to survive, let alone to live" (Avery 1990, 76). Both Walker and Avery emphasize women's perspectives, begin with women's lives. They also recognize the agency and the moral thought involved in women's actions.

Elsewhere Mary Hunt summarizes the path-breaking work of ethicist Beverly Wildung Harrison: "She stressed that women must make choices about reproductive rights both because we are legitimate moral agents, patriarchal patterns notwithstanding, and because there is an integrity to our embodied selves that is part of creation" (Hunt 1989a, 1). In addressing the issue of ecofeminism and abortion, we are offered an alternate view of creation—one that emphasizes women's embodiedness and agency, rather than a static representation of woman. The woman/nature analysis that is central to ecofeminism means that we must look both at nature *and* women. The conversation that follows places women central to the discussion about abortion.

Historically speaking, this conversation represents an early attempt to have a multicultural dialogue on this question as catalyzed by ecofeminist concerns. If either Byllye or Mary were sitting down to write an individual article for this volume, we would have had a very different piece. But that is not what was needed. The model of women coming together across race and class to discuss these issues is a crucial model for ecofeminism. In addition, context is a central principle for ecofeminism; ecofeminists tend to avoid universalistic claims such as the seamless garment argument. A dialogue such as this one enacts the sort of methodology consistent with ecofeminism's emphasis on context. Yet the fact that the context for this article is a conversation makes this piece an anomaly in this anthology, offering its readers a more personal or informal tone of voice.

This conversation took place at Byllye's home in Dorchester, Massachusetts, one evening in October 1991. Both Mary and Byllye refer to the landmark 1973 *Roe v. Wade* Supreme Court decision. At the time of the discussion, *Roe v. Wade*'s scope had been seriously eroded by subsequent decisions, and it was presumed that the court was waiting for an appropriate case that would allow it to invalidate the decision that legalized abortion.

The meaning of women as "natural resources" appears to change during the conversation. At first the concept is seen disapprovingly. Women have been natural resources in several ways, most prominently as producers of babies. Women, like the rest of nature, are used instrumentally. But then the concept takes on positive connotations: Women are natural resources to be treasured. It is the speculum that transforms this view of women as natural resources. In conversation, the radicalizing experience of seeing one's own cervix emerges.

By enabling women to see our own cervixes, the speculum brings about the consciousness of "our bodies, ourselves."

Byllye and Mary see women as moral agents and argue that, for women, respect for life includes assessing whether we can nurture that life. Can a woman respect that life if she can't nurture it? They do not see abortion as a finite experience, but place it within the whole of a woman's life and her relationship to her community. Through the use of the metaphor of recycling, they overcome the presumed finitude of abortion, interpreting both abortion and pregnancy as relational, and directing us to think of the spirituality of recycling experiences.

This dialogue exemplifies the type of process affirmed by ecofeminism. There is no suggestion by either of the women involved that this is their final word on the subject. In this sense the conversation is unfinished, or in another sense, still evolving. It is an example of what happens when ecofeminism brings women from diverse backgrounds into the dialogue about how a patriarchal culture "naturalizes" women. Its purpose is to provoke ecofeminist discussion on this subject, to push ecofeminism to become more explicit theoretically about the issue. The challenge of this conversation to us is to continue the process, to sit down with one another, to engage in conversation. We are all invited into the conversation and into the process.

THE DIALOGUE

HUNT: I'm a feminist theologian. Since I'm a Catholic by tradition, I've been working on the abortion issue as a Catholic theologian, although I'm not a practicing Catholic in the institutional sense. It's very important to acknowledge and claim Catholic roots when the Catholic Church still has an enormous amount of clout, and especially in Washington, where the major opposition on the abortion question issue now comes from the Catholic Bishops. We are their more-than-equal competition in the sense that we're using our skills to work theologically and ethically. We at WATER also have a kind of pastoral dimension and ritual work, too.

AVERY: I am in Boston, working on health-care access and related issues for African-American women. We are an understudied population. I am working in conjunction with the Harvard School of Public Health; they have the research equipment, and we of the National Black Women's Health Project are connected with the many women who need to be part of national studies for our well-being.

HUNT: This interview is occurring because Carol Adams thought that you and I might have a useful conversation from your perspective as an activist and especially in the African-American community, and my perspective as a white Catholic, also an activist. Since both of us also do theoretical work, Carol suggested that we look at the question of ecofeminism and women as natural resources, and how that issue might inform an analysis and a practice of abortion.

AVERY: Men always thought of women as a resource. The whole right to own one's body—it's just second nature to me, because men felt like we never owned our bodies in the first place.

HUNT: So it really was a question of whether it was *this* man or *that* man who owned it.

AVERY: It was a man only. The point was that *we never owned it.* I was thinking today, coming home in the car, how right the title "Our Bodies, Ourselves" was. It is about sexuality, and it is about claiming and owning who I am and how that doesn't happen. That is just incredible.

My daughter Sonia is 25. She works at the Feminist Women's Health Center. She goes between loving her work, supporting the women, providing that service, to being angry with the women because they wait so long and angry with all of us as a collective body of people because these women know nothing about their bodies. It's like they almost don't know where their vaginas are.

She told me the other day that someone was back in the physician's room saying that she came in so they couldn't kill any babies today. She said they had to drag her outside and they threw her out. Then they came and got a man and threw him out the door!

HUNT: Are these Operation Rescue types?

AVERY: Yes, who are there every day.

HUNT: They seem to fetishize the fetus, as if the life of the pregnant woman did not have some moral priority. After all, if the woman were not carrying it, the fetus would not exist. But that does not make the fetus a natural resource—rather, the woman.

AVERY: I have talked with my daughter about this. She has hard feelings with dealing with the products of conception: "I can't say this is not a baby." I said, "You're right, it is. You can't say that it's not; you have to call it for what it is." She said, "Well, Mama, it had its feet and it had its eyes." I say, "Absolutely, you have to own up to what it is that you are doing. You've got to understand that."

HUNT: You're talking about late-term abortions?

AVERY: Or even some of the early ones. You know, you can make out what it is when you see it.

HUNT: It's not a rock.

AVERY: You know it ain't a rock, it ain't a little blob of jelly. You see things in there. I saw them twenty years ago. You know, you do see them. And so you have to come to grips with it.

HUNT: And what do you say to her about that? When she says to you "What is it?" especially in terms of late-term abortions. How do you cope with that question?

AVERY: I say to her that it is the taking of a potential life. That is exactly what it is. This baby can't live by itself. I say even if the woman had it full term and left it somewhere it couldn't live by itself. It has to have some type of relationship with something.

HUNT: These are the kinds of questions for which a new analysis is necessary, and the new analysis begins, in my judgment, in honesty. So while I would never want to give the anti-choice forces any encouragement, neither would I want to pass over the important question of the reality and value, albeit limited and developmental, of fetal life.

AVERY: Absolutely.

HUNT: This leaves me with the question, thinking about Carol's analysis in terms of natural resources, that the argument could also be turned around by people who say, "Wait a minute, now you're squandering another natural resource?" That's the horror story. The Operation Rescue approach to it. I try to be thorough in terms of how I think about these things, and obviously that would not be my own position. Could somebody turn around and say "Okay, fine, you don't want us to treat women as natural resources to be squandered, then why do you people treat fetuses or embryos or pre-embryos as natural resources?" Doesn't the same analysis apply?

AVERY: I think that the same analysis does not apply, because what we're talking about is quality of life. It's like we say to young black women who are having babies to increase the race, having unhealthy babies who have neurological impairment, who are born much much too small. We say you're not doing the race any good, you're not doing anything for the race because of the quality of what it is that is being born.

Quality involves how well will I—emotionally, spiritually, and financially—be able to provide for this charge? I think bringing another human being into the world is probably the most profound, the most serious thing that we can do. Giving birth to another human being needs to be carefully thought about. It needs to be taken with that seriousness, and it needs to be within that individual to be able to provide and to make that sacrifice. Some people can't do that for emotional reasons. They can't do it for financial reasons. It doesn't mean that they will never be able to do it, but it means at this point in time in their lives they are unable to do it. We do know that quite often women have abortions that can lead to a later birth that is prepared for, planned, a taken-care-of kind of birth. That's why that option needs to be there. We're not having litters. We were not put here to just spit them out, spit them out; they need to be done with care. Women are natural resources to be treasured, not used.

HUNT: We begin with the notion that pregnancy and childbirth is by its nature a relational act. That's what makes gestation and childbirth quite different. Until we come to a point where some machine can do it, the fact is that it is without question a relational experience for which the woman has the ultimate responsibility to enter into that relationship in a way that is appropriate to her circumstances. Insofar as she can't, then the option for choice becomes obvious. This is what I would say to antiabortion activists: What you're talking about has nothing to do with the reality of the physical experience we're talking about.

AVERY: They would then come back and say that she should be able to carry the baby and put it up for adoption. That's what they would come back with. They are not saying that she needs to be forced to raise the child.

HUNT: Then that plays back into the notion that the woman is not a moral agent but that she is a natural resource to be used for those nine months.

AVERY: That's right. You are just a vessel. You're not a person. I think we just up-front say that it's something that we respect and we know, that's why we are trying to protect it. I think, to take the other side of that, that what terminating this one pregnancy is is really protecting another pregnancy. It is ensuring the right quality of life for a person. I think every sperm and every egg that are made are not meant to be a human being. Let's give the Creator credit for having more sense than that. I mean, does that make sense? I think about how abortion must be looked at in terms of how it fits in with the whole world picture.

HUNT: On an earth of four and one-half billion people.

AVERY: Yes. We look at it in terms of the whole functioning of the world, and the use of our natural resources, of which women are only one segment. But what I can't understand about the use of resources is that we have people who are already here who are allowed to be hungry, who can't find work. No attention is being paid to alleviating those conditions that cause stresses on our lives. There just seems to be a point there that we need, as a nation of people, to ensure a basic quality of life for everybody. There should be things that are sacred. When you take that view, you look at working to upgrade the quality of life for everyone.

You know, you get the young people and say, "Well, you've had four babies. Why didn't you have an abortion?" They will say, "I didn't know that was an option." I mean there are actually young girls who don't know that abortion is still legal. When they hear people talking about abortion becoming illegal, they think it's already happened. You don't even know how they hear the word *illegal*, whether they even hear "illegal" or whether they even have "legal" and "illegal" straight in their minds.

HUNT: What's important is that they have the message communicated to them in sufficiently negative terms that they don't even ask.

AVERY: But what happens for a lot of women is that their daughters have unwanted pregnancies in the exact same way they did. People start identifying with what happens once a child is born and they can't look at what might have happened if the child had not been born. When you're talking about people who struggle on lower incomes, the shit is so thick in front of your eyes that it's just impossible for you to see past that and look over where the sun might be shining.

Then there's the other part, where you will do what you have to do. You get support through an aunt or a cousin or somebody who'll say, "If you get pregnant, you let me know," which is as much as saying, "I will help you."

HUNT: They find their way to those people.

AVERY: Yes. One of the best gifts a young girl can have is to have a person who tells her that, so she'll know she has options. Sometimes someone will offer her support who knows that the mother might have trouble doing it. Or the mother might have said that she won't be able to do it. There are all different ways in which women support and help each other. I think that sometimes we don't talk enough about the positive ways in which women support each other, especially in our community, around abortion. We all need to think more about it.

HUNT: One of my particular interests is to see how in your work you've put together, or how you see women that you work with putting together, the religious component of who they are. I want to contrast it in a way with some of the Catholic women's stuff, because I think there may be some similarities.

AVERY: You know, what's interesting to me about the project of women coming together is how we are able to be there in all of our diversity. Because we have Muslim women and some very fundamentalist women. To tell you the truth, I don't know what they do with some of it in their heads, but they don't *not* come to health-related meetings, they don't *not* struggle. That's why I think the women's movement needs to include all women. The problems arise when for some reason women feel that they are not a part of it. Some women act like everybody's got to feel the same way, everybody's got to be the same, instead of saying one is a part of the women's movement because one is a woman. It gives us a better chance to help shape and direct that woman's thinking when we have her ear.

For us at the Black Women's Health Project, the women felt like they could be there no matter what church they are in. We have to accept each other along this gigantic continuum that we all fit on. We had one program, a celebration of us where we had one sister from the Caribbean who read a poem about "I am a Black Lesbian" and every single line in that poem started off with "I am a Black Lesbian"—every single line. She sat down. Another woman got up and sang this wonderful song about loving Jesus Christ. She was into her thing, and then the next one got up and did whatever she was doing. I thought, "Lord have mercy!" I mean, nobody was dying! I think once we set the stage of general acceptance and really tap into places where people are in pain, we'll get a different kind of thing happening with spirituality.

HUNT: Yes, pain, and I would even say tears, are compelling for women. We are the experts. I'm trying to invite women to really trust our tears and to see the patriarchal reversal around this. That's why abortion is such a good example. I don't know a woman who ever has had an abortion who hasn't had tears of relief, even if she had tears of regret or pain or whatever.

AVERY: That's right. That's what I had. I laughed until I cried. I was hysterical in the office. Luisah Teish says that when the rain comes, when the water hits the air and the sand, that is when we start to heal. She says if we don't have those three things happening, the water, the air, and the sand, that the healing will never start. And I've always just carried that with me.

HUNT: That's lovely. One of the insights that came from a group I belong to is that among us nothing is wasted. An idea that's thrown out now gets picked up an hour from now. .

I have never met a woman who had an abortion lightly. The experience is taken seriously by women. The experience itself is part of the sharing, the socializing of women. We support women who have abortions. Usually we come to those decisions together with a mother or a sister or a good friend, or for some women with their *compañeros.* I just think there's a way in which the sacredness of it is in the way the experience becomes part of the collective wisdom; even the pain of it becomes part of the wisdom.

I think we're pointing to another model, to an ecological model. A book or an article that you wrote gets recycled into something new. Women in this way are the ecologists of the culture. My resentment about environmentalism is it seems like it's the cleaning up after the damage done by patriarchal structures. On the other hand, I think there really is something in terms of this whole question of abortion and ecofeminism, because in fact there's a way in which abortion is really ecological. By that I don't mean that human life can be wasted.

AVERY: Right, but experience can be recycled.

HUNT: It can be recycled. The kind of natural ecology for which women have been so trustworthy is what you were talking about earlier in terms of the woman who was not in a condition to bring this pregnancy to term. There is a kind of ecology to the experience, and this is where I think the sacred question comes in. There's a kind of ecological sense in which the sum total of the experience of becoming pregnant and choosing not to bring pregnancy to term gets recycled and used as part of that individual woman and other women's way of living. For me this is an indication of something sacred.

It's a new idea, but I think we may be on to something. We literally recycle the experience among us. We talk with our kids about it; we break the silence on it, too. I see a tremendous amount of women's creativity and women's solidarity, and I call it sacred.

AVERY: Yes, we simply do not always know who is recycling what. I think that sometimes they might not even have any kids of their own, but they know that that was a good decision for them. They also know what was not in place for them to enable them to make similar decisions earlier. By their own experiences they know what they need to pass on.

HUNT: In fact, what we're talking about is not only preserving choice. Although we're up against it now with Roe on the line, the public language should not simply be preserving choice, although that is crucial. Rather, we can take the opportunity to insist abortion be made economically feasible and readily accessible, as well.

AVERY: Women need the money to go somewhere and get it or not regardless of the legal question.

HUNT: Women don't have abortions just because they will them. Somebody provides the herbs or the surgery or whatever.

AVERY: Right. The other place where we as feminists, and certainly we in the women's health movement, have missed an opportunity is when we "graduated" from gynecological self-help. We made a serious mistake. Women who come into the clinic know nothing about their bodies. The other serious mistake was when we did not plan a strategy. We went along with *Roe v. Wade* as if it were going to be with us for the rest of our lives. We knew in the 1970s it was eroding. But what we didn't start wholesale was to think about these things. The one thing I must say for the conservatives is that they form think tanks. Somebody is full-time, twenty-four hours a day, planning a strategy.

I think what we should have done, what we should have started doing in the 1970s, was to train thousands of women who would know how to do safe abortions. We knew we were going to lose this thing. We were going to talk to Asian women to get them to talk to their grandmothers about abortion. Now many of them have nobody to talk with about it. When you know how to do abortions, nobody can take that knowledge away, because it's so ingrained. When it is in the hands of women, you'd have to kill off almost every single woman in order to do away with it. That's the kind of penetration it takes to preserve choice in this culture.

HUNT: I come out of a white Irish Catholic background, and I know that in my community some of the women could not spell "abortion." I mean they had as many babies "as the Lord sent." They had an abysmal ignorance of their own bodies, absolutely no understanding of sex and pleasure, probably not a lot of sex after they stopped having their children. So this is another place where the repression around these things is phenomenal and the information isn't there. But it doesn't mean that those women didn't have abortions. A lot of them did, but the wall in terms of the communication is huge.

There is still a great deal of pernicious Catholic influence on what can be taught in schools and what's permissible in society. The classic case now is condom distribution in the New York City school system. The Cardinal of New York, John O'Connor, announced that one of the best law firms in New York is offering pro bono legal work to any parent who wants to argue in court that his or her child was given condoms without the parents' permission.

AVERY: Why doesn't he talk about the kid who gets AIDS for not using the condom? I don't understand it.

HUNT: There's nothing to understand. There is no logic to it. I have written about these things as theological pornography. They are like pornography in three ways: they objectify women, they trivialize sexuality, and they lead to violence. That's just what secular pornography does. The Catholic teaching on abortion is what I would call theological pornography: It objectifies women as natural resources, it trivializes sexuality as connected only with reproduction, and it leads to violence against women and against the whole community (see Hunt 1989b). The parallels are straight up and down. That's why I have such rage on this, because I work as a theologian with people for whom these things are important.

The notion of women as natural resources is very close to the Catholic line. The reason for women to exist and the reason for marriage is to bear babies, and lots of them.

AVERY: Every time I give speeches at abortion rallies, I know there are some anti-choice people there. I don't do programs with such people any more. It is a waste of my time. It confuses the audience. Nobody comes away looking right.

HUNT: We should be setting up round tables, forming teams. Women as moral agents with the right to bodily integrity is Beverly Wildung Harrison's (1983) work. It is like Carol Adams's (1991a and b) work on animals, their bodily integrity.

AVERY: It is a tough climate, politically.

HUNT: Yes, and the Catholic Church does not help. I am persuaded that the Catholic opposition to abortion may explain some of the other right-wing opposition. I do think there are credibility problems, that some people who oppose women's right to choose are disingenuous. The reason I say that is because I haven't seen a shred of evidence from those who oppose abortion that they really favor women's well-being.

My sense is that we are in a situation where those people in the institutional church who were the guardians of morals and ethics in the society over a long period of time, at least from the Middle Ages on, had moral authority in areas of economics, military matters, the larger politics. Now that authority is gone. The only way they can really shore up any kind of authority, any reason for being, any reason to have anybody contribute a nickel to them, is on the back of a pregnant fourteen-year-old. They really are, literally, putting their moral eggs in her basket, and all because they really don't make any difference any more in the society in terms of military, economic, or political issues.

AVERY: Right.

HUNT: I would be more persuaded if I thought that these same people who were arguing against abortion were arguing in terms of the sacredness of life in a range of places.

AVERY: No, they're not.

HUNT: Not at all; to the contrary. The analysis of legislators and their voting records which Catholics for a Free Choice has done proves that the same elected officials who vote against choice vote against WIC programs, against health-care issues in general for women and children. If they would just say that they support fetal life and all forms of life, and vote accordingly, I might be impressed. But to use this issue as the only place where they put their moral authority is to lose it.

AVERY: You can't have respect because these are also the same people who through the electronic church bleed old people to death. Have they ever shown up to say that we are tired of black babies dying at the rate twice the white babies? Are they ever there for that? They support the death penalty. It's crazy. It's hard to understand.

HUNT: The Catholic approach to this has been what is called the "seamless garment" argument, meaning that one who is against abortion is also against nuclear war, the death penalty, and the like.[1] It is exemplified by Catholic left antiwar folks, for example, the Berrigan brothers, who are reported to have tried to close an upstate New York abortion clinic and to leap the fence at the Seneca Army Depot the same day, to show the connection between abortion and nuclear war. The reverse logic would never occur to us, that is, to keep clinics open and to encourage the makers of weapons. God help the day when we who are pro-choice go to a weapons factory and say, "Let's keep this open."

There is something appealing about the "seamless garment," of course. Who would not want to develop a position that is consistent and neat, covering all issues in like fashion? But there are serious problems with it, beginning with the fact that in the case of abortion, such a position implicitly assumes that women are not moral agents.

I would prefer to argue that to be prowoman in a patriarchal society is equally consistent as, say, the pronatalist approach. This points out that in fact the real issue is not whether the garment has seams—in fact, nice clothes do—but who is wearing the dress. There just seems to be a consistent passing over of women.

AVERY: At the Feminist Women's Health Clinic where Sonia works, she tells me about the women who come in because their mothers have brought them in, because their husbands have brought them in, because their boyfriends have brought them in, and they don't want to have an abortion. What these women do, is they will keep that woman in the clinic for thirty minutes or so, and then send her back out. Or, if she's afraid of those people out there, they will slip her out the back door, then go out and tell them later on that she's gone. Their job is to help the woman get what she wants. And so it does not mean that everybody who comes into the abortion clinic gets an abortion. People don't seem to understand that. Women are told to go and think about this again.

HUNT: We can't forget that an abortion clinic in most instances is the only health-care institution some women visit. They can walk into that clinic and get someone who takes their blood pressure. Yet when you sit down with women, there are very few of them who are finally anti-choice. I mean there are the Phyllis Schlafley's and those people in Operation Rescue, but I really think if we're honest, their numbers are very small.

AVERY: But, see, we don't ever take to the streets and go knocking on people's doors.

HUNT: Assuming we lose Roe, which I'm sorry to say I think is a good assumption at this stage of the game, I just think we have to see this for the long haul. You talked earlier about whether we are going to have to spend the other half of our lives on this?

AVERY: The truth is, *we are.*

HUNT: The truth is, we are going to be going over territory that we've gone over before. We're going to be going backwards—you know—we're going to make the two steps back to go one step forward.

AVERY: We should have pushed to have gynecological self-help in every high school curriculum. We should have kept on that tactic until it got into our institutions of learning. We would have had a whole nation of women who would understand how their bodies work and who would be less apt to allow their bodies to be used as the resources of men. That's my cut on this thing about women and resources. It's a radicalizing experience to look at one's cervix. It's one that makes you definitely understand and feel connected to yourself. It is no longer a part of your body that you don't know what it looks like and it feels foreign from you. You will not let anybody else own it.

NOTES

1. Hentoff 1985 18, 20, represents this perspective. Ellen Willis 1985, 15-16, 24 offered a feminist response to the seamless garment argument. An article responding to the "seamless garment" argument within the animal rights movement is Adams 1991a and b.

19

Taking Life or "Taking on Life"?

Table Talk and Animals

CAROL J. ADAMS AND MARJORIE PROCTER-SMITH

How do we, as feminist theologians, understand our vegetarianism? What do we make of the central images regarding lambs that accompany Christian communion? How does our understanding of the theological imperative of solidarity with the oppressed work itself out when we expand the category of oppression beyond that of human beings? How can ecofeminism help us in thinking about these issues?

This essay begins the process of answering these questions. We see this process as a collective venture represented, to begin with, in our coauthorship of this essay, and furthered, we hope, in discussion, dialogue, and response to our writings. The invitation to reflect upon what we do to animals is an invitation to a table talk in both metaphorical and actual terms. Where are animals, when we sit at the table? This invitation extends to all those who have begun the

Carol J. Adams is the author of *The Sexual Politics of Meat: A Feminist-Vegetarian Critical Theory* which was awarded the first Continuum Women's Studies Award. She is completing books on *Pastoral Care and The Problem of Abusive Men* and *Abortion Rights and Animal Rights*. She is also editing with Josephine Donovan and Susanne Kappeler an anthology on feminist theory and animal rights. She has written several articles on the position of animals and animal rights in ecofeminism.

Marjorie Procter-Smith is associate professor of liturgy and worship at Perkins School of Theology, Southern Methodist University, Dallas, Texas, where she also teaches courses in feminist worship and spirituality. She is the author of *In Her Own Rite: Constructing Feminist Liturgical Tradition* and numerous articles on feminism and worship. She is co-editing with Janet Walton a *Women's Worship Commentary* and is working on a study of feminist prayer as an act of resistance.

process of dialogue between the social and the theological, between our diverse experiences of the world as women and that which we call holy, all those engaged in feminist, womanist, mujerista, Asian, Native American, liberation theologies and thealogies. When we refer to *theology* in this essay in any unmarked form, it is to this group of theologies that we are addressing ourselves, not conventional theology as it is generally conceived of. In this essay, we are not outlining the primary arguments for animal rights, but asking, given these arguments, what has theology to say on the matter?[1] We also presume that animals are explicitly a part of environmental feminist theology, and do not argue that point here (See Adams, Kheel, Donovan).

Theology recognizes that once the nonidentified, the nonpersons, are identified and heard, the transformation of history and reality occurs, because new theological subjects emerge. But so far these new theological subjects have been human beings, and what they have disrupted has not been the human-nonhuman animal relationship. They have not challenged the understanding of human nature as intrinsically unique or superior to the other animals. They have not proposed that animals themselves are new theological subjects. Thus within theology, unlike ecofeminism, animals currently are the nonidentified and the voiceless.

EXPLAINING THE ABSENCE OF ANIMALS FROM THEOLOGY

Feminist consciousness is, inherently, political consciousness. Ecofeminist consciousness about the ways people treat animals may at times be felt to clash with, rather than extend, this politicized consciousness.

As ecofeminism makes clear, women in Western cultures have been more closely associated with animals and other aspects of nonhuman nature than men. Yet, ecofeminist attempts to establish animals as subjects of their own lives may conflict with the feminist need to establish women's difference from animals to achieve women's own liberation into personhood. Furthermore, feminist consciousness may accept prevailing definitions of consciousness that posit it as something possessed only by human beings. Unlike ecofeminism, feminism proper may accept an anthropocentric definition of subjectivity such as that outlined by Paolo Freire in his classic book *Pedagogy of the Oppressed* (1972, 1978):

Unable to decide for themselves, unable to objectify either themselves or their activity, lacking objectives which they themselves have set, living "submerged" in a world to which they can give no meaning, lacking a "tomorrow" and a "today" because they exist in an overwhelming present, animals are ahistorical. . . . For the animal, the world does not constitute a "not-I" which could set him [sic] apart as an "I". . . . Their life is not one of risk-taking, for they are not aware of taking risks. . . . Consequently, animals cannot commit themselves. Their ahistorical condition does not permit them to "take on" life. Because they do not "take it on", they cannot construct it; and if they do not construct it, they cannot transform its configuration. Nor can they know themselves to be destroyed by life. (70)

Women struggle to overcome that which submerges us in a world that gives no meaning to women; they may, however, accept the notion that animals simply cannot take on life the way that self-conscious human beings can.

It should be observed that the idea of what is human has been generally based on upper- and middle-class white male experience. For many, consciousness is what defines us as human. To have consciousness means, precisely, to know oneself as more than "animal." If consciousness is something that only humans can possess, then whatever signs of inwardness, mental states, ideas, or values animals exhibit, they can never be called consciousness. If we recognize that animals have consciousness, we lose one of the central demarcations that define us as human and not animal.

Furthermore, feminist theory has accorded modernity's ability to transform nature ambivalent status. Some feminists may wish to transform women from the status of being "nature," and thus transformable by culture's agents, into being, along with men, those who transform nature. This view of nature may have been absorbed from the Marxist view of nature, and would explain the exclusion of animals from feminist consciousness. The human ability to transform nature is a central feature of the Marxist conceptualization of what is distinct about human beings (see Schmidt 1971). The Marxist emphasis on production, reason, and (human) sociality is profoundly anthropocentric. In addition, it posits animalness as the antithesis of humanness (Noske 1989, 77–80). From the Marxist point of view, animals can be neither social nor cultural, "they solely belong to the realm of necessity, i.e., natural history, the laws of matter and motion. While humans are free agents, in making their own sociocultural history, animals are unfree in that their (natural) history is made *for* them" (Noske 1989, 76; see Benton 1988). According to this view, animals, like nature, can be acted upon, but are not actors.

Along with other critics, ecofeminism challenges this view of animals and production. Should production be the basis for differentiating us from the other species? Isn't it possible that animals, too, gain and enact conscious intentionality through their interaction with the natural world, for example, through production (Ingold 1983)? Is it accurate to define production anthropocentrically? For instance, at one point, tool use was seen as solely a human capacity that catalyzed instrumental rationality. When it was discovered that some animals did indeed use tools, it was then argued that what was uniquely human was using tools to make tools. Yet, how does this equation of tool use, cognitive ability, and humanness account for the fact that some of the most intelligent animals, such as whales and dolphins, have no limbs and are sound oriented rather than tool users (Noske 1989, 151)?

While ecofeminism, along with several important developments in feminist philosophy, has challenged the positivistic scientific views of the other animals that have characterized our culture, it is clear that other feminists accept this characterization. Since it is equipped only to measure observable phenomena, and its explanatory apparatus of natural selection focuses on the individual organic level, this scientific view discounts animals' culture. It strips the other animals of consciousness, inventiveness, and cultural context. What we have is "a de-animalized biological construct rather than a mirror of animal reality" (Noske 1989, 88). It becomes, however, the prevailing viewpoint.

This prevailing viewpoint of the de-animalized animal is furthered by the practice of de-animalizing animals through meat eating. In our cultures, *meat* operates as a mass term, defining entire species of animals. Mass terms refer to things such as water or colors: No matter how much you have of it or what type of container it is in, it is still water. You can add a bucket of water to a pool of water without changing it at all. Objects referred to by mass terms have no individuality, no uniqueness, no specificity, no particularity. When we turn an animal into "meat," someone who has a very particular, situated life, a unique being, is converted into something that has no distinctiveness, no uniqueness, no individuality. When you add five pounds of hamburger to a plate of hamburger, it is more of the same thing, nothing is changed. But to have a living cow in front of you, and you kill that cow, and butcher that cow, and grind up her flesh, you have not added a mass term to a mass term and ended up with more of the same.[2] Because of the reign of *meat* as a mass term, it is not often while sitting at a table and eating meat that one thinks: "I am now interacting with an animal." We do not see our own personal meat eating as contact with animals because it has been renamed as contact with food.

But what is on the table in front of us is *not* devoid of specificity. It is the dead flesh of what was once a living, feeling being. The crucial point here is that we make some*one* who is a unique being, and therefore not the appropriate referent of a mass term, into some*thing* that is the appropriate referent of a mass term. We do so by removing any associations that might make it difficult to accept the activity of rendering a unique individual into a consumable thing. Not wanting to be aware of this activity, we accept this disassociation, this distancing device of the mass term *meat.*

According to Italian Marxist Antonio Gramsci, *hegemony* names that point at which power becomes so diffuse and invisible that it appears to dominated people as "common sense." Such a hegemony also exists in the culturally constructed view of animals by their dominators. Human use of animals is seen as so much common sense, whether it is because of enjoyment of their bodies as food or the presumed benefits of using them as research tools. What occurs with animals is a twist on this conceptualization of hegemony: People may be either dominated or dominators in other relationships, but in relationship with animals, all dominated people, along with their oppressors, become dominators of animals. Theology fails to critique this aspect of society that has become so diffuse and invisible.

CONSIDERING THE OTHERNESS OF ANIMALS

Theology emphasizes the importance of speaking from experience and listening to the voice of the oppressed. This viewpoint recognizes that solidarity does not require complete understanding of this experience; it requires respect. It means that we take the "Other" seriously. The next step is to recognize that the category of Other includes the other animals.

To recognize the animal as theological subject, as an Other, requires first a recognition of the way that these human- and male-centered categorizations have contaminated our thinking about them. Categories repel the natural from the human. Categories such as meat pre-existed our own individual relationships with animals, both providing a blueprint and an alibi for our transgressions against the other animals.

Here ecofeminism provides an important conceptual approach. Ecofeminism concerns itself with false categories of patriarchal culture, such as male-female, culture-nature, human-animal, subject-object, consciousness-instinct. Ecofeminism has observed the ways that anthropocentrism, human-centeredness, has intersected with androcentrism, male-centeredness. Traditionally, men have been associated with culture, with what characterizes us as human, with production, and with consciousness about these activities. Women have been associated with what links us with the other animals, reproduction, nature, instinct. These associations, like most universal claims, are riddled with flaws. For instance, feminists have noted how procreative and reproductive activities are seen as "natural" and "unskilled." In the same way that women's child-raising activities were rendered natural rather than social, instinctual rather than skillful, so have any signs of animals' sociality been interpreted as instinctual. This results in "distorted accounts of the social dynamics of various human and animal groups" (Nelson 1990, 208).

Among other things, the emerging theologies we are concerned with have interpreted sin as domination. Our attention is directed to *structures* of domination and exploitation. The process of theology is to raise consciousness about these structures and our participation in them, in order to empower ourselves to change them and repent of them. What has been a blueprint and an alibi is seen as partial and false. To recognize animals as Others requires that we stop colluding with the structures of domination. In other words, animals cannot be theological subjects as well as food on our tables or clothes on our back. And why should we not see them as theological subjects in light of emerging information on their consciousness and sociality? (See Bailey 1986, Clark 1982, Griffin 1990, 1991, Rollin 1981, 1990).

When new theological subjects appear, we must confront our own situation. Poor people direct us to our complicity in gaining wealth at their expense; people of color direct us to the white racism in our economic and cultural system that benefits white people; women challenge the sexist benefits of a patriarchal system. And what would animals as theological subjects do? They would require of us that static and universal categories be eliminated, that we cease believing in their lack of consciousness and sociality. They would have us confront the way we benefit from their oppression, that we recognize that we are not neutral parties to their situation, but that in eating them or in other ways benefitting from their object status, we have already taken sides.

SOLIDARITY AND INTERLOCKING OPPRESSIONS

We recognize that expanding the category of Other to include the other animals must be done carefully. If it is not, it could provide an escape for white middle-class women from engaging in solidarity with oppressed people, by focusing instead solely on oppressed animals. This would be completely inappropriate. To set up a hierarchy between the two issues is a false choice. That is not our focus, nor do we endorse such a response to this essay.[3] In fact, the oppression of people because of race, sex, and class and the oppression of animals are interwoven. Because consumption of animals' bodies is experienced separately from production of these dead bodies, consumers do not see the interwoven relationship between treatment of workers and animals. They see consumption as an end in itself, and do not consider what have been the means to that end. For instance, eating (a dead) chicken at a fast-food restaurant is disassociated from the experience of black women who, as "lung gunners," must each hour scrape the insides of 5,000 chickens' cavities and pull out the recently slaughtered chickens' lungs. Ninety-five percent of all poultry workers are undereducated black and Hispanic women who face carpal tunnel syndrome and other disorders caused by repetitive motion and stress (Clift 1990; Lewis 1990, 175; Davis forthcoming). Both women workers and the chickens themselves are means to the end of consumption.

As Rosemary Ruether has observed, environmental exploitation is not unmediated: "The exploitation of natural resources does not take place in an unmediated way. It takes place through the domination of the bodies of some people by other people" (Ruether 1981, 61). Those most oppressed because of race, sex, and class are those who become the mediators, the transformers of animals into food. For instance, Frank Perdue not only produces chicken meat for human consumption, as is well known, but he is a "self-professed union buster," a fact much less well known ("The P. Word" 1992, 14):

> Perdue's slaughterhouse workers are mostly poor women who work for approximately $5.50/hour. One North Carolina worker said, "Most of us treat our pets better ... than Perdue treats its workers." She detailed filthy working conditions, sexual harassment and ignored or poorly treated employee injuries.

A fire in a chicken processing plant in North Carolina in 1991 resulted in the death of twenty-five workers, most of whom were poor women. Indeed, meat packing is considered one of the ten worst jobs in the United States.

The centralized nature of the meat-packing industry means that a few huge corporations that are anti-union have driven down industry wages and benefits. In addition, increased technology "has forced an industry-wide speedup, resulting in some of the most dangerous jobs in America" (Juravich 1991). According to the United States Department of Labor, "almost one fourth of the workforce in the poultry industry suffers each year from industrial injuries" (Fox 1986,

41n.). Partly because of the frequent injuries, the annual United States and Canadian meat-packing plant employee turnover rate is around 60 percent, running as high as 100 percent in poultry plants (Clifton 1991, 11). There are approximately 54,000 nonunionized North American meat-packing workers — almost all of whom are women with a high school education or less, of black, Hispanic, or French-speaking ethnic background.[4]

Theology and ecofeminism as we understand them thus share commonalities in their justice-seeking efforts. Most workers who produce dead animals for consumption have not actively chosen these jobs: As African-American activist and writer Beverly Smith observes about the poor Black women who work in chicken factories:

> Their health was tremendously compromised by what they were doing, but they didn't have control over how they were going to earn a living, or over their work lives. It's not like they decided, "Well, I'll clean toilets even though I could be a corporate lawyer" or "I'll go cut up chickens though I could go and be a college professor" (Lewis 1990, 175-76).

It is white middle- and upper-class Euro-Americans who benefit most directly from exploitation of the environment and marginalized people. We have the choice not to work in chicken slaughterhouses, and we have the financial ability to purchase chicken meat, thus supporting a structure to which we do not need to submit ourselves. Recognizing that theology calls us to specific acts of solidarity and resistance and that we must include animals within environmental activism makes it transparent that what are simplistically or insufficiently called "life-style" issues are actually political actions.

THE WORD AND WORDS

Theology arises from the recognition that the oppressed have the power to speak. In refusing to hear the voice of the oppressed, the oppressors insure their marginality. Thus for all purposes they have been denied a voice, are denied words. Underlying the concern for hearing the words of the oppressed is the theological centrality of the Word in Christian and Jewish thought.

This preoccupation militates against recognizing animals as subjects of their own lives. Whether used literally (in the sense of valuing spoken and written words over other forms of communication), or metaphorically (in the identification of Jesus Christ as God's definitive "Word"), it has the effect of marginalizing and objectifying those who have no words. Although God speaks in other, nonverbal ways in scripture — whirlwind, fire, political upheaval, military victory or defeat — God's definitive communication is in the form of words: the Decalogue, the Law, Scripture. Speaking thus becomes identified with holy power. Language provides us with both a sense of affinity with God and subject status, while simultaneously confirming the object status of those who have no speech. The way language is tied to notions of the human person is suggested by Oliver Sachs when he refers to cases in which deaf individuals, in earlier centuries, could not inherit or own property, that is, they were not recognized under the law as persons (see Sachs 1989, 1990, 14-15).

As the title of the play *Children of a Lesser God* conveys, deaf persons are experienced by the hearing world as not fully human, as illegitimate children of God. Consider these synonyms: *dumb, mute, speechless, voiceless.* These adjectives refer to the absence of speech. *Dumb* applies both to animals and in popular use conveys intellectual weakness. When we say "I was speechless" we mean "I was powerless; I was helpless."

Those without speech and without power cannot name themselves; they are instead given names by those with power and speech. The interrelated absence of language and power is denoted in the Genesis story of Adam naming the animals and woman. As feminists, we have objected to the latter; as ecofeminists we object to the former.

SUBJUGATED KNOWLEDGE

Central to theology is the re-situating of expertise. The voice of the voiceless offers a truth that the voice of the expert can never offer: It offers the memory of suffering and the truths of subjugated knowledge (see Welch 1985). The problem, of course, is that animals can never claim a voice in human discourse. They are unable to give human voice to their suffering or to verbalize any knowledge — subjugated, primitive, and inadequate or powerful, sophisticated, and supposedly comprehensive. Human speech and the ability to communicate any form of knowledge separates us from the other animals.

Subjugated knowledge can incorporate our understanding of animals' suffering. Foucault argues that subjugated knowledge includes "the memory of hostile encounters which even up to this day have been confined to the margins of knowledge" (Welch 1985, 19). Fiction writers have cast human-animal relations as hostile encounters for years. Consider the pig in one novel who has just been told that he will soon be the best barbecue in the state: "The pig stopped eating. He blinked. Barbecue? *'Me?'* he cried. But the farmer only heard a regular pig squeal" (Stolz 1985, 5). If we re-situate our perspective onto the margins or into the pigpens or factory farms — where most dominated animals are — we see that being killed to be food or clothes or for sport or to be studied represents a hostile encounter. Animals do have voices; they simply don't have human words. Pigs may be crying, but we hear only their regular squeal.

Naming establishes individuality. In Mary Stolz's story, the pig escapes becoming a barrow and then barbecue by donning clothes. He discovers he has acquired a human voice as well, and passes as a young man. When asked his name, he is stumped. "My what?" he responds. He stalls for time, attempting to come up with a name, realizing that the farmer "who'd given a name to his horse and a name to his dog, hadn't bothered giving such a — such a *permanent* thing to his pig" (Stolz 1985, 10). Having taken on his own life, he proceeds to name himself. This fictional representation of naming hints at actual acts of naming by animals: "some animals may have 'unnamed names' for other animal individuals as well as for familiar humans" (Noske 1989, 150). In contrast, advice to family farmers cautions against naming: "If you're going to eat it [sic], don't give it [sic] a pet name. Try something like 'Porky' or 'Chops' or 'Spareribs' if the urge to name is too strong" (Kellogg 1985, 13). Granting a name has disastrous results, as the authors of *Chickens in Your Backyard* caution:

> The first rule to remember if you plan on raising chickens for meat is never to name a bird you intend to eat! Either you won't be able to "do it" when the time comes, or that beautiful roast chicken will sit on the table while you and the kids sit around with tears in your eyes. If you must name your future meal, call it [sic] Colonel Sanders or Cacciatore. (Luttmann 1976, 101)

This is the prevailing table talk.

Unlike family farmers, most people who consume animals do not need to confront their urge to name because of the material conditions that produce animals as meat. Just as theology demonstrates that the upper class do not go where they can listen to the poor, so most human beings do not go where they can hear the animals before slaughter. While Upton Sinclair reported the pigs' pre-slaughter cries as "so very human in their protests" (Sinclair 1906, 1973, 40) they actually possess their own unique way of protesting: "there are seven distinct sounds of a pig in the successive stages of its [sic] slaughter" (Giehl 1979, 128). In either case, by holding to some linguistic standard for communication we forget that "the most eloquent signs of pain, human *or* animal, are non-linguistic" (Rollin 1981, 32). Moreover, because we have separated animals who suffer from our daily lives, we simply do not hear them. In this we recapitulate the traditional oppressed-oppressor model of separating those who suffer from the beneficiaries of their suffering.

HEARING NEW THEOLOGICAL SUBJECTS

It may be that as oppressors we are unequipped to hear the animals. While we privilege hearing, human capacity to hear, compared to many species of animals, is inferior. "Animals such as wolves, dogs, whales, dolphins, and elephants (to name just a few) are all capable of vocalizing above or below the range of human registry. . . . Our brain can handle about one-tenth of the acoustic information a dolphin's brain can" (Noske 1989, 134-35).

Compounding the physiological limits of human hearing, of course, is the supposition that there is nothing to hear from the voiceless. But just as the women's liberation movement of the 1970s demonstrated the phenomenon of hearing to speech of those seen as inarticulate and voiceless (Morton 1985), so must theology participate in the resubjectifying of animals by acknowledging their own speech acts.

An example from the nineteenth-century women's movement offers insight on this:

When Pundita Ramabia was in this country she saw a hen carried to market with its head downward. This Christian method of treating a poor, dumb creature caused the heathen woman to cry out, "Oh, how cruel to carry a hen with its head down!" and she quickly received the reply, "Why, the hen does not mind it"; and in her heathen innocence she inquired, "Did you ask the hen?" (Anthony and Harper 1902, 1969, 245)

In her answer, Pundita Ramabia allows the hen to take on her own life. This response could only be read by the white women reporting it as "heathen innocence," rather than as subjugated knowledge. In asking the hen, or any other animals, we must accept their voices on their terms, for this is the only true way of recognizing new theological subjects. As Barbara Noske elaborates, "the basic question should not be whether animals have or have not humanlike language. In having to pass *our* tests as measured by *our* yardsticks, they will come second best, namely, as reduced humans. The real question to be posed is how the animals themselves experience the world and how they organize this experience and communicate about it" (Noske 1989, 143-44).

DANGEROUS MEMORY

This brings us to the question: How do animals experience our table talk? What, specifically, is the meaning for animals of communion language that refers to the blood of the lamb? Does the application of sacrificial language to the Christian meal and to the death of Jesus bring an end to sacrifice and suffering, not only for humans, but also for nonhuman animals? Or do these metaphors serve to justify structures of dominance, aggression, and violence? We believe that the focus on eucharist as memorializing suffering and the paradigm of the lamb, rather than disrupting suffering, acts to sanctify literal lamb eating.

When we confront our own complicity in the oppression of animals we must come to terms with their suffering. Rebecca S. Chopp says that the suffering of the modern period is so massive, so public, and so preventable, that it cannot be "fully expressed in theory or fully represented in symbol." This modern suffering therefore has what Chopp calls a "nonidentity character." It is too disruptive to be forgotten and too enormous to be located in a concept of history which is progressive and hopeful (Chopp 1986, 2). It is the "dangerous memory" of this massive suffering which disrupts traditional middle-class belief in progressive history and generates questions about God, about human identity, and about the meaning of Jesus Christ.

Chopp, as well as other theologians, refers to *human* suffering, of course: "There is no way to correct or make right the suffering of even one innocent victim, no theory to explain how one human created by God is destroyed by another human" (119). What epitomizes the nonidentity character of suffering to us, however, is most blatantly revealed in the unidentified suffering of the other, unnamed, animals. While sociologists tend to reduce animal rights theory to this concern over suffering and thus render it an emotional response to animals, we believe that theology demonstrates that attention to such suffering is precisely what makes us ethically responsible. Only oppressors can deny the importance of suffering to the individuals who suffer or who respond to that suffering. The dangerous memory of this massive suffering of subjugated animals disrupts belief in human moral superiority over the other animals.

Perhaps the focus has remained traditionally on human suffering because of the reliance on the central symbol of the cross, or to be more precise, the representative suffering of the human man Jesus on the cross and his subsequent resurrection from the dead. The question must be asked for the purposes of this essay, however, whether Jesus' sufferings as a human being are capable of representing the suffering of nonhuman animals. Is the "dangerous memory" of the suffering of innocent nonhuman animals also grounded in a promise of future freedom? Do the dead animals whose bodies human beings have consumed, used for clothing, or used in biomedical or cosmetics testing have an unrealized meaning which is somehow related to the meaning of the death and resurrection of Jesus? In pursuit of these questions we must consider the Christian eucharistic ritual, in which Jesus' suffering, death, and resurrection are memorialized and symbolized in word, action, and material objects. Although the memorial portion of the eucharistic liturgy at times in the church's history has "remembered" such diverse aspects of Jesus' life as his incarnation, his ministry, his resurrection, his sending of the Holy Spirit, his ascension, and even, proleptically, his expected return, from the Middle Ages until the present day the heaviest emphasis has been on eucharist as a memorial of his passion.

EUCHARIST AS MEMORY OF SUFFERING

Jesus' words "Do this in memory of me" form the foundation for the Christian claim that the eucharistic meal, or Lord's Supper, is (among other things) a meal which is intended to bring Jesus to memory. In particular, it is the suffering and death of Jesus which is to be remembered in this ritual meal, since its origins are associated with the beginning of his passion: "on the night when he was betrayed, Jesus took bread ... " (1 Cor. 11:23).

A central symbol for the innocent suffering of Jesus has been the Passover lamb, with whom Jesus becomes identified very early in Christian thought.[5] In the gospel of John, the death of Jesus occurs at the same time as the sacrifice of the Passover lambs in the Temple in Jerusalem. Paul writes to the church at Corinth, "For Christ, our passover lamb, has been sacrificed. Let us, therefore, celebrate the festival" (1 Cor. 5:7-8). The visionary John, in his Book of Revelation, records seeing "a Lamb, standing, as though it had been slain," before whom the heavenly assembly fell on their faces and worshiped, a figure which has been interpreted as the slain and resurrected Christ. And the author of the Book of Hebrews describes Jesus as the eternal high priest who offers up not the blood of slain animals, but his own blood:

But when Christ appeared as a high priest of the good things that have come, then through the greater and more perfect tent (not made with hands, that is, not of this creation) he entered once for all into the Holy Place, taking not the blood of goats and calves but his own blood, thus securing an eternal redemption. (Hebrews 9:11–12)

Thus for the author of Hebrews explicitly, and for the other users of the symbol implicitly, the suffering and death of Jesus, interpreted as sacrifice, is seen as bringing an end to animal sacrifices. Jesus, particularly in his suffering and death, is understood to represent the suffering and dying animal *victim*, a technical term originally applied to animals to be sacrificed, also applied to Jesus. A sign of this cessation of all animal sacrifices is reflected in the fact that the foods used for the Christian eucharistic meal are vegetarian foods: bread and wine. The problem in this interpretation is to assume that animals are not being sacrificed in other, more quotidian, ways by our own unexamined actions.

The tradition of animal sacrifice continues to exercise its influence on the symbolic language which came to be applied to the eucharistic meal and its nonanimal food elements. As the identification of the bread and wine with the presence of Christ becomes more and more the focus of theological reflection, the language becomes increasingly reminiscent of the eating of meat. At the scholastic level, medieval theologians were able to speak of the bread becoming the real flesh of Christ and the wine his blood, a change which was brought about by the so-called "Words of Institution": "this is my body," "this is my blood." At the devotional level, tales of bleeding hosts (eucharistic bread; Latin *hostia* means "an animal slain in sacrifice") were popular and widespread. Thus earlier notions that Jesus' death brought an end to sacrifice were replaced by the notion that the Mass was a repetition (in some sense) of Jesus' sacrifice, which moreover was understood as a kind of animal sacrifice.

The commemoration of Jesus' death as voluntary sacrifice has already been problematized by some feminist theologians who recognize the connection between valuing sacrifice and seeing suffering as redemptive, on the one hand, and justification of violence against women, on the other (see Brown and Parker 1989). Feminist efforts to reconceive Christian eucharistic prayers often include a rejection of traditional symbols of bread as body and wine as blood, reclaiming bread as bread and replacing wine with water.[6] Such efforts recognize the acceptance of violence inherent in traditional interpretations of Jesus' death.

Was Jesus' death a sacrifice or a murder? Is the destruction of animals for food, clothing, or experimentation sacrifice or murder? The violent death of a living being is interpreted and named based on the perceived function or value of the victim. The killing of a king is regicide; the killing of a president or a public figure is assassination; where Jesus is understood to be God, his death is deicide. For someone to be designated a "sacrifice," she or he must be understood to be an "appropriate victim." Jesus' sacrificial function is based on the interpretation of him as "innocent," as the "spotless lamb." But innocence, in the case of ritual sacrifice, is often determined by objectifying the victim. Godfrey Ashby (1988, 8) objectifies the victim even by rejecting the use of the term *victim*:

It is perhaps best to avoid the technical term "victim," since this has acquired emotive overtones which are usually absent from sacrifices. . . .

It is essential to appreciate that, even in human sacrifice, the death of the living creature is not seen as a tragedy, any more than the death of a sheep is today seen as a tragedy before roast mutton.

Thus the lamb, goat, or human person must be objectified as "victim," which means that they are reduced to their function: "roast mutton" or "sacrifice." The "death is incidental," as Ashby argues, serving merely as a means to an end, "the gate through which relationship flows in both directions [between God and humans]" (24). Although Ashby admits that normally there is a relationship between the offerer and the sacrifice offered, he rejects any notion of kinship between the two as "too strong a term" (10). In any case, it is clear that the primary relationship is between the offerer and the deity (or ancestor); the victim is merely a means.

Whether the "appropriate victim" is a battered woman, an abused child, a political prisoner, or a nonhuman animal destroyed for food or some other purpose, in each case a process of objectification is necessary to protect those who offer the sacrifice from the necessity of feeling guilt. As the lamb becomes appropriated into metaphor for Jesus' sacrifice, the reality of the suffering of individual lambs who are slaughtered for food is forgotten. Thus lambs are rendered appropriate victims at the same time that their victimization disappears. Evidence of this is that the name for a lamb who is alive is the same as the name of that which is served on a platter: as *The Meat Book* informs us, "lamb is the meat of the sheep under one year of age" (Evans and Greene, 113). Lamb, thus, is not defined as an animal taking on his or her own life. Calling lambs alive or dead the same name, like calling the destruction of animals "sacrifice" (or "meat"), creates a "facade of innocence" which obscures the sinful reality of human domination and exploitation.

Another problem with comparing Jesus' suffering and death to animal sacrifice is that Jesus' death is traditionally and liturgically interpreted as voluntary. Although Brown and Parker have challenged this interpretation, focusing on the story of Jesus' struggle in the Garden of Gethsemane, other theologians have argued that suffering and self-giving are often characteristic of the lives of oppressed people, particularly women of color who make difficult choices for themselves in order to benefit their children or their people as a whole (see Grant 1989, Cannon 1988). However, the opportunity to make a moral choice to sacrifice oneself to others is not offered to nonhuman animals who come to our tables in the form of meat, or whom we use for clothing or for research. This reality demonstrates the risk of the application of sacrificial language for those who are granted no moral agency.

The creation of community through a symbolic act that engenders memory of another act, refers to, and yet seems to continually deny, our assumptions about lambs. Communion presupposes not only a biblical consciousness about history but an ongoing relationship with lambs, in which their normative experience is rendered meaningless except as we determine it. The lamb in Christian communion becomes doubly removed, first by being slaughtered and then by being resymbolized as a human male. When Christians use lamb language, they are not talking about lambs, they are not thinking about lambs, they are thinking about Jesus. "Washed in the blood of the lamb" does not literally means lamb's blood, nor is it literally referring to a form of meat. Communion relies on taking vegetarian food and re-imaging it. Meat eating involves the "animalizing" of vegetable food: Animals take this food and transform it into their bodies, which are then eaten. But in communion, not only is the vegetable food animalized, it is masculinized through the imagery that this is the body and blood of Jesus.

Lack of consciousness about eating animals makes this imagery meaningful rather than disturbing. Christians are often disturbed by cannibalism in eucharist symbolism but not by meat-eating symbolism. Indeed, Christians' own meat eating is unproblematic, theologically speaking. Yet, any perusal of animal slaughtering texts provides the literal depiction of the fate of animals upon which eucharistic symbolism builds. In eating the eucharist, Christians believe they are taking on Jesus' life; in eating lambs, we are taking their lives:

A sharp blow on top of the poll will stun sheep that do not have horns. The use of the captive bolt with the mushroom head is recommended.

Place the stunned sheep on a table, on a sheep and veal rack, or on a platform. Grasp the jaw with the left hand, insert the knife behind the jaw, blade-edge outward, and draw the knife out through the pelt. Do not allow the sheep to kick about and get bloody; that is the reason for keeping it [*sic*] off the floor with the head over the edge of the rack or table. (Zielger 1962, 1966, 100)

When communion provides the metaphor of a suffering lamb for Jesus' suffering, what transpires is precisely the normalizing of lamb eating. As one meat textbook informs us, "There is less religious prejudice against lamb and mutton than any other meat except fish" (Ziegler 1962, 1966, 110).

ACTS OF RESISTANCE AND SOLIDARITY

What then do we do in the presence of "meat"? Consider the story of Louis, a butcher, whose father and grandfather were butchers before him: "Louis was not a happy man. He hated meat. From the time he was a little boy he was always surrounded by meat. . . . Louis did anything to get away from the meat. He got a job afternoons, cleaning fish tanks" (Yorinks 1980, n.p.). But soon his idyll ended, and he was put to work in his father's store. After his parents died, Louis took over the butcher shop. He preferred sketching fish to chopping meat.

At night Louis had trouble sleeping. One night in May, he had bad dreams. He dreamt he was walking down the street and he was attacked. Hamburgers were punching him. Salamis kicked him. Lamb chops, roast beefs, and briskets all ganged up on him. He yelled for help, but no one came.

That morning Louis woke up feeling cold and wet. He was a fish.

This children's story is instructive in a number of ways. It could be argued that Louis's transformation enacts the recognition that we humans are animals, too. Louis demonstrates a certain fantastical solidarity with his animal victims. Moreover, he recognizes that animals do not like being objects and rebel against the loss of life. Finally, this story illuminates Rosemary Ruether's observation that environmental exploitation is not unmediated, an observation that we discussed as we identified the intersection between theology and ecofeminism. The exploitation of animals is mediated through butchers and experimenters, through people such as Louis, who may not like their assigned roles.

Not eating animals is an act of resistance that arises once a sense of solidarity with other animals is experienced. Again, a fictional depiction of a person who becomes an animal, in this case a dog, offers a vision of such solidarity:

> She decides she will not eat any sort of meat ever again. . . . She makes a silent vow to be a vegetarian from now on even if she has to starve to do it. Better that than even the remote possibility of eating one's friends and fellow sufferers. . . . Pooch wonders, does not some atavistic need exist in all of us to save the world, exactly to the degree that we would save ourselves, for aren't we "the world" as much as any other piece in it? Perhaps the more animal we are . . . that is, Pooch thinks, that I should keep my basic nature even while becoming (or, rather, hoping to become) an intellectual . . . if I could retain strong links to my animal past. Never forget what I am and where I come from. . . . (Emshwiller 1990, 16, 63)

It may be that the most comfortable way to deflect attention from the need for our resistance to the oppression of animals and solidarity with animals is imagining that animals can save themselves. It may be, though, that such representations as found in *Animal Farm, The Birds, Mrs. Nimby and the Rats of NIMH, Charlotte's Web,* and other fictions only appease the guilt we have for failing to resist. After all, most animals cannot fight collectively against human oppressors, and the lack of struggle cannot be taken as absence of resistance or acceptance of domination. Collective action on the part of the other animals for their own liberation will not occur in the absence of people's stopping their own acts of oppression. Animals cannot take on their own lives until humans stop taking their lives.

But we are not entirely pessimistic about this. Recall the reference to those family farmers for whom "the urge to name is too strong." The fear expressed by the authors of the text on growing animals for slaughter was that such naming would bring about feelings of connection, of some sort of solidarity with the animals, and thus prevent the inevitable, the taking of the animal's life for food. This appreciation of the strength of the urge to know a name when in relationship with others, including animals, is the beginning of acknowledging new theological subjects, of creating a new table talk. It must be followed, though, by the recognition that human names are inadequate for these new subjects. If Freire is correct in saying "To exist, humanly, is to *name* the world, to change it" (Freire 1972, 1978, 61), then to exist as humans in relationship with animals we must allow them their unnamed names. In Ursula LeGuin's short story "She Unnames Them," Eve unnames herself and the animals, and discovers solidarity: "They seemed far closer than when their names had stood between myself and them like a clear barrier" (LeGuin 1987, 235). On the model of unnaming, releasing animals from oppression requires withdrawing our control, repudiating those expectations that we can eat, wear, experiment upon, or constrain animals to provide entertainment for us at circuses or zoos. Only then can they productively take on their own lives.

NOTES

Thanks to Millicent Feske, Mary E. Hunt, and Jay McDaniel for reading and responding to earlier versions of this essay. Thanks also to Karen Davis of United Poultry Concerns (P.O. Box 59367, Potomac, MD 20859), who called our attention to *Chickens in Your Backyard* and provided information on women in the poultry industry.

1. See Birch et al. (1990) for a volume that pursues similar questions in a different way. See Singer (1990), Regan (1983), Linzey (1987), and Adams (1990, 1991a and b) for texts that examine the use of the other animals by human beings.

2. This example is based on an explanation offered by Nancy Tuana.

3. John Cobb (1985) also notes that interest in the nonhuman world risks benefitting the middle class at the expense of the poor, but he argues that a closer examination of environmental issues reveals that these interests are not really in basic conflict. This point is explored in various ways as well in Birch et al. (1990).

4. "American Dream," winner of the 1991 Best Documentary Oscar about a strike at a Hormel meat-packing plant, showed that "juxtaposition of images of workers chopping up hogs with the tense union-management negotiations produces an apt metaphor for Hormel's attitude toward its employees" (Kronke).

5. Jewish vegetarians are creating alternate ways of commemorating Passover. See, for instance, Kalechofsky 1988.

6. Unpublished eucharistic prayers written by Cheryl Jordan and Sue Ann Hill.

20

Ecofeminist Education

Adolescence, Activism, and Spirituality

ZOE WEIL

I have been an animal rights and environmental educator for seven years, focusing most of my attention on adolescents. This essay grows out of my experience working with teenagers whose particular needs, issues, and concerns pose interesting challenges and call for an expanded approach to education. As an advocate and educator, my goal is dual: to help animals and nature by encouraging appreciation for them and concern about their exploitation, and to help my students by fostering values consonant with a healthy, meaningful, just, thoughtful, and compassionate life-style. My methods toward this goal are varied, reflecting my conviction that heart, mind, and spirit all need to be involved in the process of learning, growing, and developing a value system by which to live.

I use what I feel is an ecofeminist pedagogy—a perspective which challenges the domination and hierarchical systems of oppression that underlie the patriarchal structures and philosophies of the dominant culture, and a methodology which attempts to untangle and disarm patriarchal indoctrination as it relates to various aspects of our life-styles, beliefs, ideas, and behaviors. In addition, my experience as a divinity school student has led me to realize that an expanded approach to education, which makes room for spiritual, emotional,

Zoe Weil directs ANIMALEARN, the educational division of the American Anti-Vivisection Society. She is the author of *Animals in Society: Facts and Perspectives on Our Treatment of Animals*, a text for secondary school students. She has a master of theological studies from Harvard Divinity School and a master of arts in English Literature from the University of Pennsylvania.

and moral, as well as intellectual development, is imperative. Challenging pervasive systems of oppression in our culture (be they oppressive to women, minorities, animals, or nature) requires that we excavate not only our culture but also ourselves—our beliefs, values, and assumptions. Adolescents are at a stage where they are often eager to question and understand themselves and their world. The growth that takes place when they look within as well as without is intellectual, emotional, and spiritual. When I teach, I try to provide room for this developmental gestalt. My courses are designed to provide information, to encourage activism, to practice articulating new positions and views, to challenge cultural and personal belief systems, and to nourish spiritual and emotional development as it relates to animals, the earth, and society in general.

I encourage these many "ways of knowing" (see Belenky et al. 1986) because I ascribe to the feminist belief that emotions, intuitions, rational thinking, and spiritual insight are all important sources of knowledge and should all be respected and honored for their validity, power, and truthfulness. As a feminist, I reject the patriarchal view that rational thought is the *only* basis for knowledge and morality, and I advocate a pedagogy which acknowledges and supports the education of the whole person.

A dozen teenagers plan a protest in front of Jim's Steaks restaurant for the Great American Meatout. Several have to obtain permission to leave school for the event. A group of high school girls takes two trains, spends ten dollars per person and over an hour in traveling time, to stand in front of the Philadelphia Spectrum protesting the circus. Another group of adolescents hands out leaflets at their school cafeteria to inform their peers about the suffering endured by the animals served up as lunch. Some refuse to dissect animals in biology class despite threats of failing grades from teachers and administrators. After their school day, a number of them then go home to encounter derision, hostility, and accusations about their convictions. A few are told by their parents that if they do not eat the animals on their plate, they cannot participate in their school's animal rights group or go to animal rights classes.

These activities can be contrasted with the experience of a young boy depicted in the CBS documentary on hunting, *The Guns of Autumn*. In the film, a group of hunters is interviewed around their campfire. One of the members of the group is a twelve-year-old boy, whose father answers the question "Do you expect [your son] to be a hunter?" with "I'd just be very unhappy if he won't be." A fellow hunter adds that he enjoys seeing his sons kill. This dialogue occurs in front of the boy, who is then asked whether he likes to hunt. Whatever feeling for animals this twelve-year-old may have experienced has to be suppressed in order to please his father and fulfill his expectations.

The vast majority of young animal activists (like animal advocates in general) are female, which raises several questions: Do girls relate to animals because, like women in our society, animals are oppressed and victimized within patriarchal structures?[1] Is compassion for animals a natural human emotion that is repressed by boys in their effort to be perceived as masculine?[2] Would boys respond in equal numbers to the exploitation and suffering of animals if they were not encouraged, or forced, to suppress their nurturing, compassionate, and humanitarian inclinations? Even in communities where hunting is prevalent, girls are rarely taught or expected to kill for sport, and they are less frequently castigated for displaying emotion when animals are killed, injured, sick, abused, or exploited. In our society, boys and men are often taught to kill, while girls and women are raised to nurture and care for others, including the orphaned sparrow or fawn, the injured cat, or the ill dog. At the same time, characteristics of care-giving are not respected in our culture, so the nurturing and compassionate feelings and humanitarian opinions of girls are not usually taken seriously. When young women take political action on behalf of animals, they and their cause are often denied credibility and attention. When boys express humanitarian concerns, however, their opinions are accorded more weight. Because our society so often denies girls respect and support, they may feel less empowered than boys to effect change. So while boys may be less involved in the animal movement because they have repressed their caring impulses, when they do become active, they hold leadership positions in significant disproportion to their numbers. The Philadelphia area group, SPARE (Students Protecting Animals' Rights and the Environment), is a case in point. The group is comprised almost entirely of concerned and caring young women, but is led by an extremely motivated, hardworking, determined, well-respected young man.

How can an ecofeminist pedagogy resist and counteract the effects of gender to help empower young women and involve more fully young men? In order to combat the societal forces surrounding gender roles, as well as to actively involve young people in social change, I encourage students to explore their own relationship with and feelings toward animals and nature, as well as to take responsibility for their behavior and for social change in general. For the girls the new element in this approach is often action and responsibility; for the boys it is often connection with nature and the relinquishing of domination, which they are especially heir to.

Each of my classes includes a lecture which introduces the topic at hand (animal liberation philosophy, hunting and trapping, animal agribusiness, vivisection, and so forth). The lectures present facts that challenge many of the prevailing myths of our culture, such as "hunting is necessary to prevent animals from starving to death" or "vivisectors care about the animals they use" or "Frank Perdue's chickens live in 'chicken heaven.' "[3] I also show videos that depict actual animal abuse in these various industries.[4] After warning students that the footage is graphic, I invite them to leave the room or close their eyes if they wish. The footage, though disturbing, often elicits compassion as the students hear the animals' cries and see, perhaps for the first time, the detachment the exploiter demonstrates when he or she beats, shocks, laughs at, or kills the animals under his or her power and control. Following the video, the students discuss their impressions, feelings, and opinions, and we then do role plays to practice voicing our perspectives and responding to different positions. Each class ends with some form of activism, either writing letters to legislators, to CEOs of corporations, or planning community demonstrations or actions in school.

I have constructed the above format for classes because I believe that the students ought to be engaged on several levels. It is important that they have well-documented fact sheets and articles so that they can be fully informed and then convince others of the veracity of their statements. They participate in role plays in order to learn to speak articulately, to respond to hostility and derision, and to stand up for themselves and their opinions. The classes also provide room for personal reflections on animals and encourage the students' emotional relationship with and empathy for animals. The activism at the end of class is meant to empower them and to drive home the idea that they can *do* something to prevent the exploitation of animals. While adolescents are not accorded the rights of adults and are subjected to the rules, regulations, and social directives dictated by parents, teachers, and various institutions, they can be quite vocal as consumers. Millions of products are marketed directly toward them, and they actually hold significant power to affect corporate and government policies by exercising their political and economic voice.

When asked why they are coming after school every week to learn about animal issues, most of my students say that it is because they love animals. Among animal advocates, passion for animals is often the motivating force that leads to action. While one might admire the person who challenges her own speciesism[5] from an intellectual or theoretical standpoint, there is no doubt that many, if not most, animal advocates come to our convictions and change their speciesist behaviors because of an emotional connection to or appreciation for animals. Here, too, however, gender differences are apparent. Boys may indeed become committed to animal liberation, but often not because they love animals; rather, they may express concern about "justice" and "doing what is right." Only later might they demonstrate more overt *feelings* toward animals.

There need not be a dichotomy between justice and compassion, or theory and feeling. The animal advocate's belief that "it is not right to exploit animals or cause them to suffer" may stem from empathy with suffering, intellectual awareness that exploitation is unjust and immoral, or both. When ascribing merit to motivations, however, the theoretical perspective (more often advocated by the boys) is usually viewed with more validity and seriousness than the emotional perspective (more often advocated by the girls). Despite Carol Gilligan's exposé of the false hierarchies regarding gender and moral development (Gilligan 1982), the view that emotional motivation is inferior to intellectual or theoretical motivation persists. Thus, the girls, who readily sympathize with the animal movement's goals and beliefs, are often discredited *because* of that sympathy.

Although love or deep affinity may be most people's initial motivation for protecting animals or nature from destruction, it is true that these feelings are an unreliable foundation for moral theory or justice. Feelings for animals and the environment may incite us to action, but they are an arbitrary basis for granting protection or equal consideration. For example, it is common for people to believe that dogs and parrots should have certain rights (a right to a home, to food, to water; a right of protection from abuse or cruelty, and so forth), yet be unwilling to extend these basic rights to pigs or chickens, *simply because they like dogs and parrots whereas they do not like pigs and chickens.* Nevertheless, love of a dog may inspire someone to realize dogs' profound plight in our society.[6] This insight may then lead to compassion which extends to cats or to rabbits or to wildlife. As this person is challenged by the animal liberation movement, she may soon come to realize that a prejudice underlies her relationship with animals, and may further extend her circle of compassion to include animals she does not necessarily like, such as those whom people eat, wear, or vivisect. In other words, empathy may be informed and expanded through intellectual development.

Since many young people come to the animal liberation movement because of their emotional connection to animals or to nature, this passion must be continually nurtured and tapped for its potential power to effect change. At the same time, these adolescents are still in the early stages of building the elaborate defense mechanisms necessary to survive emotionally in a world with such violence and suffering. They are therefore susceptible to the whole range of often-damaging emotions as they are exposed to the horrifying facts about animal exploitation, the staggering suffering and death toll of billions of animals every year, and the destruction of the natural world on which all species depend. As these teenagers become informed about animal exploitation, feelings of despair, impotence, and inertia are common, as are rage and hatred. Rage may have its place as a motivator for action, yet one treads a precarious ground if one's source of inspiration is more a reflection of hatred and anger than love.

These young animal activists face a daunting task. They are challenging pervasive systems of oppression and victimization but are disempowered by their society, which does not yet recognize them as adults. They cannot vote, nor can they necessarily make many significant personal choices (often including what they will eat). They are also at an age where conformity is most compelling, so those who fight for animals while their peers are scoffing face difficulties not shared by their adult counterparts. Adolescence may be a rebellious stage in life, but usually adolescents rebel *with* their peers against the conventions of their parents or dominant culture. Many students who become politically active in animal rights, however, do not have the support of their friends and are alone in their convictions, facing ridicule rather than peer acceptance and popularity. Their love of and respect for animals leads them to confront the reality of extreme animal cruelty and suffering that most others neither concern themselves with nor even acknowledge. As the animal liberation movement grows, these teenagers are beginning to find communities of like-minded individuals, but for many, especially those in rural, farming, or sport-hunting areas, the struggle is profoundly lonely. The internal battle between despair and hope, between helplessness and righteous anger and action, rages furiously in these young people.

Amidst the emotional turmoil of adolescence, during which teenagers are defining their identities and challenging the traditions and belief systems in which they have been raised, spiritual forces may come into play to combat both despair and hatred. For some young people, established faiths may provide a grounding or perspective that is valuable; for others, spirituality may be less defined or institutionalized, but equally compelling. Their commitment to social change may be informed and sustained by many forces, many feelings, many beliefs, and many ideas. Nurturing growth of the spirit and calling upon powers other than those that stem from fluctuating emotions, trends, or beliefs—be they divine powers, those that infuse nature, or powers that derive from the wise part of oneself—are usually worthwhile and meaningful for those who care to change themselves and the world. When spiritual beliefs and feelings underlie and sustain young animal advocates, the boundaries between action and passion, between faith and works, become fluid, one informing and inspiring the other; one providing the nourishment for the other's deeds.

Because I believe that nourishing the spirit is as important as nourishing the mind and heart, I try to incorporate and invite spirituality into the process of education and personal growth.[7] During the last session of my animal issues course, I hold a Council of All Beings.[8] The council is an experiential workshop designed to deepen connections with the natural world and the animals who share it with us. The students, who have up to that point learned a great deal about the pain and suffering animals endure and the frightening destruction of our environment, have an opportunity to explore their understanding and appreciation from a different vantage.

The council begins with an invocation and meditation, during which I ask the students to allow an image of an animal, landscape, plant, or other aspect of nature to enter their consciousness, to visit them in their imaginations. They are instructed not to choose this Being, but rather to let the Being choose them. In this way, they invite the wise and compassionate parts of themselves (which may be more unconscious than conscious) to be heard. During the meditation, I ask the students to enter the Being, to become it. I offer suggestions for questions they might ask themselves as this Being: How do I feel? What is the world like for me? How do I know things? What is happening to me? What are my experiences of the world? What are humans doing to me? What do I want humans to do or not do? Finally, I ask them what gift, talent, or quality they bring to the world that they could offer to humans to help ease their own suffering, human suffering, and the world's suffering.

After leading them back to an awareness of the present, we silently make masks to represent ourselves. Sitting in a circle, masks in front of our faces, we share our experiences. Cow may speak of her misery when her calf is wrenched from her teat at one-day-old to be sold for veal production, while Tree may speak about her body dying from the acid in rain. Each Being is able to tell humans what she wishes, and ultimately, each offers humans her particular wisdom. Hawk may offer the wisdom of perspective and clear vision, and Mountain may give the gift of patience. We listen to every Being with attention. Several are moved to tears. Some who have been reticent in class suddenly speak eloquently when the mask is before their face—no small feat for a shy adolescent.

At the end of the council, I ask that each of us make a promise to change one of our behaviors to help the Being for whom we have spoken. I stress that the promise be small, because it will be a sacred promise not to be broken for lack of will or forgetfulness. The promise may be as simple as not littering, recycling cans and bottles, or eliminating veal from one's diet. There is always time for more councils and more promises, as long as each council and each promise is viewed with respect and seriousness.[9]

The promises are meant to link spiritual experiences with purposeful action and responsibility. The students expect to make such promises and do not seem to find them out of place in the spiritual setting of the council. Action and behavior changes make sense to them because the course has always encouraged personal responsibility for global change. Promises to help are sustaining, feeding their own self-esteem and empowering them as they are protecting others. They reflect not only respect for the earth and animals, but for themselves.

The council has the ability to empower and to touch, to remind and to make wise. The young people who care to learn about what is happening to our earth often need their anger tempered by their love, their rage tempered by their wisdom. Calling upon the earth and the animals to offer that wisdom (through the council format) often helps. Those they would protect—the animal or part of nature for whom they spoke—provide, in a spiritual sense, power and guidance. The passion for animals is nurtured with both knowledge and connection.

Most of these council participants are girls, but I have also held councils with groups comprised predominantly of adolescent boys. At the end of one course that I gave to an environmental club (about half male), I was concerned that the seventeen-year-old boys who had been very critical and "tough" during the classes would find the council too weird and "touchy-feely." Quite to the contrary, the boys were very moved and moving, and they spoke poetically and with deep feeling. When the council was over and I thanked the participants, one young man told me that he might sound corny, but he thought that when he looked back on high school, this would stand out as an especially meaningful, memorable, and significant experience. For many boys, the council provides room for spiritual and emotional growth and exploration, which is often denied to them in our culture. Since boys' feelings of love for and connection to animals and nature are continually challenged by a society that encourages them to be oppressors and constantly exposes them to the propaganda of our culture (which teaches that deer are meant to be targets, cows are meant to be eaten by real men, and nature is meant to be exploited), the council may reawaken emotions long since suppressed. For many girls, the council gives voice. In a literal sense the girls become spokespeople for animals and nature. Feeling a connection to animals may not be new, but speaking up for themselves (as an animal or part of nature) may be quite new, and quite empowering.

I have met many an adult animal activist who derides councils and other similar spiritual activities because they know people who sing of the earth and hug trees but eat animals and wear furs. In their view, such spiritual endeavors are shallow, self-serving experiences, unconnected to the real work of saving the earth and the animals. For those who reject such experiences, I can only offer my observation that the council not only enriches the participants, but often empowers and motivates them to act, as well. Since adolescents often respond very negatively to hypocrisy, there is even less room for them to profess beliefs to which they do not adhere. In addition, their life-style choices are in flux, and personal changes are not only easier for them than for adults, but are also integral to their development.

In contrast, I have also met many aggressive and embittered animal activists (adult and teen) who hurl insults upon the unsuspecting fur coat wearer or veal eater. Their anger and hatred help neither the animals nor the animal exploiters, who will not change in the face of such nasty and inhumane interactions. Perhaps a taste of tree hugging, earth singing, or speaking in councils would be worthwhile for these activists, whose spiritual development might enhance the efficacy of their activism.

Inspiring saintliness is not a realizable goal, but encouraging successful and sustaining lives for my students is. Success cannot be measured simply by how many companies stop testing their products on animals or how many activists show up for a protest. It must also be measured by how many people begin to challenge their own prejudices, expand their compassion, change their behaviors, sustain their commitment and dedication, and transform the underlying systems of oppression that govern our society and victimize those without voice.

The spiritual connection to nature and animals that I try to offer my students often helps to sustain lives and to blend patience with vigorous action. Those whose spiritual relationship with the earth is integral to their being often have good medicine for burnout, hatred, and feelings of impotence. For adolescents, whose rage and passion may be at its peak, the need for celebrations of life and love is very real. Disconnection from family and friends, lack of faith or hope, and isolation can be extremely debilitating. Whether it is with a group of friends singing a song about saving the rain forests, alone with a howling coyote crying in the distance, or speaking in councils, the spiritual and powerful connections to the earth ought to be nurtured and encouraged, for not only do they keep the young activist centered, compassionate, committed, and open, they also pave the way for successful, mature, and wise adult activism.

NOTES

1. While I will not be examining this question here, for further information please see Carol Adams, *The Sexual Politics of Meat* (1990), Charlene Spretnak, *The Politics of Women's Spirituality* (1982), Andrée Collard, *The Rape of the Wild* (1988), and the work of Ynestra King and Marti Kheel.

2. Although some may argue that compassion is not elemental, but rather learned, I believe that compassion is innate in all humans. For a discussion of research that supports this position, see Ferrucci 1990, 81.

3. For information on hunting you can write to The Fund for Animals, 850 Sligo Ave. Suite LL2, Silver Spring, MD 20910. For information on vivisection you can contact The American Anti-Vivisection Society, 801 Old York Rd., Jenkintown, PA 19046. Information on current animal agricultural practices is available from Farm Sanctuary, P.O. Box 150, Watkins Glen, NY 14891; Humane Farming Association, 1550 California St., San Francisco, CA 94109; Farm Animal Reform Movement, P.O. Box 70123, Washington, DC 20088; Animal Rights International, P.O.

Box 214, Planetarium Station, New York, NY 10024; and United Poultry Concerns, P.O. Box 59367, Potomac, MD 20859. Pertinent books include: Singer 1990; Robbins 1987; and Mason and Singer 1990.

4. Videos are available from People for the Ethical Treatment of Animals, P.O. Box 42516, Washington, DC 20015; Farm Sanctuary (see note above); and Focus on Animals, P.O. Box 150, Trumbull, CT 06611.

5. Speciesism, a term coined by Richard Ryder and later popularized by Peter Singer, is "a prejudice or attitude of bias in favor of the interests of members of one's own species and against those of members of other species." Singer further elucidates the word's meaning by comparing it to other "isms" such as racism and sexism. "It should be obvious that the fundamental objections to racism and sexism made by Thomas Jefferson and Sojourner Truth apply equally to speciesism. If possessing a higher degree of intelligence does not entitle one human to use another for his or her own ends, how can it entitle humans to exploit nonhumans for the same purpose" (Singer 1990).

6. The buying, selling and breeding of dogs (and other animals) have resulted in a severe overpopulation problem. Millions of dogs are killed every year in pounds and shelters because there are not enough homes for them. Millions more die of starvation or disease or are hit by cars on the streets. Puppy mills abound, and dogs have been overbred so that among a variety of breeds, many suffer from deformities and health problems. Greyhounds are raced for entertainment, then killed or sold for research, while beagles and other breeds are bred for laboratory experiments. They are also used in military experiments, in law enforcement, and on battlefields during wars.

7. I wish to stress that I am not suggesting any insidious form of proselytism here. I invite exploration of the spirit without advocating any particular religion or faith. The experiences in which I invite students to participate do not advance specific beliefs about God or divinity, rather they permit the individual to relate to nature, animals, and the sacred in whatever way she or he wishes.

8. The Council of All Beings was developed in Macy et al. (1988).

9. If any readers choose to lead councils within this structure, it is important to be aware that it is difficult to make new, sincere promises regularly. I would welcome any comments or advice on the problem of being fully and honestly present, involved, and committed to examining and changing one's behavior within this context.

Bibliography

Ackelsberg, Martha. 1986. "Spirituality, Community, and Politics: B'not Esh and the Feminist Reconstruction of Judaism." *Journal of Feminist Studies in Religion* 2 (Fall).

Adams, Carol J. 1990. *The Sexual Politics of Meat: A Feminist-Vegetarian Critical Theory.* New York: Continuum.

———. 1991a. "Ecofeminism and the Eating of Animals." *Hypatia* 6(1): 125-45.

———. 1991b. "Abortion Rights and Animal Rights." *Between the Species: A Journal of Ethics* 7(4): 181-89.

Aitken, Robert. 1986. "Kanzeon." In *Not Mixing Up Buddhism: Essays on Women and Buddhist Practice.* Fredonia, N.Y.: White Pine Press.

Allen, Jeffner. 1984. "Motherhood: The Annihilation of Women." In Joyce Trebilcot, ed. *Mothering: Essays in Feminist Theory.* Totowa, N.J.: Rowman.

Allen, Paula Gunn (Laguna Pueblo/Lakota). 1986a. "Raven's Road." In Mary Bartlett, ed. *The New Native American Novel: Works in Progress.* Albuquerque: University of New Mexico Press.

———. 1986b. *The Sacred Hoop: Recovering the Feminine in American Indian Traditions.* Boston: Beacon Press.

Alpert, Rebecca T., and Arthur Waskow. 1987. "Toward an Ethical Kashrut." *The Reconstructionist* (March-April): 9-13.

Anthony, Susan B., and Ida Husted Harper. 1902, 1969. *The History of Woman Suffrage,* vol. 4, 1883-1900. Reprint. New York: Arno Press.

Ashby, Godfrey. 1988. *Sacrifice: Its Nature and Purpose.* London: SCM Press.

Atwood, Margaret. 1985. *The Handmaid's Tale.* New York: Fawcett.

Austin, Richard Cartwright. 1988. *Hope for the Land: Nature in the Bible.* Atlanta: John Knox Press.

Avery, Byllye. 1990. "A Question of Survival/A Conspiracy of Silence: Abortion and Black Women's Health." In Marlene Gerber Fried, ed. *From Abortion to Reproductive Freedom: Transforming a Movement.* Boston: South End Press.

Awiakta, Marilou. 1986. "Baring the Atom's Mother Heart." In Douglas Paschall and Alice Swanson, eds. *Homewords: A Book of Tennessee Writers.* Knoxville: Tennessee Arts Commission and the University of Tennessee Press.

Bach, Bob. 1984. "Letter to the Editor." *New York Times* (Feb. 2), A18.

Badiner, Allan Hunt, ed. 1990. *Dharma Gaia: A Harvest of Essays in Buddhism and Ecology.* Berkeley: Parallax Press.

Bagby, Rachel. 1990. "Daughters of Growing Things." In Irene Diamond and Gloria Feman Orenstein, eds. *Reweaving the World: The Emergence of Ecofeminism.* San Francisco: Sierra Club Books.

Bailey, Marian Breland. 1986. "Every Animal Is the Smartest: Intelligence and the Ecological Niche." In R. J. Hoagg and Larry Goldman, eds. *Animal Intelligence:*

Insights into the Animal Mind. Washington, D.C.: Smithsonian Institution Press.

Baker, Mark. 1982. *Nam: The Vietnam War in the Words of the Men and Women Who Fought There.* New York: Morrow and Company.

Banerjee, Nikunjavihari. 1980. *Studies in the Dharmasastra of Manu.* New Delhi: Munshiram Manoharlal Publishers.

Barbour, Ian G. 1974. *Myths, Models and Paradigms: A Comparative Study in Science and Religion.* New York: Harper and Row.

Barker, Clive. 1989. *The Great and Secret Show.* New York: Harper & Row.

Beauvoir, Simone de. 1949, 1952. *The Second Sex.* Trans. H. M. Parshley. New York: Knopf.

Beck, Peggy V., and Anna L. Walters (Pawnee/Otoe). 1977. *The Sacred Ways of Knowledge: Sources of Life.* Tsaile, Ariz.: Navajo Community College Press. Tsaile RPO, Navajo Nation, AZ 86556.

Begg, Ean. 1985. *The Cult of the Black Virgin.* Boston: Arkana.

Belenky, Mary Field, et al. 1986. *Women's Ways of Knowing: The Development of Self, Voice and Mind.* New York: Basic Books.

Benton, Ted. 1988. "Humanism-Speuesism. Marx on Humans and Animals." *Radical Philosophy* 50: 4-18.

Bernstein, Ellen. 1987. "The Trees' Birthday: A Celebration of Nature." Philadelphia: Turtle River Press. Available from FRCH, Church Road and Greenwood Ave., Wyncote, PA 19095.

Berry, Thomas. 1988. *The Dream of the Earth.* San Francisco. Sierra Club Books.

Bhattacharji, Hansanarayan. 1982 *Hinuder Dev Devi: Udvab o Kromovikash, Tritiya Parva.* Calcutta, Firma KLM Private Ltd.

Bill Haley and His Comets (Performers). 1957. "Thirteen Women . . . And Only One Man in Town" (Song). *Rock Around the Clock,* Decca DL 78225.

Birch, Charles, William Eakin, and Jay B. McDaniel. 1990. *Liberating Life: Contemporary Approaches to Ecological Theology.* Maryknoll, N.Y.: Orbis Books.

Bizot, Judithe. 1992. "Raising Our Voices: An Interview with Bella Abzug." *UNESCO Courier* 45 (March): 36-37.

Black Elk, Wallace (Lakota), and William S. Lyon. 1990. *Black Elk: The Sacred Ways of a Lakota.* New York: Harper & Row.

Blofeld, John. 1978. *Boddhisattva of Compassion: The Mystical Tradition of Kwan Yin.* Boulder, Colo.: Shambhala Books.

Blonsky, Marshall. 1989. "A Literary High-Wire Act." *New York Times Magazine* (Dec. 10).

Boucher, Sandy. 1985. *Turning the Wheel: American Women Creating the New Buddhism.* San Francisco: Harper and Row.

Boyer, Paul. 1985. *By the Bomb's Early Light: American Thought and Culture at the Dawn of the Atomic Age.* New York: Pantheon.

Brandon, William. 1974. *The Last Americans: The Indian in American Culture.* New York: McGraw Hill.

Brelis, Matthew. 1990. "Neighbors, Relatives Express Shock at Arrests of Youthful Suspects." *The Boston Globe* (Nov. 21).

Brians, Paul. 1988. *Nuclear Holocausts: Atomic War in Fiction, 1895-1984.* Kent, Ohio: Kent State University Press.

Broder, David. 1989. *Chicago Tribune* (May 31), sec. 1, 17.

Brooke-Rose, Christine. 1986. "Woman as a Semiotic Object." In Susan Rubin

Suleiman, ed. *The Female Body in Western Culture.* Cambridge, Mass.: Harvard University Press.

Brown, Joanne Carlson, and Rebecca Parker. 1989. "For God So Loved the World?" In Joanne Carlson Brown and Carole R. Bohn, eds. *Christianity, Patriarchy, and Abuse: A Feminist Critique.* New York: Pilgrim Press.

Brown, Lester R., ed. 1990. *State of the World: A Worldwatch Institute Report on Progress Toward a Sustainable Society.* New York: W. W. Norton.

Buber, Martin. 1963. *Israel and the World: Essays in a Time of Crisis.* New York: Schocken Books.

Buchanan Brothers (Performers). 1946. "Atomic Power" (Song). *Atomic Cafe,* Rounder Records 1034.

Bullard, Robert. 1990. *Dumping in Dixie: Race, Class and Environmental Quality.* Boulder, Colo.: Westview Press.

Caillois, Roger. 1959. *Man and the Sacred.* Trans. Meyer Barash. Glencoe, Ill.: The Free Press.

Caldicott, Helen. 1984. *Missile Envy: The Arms Race and Nuclear War.* New York: William Morrow.

Cannon, Katie Geneva. 1988. *Black Womanist Ethics.* Atlanta: Scholars Press.

Capra, Fritjof, and Charlene Spretnak. 1984. *Green Politics: The Global Promise.* New York: E. P. Dutton.

Caputi, Jane. 1987. *The Age of Sex Crime.* Bowling Green, Ohio: Bowling Green State University Press.

————. 1988a. "Films of the Nuclear Age." *Journal of Popular Film and Television* 16(3): 100-7.

————. 1988b. "Seeing Elephants: The Myths of Phallotechnology." *Feminist Studies* 16(3): 487-524.

————. 1990. "Interview with Paula Gunn Allen." *Trivia: A Journal of Ideas* 16/17: 50-67.

————. 1991. "Metaphors of Radiation: Or, Why a Beautiful Woman Is Like a Nuclear Power Plant." *Women's Studies International Forum.* 14, no. 5: 423-442.

Carlsen, Carol F. 1980. *The Devil in the Shape of a Woman: The Witch in 17th Century New England.* Ph.D. Diss. New Haven, Conn.: Yale University.

Carlsen, Torv, and John Magnus (Directors). 1988. *Knocking on Armageddon's Door* (Film). PBS Broadcast, July 19.

Carnes, Patrick. 1983. *Out of the Shadows: Understanding Sexual Addiction.* Minneapolis: CompCare.

Castleman, Michael. 1985. "Toxins and Male Infertility." *Sierra* (March/April): 49-52.

Chapman, Abraham, ed. 1975. *The Literature of the American Indians.* New York: A Meridian Book.

Chardin, Pierre Teilhard de. 1964. "Some Reflections on the Spiritual Repercussions of the Atom Bomb." In *The Future of Man.* Trans. N. Denny. New York: Harper and Row.

Charles, R. H. 1913. *The Pseudepigrapha of the Old Testament.* Oxford: Clarendon Press.

Cheney, Jim. 1987. "Eco-Feminism and Deep Ecology." *Environmental Ethics* 9(2) (Summer): 115-46.

Chernus, Ira. 1986. *Dr. Strangegod: On the Symbolic Meaning of Nuclear Weapons.* Columbia, S.C.: University of South Carolina Press.

Chopp, Rebecca. 1986. *The Praxis of Suffering: An Interpretation of Liberation and Political Theologies.* Maryknoll, N.Y.: Orbis Books.

Christ, Carol. 1987. *Laughter of Aphrodite: Reflections on a Journey to the Goddess.* San Francisco: Harper and Row.

———. 1990. "Rethinking Theology and Nature." In Irene Diamond and Gloria Feman Orenstein, eds. *Reweaving the World: The Emergence of Ecofeminism.* San Francisco: Sierra Club Books.

Christ, Carol, and Judith Plaskow, eds. 1979. *Womanspirit Rising: A Feminist Reader in Religion.* New York: Harper and Row.

Christian, Barbara. 1985. *Black Feminist Criticism.* New York: Pergamon Press.

Cixous, Hélène, 1980. "The Laugh of the Medusa." In Elaine Marks and Isabelle de Courtivron, eds. *New French Feminists.* New York: Schocken Books.

Clark, Stephen R. L. 1982. *The Nature of the Beast.* New York: Oxford University Press.

Clift, Elayne. 1990. "Advocate Battles for Safety in Mines and Poultry Plants." *New Directions for Women* (May/June): 3.

Clifton, Wallace B. 1984. *Jung and Christianity.* New York: Crossroad.

Cobb, John B. 1985. "Points of Contact Between Process Theology and Liberation Theology." *Process Studies* 14: 124-41.

Cocks, Jay. 1984. "Why He's a Thriller." *Time* (March 19), 54-60.

Coe, Michael D. 1980. *The Maya.* Rev. ed. New York: Thames & Hudson.

Cohn, Carol. 1987. "Sex and Death in the Rational World of Defense Intellectuals." *Signs: Journal of Women in Culture and Society* 12: 687-718.

———. 1989. "Sex and Death in the Rational World of Defense Intellectuals." In Diana E. H. Russell, ed. *Exposing Nuclear Phallacies.* New York: Pergamon Press.

Collard, Andrée with Joyce Contrucci. 1988. *The Rape of the Wild.* Bloomington: Indiana University Press.

Collins, Patricia Hill. 1990. *Black Feminist Thought: Knowledge, Consciousness, and the Politics of Empowerment.* Boston: Unwin Hyman.

Collins, Sheila D. 1974. *A Different Heaven and Earth.* Valley Forge, Penn.: Judson Press.

Committee for Abortion Rights and Against Sterilization Abuse (CARASA). 1988. *Women Under Attack: Victories, Backlash and the Fight for Reproductive Freedom.* Boston: South End Press.

Condorcet, Antoine-Nicholas de. 1794. *Sketch for a Historical Picture of the Progress of the Human Mind.*

Condren, Mary. 1989. *The Serpent and the Goddess: Women, Religion, and Power in Celtic Ireland.* San Francisco: Harper and Row.

Conrad, Paul (Artist). 1987. Cartoon. *Los Angeles Times* (Feb. 22), V5.

Cook, Francis H. 1989. "The Jewel Net of Indra." In J. Baird Callicott, and R. T. Ames, eds. *Nature in Asian Traditions of Thought.* Albany, N.Y.: State University of New York Press.

Cope-Kasten, Vance. 1989. "A Portrait of Dominating Rationality." American Philosophical Association. *Newsletter on Feminism and Philosophy.* 88(2): 29-34.

Cortez, Jayne. 1984. "Tell Me." *Coagulations: New and Selected Poems.* New York: Thunder's Mouth Press.

Courlander, Harold with Hopi Spokespeople. 1971. *The Fourth World of the Hopi.* Greenwich, Conn.: Fawcett Publications.

Crouse Group of Companies. 1976. Advertisement. *Nuclear News Buyer's Guide,* (Mid-February): 102.

Culpepper, Emily Erwin. 1986. "Ancient Gorgons: A Face for Contemporary Women's Rage." *Woman of Power: A Magazine of Feminism, Spirituality, and Politics* 3: 22-24, 40.

Dallery, Arleen B. 1989. "The Politics of Writing (the) Body." In Alison M. Jaggar and Susan R. Bordo. *Gender/Body/Knowledge: Feminist Reconstructions of Being and Knowing.* New Brunswick, N.J.: Rutgers University Press.

Daly, Mary. 1973. *Beyond God the Father: Toward a Philosophy of Women's Liberation.* Boston: Beacon Press.

———. 1978. *Gyn/Ecology: The Metaethics of Radical Feminism.* Boston: Beacon Press.

———. 1984. *Pure Lust: Elemental Feminist Philosophy.* Boston: Beacon Press.

———. 1989. "Be-Friending." In Judith Plaskow and Carol P. Christ, eds. *Weaving the Visions.* San Francisco: Harper and Row.

Daly, Mary, with Jane Caputi. 1987. *Webster's First New Intergalactic Wickedary of the English Language.* Boston: Beacon Press.

Darian, Steven G. 1978. *The Ganges in Myth and History.* Honolulu: The University Press of Hawaii.

Davies, Katherine. 1988. "What Is Ecofeminism?" *Women and Environments* 10(3): 4-6.

———. 1987. *Tree of Life: Buddhism and Protection of Nature.* Hong Kong: Buddhist Perception of Nature Project.

Davies, Shannon, ed. 1987. *Three of Life: Buddhism and Protection of Nature.* Hong Kong: Buddhist Perception of Nature Project.

Davis, Karen. Forthcoming. " 'We're Treated Like Animals': Women in the Poultry Industry." *Feminists for Animal Rights Newsletter.*

Day, Barbara, and Kimberly Knight. 1991. "The Rain Forest in Our Back Yard." *Essence* 21 (Jan.): 75-77.

de la Pena, Nonny, and Susan Davis. 1990. "The Greens Are White: And Minorities Want In." *Newsweek* 116 (Oct. 15): 34.

Deloria, Vine, Jr. 1973. *God is Red.* New York: Grosset and Dunlap.

D'Eaubonne, Francoise. 1980. "Feminism or Death." In Elaine Marks and Isabelle de Courtivron, eds. *New French Feminists: An Anthology.* Amherst, Mass.: University of Massachusetts Press.

Deutscher, Isaac. 1968. *The Non-Jewish Jew and Other Essays.* London: Oxford University Press.

Devall, Bill. 1990. "Ecocentric Sangha." In Alan Hunt-Badiner, ed. *Dharma Gaia.* Berkeley: Parallax Press.

Devall, Bill, and George Sessions. 1985. *Deep Ecology: Living as if Nature Mattered.* Salt Lake City: Peregrine Smith Books.

Diamond, Irene, and Gloria Feman Orenstein, eds. 1990. *Reweaving the World: The Emergence of Ecofeminism.* San Francisco: Sierra Club Books.

Dogan Zenji. 1985. "Mountains and Waters Sutra." In Kaz Tanahashi, ed. *Moon in a Dewdrop.* San Francisco: North Point Press.

Donovan, Josephine. 1990. "Animal Rights and Feminist Theory." *Signs: Journal of Women in Culture and Society* 15(2): 350-75.

Doubiago, Sharon. 1989. "Mama Coyote Talks to the Boys." In Judith Plant, ed.

Healing the Wounds: The Promise of Ecofeminism. Philadelphia, Pa.: New Society Publishers.

Douglas, Mary. 1979. *Purity and Danger: An Analysis of Concepts of Pollution and Taboo.* London: Routledge & Kegan Paul.

The Earth Works Group. 1989. *50 Simple Things You Can Do to Save the Earth.* Berkeley: EarthWorks Press.

Easlea, Brian. 1980. *Witchhunting, Magic and the New Philosophy.* Highlands, N.J.: Humanities Press.

———. 1981. *Science and Sexual Oppression: Patriarchy's Confrontation with Women and Nature.* London: Weidenfeld and Nicholson.

———. 1983. *Fathering the Unthinkable: Masculinity, Scientists and the Nuclear Arms Race.* London: Pluto Press.

Easterbrook, Gregg. 1990. "Everything You Know About the Environment Is Wrong." *New Republic* 30 (April): 14-27.

Ecofeminist Visions Emerging (EVE) Newsletter for a Spiritual Politic and a Political Spirituality. 1992. 17 (June).

Edge, David O. 1973. "Technological Metaphor." In David O. Edge and James N. Wolfe, eds. *Meaning and Control.* London: Tavistock.

Ehrlich, Paul R., et al. 1973. *Human Ecology: Problems and Solutions.* San Francisco: W. H. Freeman Co.

Eisenberg, Evan. 1990. "The Call of the Wild." *The New Republic.* 30 (April).

Eisenstein, Zillah, ed. 1979. *Capitalist Patriarchy and the Case for Socialist Feminism.* New York: Monthly Review Press.

Eisler, Riane Tennenhaus. 1987. *The Chalice and the Blade: Our History, Our Future.* San Francisco: Harper and Row.

———. 1990. "The Gaia Tradition and the Partnership Future: An Ecofeminist Manifesto." In Irene Diamond and Gloria Feman Orenstein, eds. *Reweaving the World: The Emergence of Ecofeminism.* San Francisco: Sierra Club Books.

Ellemont, John, and Sean P. Murphy. 1990. "Police Defend Low Profile Handling of Franklin Field Murder: Critics Say Community Should Have Been Warned." *The Boston Globe* (Nov. 21).

Ellsberg, Patricia, and Elissa Melamed. 1989. "Seeing Through the Emperor's New Clothes: Two Women Look at the Nuclear Issue." In Diana E. H. Russell, ed. *Exposing Nuclear Phallacies.* New York: Pergamon Press.

Emshwiller, Carol. 1990. *Carmen Dog.* San Francisco: Mercury House.

Ervin, Michael. 1992. "The Toxic Doughnut." *Progressive* 56 (Jan.): 15.

Evans, Travers M., and David Greene. *The Meat Book.* New York: Charles Scribner's Sons.

Falk, Marcia. 1986. Response to "Feminist Reflections on Separation and Unity in Jewish Theology." *Journal of Feminist Studies in Religion* 2 (Spring).

Farley, Margaret A. 1986. *Personal Commitments.* San Francisco: Harper and Row.

Ferguson, Kathy E. 1984. *The Feminist Case Against Bureaucracy.* Philadelphia: Temple University Press.

Ferrucci, Piero. 1990. *Inevitable Grace.* New York: Jeremy Tarcher.

Fields, Rick. 1981. *How the Swans Came to the Lake: A Narrative History of Buddhism.* Boulder, Colo.: Shambhala Publications.

———. "Buddhist Journal Beat." *Tricycle: The 1989 Buddhist Review* 1(2): 80-81.

Fine, Lawrence. 1987. "The Contemplative Practices of the Yihudim in Lurianic

Kabbahal." In Arthur Green, ed. *Jewish Spirituality from the Sixteenth Century Revival to the Present.* New York: Crossroad.

Five Stars (Performers). 1957. "Atom Bomb Baby" (Song). *Atomic Cafe.* Rounder Records 1034.

Forte, Dianne J. 1992. "SisteReach . . . Because 500 Years Is Enough." *Vital Signs: News from the National Black Women's Health Project* 1 (Spring): 5.

Fourez, Gerrard. 1982. *Liberation Ethics.* Philadelphia: Temple University Press.

Fox, Michael W. 1986. *Agricide: The Hidden Crisis that Affects Us All.* New York: Shocken.

Freire, Paulo. 1972, 1993. *Pedagogy of the Oppressed.* New York: Continuum.

French, Marilyn. 1985. *Beyond Power: On Women, Men and Morals.* New York: Summit Books.

Freud, Sigmund. 1955. "Medusa's Head." In J. Strachey, trans. and ed. *The Standard Edition of the Complete Psychological Works of Sigmund Freud,* vol. 18. London: Hogarth Press (written 1922, post-humously published 1940).

Friedman, Lenore. 1987. *Meetings with Remarkable Women.* Boston: Shambhala.

Gadon, Elinor W. 1989. *The Once & Future Goddess: A Symbol for Our Time.* San Francisco: Harper and Row.

Galland, China. 1990. *Longing for Darkness: Tara and the Black Madonna.* New York: Viking.

Garb, Yaakov Jerome. 1990. "Perspective or Escape? Ecofeminist Musings on Contemporary Earth Imagery." In Irene Diamond and Gloria Feman Orenstein, eds. *Reweaving the World: The Emergence of Ecofeminism.* San Francisco: Sierra Club Books.

Gatens, Moira. 1991. *Feminism and Philosophy: Perspectives on Difference and Equality.* Bloomington, Ind.: Indiana University Press.

Geller, Laura, and T. Drorah Setel. 1986. "What Kind of Tikkun Does the World Need?" *Tikkun* 1: 16ff, 114-15.

Giehl, Dudley. 1979. *Vegetarianism: A Way of Life.* New York: Harper and Row.

Gilligan, Carol. 1982. *In a Different Voice.* Cambridge, Mass.: Harvard University Press.

Gilman, Sander L. 1985. "Black Bodies, White Bodies: Toward an Iconography of Female Sexuality in Late Nineteenth-Century Art, Medicine and Literature." *Critical Inquiry* 12 (Autumn): 205-43.

Gimbutas, Marija. 1974. *The Gods and Goddesses of Old Europe: 7000-3500 B.C.* Berkeley: University of California Press.

———. 1989. *The Language of the Goddess.* San Francisco: Harper & Row.

———. 1991. *Civilization of the Goddess: The World of Old Europe.* San Francisco: Harper & Row.

Golden Gate Quartet (Performers). 1946. "The Atom and Evil" (Song). *Atomic Cafe.* Rounder Records 1034.

Gordon, Linda. 1976. *Woman's Body, Woman's Right: Birth Control in America.* New York: Penguin.

Grant, Jacquelyn. 1989. *White Women's Christ and Black Women's Jesus.* Atlanta: Scholars Press.

Graves, Robert. 1955, 1960. *The Greek Myths.* Mt. Kisco, N.Y.: Moyer Bell Limited.

Gray, Elizabeth Dodson. 1982. *Patriarchy As A Conceptual Trap.* Wellesley, Mass.: Roundtable Press.

———. 1979a. *Why the Green Nigger? Re-Mything Genesis.* (Succeeding editions published as *Green Paradise Lost.*) Wellesley, Mass.: Roundtable Press.

————. 1979b. *Green Paradise Lost.* Wellesley, Mass.: Roundtable Press.

Grey, Mary. 1991. "Claiming Power in Relation: Exploring the Ethics of Connection." *Journal of Feminist Studies in Religion* 7(1): 7-18.

Griffin, Donald R. 1990. "Foreword." In Marc Bekoff and Dale Jamieson, eds. *Interpretation and Explanation in the Study of Animal Behavior.* Vol 1: *Interpretation, Intentionality, and Communication.* Boulder, Colo.: Westview Press.

————. 1991. "The Problem of Distinguishing Awareness from Responsiveness." In D. G. M. Wood-Gush, M. Dawkins, R. Ewbank, eds. *Self-Awareness in Domesticated Animals: Proceedings of a Workshop Held at Keble College, Oxford.* Hertfordshire, England: The Universities Federation for Animal Welfare.

Griffin, Susan. 1978. *Woman and Nature: The Roaring Inside Her.* San Francisco: Harper and Row.

————. 1988. "Split Culture." *The Creative Woman* 8: 4-9.

Gross, Rita. 1986. "Buddhism and Feminism: A Personal Synthesis." In *Not Mixing Up Buddhism: Essays on Women and Buddhist Practice.* Fredonia, N.Y.: White Pine Press.

————. 1991. "Buddhism after Patriarchy?" In Paula M. Cooey, William R. Eakin, and Jay B. McDaniel, eds. *After Patriarchy.* Maryknoll, N.Y.: Orbis Books.

Gunn, John M. 1917, 1977. *Schet-Chen: History, Traditions and Narratives of the Queres Indians of Laguna and Acoma.* Albuquerque: Albright and Anderson. Reprint. New York: AMS Press, 1977.

Gupta, Lina. 1991. "Kali, the Savior." in Paula Cooey, William R. Eakin and Jay B. McDaniel, eds. *After Patriarchy: Feminist Transformations of the World Religions.* Maryknoll, N.Y.: Orbis Books.

Gustafson, James M. 1981. *Ethics from a Theocentric Perspective.* Vol. 1: *Theology and Ethics.* Chicago: University of Chicago Press.

Gutiérrez, Gustavo. 1973. *A Theology of Liberation.* Maryknoll, N.Y.: Orbis Books.

Halifax, Joan. 1990. "The Third Body: Buddhism, Shamanism, and Deep Ecology." In Alan Hunt-Gadiner, ed. *Dharma Gaia.* Berkeley: Parallax Press.

Hall, Nor. 1980. *The Moon & the Virgin: Reflections on the Archetypal Feminine.* New York: Harper and Row.

Hamilton, Cynthia. 1990. "Women, Home and Community: The Struggle in an Urban Environment." In Irene Diamond and Gloria Feman Orenstein, eds. *Reweaving the World: The Emergence of Ecofeminism.* San Francisco: Sierra Club Books.

Hanmer, Jalna. 1983. "Reproductive Technology: The Future for Women?" In Joan Rothschild, ed. *Machina Ex Dea: Feminist Perspectives on Technology.* New York: Pergamon.

Hanson, Paul. 1975. *The Dawn of Apocalyptic: The Historical and Sociological Roots of Jewish Apocalyptic Eschatology.* Philadelphia: Fortress Press.

Harding, Sandra. 1986. *The Science Question in Feminism.* Ithaca, N.Y.: Cornell University Press.

Harman, Willis. 1988. *Global Mind Change: The New Age Revolution in the Way We Think.* New York: Warner Books.

Harris, Adrienne, and Ynestra King, eds. 1989. *Rocking the Ship of State: Toward a Feminist Peace Politics.* Boulder, Colo.: Westview Press.

Harris, Maria. 1989. *Dance of the Spirit: The Seven Steps of Women's Spirituality.* New York: Bantam Books.

Harrison, Beverly Wildung. 1983. *Our Right to Choose: Toward a New Ethic of Abortion.* Boston: Beacon Press.

———. 1985. "The Power of Anger in the Work of Love." In Carol S. Robb, ed. *Making the Connections.* Boston: Beacon Press.

Hartmann, Betsy. 1987. *Reproductive Rights and Wrongs: The Global Politics of Population Control and Contraceptive Choice.* New York: Harper & Row.

Haskins, Jim. 1978. *Voodoo and Hoodoo: Their Tradition and Craft as Revealed by Actual Practitioners.* New York: Stein and Day.

Hayward, Alan. 1973. *Planet Earth's Last Hope.* Great Britain: Cox & Wyman, Ltd.

Heath, Stephen. 1978. "Difference." *Screen* 19(3): 50-112.

Heinze, Ruth-Inge. 1991. *Shamans of the Twentieth Century.* New York: Irvington Publishers Inc.

Hentoff, Nat. 1985. "How Can the Left Be Against Life?" *The Village Voice* (July 16).

Herlihy, David. 1988. *Medieval Households.* Cambridge, Mass.: Harvard University Press.

Heschel, Abraham Joshua. 1962. *The Prophets.* New York: Harper & Row.

Hoban, Russell. 1980. *Riddley Walker.* New York: Pocket Books.

Holmes, Ronald M., and James De Burger. 1988. *Serial Murder.* Newbury Park, Calif.: Sage.

hooks, bell. 1981. *Ain't I A Woman.* Boston: South End Press.

———. 1984. *Feminist Theory: From Margin to Center.* Boston: South End Press.

———. 1989. *Talking Back: Thinking Feminist, Thinking Black.* Boston: South End Press.

———. 1990. *Yearning: Race, Gender and Cultural Politics.* Boston: South End Press.

hooks, bell, and Cornell West. 1991. *Breaking Bread: Insurgent Black Intellectual Life.* Boston: South End Press.

Hunt, Mary E. 1988. "Abortion in a Just Society." *Conscience: A Newsjournal of Prochoice Catholic Opinion* 9(4): 9-12.

———. 1989a. "Agents With Integrity." *Waterwheel* 2(2): 1, 2.

———. 1989b. "Theological Pornography." In Joanne Carlson Brown and Carole R. Bohn, eds. *Christianity, Patriarchy, and Abuse.* New York: Pilgrim Press.

———. 1991. "Packaging Feminism for the Abortion Debate." *Conscience: A Newsjournal of Prochoice Catholic Opinion* 12(4): 1, 3, 6, 7, 9.

Ingold, Tim. 1983. "The Architect and the Bee: Reflections on the Work of Animals and Men." *Man* 18: 1-20.

Irigaray, Luce. 1981. "The Sex Which Is Not One." In Elaine Marks and Isabelle de Courtivron, eds. *New French Feminists.* New York: Schocken Books.

Irving,Thomas Ballantine. 1985. *The Maya's Own Words.* Culver City, CA.: Labyrinthos.

Isasi-Diaz, Ada Maria, and Yolanda Tarango. 1988. *Hispanic Women: Prophetic Voice in the Church.* San Francisco: Harper & Row.

Iverem, Esther. 1991. "By Earth Obsessed." *Essence* 22 (Sept.): 37-38.

Jacobs, Louis. 1987. "The Uplifting of Sparks in Late Jewish Mysticism." In Arthur Green, ed. *Jewish Spirituality from the Sixteenth Century Revival to the Present.* New York: Crossroad.

Jaggar, Alison M. 1983. *Feminist Politics and Human Nature.* Totowa, N.J.: Rowman and Allenheld.

———. 1985. "Love and Knowledge: Emotion in Feminist Epistemology." In A.

Jaggar and S. Bordo, eds. *Gender/Body/Knowledge*. New Brunswick, N.J.: Rutgers University Press.

Jahn, Janheinz. 1961. *Muntu: The New African Culture*. New York: Grove Press.

Japan Graphic Designers Association. 1986. *Graphic Design in Japan*, vol. 6. Tokyo: Kodansha International Ltd.

Jones, Ken. 1989. *The Social Face of Buddhism*. Boston: Wisdom Publications.

Joyce, Christopher. 1989. "Africans Call for End to the Ivory Trade." *New Scientist* 122 (June 10): 22.

Jung, Carl. 1953-1979. *The Collective Works of C. G. Jung*. Vol. 3. Trans. R. F. C. Hull. Princeton, N.J.: Princeton University Press.

———. 1968. *Man and His Symbols*. New York: Dell Publishing Company.

Jungk, Robert. 1958. *Brighter than a Thousand Suns: A Personal History of the Atomic Scientists*. Trans. James Cleugh. New York: Harcourt, Brace and Company.

Juravich, Tom. 1991. "The 10 Worst Jobs Today Are Not the Dirtiest Ones." *The Buffalo News* (March 13).

Kabilsingh, Chatsumarn. 1990. "Early Buddhist Views on Nature." In Alan Hunt-Badiner, ed. *Dharma Gaia*. Berkeley: Parallax Press.

Kalechofsky, Roberta. 1988. *Haggadah for the Liberated Lamb*. Marblehead, Mass.: Micah Publications.

Kalupahana, David J. 1987. *The Principles of Buddhist Psychology*. Albany, N.Y.: State University of New York Press.

Karabinus, Audrey. 1987. "Women in North American Zen Buddhism." Unpublished M.A. thesis.

Kaza, Stephanie. 1985. "Towards a Buddhist Environmental Ethic." *Buddhism at the Crossroads* 1(1): 22-25.

———. 1989. "Systems Thinking: Tools for Restoration Ecology." Presented at the Society for Ecological Restoration and Management Annual Meeting, Oakland, Calif.

Keen, Sam. 1986. *Faces of the Enemy: Reflections of the Hostile Imagination*. San Francisco: Harper and Row.

Keller, Catherine. 1986. *From a Broken Web: Separation, Sexism and Self*. Boston: Beacon Press.

Kellert, Stephen. 1989. "Perceptions of Animals in America." In R. J. Hoage, ed. *Perceptions of Animals in American Culture*. Washington, D.C.: Smithsonian Institution Press.

Kellogg, Kathy, and Bob Kellogg. 1985. *Raising Pigs Successfully*. Charlotte, Vt.: Williamson Publishing.

Kheel, Marti. 1985. "The Liberation of Nature: A Circular Affair." *Environmental Ethics* 7(2): 135-49.

———. 1987. "Befriending the Beast." *Creation* (Sept./Oct.): 11-12.

———. 1988. "Animal Liberation and Environmental Ethics: Can Ecofeminism Bridge the Gap?" Paper presented at the annual meeting of the Western Political Science Association, San Francisco, March 10-12.

———. 1989. "From Healing Herbs to Deadly Drugs." In Judith Plant, ed. *Healing the Wounds: The Promise of Ecofeminism*. Philadelphia: New Society Publishers.

———. 1990. "Ecofeminism and Deep Ecology: Reflections on Identity and Difference." In Irene Diamond and Gloria Feman Orenstein, eds. *Reweaving the World: The Emergence of Ecofeminism*. San Francisco: Sierra Club Books.

King, Stephen. 1986. *It*. New York: Viking.

King, Ynestra. 1989. ."Healing the Wounds: Feminism, Ecology, and the Nature/ Culture Dualism." In Alison M. Jaggar and Susan R. Bordo, eds. *Gender/Body/ Knowledge: Feminist Reconstructions of Being and Knowing.* New Brunswick, N.J.: Rutgers University Press.

————. 1990. "Healing the Wounds: Feminism, Ecology, and the Nature/Culture Dualism." In Irene Diamond and Gloria Feman Orenstein, eds. *Reweaving the World: The Emergence of Ecofeminism.* San Francisco: Sierra Club Books.

Kinsley, David. 1987. *Hindu Goddesses: Visions of the Divine Feminine in the Hindu Religious Tradition.* Delhi: Motilal Banarasidass.

Kittay, Eva Feder. 1984. "Womb Envy: An Explanatory Concept." In Joyce Trebilcot, ed. *Mothering: Essays in Feminist Theory.* Totowa, N.J.: Rowman.

Klein, Anne. 1986. "Compassion: Gain or Drain? Buddhist and Feminist Views on Compassion." *Spring Wind* 6(1, 2, 3): 105-16.

Koen, Susan, and Nina Swaim, eds. 1980. *Ain't No Where We Can Run: A Handbook for Women on the Nuclear Mentality.* Norwich, Vt.: WAND.

Kohlberg, Lawrence. 1981. *The Philosophy of Moral Development.* San Francisco: Harper and Row.

Krafft-Ebing, Richard von. 1965. *Psychopathia Sexualis.* Trans. F. S. Klaf. New York: Stein and Day.

Krippner, Stanley. 1991. "Foreword." In Ruth-Inge Heinze. *Shamans of the Twentieth Century.* New York: Irvington Publishers Inc.

Kronke, David. N.D. "Documentary Looks at Hormel's Bid to Hog Its Profits. *Dallas Times Herald.*

Lake, Kirsopp, trans. 1919. *The Apostolic Fathers.* 2 vols. New York: G. P. Putnam's Sons.

Lame Deer, John (Fire) (Lakota), and Richard Erdoes. 1972. New York: Simon and Schuster.

Lansky, Philip S. 1990. "Health Today." *New Frontier* (June): 21.

Larsen, Elizabeth. 1991. "Granola Boys, Eco-Dudes, and Me." *Ms.* 2 (July/Aug.), 96-97.

Laurence, William L. 1945. "Eyewitness Account of Bomb Test." *New York Times* (Sept. 26), 1.

————. 1946. *Dawn Over Zero: The Story of the Atomic Bomb.* New York: Alfred A. Knopf.

Lederer, Wolfgang, 1968. *The Fear of Women.* New York: Harcourt Brace Jovanovich.

LeGuin, Ursula, 1987. *Buffalo Gals and Other Animal Presences.* New York: Roc/ Penguin Books.

Lerner, Gerda, ed. 1973. *Black Women in White America.* New York: Vintage Books.

————. 1986. *The Creation of Patriarchy.* New York: Oxford University Press.

"Let the Guy Grin. He's the New Top Gun of the Movies." 1986. *People Weekly* (Dec. 22-29), 24.

Levitt, Peter. 1990. "An Intimate View." In Alan Hunt-Badiner, ed. *Dharma Gaia.* Berkeley: Parallax Press.

Lewis, Andrea. 1990. "Looking at the Total Picture: A Conversation with Health Activist Beverly Smith." In Evelyn C. White, ed. *The Black Women's Health Book: Speaking for Ourselves.* Seattle: The Seal Press.

Lifton, Robert Jay. 1979. *The Broken Connection: On Death and the Continuity of Life.* New York: Basic Books.

Lifton, Robert J., and Richard Falk. 1982. *Indefensible Weapons: The Political and Psychological Case Against Nuclearism.* New York: Basic Books.

Linzey, Andrew. Forthcoming. "Liberation Theology and the Oppression of Animals." *Animal Theology.*

———. 1987. *Christianity and the Rights of Animals.* New York: Crossroad.

Little Caesar with The Red Callender Sextette (Performers). 1957. "Atomic Love" (Song). *Atomic Cafe.* Rounder Records 1034.

Lorde, Audre. 1983. "An Open Letter to Mary Daly." In Cherríe Moraga and Gloria Anzaldua, eds. *This Bridge Called My Back: Writings by Radical Women of Color.* New York: Kitchen Table Press.

Lovelock, James, 1979. *Gaia: A New Look at Life on Earth.* Oxford: Oxford University Press.

———. 1988, 1990. *The Ages of Gaia: A Biography of Our Living Earth.* New York: Bantam.

Lowell Blanchard with the Valley Trio (Performers). 1950. "Jesus Hits Like an Atom Bomb" (Song). *Atomic Cafe.* Rounder Records 1034.

Lugones, Maria. 1987. "Playfulness, 'World'-Travelling, and Loving Perception." *Hypatia* 2(2).

Luttmann, Rich, and Gail Luttmann. 1976. *Chickens in Your Backyard.*

Maathai, Wangari. 1991. "Foresters Without Diplomas." *Ms.* 1 (Mar./Apr.), 74-75.

McAllister, Pam, ed. 1982. *Reweaving the Web of Life: Feminism and Nonviolence.* Philadelphia: New Society Publishers.

McCarthy, Kate. 1990. "A Critique of Emptiness from the Margins." Presented at the Western Regional Meeting of the American Academy of Religion, March.

MacCormack, Carol, and Marilyn Strathern, eds. 1980. *Nature, Culture and Gender.* New York: Cambridge University Press.

McFague, Sallie. 1987. *Models of God: Theology for an Ecological, Nuclear Age.* Philadelphia: Fortress Press.

MacKenzie Brown, C. 1990. *The Triumph of the Goddess.* New York: The State University of New York Press.

McKibben, Bill. 1989. *The End of Nature.* New York: Random House.

MacKinnon, Catharine A. 1983. "Feminism, Marxism, Method, and the State: Toward Feminist Jurisprudence." *Signs: Journal of Women in Culture and Society* 8 (Summer): 635-58.

———. 1987. *Feminism Unmodified: Discourses on Life and Law.* Cambridge, Mass.: Harvard University Press.

McLuhan, Marshall. 1951. *The Mechanical Bride: Folklore of Industrial Man.* Boston: Beacon Press.

McMullen, Ann. 1977. *Electrical Review* 201(19): 47-49.

Macy, Joanne. 1977. "Perfection of Wisdom: Mother of All Buddhas." In Rita Gross, ed. *Beyond Androcentrism.* Missoula: Scholars Press.

———. 1983. *Despair and Personal Power in the Nuclear Age.* Philadelphia: New Society Publishers.

———. 1990. "The Greening of the Self." *Common Boundary* (July-August): 22-25.

———. 1991a. "Guardians of the Future." *In Context* 28 (Spring): 20-25.

———. 1991b. *Mutual Causality in Buddhism and General Systems Theory: The Dharam of Natural Systems.* Albany, N.Y.: State University of New York Press.

———. 1991c. *World as Lover, World as Self.* San Francisco: Parallax Press.

Macy, Joanna, et al. 1988. *Thinking Like a Mountain: Toward a Council of All Beings.* Philadelphia: New Society Publishers.

Marshall, Karen. 1989. "Caretakers of the Earth." *Woman of Power: A Magazine of Feminism, Spirituality, and Politics.* 14: 42-44.

Marshall, Paule. 1983. *Praisesong for the Widow.* New York: G. P. Putnam's Sons.

Martin, M. Kay, and Barbara Voorhies. 1975. *Female of the Species.* New York: Columbia University Press.

Mason, Jim, and Peter Singer. 1990. *Animal Factories.* New York: Harmony Books.

May, Elaine Tyler. 1988. *Homeward Bound: American Families in the Cold War Era.* New York: Basic Books.

Mendelsohn, Isaac, ed. 1955. *Religion in the Ancient Near East.* New York: Liberal Arts Press.

Merchant, Carolyn. 1980. *The Death of Nature: Women, Ecology, and the Scientific Revolution.* New York: Harper & Row.

———. 1989. *Ecological Revolutions: Nature, Gender, and Science in New England.* Chapel Hill, N.C.: University of North Carolina Press.

———. 1990. "Ecofeminism and Feminist Theory." In Irene Diamond and Gloria Feman Orenstein, eds. *Reweaving the World: The Emergence of Ecofeminism.* San Francisco: Sierra Club Books.

Meyer, Eugene L. 1992. "Environmental Racism: Why Is It Always Dumped In Our Backyard? Minority Groups Take a Stand." *Audubon* 94 (Jan./Feb.): 30-32.

Midgley, Mary. 1978. *Beast and Man: The Roots of Human Nature.* Ithaca, N.Y.: Cornell University Press.

Miller, Perry. 1956. "The End of the World." In *Errand into the Wilderness.* Cambridge, Mass.: Belknap Press of Harvard University Press.

Mills, Patricia Jagentowicz. 1991. "Feminism and Ecology: On the Domination of Nature." *Hypatia* 6(1): 162-78.

Moltman, Jürgen. 1979. *The Future of Creation.* Philadelphia: Fortress Press.

Moore, Alan. 1986. *The Watchmen.* New York: D.C. Comics.

Morley, Sylvanus G. 1947. *The Ancient Maya.* Stanford: Stanford University Press.

Morreale, Don. 1988. *Buddhist America.* Santa Fe: John Muir Publications.

Morton, Nelle. 1985. *The Journey Is Home.* Boston: Beacon Press.

Mullert, G. M. 1979. *Spider Woman Stones: Legends of the Hopi Indians.* Tucson: University of Arizona Press.

Murphy, Patrick D. 1988. "Sex-typing the Planet." *Environmental Ethics.* 10: 155-68.

Murphy, Yolanda, and Robert Murphy. 1974. *Women of the Forest.* New York: Columbia University Press.

Myers, Linda James. 1988. *Understanding an Afrocentric Worldview: Introduction to an Optimal Psychology.* Dubuque, Iowa: Kendall/Hunt.

Myers, Lou (Artist). 1983. Cartoon. In Steven Heller, ed. *War Heads: Cartoonists Draw the Line.* New York: Penguin.

Narayan, Uma. 1988. "Working Together Across Difference: Some Considerations on Emotions and Political Practice." *Hypatia* 3(2) (Summer): 31-47.

Nelson, Gertrude Mueller. 1986. *To Dance with God: Family Ritual and Community Celebration.* Mahwah, N.J.: Paulist Press.

Nelson, Lin. 1990. "The Place of Women in Polluted Places." In Irene Diamond and Gloria Feman Orenstein, eds. *Reweaving the World: The Emergence of Ecofeminism.* San Francisco: Sierra Club Books.

Nelson, Lynn Hankinson. 1990. *Who Knows: From Quine to a Feminist Empiricism.* Philadelphia: Temple University Press.

Nelson, Robert H. 1990. "Tom Hayden, Meet Adam Smith and Thomas Aquinas." *Forbes* (Oct. 10): 94-97.

Nequatewa, Edmund (Hopi). 1967. *Truth of a Hopi: Stories Relating to the Origin Myths and Clan Histories of the Hopi.* Arizona: Northland Press.

Nhat Hanh, Thich. 1990a. *Present Moment, Wonderful Moment.* Berkeley: Parallax Press.

——. 1990b. *Transformation and Healing.* Berkeley: Parallax Press.

Nichols, Charles. 1963. *Many Thousand Gone.* Leiden: E. J. Brill.

Nirmalananda, Swami. 1987. *Dev-Devi o Tader Vahana.* Calcutta: Impressive Impression.

Northup, Solomon. 1853. *Narrative of Solomon Northrup, Twelve Years a Slave.* Auburn, N.Y.: Derby and Miller.

Noske, Barbara. 1989. *Humans and Other Animals: Beyond the Boundaries of Anthropology.* London: Pluto Press.

Nyssa, Gregory, 1893. *On the Soul and the Resurrection.* In *Nicene and Post-Nicene Fathers.* 2nd series, vol, 5. New York: Parker.

O'Brien, Mary. 1981. *The Politics of Reproduction.* Boston: Routledge.

Oda, Mayumi. 1988. *Goddesses.* Volcano, Calif.: Volcano Press/Kazan Books.

Ogunyemi, Chikwenye Okonjo. 1985. "Womanism: The Dynamics of the Contemporary Black Female Novel in English." *Signs: Journal of Women in Culture and Society* 11 (Autumn): 63-80.

Omolade, Barbara. 1989. "We Speak for the Planet." In Adrienne Harris and Ynestra King, eds. *Rocking the Ship of State: Toward a Feminist Peace Politics.* Boulder, Colo.: Westview Press.

Orenstein, Gloria Feman. 1988. "Interview with the Shaman of Samiland: The Methodology of the Marvelous." *Trivia: A Journal of Ideas* 12 (Spring).

Origen. G. W. Butterworth, ed. 1966. *On First Principles.* New York: Harper and Row.

Ortner, Sherry. 1974. "Is Female to Male as Nature Is to Culture?" In Michelle Zimbalist Rosaldo and Louise Lamphere, eds. *Woman, Culture and Society.* Stanford, Calif.: Stanford University Press.

Ouedraogo, Josephine. 1992. "Sahel Women Fight Desert Advance." *UNESCO Courier* 45 (March): 38.

"The P. Word." 1992. *Bunny Huggers' Gazette* 13:14-15.

Parsons, Elsie Clews. 1939. *Pueblo Indian Religions.* 2 vols. Chicago: University of Chicago.

Perkins, William. 1590. *Christian Oeconomie.* London.

——. 1596. *A Discourse on the Damned Art of Witchcraft.* London.

Petchesky, Rosalind Pollack. 1984. *Abortion and Woman's Choice: The State, Sexuality, and Reproductive Freedom.* New York: Longman.

Plant, Judith, ed. 1989. *Healing the Wounds: The Promise of Ecofeminism.* Philadelphia: New Society Publishers; Toronto: Between the Lines.

——. 1990. *Standing Again at Sinai: Judaism from a Feminist Perspective.* San Francisco: Harper San Francisco.

Plaskow, Judith, and Carol P. Christ, eds. 1989. *Weaving the Visions.* San Francisco: Harper and Row.

Plato. 1937 *Timaeus.* In B. Jowett, ed. *The Dialogues of Plato.* vol. 2. New York: Random House.

Plumwood, Val. 1986. "Ecofeminism: An Overview and Discussion of Positions and Arguments." *Australasian Journal of Philosophy,* supp. to vol 64: 120-37.

———. 1991. "Nature, Self, and Gender: Feminism, Environmental Philosophy, and the Critique of Rationalism." *Hypatia* 6(1) (Spring): 3-27.

———. 1992. "Feminism and Ecofeminism: Beyond the Dualistic Assumptions of Women, Men and Nature." *The Ecologist* 22(1): 8-13.

Pollan, Michael, et al. 1990. "Only Man's Presence Can Save Nature." *Harper's* (April), 37-48.

Putter, Ruth (Photographer). 1985. Photograph. *Heresies: A Feminist Publication on Art & Politics* 5(4): back cover.

Quine, Willard Van Orman. 1960. *Word and Object.* Cambridge, Mass.: The M.I.T. Press.

Rain Crowe, Thomas. 1990. "Reweaving the Future" (Interview with Marilou Awiakta). *Appalachian Journal* (Fall): 40-54.

Ramprasad Sen. 1966. *Ramprasad's Devotional Songs.* Trans. Jadunath Sinha. Calcutta.

Reagan, Ronald. 1983. "President's Speech on Military Spending and a New Defense." *New York Times* (March 24), A20.

Regan, Tom. 1983. *The Case for Animal Rights.* Los Angeles: University of California Press.

Reik, Theodor. 1960. *The Creation of Woman.* New York: McGrawHill.

Richards, Dona. 1980. "European Mythology: The Ideology of 'Progress'." In Molefi Kete Asante and Abdulai Sa Vandi, eds. *Contempoarary Black Thought.* Beverly Hills, Calif.: Sage.

Richardson, Cyril, ed. 1953. *Early Christian Fathers* 1. Philadelphia: Westminster Press.

Riley, Shay. 1991. "Eco-Racists Use Fatal Tactics." *Daily Illini* 121 (Sept. 4), 15.

Robbins, John. 1987. *Diet for a New America.* Walpole, N.H.: Stillpoint Publishing.

Roberts, Elizabeth, and Elias Amidon, eds. 1991. *Earth Prayers from Around the World.* San Francisco: HarperCollins.

Robinson, James M., ed. 1977. *The Nag Hammadi Library.* San Francisco: Harper and Row.

Rollin, Bernard, 1981. *Animal Rights and Human Morality.* Buffalo, N.Y.: Prometheus Books.

———. 1990. *The Unheeded Cry: Animal Consciousness, Animal Pain and Science.* New York: Oxford.

Rosaldo, Michelle Z., and Louise Lamphere. 1974. *Woman, Culture and Society.* Stanford, Calif.: Stanford University Press.

Ross, Andrew. 1991. *Strange Weather: Culture, Science & Technology in the Age of Limits.* New York: Verso.

Ross, David Komito. 1991. "Eco-bodhicitta and Artful Conduct." Presented at John F. Kennedy University, Orinda, Calif., October 11.

Ruether, Rosemary Radford. 1972, 1979. "Motherearth and the Megamachine: A Theology of Liberation in a Feminine, Somatic and Ecological Perspective." *Christianity and Crisis* (April 12). Reprinted in Carol P. Christ and Judith Plaskow, eds. 1979. *Womanspirit Rising: A Feminist Reader in Religion.* San Francisco: Harper & Row.

——. 1975. *New Woman/New Earth: Sexist Ideologies and Human Liberation.* New York: Seabury.

——. 1981. *To Change the World: Christology and Cultural Criticism.* New York: Crossroad.

——. 1983. *Sexism and God-Talk: Toward a Feminist Theology.* Boston: Beacon Press.

——. 1984. "Envisioning Our Hope: Some Models for the Future." In Janet Kalven and Mary Buckley, eds. *Women's Spirit Bonding.* New York: Pilgrim Press.

——. 1986. *Women-Church.* New York: Harper and Row.

——. 1989. "Toward an Ecological-Feminist Theory of Nature." In Judith Plant, ed. *Healing the Wounds: The Promise of Ecofeminism.* Philadelphia: New Society Publishers.

——. 1990. "Eschatology and Feminism." In Susan Thistlethwaite and Mary Potter Engels, eds. *Lift Every Voice.* San Francisco: HarperSan Francisco.

——. 1990a. *Christianity and Crisis* 50:8 (May 28).

——. 1990b. "Women, Sexuality, Ecology, and the Church." *Conscience: A Newsjournal of Prochoice Catholic Opinion* 9(4): 1, 4-11.

——. Forthcoming. *Gaia and God. Toward an Ecofeminist Theology of Earth Healing.*

Russell, Diana E. H., ed. 1989. *Exposing Nuclear Phallacies.* New York: Pergamon Press.

Russell, Julia Scofield. 1990. "The Evolution of an Ecofeminist." In Irene Diamond and Gloria Feman Orenstein, eds. *Reweaving the World: The Emergence of Ecofeminism.* San Francisco: Sierra Club Books.

Sachs, Oliver. 1989, 1990. *Seeing Voices: A Journey into the World of the Deaf.* New York: HarperCollins.

Saiving, Valerie. 1992. "The Human Situation: A Feminine View." In Carol Christ and Judith Plaskow, eds. *Womanspirit Rising.* 2nd ed. San Francisco: HarperSan Francisco.

Salleh, Ariel. 1991. "Review of *Staying Alive: Women, Ecology and Development.*" *Hypatia* 6(1): 206-14.

Sanchez, Carol Lee (Laguna Pueblo/Lakota). 1989. "New World Tribal Communities: An Alternative Approach for Recreating Egalitarian Societies." In Judith Plaskow and Carol P. Christ, eds. *Weaving the Visions: New Patterns in Feminist Spirituality.* San Francisco: Harper and Row.

Sanders, Thomas E., and Walter W. Peek, eds. 1973. "The Liberated and the League: The Law of the Great Peace and the American Epic." *Literature of the American Indian.* Toronto: CollierMcMillan.

Schallert, K. L. 1992. "Speaker Examines Impact of the West on Africa" (Wagaki Mwangi). *Daily Illini* 121 (April 3), 3.

Schmidt, Alfred. 1971. *The Concept of Nature in Marx.* Trans. Ben Fowkes. London: NLB.

Scholem, Gershom. 1941. *Major Trends in Jewish Mysticism.* New York: Schocken Books.

Seager, Joni, ed. 1989. *The State of the Earth Atlas.* New York: Touchstone/Simon and Schuster.

See, Carolyn. 1987. *Golden Days.* New York: McGraw-Hill Book Company.

Seed, John, Joanna Macy, Pat Fleming, and Arne Naess. 1988. *Thinking Like a Mountain.* Philadelphia: New Society Publishers.

Sekaquaptewa, Helen (Hopi), edited by Louise Udall. 1969. *Me and Mine: The Life Story of Helen Sekaquaptewa as Told to Louise Udall.* Tucson: University of Arizona Press.

Semmelroth, Otto. 1963. *Mary: Archetype of the Church.* New York: Sheed and Ward.

Setel, T. Drorah. 1986. "Feminist Reflections on Separation and Unity in Jewish Theology." *Journal of Feminist Studies in Religions.* 2 (Spring 1986).

Shiva, Vandana. 1988. *Staying Alive: Women, Ecology, and Development.* London: Zed Press. New Delhi: Kali for Women.

Signs: Journal of Women in Culture and Society. 1991. 7:1. (Special issue on French feminism.)

Silko, Leslie Marmon. 1977. *Ceremony.* New York: New American Library, a Signet Book.

Sinclair, Upton. 1906, 1973. *The Jungle.* New York: New American Library.

Singer, Peter. 1990. *Animal Liberation.* 2nd ed. New York: New York Review of Books.

Singh, Raghubir. 1992. "Ganges." *Life* magazine. 5, no. 3 (March).

Sivaraksa, Sulak. 1991. *Seeds of Peace.* Berkeley: Parallax Press.

Sjöö, Monica, and Barbara Mor. 1987. *The Great Cosmic Mother: Rediscovering the Religion of the Earth.* San Francisco: Harper.

Smith, Andy. 1991. "For All Those Who Were Indian in Another Life." *Ms.* (Nov./Dec.), 44-45.

Smith, Mike (Artist). 1988. Cartoon. *Nevada Nuclear Waste Newsletter* 4(2) (June), 1.

Smith, Mimi (Artist). 1982. Cartoon. *Public Illumination Magazine* 21 (June), 14.

Smith-Rosenberg, Carroll. 1985. *Disorderly Conduct: Visions of Gender in Victorian America.* New York: Oxford University Press.

Snitow, Ann. 1989. "A Gender Diary." In Adrienne Harris and Ynestra King, eds. *Rocking the Ship of State: Towards a Feminist Peace Politics.* Boulder, Colo: Westview Press.

Sofia, Zöe. 1984. "Exterminating Fetuses: Abortion, Disarmament, and the Sexo-semiotics of Extraterrestrialism." *Diacritics* 14(2): 47-59.

Spirit of Memphis Quartet (Performers). 1951. "Atomic Telephone" (Song). *Atomic Cafe.* Rounder Records 1034.

Spretnak, Charlene. 1981. *Lost Goddesses of Early Greece.* Boston: Beacon Press.

———, ed. 1982. *The Politics of Women's Spirituality: Essays on the Rise of Spiritual Power Within the Feminist Movement.* Garden City, N.Y.: Anchor Press.

———. 1983. "Naming the Cultural Forces that Push Us Toward War." *Journal of Humanistic Psychology* 23(3): 104-14.

———. 1986. *The Spiritual Dimensions of Green Politics.* Santa Fe, N. Mex.: Bear and Company.

———. 1990. "Ecofeminism: Our Roots and Flowering." In Irene Diamond and Gloria Feman Orenstein, eds. *Reweaving the World: The Emergence of Ecofeminism.* San Francisco: Sierra Club Books.

———. 1991. *States of Grace: The Recovery of Meaning in the Postmodern Age.* San Francisco: HarperSanFrancisco.

———. 1992. "A Closer Look at Natural Law: An Ecofeminist Perspective on Abortion" (Abridged). *The Utne Reader* (May/June).

Stanton, William. 1960. *The Leopard's Spots: Scientific Attitudes Toward Race in America, 1815-1859.* Chicago: University of Chicago Press.

Starhawk. 1979. *The Spiral Dance: A Rebirth of the Ancient Religions of the Great Goddess*. San Francisco: Harper and Row.

———. 1982a. *Dreaming the Dark: Magic, Sex and Politics*. Boston: Beacon Press.

———. 1982b. "Ethics and Justice in Goddess Religion." In Charlene Spretnak, ed. *The Politics of Women's Spirituality: Essays in the Rise of Spiritual Power within the Feminist Movement*. Garden City, N.Y.: Doubleday, Anchor Books.

———. 1989. *The Spiral Dance*. Tenth Anniversary Edition. San Francisco: Harper & Row.

———. 1990. "Power, Authority, and Mystery: Ecofeminism and Earth-Based Spirituality." In Irene Diamond and Gloria Feman Orenstein, eds. *Reweaving the World: The Emergence of Ecofeminism*. San Francisco: Sierra Club Books.

Stivers, Richard. 1982. *Evil in Modern Myth and Ritual*. Athens, Ga.: University of Georgia Press.

Stolz, Mary. 1985. *Quentin Corn*. Boston: David R. Godine.

Stone, Merlin. 1976. *When God Was a Woman*. New York: Harcourt.

Strange, Penny. 1989. "It'll Make a Man of You: A Feminist View of the Arms Race." In Diana E. H. Russell, ed. *Exposing Nuclear Phallacies*. New York: Pergamon Press.

Strong, William Duncan. 1987. *Aboriginal Society in Southern California*. Banning: Malki Museum Press, 1987.

"Sudden Move Shifts Planet." 1990. *TV Guide* (Oct. 13-19), 36.

Summers, Montague, ed. 1928. *Malleus Maleficarum*. London: J. Rodker.

Suzuki, D. T. 1949. "Practical Methods of Zen Instruction." In *Essays in Zen Buddhism*. New York: Grove Press.

Tanahashi, Kaz, ed. 1985. *Moon in a Dewdrop: Writings of ZenMaster Dogen*. San Francisco: North Point Press.

Teish, Luisah. 1985. *Jambalaya: The Natural Woman's Book of Personal Charms and Practical Rituals*. San Francisco: Harper & Row.

Tellenbach, Hubertus, and Bin Kimura. 1989. "The Japanese Concept of Nature." In J. Baird Callicott, and R. T. Ames, eds. *Nature in Asian Traditions of Thought*. Albany, N.Y.: State University of New York Press.

"Three Minutes to Midnight." 1984. *Bulletin of the Atomic Scientists* (January), 2.

Ticktin, Esther. 1976. "A Modest Beginning." In Elizabeth Koltun, ed. *The Jewish Woman: New Perspectives*. New York: Schocken Books.

Tillich, Paul. *Systematic Theology*, 3 vols. Chicago: University of Chicago Press, 1951-63.

Titus, A. Constandina. 1986. *Bombs in the Backyard: Atomic Testing and American Politics*. Reno: University of Nevada Press.

Tobias, Michael. 1990. *Voice of the Planet*. New York: Bantam.

Todd, Judith. 1981. "On Common Ground: Native American Spirituality and Feminist Spirituality Approaches in the Sturggle to Save Mother Earth." In Charlene Spretnak, ed. *The Politics of Women's Spirituality*. Garden City: Anchor Books.

Trammps (Performers). 1977. "Disco Inferno" (Song). *Saturday Night Fever*. RSO Records RS-2-4001.

Trebilcot, Joyce, ed. 1984. *Mothering: Essays in Feminist Theory*. Totowa, N.J.: Rowman.

Trible, Phyllis. 1973. "Depatriarchalizing in Biblical Interpretation." *Journal of the American Academy of Religion* 41(1) (March).

Turner, Frederick. 1988. "A Field Guide to the Synthetic Landscape: Toward a New Environmental Ethic." *Harper's* (April), 49-55.

Turner, Frederick W. III, ed. 1974. *The Portable North American Indian Reader.* New York: Viking.

TV Guide. 1990. Advertisement for TBS cable television network (Aug. 11-17), 83.

Tyler, Hamilton A. 1964. *Pueblo Gods and Myths.* Norman: University of Oklahoma Press.

Tyson, Ray. 1991. "We're Not Going to Put Up With It." *USA Today* (Oct. 24).

United States Office of Technology Assessment. 1985. *Reproductive Health Hazards in the Workplace.* Washington, D.C.: Government Printing Office.

Vicinus, Martha. 1982. "Sexuality and Power: A Review of Current Work in the History of Sexuality." *Feminist Studies* 8: 133-56.

Vogt, Kari. 1990. "Becoming Male: A Gnostic and Early Christian Metaphor." In Kari Borresen, ed. *Image of God and Gender Models in Judaeo-Christian Tradition.* Oslo: Solum Forlag.

Walker, Alice. 1983a. *In Search of Our Mothers' Gardens: Womanist Prose.* New York: Harcourt Brace Jovanovich.

———. 1983b. "Only Justice Can Stop a Curse." In *In Search of Our Mothers' Gardens: Womanist Prose.* New York: Harcourt Brace Jovanovich.

———. 1988. "Everything Is a Human Being." In *Living by the Word: Selected Writings, 1973-1987.* New York: Harcourt Brace Jovanovich.

———. 1990. "Right to Life: What Can the White Man Say to the Black Woman?" In Marlene Gerber Fried, ed. *From Abortion to Reproductive Freedom: Transforming a Movement.* Boston: South End Press.

Walker, Barbara. 1983. *The Woman's Encyclopedia of Myths and Secrets.* San Francisco: Harper & Row.

———. 1985. *The Crone: Woman of Age, Wisdom, and Power.* San Francisco: Harper & Row.

———. 1988. *The Woman's Dictionary of Symbols and Sacred Objects.* San Francisco: Harper & Row.

Warnock, Donna. 1982. "Patriarchy Is a Killer: What People Concerned About Peace and Justice Should Know." In Pam McAllister, ed. *Reweaving the Web of Life: Feminism and Nonviolence.* Philadelphia: New Society Publishers.

Warren, Karen J. 1987. "Feminism and Ecology: Making Connections." *Environmental Ethics* 9(1) (Spring): 3-20.

———. 1988. "Toward an Ecofeminist Ethic." *Studies in the Humanities* 15: 140-56.

———. 1989. "Male Gender Bias and Western Conceptions of Reason and Rationality." American Philosophical Association. *Newsletter on Feminism and Philosophy* 88(2): 49-53.

———. 1990. "The Power and Promise of Ecological Feminism." *Environmental Ethics* 12 (3) (Summer): 125-46.

———. 1991a. "Toward A Feminist Peace Politics." *Journal of Peace and Justice Studies* 13(1): 87-102.

———. 1991b. "Feminism and the Environment: An Overview of the Issues." American Philosophical Association *Newsletter on Feminism and Philosophy* 90(3) (Fall): 108-16.

Warren, Karen J., and Jim Cheney. Forthcoming. *Ecological Feminism: A Philo-*

sophical Perspective on What it Is and Why it Matters. Boulder, Colo.: Westview Press.

Waskow, Arthur. 1983. *These Holy Sparks: The Rebirth of the Jewish People.* San Francisco: Harper & Row.

————. 1988. "Down-to-Earth Judaism: Food, Sex, and Money." *Tikkun* 3.

————. 1987. *Rainbow Sign.* Unpublished ms.

Waters, Frank and Oswald White Bear Fredericks with Hopi Spokespeople. 1963. *Book of the Hopi.* New York: The Viking Press.

Weart, Spencer R. 1988. *Nuclear Fear: A History of Images.* Cambridge, Mass.: Harvard University Press.

Weatherford, Jack. 1988. *Indian Givers: How the Indians of the Americas Transformed the World.* New York: Fawcett Columbine.

Weber, Thomas. 1988. *Hugging the Trees: The Story of the Chipko Movement.* Calcutta: Penguin.

Wehr, Demaris S. 1987. *Jung and Feminism.* Boston: Beacon Press.

Weigand, Phil C. 1978. "Contemporary Social and Economic Structure." *Art of the Huichol.* New York: The Fine Arts Museum of San Francisco/Harry N. Abrams, Inc.

Weigle, Marta. 1982. *Spiders & Spinsters: Women and Mythology.* Albuquerque: University of New Mexico Press.

————. 1989. *Creation and Procreation: Feminist Reflections on Mythologies of Cosmogomy and Parturition.* Philadelphia: University of Pennsylvania Press.

Welch, Sharon D. 1985. *Communities of Resistance and Solidarity: A Feminist Theology of Liberation.* Maryknoll, N.Y.: Orbis Books.

White, Lynn, Jr. 1967. "The Historical Roots of Our Ecologic Crisis." *Science* 155, no. 3767 (March 10): 1203-7.

Williams, Delores S. 1991. "African-American Women's Experience and Christian Notions of Redemption." In Paula M. Cooey, William R. Eakin, and Jay B. McDaniel, eds. *After Patriarchy: Feminist Transformations of the World Religions.* Maryknoll, N.Y.: Orbis Books.

Willis, Ellen. 1985. "Putting Women Back into the Abortion Debate." *The Village Voice* (July 16).

Willson, Martin. 1986. *In Praise of Tara.* London: Wisdom Publications.

Wilson, David S. 1990. "Capt. Kirk Comes Down to Earth." *TV Guide* (Oct. 13-19), 10-11.

Wilson, Francis, and Mamphela Ramphele. 1989. *Uprooting Poverty: The South African Challenge.* Capetown: David Philip.

Wong, Doris Sue. 1991. "Youth Says He Feared Gang." *The Boston Globe* (Dec. 19).

Wood, Michael. 1975. *America in the Movies: Or, Santa Maria, It Had Slipped My Mind.* New York: Basic Books.

Worldwatch. 1987. "On the Brink of Extinction." Quoted in *World Development Forum* 5 (Nov.), 3.

Yorinks, Arthur. 1980. *Louis the Fish.* Illus. Richard Egielski. New York: Farrar, Straus, Giroux.

Ziegler, P. Thomas. 1962, 1966. *The Meat We Eat.* Danville, Ill.: The Interstate Printers and Publishers.

Zimmer, Heinreich. 1962. *Myths and Symbols in Indian Art and Civilization,* ed. Joseph Campbell. New York: Harper & Row.

Zimmerman, Michael E. 1987. "Feminism, Deep Ecology, and Environmental Ethics." *Environmental Ethics* 9 (Spring): 21-44.

Of Related Interest from Continuum

Carol J. Adams
THE SEXUAL POLITICS OF MEAT
A Feminist-Vegetarian Critical Theory
$16.95 paperback   ISBN 0-8264-0513-4

"*The Sexual Politics of Meat* by Carol J. Adams examines the historical gender, race, and class implications of meat culture, and makes the links between the practice of butchering/eating animals and the maintenance of male dominance. Read this powerful new book and you may well become a vegetarian."
—*Ms.*

"A clearheaded scholar joins the ideas of two movements—vegetarianism and feminism—and turns them into a single coherent and moral theory. Her argument is rational and persuasive. New ground—whole acres of it—is broken by Adams."
—Colman McCarthy, *Washington Post Book World*

Josephine Donovan
FEMINIST THEORY
The Intellectual Traditions of American Feminism
New Expanded Edition
$18.95 paperback   ISBN 0-8264- 0617-3

This new expanded edition covers "The 1980s and Beyond": feminism and postmodernism, multiculturalism, traditional liberalism, and the environment.

"A superbly intelligent, lucid guide to one of the great movements of the modern world."
—Catharine Stimpson

"Not only an impressive piece of research, but an invaluable research guide."
—*Women's Review of Books*